THE UN

I

TWENTIETH CENTURY

Volume I: America 1900–1945

THE UNITED STATES IN THE TWENTIETH CENTURY

James S. Olson
Robert D. Marcus
David Burner
EDITORS

Volume I: America 1900–1945

Edited by
James S. Olson
Sam Houston State University

St. Martin's Press
New York

Aquisitions editor: Louise H. Waller
Manager, publishing services: Emily Berleth
Publishing services associate: Kalea Chapman
Project management: Till & Till, Inc.
Production supervisor: Joe Ford
Art director: Sheree Goodman
Cover design: Liz Driesbach

Library of Congress Catalog Card Number: 94-65246

Manufactured in the United States of America.

9 8 7 6 5
f e d c b a

For information, write:

St. Martin's Press, Inc.
175 Fifth Avenue
New York, NY 10010

ISBN: 0-312-10104-X

Acknowledgments
It is a violation of the law to reproduce these selections by any means whatsoever without the written permission of the copyright holder.

1. "The Gangs of New York City" by Jacob Riis. From: Jacob Riis, "The Gangs of New York City." From Jacob Riis, *How the Other Half Lives* (New York, 1918).

2. "The World of George Washington Plunkitt" by James S. Olson. From: James S. Olson, "The World of George Washington Plunkitt" in William Riordan, *Honest Graft* (St. James, N.Y., 1993).

3. "The Jungle" by Upton Sinclair. From: Upton Sinclair, "Living and Dying in Packington, Chicago." From Upton Sinclair, *The Jungle* (Chicago, 1905).

4. "Rose Schneiderman and the Triangle Shirtwaist Fire" by Bonnie Mitelman. From: Bonnie Mitelman, "Rose Schneiderman and the Triangle Shirtwaist Fire," *American History Illustrated* (July 1981). Reprinted through the courtesy of Cowles Magazines, publisher of *American History Illustrated.*

5. "Fighting Life in the Philippines" by Henry C. Rowland. From: Henry C. Rowland, "Fighting Life in the Philippines," *McClure's Magazine,* 19 (May 1902 to October 1902).

6. "Terrorism in the Age of Roosevelt: The Miss Stone Affair, 1901–1902" by Randall B. Woods. From: Randall B. Woods, "Terrorism in the Age of Roosevelt: The Miss Stone Affair, 1901–1902," *American Quarterly* (Fall 1979). Published by the American Studies Association. Reprinted by permission of *American Quarterly* and the author.

7. "The Anti-German Crusade, 1917–1918" by Munroe Smith. From: Munroe Smith, "The German Theory of Warfare," *North American Review* (September 1917), and Munroe Smith, "We Must Kill to Save," *North American Review* (February 1918).

Acknowledgments and copyrights are continued at the back of the book on pages 332–333, which constitute an extension of the copyright page.

Preface

If historical films, television documentaries, and best-selling books are any indication, Americans have an appreciation of history in general and of social history in particular. History is to be read and enjoyed, but selecting an appropriate text for a class can be frustrating for an instructor who wants to give her or his students material that is comprehensive in scope and at the same time readable and interesting. For those who worry that students are being asked to recall too much detail, too many small particulars, the anthology was invented.

America 1900–1945 gives students a selection of essays on such subjects as biography, gender, sexuality, crime, ethnicity, war, and sports—topics most readers will find inherently interesting. The book is designed to supplement a twentieth-century United States history textbook along with its companion volume, *America since 1945*.

This book focuses primarily on social history because undergraduate students, who should learn an appreciation for history along with the events and persons of history, seem to enjoy reading about and discussing people's lives.

Thanks are extended to the following individuals who supplied useful information to guide the selection of essays that appear in this book: Michael Bellesiles, Emory University; Nancy Conradt, College of DuPage; Richard Frey, Southern Oregon State College; George E. Hopkins, Western Illinois University; Thomas M. Jacklin, University of Baltimore; James McKee, Christian Brothers University; C. Elizabeth Raymond, University of Nevada, Reno; Ellen Schrecker, Yeshiva University; and Marcia G. Synnott, University of South Carolina.

James S. Olson

Contents

THE UNITED STATES
IN THE
TWENTIETH CENTURY

Volume I: America 1900–1945

PART ONE

PROGRESSIVE IMPULSES, 1900–1920

A great deal seemed wrong with America in the early 1900s, and an enterprising group of journalists known as "muckrakers" described those ills to avid readers of newspaper and magazines. The leading muckrakers included Henry Demarast Lloyd, whose book *Wealth and Commonwealth* (1896) described the power of corporate monopolies; Ida Tarbell, whose book *History of Standard Oil Company* (1904) exposed the machinations of the Rockefeller trust; Lincoln Steffens, whose 1904 book *The Shame of the Cities* described widespread municipal corruption; David Graham Phillips, whose work *The Treason of the Senate* (1906) focused on political corruption in high places; and Upton Sinclair, author of *The Jungle* (1906), which dealt with the problems of immigrants and working conditions in Chicago's packinghouses. Muckraker journalism provided reformers with much of the emotional and political ammunition they needed to implement federal and state legislation designed to ameliorate these problems. Since then, historians have described the early 1900s as the "Progressive Era."

Progressivism had many faces. It was a complex, diverse political movement of small businessmen, professionals, farmers, labor unions, and social workers designed to bring political and economic reform to the United States. In its most basic form, Progressivism implied a belief in the need for governmental action—at the local, state, and national level—to accomplish a wide range of goals: to prevent excesses by big business; eliminate political corruption; preserve competition and fair prices; promote good government; find the proper balance between the conservation of natural resources and economic development; reduce tariff rates; bring about some form of immigration restriction; develop proper safety net programs for the urban poor; secure some measure of control over bank credit and the money supply; and provide for consumer protection.

Although the Progressive movement sometimes found expression in third-party efforts, such as the Progressive Party of 1912 and the Progressive Party of 1924, its real influence can be found in the "Square Deal" and "New Nationalism" of people like Theodore Roosevelt and Herbert Croly; the "New Freedom" of people like Woodrow Wilson and Louis Brandeis; and such local and state reformers as Hazen Pingree and Robert La Follette. The Progressive movement—as expressed in legislation like the Interstate Commerce Act of 1887, the Sherman Antitrust Act of 1890, the Elkins Act of 1903, the Hepburn Act of 1906, the Pure Food and Drug and Meat Inspection Acts of 1906, the Mann–Elkins Act of 1909, the Federal Reserve Act of 1913, and the Clayton Antitrust and Federal Trade Commission Acts of 1914—was probably the most successful political movement in American history.

1. The Gangs of New York City

JACOB RIIS

We hear a great deal about "colors" these days, about the "Bloods," the "Crips," the "Skinheads," and the "Texas Mafia," about gangs and organized crime seizing control of American cities, making it difficult for "decent" people to live out their lives in peace and tranquility. Turf battles and drug dealing result in drive-by shootings, keeping people off the streets and forcing many of them to sleep on the floor at night, below the range of ricocheting bullets. School districts across the country are establishing their own police forces to deal with the gang problem.

But gangs are nothing new. As long as there have been cities, with large numbers of people crowded together in a limited area, and with most of those people being poor and disadvantaged, gangs have appeared as a way of making money or protecting territory. Immigration and ethnic diversity have provided another reason for people to coalesce into groups, and gangs have traditionally been one of those groups. Some historians have even seen gangs as useful institutions imposing order, rough though it may be, where none existed before. The following essay describes New York City youth gangs as they existed in the late nineteenth century. Jacob Riis, a Danish immigrant who carefully chronicled life in American cities, wrote How the Other Half Lives *in 1890.*

The "growler" stood at the cradle of the tough. It bosses him through his boyhood apprenticeship in the "gang," and leaves him, for a time only, at the door of the jail that receives him to finish his training and turn him loose upon the world a thief, to collect by stealth or by force the living his philosophy tells him that it owes him, and will not voluntarily surrender without an equivalent in the work which he hates. From the moment he, almost a baby, for the first time carries the growler for beer, he is never out of its reach, and the two soon form a partnership that lasts through life. It has at least the merit, such as it is, of being loyal. The saloon is the only thing that takes kindly to the lad. Honest play is interdicted in the streets. The policeman arrests the ball-tossers, and there is no room in the backyard. In one of these, between two enormous tenements that swarmed with children, I read this ominous notice: "All boys caught in this yard will be dealt with according to law."

Along the water-fronts, in the holes of the dock-rats, and on the avenues, the young tough finds plenty of kindred spirits. Every corner has its gang, not always on the best of terms with the rivals in the next block, but all with a common program: defiance of law and order, and with a common ambition: to get "pinched," i.e., arrested, so as to pose as heroes before their fellows. A successful raid on the grocer's till is a good mark, "doing up" a policeman cause for prosecution in New York. The police deny its existence while nursing the bruises received in nightly battles with it that tax their utmost resources. The newspapers chronicle its doings daily, with a sensational minuteness of detail that does its share toward keeping up its evil traditions and inflaming the ambition of its members to be as bad as the worst.

The gang is the ripe fruit of tenement-house growth. It was born there, endowed with a heritage of instinctive hostility to restraint by a generation that sacrificed home to freedom, or left its country for its country's good. The tenement received and nursed the seed. The intensity of the American temper stood sponsor to the murderer in what would have been the common "bruiser" of a more phlegmatic clime. New York's tough represents the essence of reaction against the old and the new oppression, nursed in the rank soil of its slums. Its gangs are made up of the American-born sons of English, Irish, and German parents. They reflect exactly the conditions of the tenements from which they sprang. Murder is as congenial to Cherry Street or to Battle Row, as quiet and order to Murray Hill. The "assimilation" of Europe's oppressed hordes, upon which our Fourth of July orators are fond of dwelling, is perfect. The product is our own. Such is the genesis of New York's gangs.

Their history is not so easily written. It would embrace the largest share of our city's criminal history for two generations back, every page of it dyed red with blood. The guillotine Paris set up a century ago to avenge its wrongs was not more relentless, or less discriminating, than this Nemesis of New York. The difference is of intent. Murder with that was the serious purpose; with ours it is the careless incident, the wanton brutality of the moment. Bravado and robbery are the real purposes of the gangs; the former prompts the attack upon the policeman, the latter that upon the citizen. Within a single week last spring, the newspapers recorded six murderous assaults on unoffending people, committed by young highwaymen in the public streets. How many more were suppressed by the police, who always do their utmost to hush up such outrages "in the interests of justice," I shall not say. There has been no lack of such occurrences since, as the records of the criminal courts show.

In fact, the past summer has seen, after a period of comparative quiescence of the gangs, a reawakening to renewed turbulence of the East Side tribes, and over and over again the reserve forces of a precinct have been called out to club them into submission. It is a peculiarity of the gangs that they usually break out in spots, as it were. When the West Side is in a state of eruption, the East Side gangs "lie low," and when the toughs along the North River are nursing broken heads at home, or their revenge in Sing Sing, fresh trouble breaks out in the tenements east of Third Avenue. This result is brought about by the very efforts made by the police to put down the gangs. In spite of local feuds, there is between them a species of ruffianly Freemasonry that readily admits to full fellowship a hunted rival in the face of the common enemy.

The gangs belt the city like a huge chain from the Battery to Harlem—the collective name of the "chain gang" has been given to their scattered groups in the belief that a much closer connection exists between them than commonly supposed—and the ruffian for whom the East Side has become too hot, has only to step across town and change his name, a matter usually much easier for him than to change his shirt, to find a sanctuary in which to plot fresh outrages. The more notorious he is, the warmer the welcome, and if he has "done" his man he is by common consent accorded the leadership in his new field. From all this it might be inferred that the New York tough is a very fierce individual, of indomitable courage and naturally as blood-thirsty as a tiger. On the contrary he is an errant coward. His instincts of ferocity are those of the wolf rather than the tiger. It is only when he hunts with the pack that he is dangerous. Then his inordinate vanity makes him forget all fear or caution in the desire to distinguish himself before his fellows, a result of his swallowing all the flash literature and penny-dreadfuls he can beg, borrow, or steal—and there is never any lack of them—and of the strongly dramatic element in his nature that is nursed by such a diet into rank and morbid growth.

He is a queer bundle of contradictions at all times. Drunk and foul-mouthed, ready to cut the throat of a defenseless stranger at the toss of a cent, fresh from beating his decent mother black and blue to get money for rum, he will resent as an intolerable insult the imputation that he is "no gentleman." Fighting his battles with the coward's weapons, the brass-knuckles and the deadly sandbag, or with brick-bats from the housetops, he is still in all seriousness a lover of fair play, and as likely as not, when his gang has downed a policeman in a battle that has cost a dozen broken heads, to be found next saving a drowning child or woman at the peril of his own life. It depends on the angle at which he is seen, whether he is a cowardly ruffian, or a possible hero with different training and under different social conditions. Ready wit he has at all times, and there is less meanness is his make-up than in that of the bully of the London slums.

I have a very vivid recollection of seeing one of his tribe, a robber and murderer before he was nineteen, go to the gallows unmoved, all fear of the rope overcome, as it seemed, by the secret, exultant pride of being the center of a first-class show, shortly to be followed by that acme of tenement-life bliss, a big funeral. He had his reward. His name is to this day a talisman among West Side ruffians, and is proudly borne by the gang of which, up till the night when he "knocked out his man," he was an obscure though aspiring member. The crime that made McGloin famous was the cowardly murder of an unarmed saloonkeeper who came upon the gang while it was sacking his bar-room at the dead of night. McGloin might easily have fled, but disdained to "run for a Dutchman." His act was a fair measure of the standard of heroism set up by his class in its conflicts with society. The finish is worthy of the start.

The first long step in crime taken by the half-grown boy, fired with ambition to earn a standing in his gang, is usually to rob a "lush," i.e., a drunken man who has strayed his way, likely enough is lying asleep in a hallway. He has served an apprenticeship on copper-bottom wash-boilers and like articles found lying around loose, and capable of being converted into cash enough to give the growler a trip or two; but his first venture at robbery moves him up into full fellowship at once. He is no longer a "kid," though his years may be few, but a tough with the rest. He may even in time—he is reasonably certain of it—get his name in the papers as a murderous scoundrel, and have his cup of glory filled to the brim. I came once upon a gang of such young rascals passing the growler after a success-ful raid of some sort, down at the West Thirty-seventh Street dock, and, having my camera along, offered to "take" them. They were not old and wary enough to be shy of the photographer, whose acquaintance they usually first make in handcuffs and the grip of a policeman; or their vanity overcame their caution.

It is entirely in keeping with the tough's character that he should love of all things to pose before a photographer and the ambition is usually the stronger the more repulsive the tough. These were of that sort, and accepted the offer with great readiness, dragging into their group a disreputable-looking sheep that roamed about with them (the slaughter-houses were close at hand) as one of the band. The homeliest ruffian of the lot, who insisted on being taken with the growler to his "mug," took the opportunity to pour what was left in it down his throat and this caused a brief unpleasantness, but otherwise the performance was a success. While I was getting the camera ready, I threw out a vague suggestion of cigarette-pictures, and it took root at once. . . .

One of them tumbled over against a shed, as if asleep, while two of the others bent over him, searching his pockets with a deftness that was highly suggestive. This, they explained for my benefit, was to show how they "did the trick." The rest of the band were so impressed with the importance of this exhibition that they insisted on crowding into the picture by climbing upon the shed, sitting on the roof with their feet dangling over the edge, and disposing themselves in every imaginable manner within view, as they thought. Lest any reader be led into the error of supposing them to have been harmless young fellows enjoying themselves in peace, let me say that within half an hour after our meeting, when I called at the police station three blocks away, I found there two of my friends of the "Montgomery Guards" under arrest for robbing a Jewish pedlar who had passed that way after I left them, and trying to saw his head off, as they put it, "just for fun. The sheeny cum along an' the saw was there, an' we socked it to him." The prisoners were described to me by the police as Dennis, "the Bum," and "Mud" Foley.

It is not always that these little diversions end as harmlessly as did this, even from the standpoint of the Jew, who was pretty badly hurt. Not far from the preserves of the Montgomery Guards, in Poverty Gap . . . a young lad, who was the only support of his aged parents, was beaten to death within a few months by the "Alley Gang," for the same offense that drew down the displeasure of its neighbors upon the pedlar: that of being at work trying to earn an honest living. I found a part of the gang asleep the next morning, before young Healey's death was known, in a heap of straw on the floor of an unoccupied room in the same row of rear tenements in which the murdered boy's home was. One of the tenants, who secretly directed me to their lair, assuring me that no worse scoundrels went un-hung, ten minutes later gave the gang, to its face, an official character for sobriety and inoffensiveness that very nearly startled me into an unguarded rebuke of his duplicity. I caught his eye in time and held my peace. The man was simply trying to protect his own home, while giving such aid as he safely could toward bringing the murderous ruffians to justice. The inci-dent shows to what extent a neighborhood may be terrorized by a deter-mined gang of these reckless toughs.

In Poverty Gap there were still a few decent people left. When it comes to Hell's Kitchen, or to its competitors at the other end of Thirty-ninth Street over by the East River, and further down First Avenue in "the Vil-lage," the Rag Gang and its allies have no need of fearing treachery in their periodical battles with the police. The entire neighborhood takes a hand on these occasions, the women in the front rank, partly from sheer love of the "fun," but chiefly because husbands, brothers, and sweethearts are in the fight to a man and need their help. Chimney-tops form the staple of ammunition then, and stacks of loose brick and paving-stones, carefully hoarded in upper rooms as a prudent provision against emergencies. Regular patrol posts are established by the police on the housetops in times of trouble in these localities, but even then they do not escape whole-skinned, if, indeed, with their lives; neither does the gang. The policeman knows of but one cure for the tough, the club, and he lays it on without stint whenever and wherever he has the chance, knowing right well that, if caught at a disadvantage, he will get his outlay back with interest.

Words are worse than wasted in the gang-districts. It is a blow at sight, and the tough thus accosted never stops to ask questions. Unless he is "wanted" for some signal outrage, the policeman rarely bothers with arresting him. He can point out half a dozen at sight against whom indictments are pending by the basketful, but whom no jail ever held many hours. They only serve to make him more reckless, for he knows that the political backing that has saved him in the past can do it again. It is a commodity that is only exchangeable "for value received," and it is not hard to imagine what sort of value is in demand. The saloon, in ninety-nine cases out of a hundred, stands behind the bargain. For these reasons, as well as because he knows from frequent experience his own way to be the best, the policeman lets the gangs alone except when they come within reach of his long night-stick. They have their "club-rooms" where they meet, generally in a tenement, sometimes under a pier or a dump, to carouse, play cards, and plan their raids; their "fences," who dispose of the stolen property. When the necessity presents itself for a descent upon the gang after some particularly flagrant outrage, the police have a task on hand that is not of the easiest. The gangs, like foxes, have more than one hole to their dens. In some localities, where the interior of a block is filled with rear tenements, often set at all sorts of odd angles, surprise alone is practicable. Pursuit through the winding ways and passages is impossible. The young thieves know them all by heart. They have their runways over roofs and fences which no one else could find. Their lair is generally selected with special reference to its possibilities of escape. Once pitched upon, its occupation by the gang, with its earmark of nightly symposiums, "canrackets" in the slang of the street, is the signal for a rapid deterioration of the tenement, if that is possible. Relief is only to be had by ousting the intruders.

An instance came under my notice in which valuable property had been well-nigh ruined by being made the thoroughfare of thieves by night and by day. They had chosen it because of a passage that led through the block by way of several connecting halls and yards. The places came soon to be known as "Murderers Alley." Complaint was made to the Board of Health, as a last resort, of the condition of the property. The practical inspector who was sent to report upon it suggested to the owner that he build a brick-wall in a place where it would shut off communication between the streets, and he took the advice. Within the brief space of a few months the house changed character entirely, and became as decent as it had been before the convenient runway was discovered. This was in the Sixth Ward, where the infamous Whyo Gang until a few years ago absorbed the worst depravity of the Bend and what is left of the Five Points. The gang was finally broken upon when its leader was hanged for murder after a life of uninterrupted and unavenged crimes, the recital of which made his father confessor turn pale, listening in the shadow of the scaffold, though many years of labor as chaplain of the Tombs had hardened him to such rehearsals. The great Whyo had been a "power in the ward," handy at carrying elections for the party or faction that happened to stand in need of his services and was willing to pay for them in money or in kind. . . .

The exploits of the Paradise Park Gang in the way of highway robbery showed last summer that the embers of the scattered Whyo Gang, upon the wreck of which it grew, were smouldering still. The hanging of Driscoll broke up the Whyos because they were a comparatively small band, and, with the incomparable master-spirit gone, were unable to resist the angry rush of public indignation that followed the crowning outrage. This is the history of the passing away of famous gangs from time to time. The passing is more apparent than real, however. Some other daring leader gathers the scattered elements about him soon, and the war on society is resumed. A bare enumeration of the names of the best-known gangs would occupy pages of this book. The Rock Gang, the Rag Gang, the Stable Gang, and the Short Tail Gang down about the "Hook" have all achieved bad eminence, along with scores of others that have not paraded so frequently in the newspapers. By day they loaf in the corner groceries on their beat, at night they plunder the stores along the avenues, or lie in wait at the river for unsteady feet straying their way. The man who is sober and minds his own business they seldom molest, unless he be a stranger inquiring his way, or a policeman and the gang twenty against the one. The tipsy wayfarer is their chosen victim, and they seldom have to look for him long. One has not far to go to the river from any point in New York. The man who does not know where he is going is sure to reach it sooner or later. Should he foolishly resist or make an outcry—dead men tell no tales. "Floaters" come ashore every now and then with pockets turned inside out, not always evidence of a post-mortem inspection by dock-rats. Police patrol the rivers as well as the shore on constant look-out for these, but seldom catch up with them. If overtaken after a race during which shots are often exchanged from the boats, the thieves have an easy way of escaping and at the same time destroying the evidence against them; they simply upset the boat. They swim, one and all, like real rats; the lost plunder can be recovered at leisure the next day by diving or grappling. The loss of the boat counts for little. Another is stolen, and the gang is ready for business again. The fiction of a social "club," which most of the gangs keep up, helps them to a pretext for blackmailing the politicians and the storekeepers in their bailiwick at the annual seasons of their picnic, or ball. The "thieves' ball" is as well known and recognized an institution on the East Side as the Charity Ball in a different social stratum, although it does not go by that name, in print at least. Indeed, the last thing a New York tough will admit is that he is a thief. He dignifies his calling with the pretense of gambling. He does not steal: he wins "your money or your watch," and on the police returns he is a "speculator." If, when he passes around the hat for "voluntary" contributions, any storekeeper should have the temerity to refuse to chip in, he may look for a visit from the gang on the first dark night, and account himself lucky if his place escapes being altogether wrecked. The Hell's Kitchen Gang and the Rag Gang have both distinguished themselves within recent times by blowing up objectionable stores with stolen gunpowder.

But if no such episode mars the celebration, the excursion comes off and is the occasion for a series of drunken fights that as likely as not end in murder. No season has passed within my memory that has not seen the police reserves called out to receive some howling pandemonium returning from a picnic grove on the Hudson or on the Sound. At least one peaceful community up the river, that had borne with this nuisance until patience had ceased to be a virtue, received a boat-load of such picnickers in a style befitting the occasion and the cargo. The outraged citizens planted a howitzer on the dock, and bade the party land at their peril. With the loaded gun pointed dead at them, the furious toughs gave up and the peace was not broken on the Hudson that day, at least not ashore.

It is good cause for congratulation that the worst of all forms of recreation popular among the city's toughs, the moonlight picnic, has been effectually discouraged. Its opportunities for disgraceful revelry and immorality were unrivalled anywhere. In spite of influence and protection, the tough reaches eventually the end of his rope. Occasionally—not too often—there is a noose on it. If not, the world that owes him a living, according to his creed, will insist on his earning it on the safe side of a prison wall. A few, a very few, have been clubbed into an approach to righteousness from the police standpoint. The condemned tough goes up to serve his "bit" or couple of "stretches," followed by the applause of his gang. In the prison he meets older thieves than himself, and sits at their feet listening with respectful admiration to their accounts of the great doings that sent them before. He returns with the brand of the jail upon him, to encounter the hero-worship of his old associates as an offset to the cold shoulder given him by all the rest of the world.

Even if he is willing to work, disgusted with the restraint and hard labor of prison life, and in a majority of cases that thought is probably uppermost in his mind, no one will have him around. If, with the assistance of Inspector Byrnes, who is a philanthropist in his own practical way, he secures a job, he is discharged on the slightest provocation, and for the most trifling fault. Very soon he sinks back into his old surroundings, to rise no more until he is lost to view in the queer, mysterious way in which thieves and fallen women disappear. No one can tell how. In the ranks of criminals he never rises above that of the "laborer," the small thief or burglar, or general crook, who blindly does the work planned for him by others, and runs the biggest risk for the poorest pay. It cannot be said that the "growler" brought him luck, or its friendship fortune. And yet, if his misdeeds have helped to make manifest that all effort to reclaim his kind must begin with the conditions of life against which his very existence is a protest, even the tough has not lived in vain. This measure of credit at least should be accorded him, that, with or without his good-will, he has been a factor in urging on the battle against the slums that bred him. It is a fight in which eternal vigilance is truly the price of liberty and the preservation of society.

2. The World of George Washington Plunkitt

JAMES S. OLSON

An old axiom in English politics states that "Power corrupts, and absolute power corrupts absolutely." Eventually, according to this point of view, every politician becomes corrupted by the political power he or she possesses. Sooner or later, they use their power to benefit themselves, becoming rich because of the office they hold. If history proves anything, it demonstrates clearly that politics and scandal peacefully coexist at all levels of society. When the public discovers that a politician has used public office for personal gain, there is an outpouring of righteous indignation. Newspapers print lurid headlines, preachers pound the pulpit, and teachers bemoan the disappearance of public morality. Opposition political parties use the scandal to put themselves into office, and the whole cycle begins again.

*During the Progressive Era, Americans were particularly concerned about political corruption in city governments. Lincoln Steffens, the famous muckraking journalist, wrote a best-selling book—*The Shame of the Cities—*in 1904 exposing urban corruption. But George Washington Plunkitt, a public official who was part of the Tammany Hall political machine in New York City, argued that graft was not bad, as long as it was "honest graft." In the following article, historian James S. Olson describes the political world of George Washington Plunkitt, one of the Progressive Era's most corrupt politicians.*

George Washington Plunkitt was usually perched on the high chair of Anthony Graziano's shoeshine-bootblack stand in the Old New York County Courthouse—Tweed Courthouse—off Foley Square in New York City. From there he ruled one of the most lucrative political fiefdoms in the country. On ceremonial occasions, Plunkitt dressed up in a long, formal coat and top hat, but far more often than that he was high on his throne at Graziano's, decked out in shirtsleeves and suspenders, smoking an expensive cigar, looking out on New York City from under the shadow of a flat-topped, circular straw hat. It was 1903 and even though Plunkitt was a multimillionaire, he came to Graziano's every day and expected a free shoeshine. Graziano was happy to oblige. A deal was a deal. George Washington Plunkitt made sure that Graziano's permit to keep the bootblack stand in front of the courthouse was renewed each year. In return, Plunkitt wanted his boots touched up regularly. One journalist was later to write that Plunkitt, on the bootblack stand, "received reports from his henchmen, distributed patronage, and adjusted complaints from his district. His filing cabinet was the sweatband on his hat."

Plunkitt was a living symbol of the rags-to-riches Horatio Alger story so many poor people yearned to fulfill. He had been born in 1842 in Nanny Goat Hill, a poor Irish shantytown on the upper west side of Manhattan, at a time when New Yorkers still grew crops in small patches of their yards and kept chickens and goats and even cows in makeshift sheds. Plunkitt's immigrant parents were dirt poor but they were dreamers. And the name they picked for their son was no coincidence. With a name like George Washington, they knew their boy was going to succeed in America. He did not make his fortune in business like Andrew Carnegie or John D. Rockefeller. George Washington Plunkitt made his money in politics. He was a Sachem of Tammany Hall.

When he was a boy, Plunkitt tired of school after "three winters of it" and went to work in a butcher shop. Year after year he came home tired and frustrated, his clothes covered in blood and his fingers cut up from accidental knife wounds, but he also learned the business, and in 1866 Plunkitt went off on his own, opening a butcher shop in Washington Square that soon prospered. But it was a limited prosperity—the good life that often comes to small businessmen who slave away in their shops for fifteen hours a day, seven days a week. Plunkitt wanted more, and one way for the son of Irish immigrants to grab more in America was politics. Arriving during the Jacksonian era, when property barriers to voting had collapsed, the Irish became a powerful voting bloc. Lacking industrial skills, they were equipped with centuries of experience in life-or-death political battles with the English. In Ireland mass and direct action politics had gone on for years; and slowly, between 1820 and 1880, the Irish constructed their famous American political machines. Working with ethnic and religious unity through local Roman Catholic parishes and saloons, Irish politicians first became street captains and later district and precinct leaders, aldermen, and state and national legislators. Using police, fire department, sanitation, and public works jobs as patronage, they attracted the loyalty of voters economically dependent upon the political success of the machine. And by championing the workingman and the poor, Irish Catholic politicians became very influential in the Democratic Party. In Boston, Cleveland, Chicago, Pittsburgh, Baltimore, St. Louis, and New Orleans, Irish political machines were powerful, and power eventually translated into a shaky respectability.

The premier symbol of Irish-American political power in the United States was New York's Tammany Hall. Tammany Hall was the most powerful urban political machine in American history. William Mooney, a soldier during the American Revolution and a prominent anti-Federalist in New York City, had founded Tammany in 1789. He named the organization the Society of Saint Tammany, after a legendary Delaware Indian chief who supposedly concluded with William Penn the treaty handing all of Pennsylvania over to the Quakers. Naively hoping to become a national political movement, Tammany leaders organized thirteen "tribes," one in each of the thirteen states, and designated their leaders by such Indian titles as "Sachem" and "Sagamore." They called their meeting places "Wigwams." During its early years, Tammany was more of a fraternal organization than a political party, complete with oaths, covenants, secret grips and handshakes, and elaborate symbols whose meaning could be divined only by members. By the early 1800s, Tammany Hall had all but disappeared except in New York City, where it became the organizational engine—the "machine"—driving the Democratic Party. Tammany was a kind of shadow government. More often than not its own members ran for political office, but even when Democrats who were not members of Tammany sought political office, they needed the backing of "The Hall." Otherwise, they did not have a prayer of being elected. The decades of Jeffersonian and Jacksonian Democracy in the early 1800s allowed Tammany to cloak itself in the robes of reform—supporting the campaign for manhood suffrage without property qualifications, calling for the abolition of debtors' prisons, and backing President Andrew Jackson in his righteous crusade against the Second Bank of the United States in 1832. Tammany assumed national political stature in 1836 when Martin Van Buren, the vice-president of the United States and its own Grand Sachem, was elected president of the United States.

Tammany Hall's seventy-year reign of political dominance in New York City began in 1855 when Fernando Wood, one of its own, was elected mayor. Political opponents—particularly middle- and upper-class Republicans along with corporations—accused Wood and his cronies of graft and corruption, and those complaints reached a crescendo in 1868 when William Marcy "Boss" Tweed was elected Grand Sachem of Tammany. The new mayor—A. Oakey Hall—was little more than a Tweed stooge, and the Tweed Ring was charged with looting city coffers of $45 million and costing the city another $200 million in lost tax revenues through shady bond deals and by granting tax exemptions to individuals and businesses in return for kickbacks and political favors to the machine. Thomas Nast, the political cartoonist for *Harpers' Weekly,* drew a series of devastating, satirical cartoons of Tweed and his stooges, portraying the bosses as sleazy, greedy opportunists growing rich and fat at public expense.

Samuel Jones Tilden, chairman of the New York State Democratic Party, launched an investigation of the Tweed Ring, and the sensational exposé of Tammany graft drove the Hall from power in 1871. Boss Tweed died in prison a few years later. Tammany remained a potent force in city politics, however, and its banishment from the seat of power was only temporary. In 1874 John Kelly was elected Grand Sachem and Tammany regained control of city government. Richard Croker succeeded Kelly as Grand Sachem in 1886. Republicans resurrected their charges of graft and corruption over the years, and in 1894 the state legislature appointed the Lexow Commission to investigate charges of Tammany corruption. The heat was on again and Croker had to resign his Tammany post. A reform administration governed city politics for three years, but by 1897 Croker was back in charge of Tammany and Tammany was in charge of New York City. Seth Low, a progressive reformer, once again accused Tammany of political corruption, and in 1901 New York City voters rejected Tammany candidates. The divorce, however, lasted only two years. Charles Francis Murphy became Grand Sachem in 1902 and in 1903 voters returned Tammany to power.

For the next thirty years, Tammany Hall ruled New York City with an iron hand. Charles Murphy remained Grand Sachem until his death in 1924, when Judge George W. Olvany succeeded him. Jimmy Walker, the Tammany candidate, was elected mayor in 1926, but charges of corruption soon surfaced against him. Samuel Seabury led a state investigation of Tammany Hall, and the evidence of corruption was so overwhelming, and the news stories so sensational, that in 1932 Walker was forced to resign as mayor. Fiorello La Guardia, an anti-Tammany candidate for the Fusion Party, was elected mayor in 1933, and he remained in power for the next twelve years, wreaking havoc with Tammany Hall. The machine never re-gained its power, at least not as the dominating political force it had been from the mid-1850s to the early 1930s.

But during its seven-decade reign of power in New York City, Tammany Hall seemed to have more lives than the proverbial cat. Middle- and upper-class Republicans continually accused Tammany of buying votes, always insisting that New York City deserved better, that the good old boys down at the Hall should be turned out, that power should reside in those destined by breeding and education to rule—middle- and upper-class Republicans. Now and then, their accusations hit a responsive chord and voters sent Tammany a message, but the Hall always rose out of its ashes, working its political magic through the hundreds of thousands of working-class New Yorkers who were part of the organization.

What was most frustrating—at least to the upper classes—about Tammany Hall's political power was its quasi-legal status. The Tammany organization was unique among the major urban machines in the late nineteenth and early twentieth centuries. The reformers could never charge Tammany Hall with stealing an election by stuffing the ballot boxes with illegal votes. The Hall did not make it a continuing practice to register dead people and mark ballots for them; the Hall did not rely on getting its minions to vote two or three or four times; the Hall did not cheat when the votes were tallied. The Hall rarely stooped to voter fraud, for it did not need to. Tammany Hall enjoyed the genuine support of the people of New York City.

In 1901 Seth Low ousted Tammany in a reform crusade. Low had inherited a fortune from the family tea and silk importing business, but his real interest was good government. Elected twice as mayor of Brooklyn (1882–1885), Low emphasized efficiency, honesty, and merit in his admin-istration of the city. He became president of Columbia University in 1889 and continued to promote the interests of reform in city government. Low left Columbia in 1901 when he decided to take on Tammany Hall and run for mayor of New York City. The campaign was a sensational one. Low accused Tammany of robbing the city blind, and he managed to win the election. The next year Lincoln Steffens, managing editor of *McClure's Magazine,* began writing a series of exposés of corruption in American city government. One of his targets was Tammany Hall. The articles brought Steffens national attention, making him the most prominent muckraker in the United States, and formed the basis of his best-selling *The Shame of the Cities* in 1904. Steffens wrote: "Tammany is bad government; not ineffi-cient, but dishonest; not a party, but a delusion and a snare, hardly known by its party name—Democracy; having little standing in the national coun-cils of the party and caring little for influence outside of the city. Tammany is Tammany, the embodiment of corruption. All the world knows and all the world may know what it is and what it is after."

When Steffens was writing his essay on New York City, Tammany Hall was reasserting itself after its 1901 defeat. As far as Lincoln Steffens was concerned, Low had been the best of mayors—"conscientious and experi-enced and personally efficient" and New York City had the opportunity to show whether it had "that sustained good citizenship which alone can make democracy a success." The people of New York were going to decide whether they wanted good government or Tammany Hall. Seth Low thought he was a sure bet for a second term. The Fusion Party renominated him. Lincoln Steffens's revelations had excited the nation, and Low's first term had been a model of efficiency and honesty. He epitomized the reform spirit of the Progressive Era. The mayor thought he had brought good government to the city and believed that the people of New York City appreciated it. Tammany Hall nominated George B. McClellan to oppose Seth Low's candidacy. The election was not even close. McClellan won a 56 percent plurality, defeating Low by 314,782 votes to 252,086 votes. The people of New York City did not want good government or reform or efficiency or honesty or merit. They wanted Tammany Hall.

Seth Low's defeat came as no surprise to Lincoln Steffens. He understood the system. In *The Shame of the Cities,* he wrote, "Foreigners marvel . . . at us, and . . . cannot understand why we New Yorkers regard Tammany as so formidable. I think I can explain it. Tammany is corruption with consent; it is bad government founded on the suffrages of the people. . . . Tammany used to stuff the ballot boxes and intimidate voters; today there is practically none of that. Tammany rules . . . by right of the votes of the people of New York. Tammany corruption is democratic corruption. . . . Tammany's power is positive. . . . Tammany's democratic corruption rests upon the corruption of the people, the plain people, and there lies its great significance; its grafting system is one in which more individuals share than any I have studied."

Tammany's power rested on its ability to deliver. In 1870, when the population of New York City just exceeded one million people, Tammany Hall controlled nearly 14,000 municipal jobs. Later in the nineteenth century, when the city expanded geographically to include the Bronx, Queens, and Brooklyn, the population needing Tammany's service multiplied, but so did the volume of available resources. Although it is impossible to make any exact estimates, simple arithmetic throws some light on why Tammany enjoyed such extensive popular support even though its penchant for graft and corruption was widely known. If there were six members in the family—husband, wife, and four children—of each Tammany employee, then 84,000 people in the 1870s benefited directly, every day of the week, from the machine's power. To that number must be added thousands, perhaps even tens of thousands, of small businessmen like Anthony Graziano—bootblacks, pushcart operators, barbers, grocers, restaurant and cafe owners, taxi drivers, newspaper and magazine sellers, pharmacists, peddlars, and building contractors—who received licenses and exclusive concessions from the city. Those small businessmen and their families, as well as their employees and their employees' families, often viewed Tammany as a lifeline, a benefactor that kept them alive financially in a capricious economic world.

Beyond those hundreds of thousands of lower- and working-class New Yorkers who saw a direct connection between their own welfare and that of Tammany Hall, there were tens of thousands of other New Yorkers who had been on the receiving end, more than once, of Tammany largesse—a turkey at Thanksgiving when the dinner table would have been empty otherwise, bail money for a son or father incarcerated for public intoxication or brawling after a night on the town, a pair of boots for a man about to start a new job, a hotel room for a family burned out of its house, a bucket of coal when there was no fuel in the oven, several boxes of groceries for new immigrants just off the boat from Europe, a casket and funeral for a dead child, a few dollars to pay a doctor's bill, or a good word to a banker or a loan shark or a bill collector about to get even with a poor family. At almost any time in the late nineteenth century and the early twentieth, most of the poor and working-class people of the city received what they considered real, tangible benefits from Tammany Hall. All Tammany asked in return was their votes. Lincoln Steffens, even while condemning the corruption and autocracy he found in Tammany Hall, had a detached respect for the success of its democratic corruption, for the efficiency in which its leaders dispensed benefits to the multitudes: "The leader and his captains have their hold because they take care of their own. They speak pleasant words, smile friendly smiles, notice the baby, give picnics up the River or Sound, or a slap on the back; find jobs, most of them at city expense, but they have also newsstands, peddling privileges, railroad and other business places to dispense; they permit violations of the law, and, if a man has broken the law without permission, see him through the court. Though a blow in the face is as readily given as a shake of the hand, Tammany kindness is real kindness, and will go far, remember long, and take infinite trouble for a friend." Steffens also knew how Tammany defined friendship. A real friend, a true friend, was anybody who voted for Tammany Hall, who actively participated in the work to perpetuate the machine.

George Washington Plunkitt had been the most active of participants. From his butcher shop on Washington Square in the 1860s, he formed the George Washington Plunkitt Association, a group of people who agreed to cast their votes at his bidding. In return, Plunkitt made sure that they got the best cuts of pork or beef when they made their purchases, credit when they were short of cash, and even some free pork fat and soup bones when they were down and out. Soon the word was out around Washington Square that Plunkitt could deliver sixty votes. That attracted the interest of Tammany Hall. The head of the local election district named Plunkitt a "block captain"—head of the Tammany organization for one city block. The appointment gave him access to Tammany resources—the turkeys, bail money, coal, hotel rooms, or whatever he needed to assist "his" sixty voters. It was the beginning of a long, successful career for Plunkitt.

The Tammany Hall machine was an extraordinarily well-developed political organization. Its smallest unit was the tenement-house captain, the Tammany man within each working-class apartment house in the city. Twelve to fifteen tenement-house captains made up the block committee, headed by a block captain, and dozens of blocks formed an election district led by an election district committee and an election district captain. An assembly district, headed by an assembly leader and district committee, was composed of any number of election districts. The assembly district leaders had to stand for election in the Democratic Party primaries, and they had the power to select the election district leaders. The district leaders together formed the county executive committee, which was headed by a chairman. At the top of it all was the Grand Sachem of Tammany Hall. By the early 1900s, when New York City included Manhattan, Staten Island,

Queens, Brooklyn, and the Bronx, more than 32,000 people enjoyed formal political appointments at the election district committee level and above. With the addition of tenement-house captains and block committees, the number probably approached 100,000 people. It was an extraordinary political organization.

The opportunity to construct such an elaborate political machine in the United States was comparatively recent in origin. Early in the nineteenth century, American cities had been run by the Anglo-Protestant elites who owned property and who maintained their political power because poor and working-class people living in cities were not allowed to vote. Elite political values, and their economic corollaries, found expression in the National Republican Party of the 1820s, the Whig Party of the 1830s and 1840s, and the Republican Party of the 1850s. City services—public schools, road and bridge construction, water and sewage systems, garbage pick-up, and police and fire protection—all catered to the middle- and upper-class Anglo-Protestants.

But Jacksonian democracy and mass immigration from Europe undermined the urban political status quo. During the Age of Jackson, property requirements for voting disappeared state by state, allowing all white men to vote, including the lower classes. The number of people casting ballots in city elections increased geometrically, and most of the new voters found their way to the Democratic Party, which was more sympathetic to their status. The same was true of the millions of immigrants who poured into the United States from Germany and Ireland in the nineteenth century. The Whig and later the Republican parties were unable to attract the loyalties of the new immigrants, primarily because many upper-class Anglo-Protestants were anti-Catholic nativists. In New York City, the immigrants turned to the Democratic Party for support, and Tammany Hall was only too happy to provide it.

Within a generation, from the 1830s to the 1850s, the elite that had traditionally controlled New York City government found itself vastly outnumbered and politically overwhelmed by Tammany's supporters. The Hall's ability to maintain the loyalties of so many people was directly connected to the physical growth of the city. Every year, beginning in the 1830s, thousands and then tens of thousands of new residents settled in New York City. They came from upstate New York, southern New England, and New Jersey farms, as well as from Ireland, Germany, and later Poland, Italy, Austria-Hungary, and Russia. The demand to house, feed, transport, educate, and protect these millions created a construction boom and a boom in city services that lasted throughout the nineteenth and into the twentieth century. Because the city either issued construction permits or directly contracted new building projects, there was a strong political component to the economic boom. Tammany Hall controlled the issuance of those building permits and construction contracts, as well as the tens of thousands of jobs associated with them. As George Washington Plunkitt remarked to journalist William Riordon in 1904, "I seen my opportunities and I took 'em."

Take them he did. By the mid-1870s Plunkitt was a well-known Tammany Hall operative in the Fifteenth Assembly District around Washington Square. He was captain of an election district and knew that the city was about to begin construction of huge dock and wharf facilities in lower Manhattan. Plunkitt sold his butcher shop and used the capital to become a building contractor. These were the days before the era of competitive bidding, and Tammany Hall made sure that Plunkitt got his share of the projects, something befitting the needs of a powerful man on the make. Plunkitt himself made sure, of course, that all of his friends and his friends' friends got subcontracts and jobs on the projects. In 1868 he was elected to the state legislature, and in 1870 he began several terms as a city alderman. Plunkitt later bragged that he was the only person in New York City history to hold four different political offices at the same time—assemblyman, supervisor, alderman, and police magistrate. In 1883 Plunkitt won a seat in the state senate. Within a few years, George Washington Plunkitt was a millionaire and chairman of the Fifteenth Assembly District. The other Tammany assembly district chairmen—the exalted sachems—also became rich men.

The wealth of Tammany's leaders seemed ill-gotten gain to the Anglo-Protestant elites who had made their money on land in the early days of the republic or corporate profits in the industrial era. For them, the sleaziest form of scandal was exploiting political power and public office for personal gain. Self-righteous criticism of Tammany Hall corruption became the conventional wisdom of upper-class patricians and their voices in the intellectual community. In 1888 the British observer James Bryce, in his book *The American Commonwealth,* argued that "there is no denying that the government of cities is the one conspicuous failure of the United States." Andrew White, president of Cornell University, wrote in 1890 that "the city governments of the United States are the worst in Christendom—the most expensive, the most inefficient, and the most corrupt." In 1894 Edwin Godkin, editor of *The Nation,* declared that "the present condition of city governments in the United States is bringing democratic institutions into contempt the world over, and imperiling some of the best things in our civilization."

Since the times of the Founding Fathers in the late 1700s, Americans had been suspicious of political organizations. Classical democratic theory rejected the need for political parties of any kind, let alone organizational machines rich in resources. Citizens were expected to vote their consciences and to exercise the franchise directly, without the need for intermediaries between them and those they elected to serve. Tammany Hall seemed to contradict such high-minded values at every turn, and throughout its years of dominance in New York City, the Anglo-Protestant elites who had been driven from the seats of power raged against the Hall in self-righteous indignation, condemning machine politics as a "cancer of corruption" or a "moral depravity." Good government was detached and disinterested, efficient and fair, loyal to established procedures and regulations, with an educated electorate making rational choices about those who should govern them.

But what is rational to one person may not seem rational to another. Tammany Hall maintained its political control because it was eminently rational to most New York City voters. In the late nineteenth and early twentieth centuries, Tammany Hall was far more than a disinterested, detached city government for several million poor, working-class New Yorkers.

It was also a successful city government delivering municipal services, a social welfare agency assisting the immigrant poor and their children in adjusting to the new country, a political interest group giving working-class people at least a modest voice in an economic world increasingly dominated by rich corporations, and a business with tens of thousands of employees. In spite of the reform rhetoric, Tammany Hall was remarkably successful in managing the city's enormous growth. The New York City population increased from approximately 515,000 people in 1850 to more than seven million people in 1935. The city also expanded spatially, and its new residents demanded all the city services enjoyed by the people of central Manhattan—paved roads, street lights, electricity, water and sewage systems, fire and police protection, bridges, parks, libraries, schools, and public transportation. Tammany managed to supply those services.

Historian Jon Teaford has argued that American cities in general—New York City included—enjoyed "as high a standard of public services as any urban residents in the world." In 1883 Tammany officials authorized a new Croton aqueduct system, and in 1905 they began developing the Catskill aqueduct, both of which gave New York City the finest water supply of any city on earth. Tammany built the bridges and tunnels—Brooklyn Bridge (1883), Williamsburg Bridge (1903), Manhattan Bridge (1909), Queensborough Bridge (1909), and Holland Tunnel (1927)—that linked Manhattan with New Jersey and Long Island. The organization completed Penn Station in 1910 and Grand Central Station in 1913. Tammany officials brought the elevated railroad and then the subway system to New York City. By the 1920s, after more than a half-century of Tammany rule, New York City's system of public transportation, public education, and higher education was the envy of the world. And in spite of all the charges of mismanagement and corruption, Tammany managed to govern the city without ever declaring bankruptcy or defaulting on its obligations, even during the panics and depressions of 1873, 1893, and 1907. During Tammany's reign, New York City bonds enjoyed AAA ratings. The financial community considered them to be one of the best, safest, and most liquid investments in the world.

But Tammany was more than a political organization and a government to New York City residents, especially to the immigrant poor. During the years of Tammany power, millions arrived in New York City, Irish, Germans, Italians, Jews, Greeks, and African Americans. By 1900, three out of four people in the city were either immigrants or the children of immigrants. For most of them, politics did not revolve around larger-than-life, complex issues like slavery or imperialism or free silver or civil service. Politics was tangible and personal, just as it had been in the Old World villages, where politicians were local people who could help you or hurt you. It was the same in New York City. When you had a problem, you took it to your block leader or election district chairman; all he wanted in return was your vote. Most Tammany leaders were second-generation Americans who understood the streets and the challenges of immigrant life. And poor people understood them. In an era when there were no formal government safety-net programs, Tammany acted as a social welfare agency to new immigrants. It was the purest form of representative government—local, responsive, and personal.

Tammany Hall was much more than a social welfare agency. It also served as an interest group—the only interest group—for a working-class constituency. Between 1870 and 1920, virtually every section of American society, in attempts to cope with the industrial revolution, began to look outward and to form communities of interest. Businessmen established corporations to protect their capital, engaged in vertical and horizontal integration to increase profit margins, and established trade associations and groups like the Chamber of Commerce or the National Association of Manufacturers to promote their interests. Middle-class professionals formed organizations like the American Medical Association, the American Bar Association, or the American Dental Association. Eventually labor unions would emerge to perform the same services for workers, but unions—especially unions for mass-production workers—were in their infancy in the late 1800s and early 1900s. Working-class people confronted an increasingly organized economy without interest groups of their own. They were at the mercy of organized upper- and middle-class power brokers. What working-class people in New York City realized, however, was that those power brokers, if they were going to be successful economically, had to deal with Tammany Hall, and the sachems of the Hall would see to it that those benefits were widely distributed to the faithful.

Finally, Tammany Hall was a business, a big business, a way for talented, enterprising poor people to fulfill the American dream. Later generations would use sports and entertainment to get out of the ghetto; in the late 1800s and early 1900s, Tammany Hall was a way out. The city had an income of more than $100 million in 1904, and it spent that money providing services to its constituents. The sachems of Tammany Hall were its executives, the people who managed the business. They signed the contracts, controlled the cash flow, and watched the margins. They worked eighteen-hour days, seven days a week, just like upper management businessmen today. And like the CEOs of the major corporations, they also took care of themselves, making the kind of money consistent with the huge operation they were running. Nobody expected them to live on their city salaries. Over and over again, at every opportunity, Plunkitt used the inside information about impending city construction projects to make prudent investments or to demand kickbacks. He said disarmingly about the system: "I don't think you can easily find a better example than I am of success in politics. After forty years' experience at the game I am—well, I'm George Washington Plunkitt. Everybody knows what figure I cut in the greatest organization on earth, and if you hear people say that I've laid away a million or so since I was a butcher's boy in Washington Market, don't come to me for an indignant denial. I'm pretty comfortable, thank you."

Tammany Hall did not need to rig elections or steal from the public treasury. Even Lincoln Steffens, one of Tammany's most hostile critics, said that "hypocrisy is not a Tammany vice. Tammany is for Tammany, and the Tammany men say so. Other rings proclaim lies and make pretensions; other rogues talk about the tariff and imperialism. Tammany is honestly dishonest. Time and again, in private and in public, the leaders, big and little, have said they are out for themselves and their own. . . . Tammany rules, when it rules, by right of the votes of the people of New York." This was honest graft. In the Declaration of Independence, Thomas Jefferson wrote the noble words that government "derived its just powers from the consent of the governed," but George Washington Plunkitt said it even better: "Tammany . . . looked after their friends, within the law, and gave them what opportunities they could to make honest graft. Now, let me tell you that's never goin' to hurt Tammany with the people. Every good man looks after his friends, and any man who doesn't isn't likely to be popular. If I have a good thing to hand out in private life, I give it to a friend. Why shouldn't I do the same in public life?"

3. The Jungle

UPTON SINCLAIR

During the spring of 1993, a scare rippled through the Pacific Northwest when several people died of food poisoning after eating hamburgers at Jack-in-the-Box franchise outlets. The Food and Drug Administration quickly launched an investigation and discovered that a beef wholesaler had supplied Jack-in-the-Box with bacterially tainted beef. Government regulation of the meat-processing industry has been the norm since Congress passed the Meat Inspection Act back in 1906. That year, Upton Sinclair's The Jungle *was a best-selling novel. Ironically, Sinclair wanted the book to be remembered for its portrayal of how desperate life could be for an immigrant family living in Chicago. But what people really remembered about the novel was its description of the slaughterhouses and meat-processing plants in Chicago, and just what went into the hot dogs, sausages, and bologna that Americans were eating. President Theodore Roosevelt read the novel and was equally appalled. He then threw his support behind the Meat Inspection Act and saw to its passage in Congress. The following selection comes from* The Jungle.

During this time that Jurgis was looking for work occurred the death of little Kristoforas, one of the children of Teta Elzbieta. Both Kristoforas and his brother, Juozapas, were cripples, the latter having lost one leg by having it run over, and Kristoforas having congenital dislocation of the hip, which made it impossible for him ever to walk. He was the last of Teta Elzbieta's children, and perhaps he had been intended by nature to let her know that she had had enough. At any rate he was wretchedly sick and undersized; he had the rickets, and though he was over three years old, he was no bigger than an ordinary child of one. All day long he would crawl around the floor in a filthy little dress, whining and fretting; because the floor was full of drafts he was always catching cold, and snuffling because his nose ran. This made him a nuisance, and a source of endless trouble in the family. For his mother, with unnatural perversity, loved him best of all her children, and made a perpetual fuss over him—would let him do anything undisturbed, and would burst into tears when his fretting drove Jurgis wild.

And now he died. Perhaps it was the smoked sausage he had eaten that morning—which may have been made out of some of the tubercular pork that was condemned as unfit for export. At any rate, an hour after eating it, the child had begun to cry with pain, and in another hour he was rolling about on the floor in convulsions. Little Kotrina, who was all alone with him, ran out screaming for help, and after a while a doctor came, but not until Kristoforas had howled his last howl. No one was really sorry about this except poor Elzbieta, who was inconsolable. Jurgis announced that so far as he was concerned the child would have to be buried by the city, since they had no money for a funeral; and at this the poor woman almost went out of her senses, wringing her hands and screaming with grief and despair. Her child to be buried in a pauper's grave! And her stepdaughter to stand by and hear it said without protesting! It was enough to make Ona's father rise up out of his grave to rebuke her! If it had come to this, they might as well give up at once, and be buried all of them together!

In the end Marija said that she would help with ten dollars; and Jurgis being still obdurate, Elzbieta went in tears and begged the money from the neighbors, and so little Kristoforas had a mass and a hearse with white plumes on it, and a tiny plot in a graveyard with a wooden cross to mark the place. The poor mother was not the same for months after that; the mere sight of the floor where little Kristoforas had crawled about would make her weep. He had never had a fair chance, poor little fellow, she would say. He had been handicapped from his birth. If only she had heard about it in time, so that she might have had that great doctor to cure him of his lameness! Some time ago, Elzbieta was told, a Chicago billionaire had paid a fortune to bring a great European surgeon over to cure his little daughter of the same disease from which Kristoforas had suffered. And because this surgeon had to have bodies to demonstrate upon, he announced that he would treat the children of the poor, a piece of magnanimity over which the papers became quite eloquent. Elzbieta, alas, did not read the papers, and no one had told her; but perhaps it was as well, for just then they would not have had the carfare to spare to go everyday to wait upon the surgeon, nor for that matter anybody with the time to take the child.

All this while that he was seeking for work, there was a dark shadow hanging over Jurgis; as if a savage beast were lurking somewhere in the pathway of his life, and he knew it, and yet could not help approaching the place. There are all stages of being out of work in Packingtown, and he faced in dread the prospect of reaching the lowest. There is a place that waits for the lowest man—the fertilizer-plant!

The men would talk about it in awe-stricken whispers. Not more than one in ten had ever really tried it; the other nine had contented themselves with hearsay evidence and a peep through the door. There were some things worse than even starving to death. They would ask Jurgis if he had worked there yet, and if he meant to; and Jurgis would debate the matter with himself. As poor as they were and making all the sacrifices that they were, would he dare to refuse any sort of work that was offered to him, be it as horrible as ever it could? Would he dare to go home and eat bread that had been earned by Ona, weak and complaining as she was, knowing that he had been given a chance, and had not had the nerve to take it?—And yet he might argue that way with himself all day, and one glimpse into the fertilizer-works would send him away again shuddering. He was a man, and he would do his duty; he went and made application—but surely he was not also required to hope for success.

The fertilizer-works of Durham's lay away from the rest of the plant. Few visitors ever saw them, and the few who did would come out looking like Dante, of whom the peasants declared that he had been into hell. To this part of the yards came all the "tankage" and waste products of all sorts; here they dried out the bones—and in suffocating cellars where the daylight never came you might see men and women and children bending over whirling machines and sawing bits of bone into all sorts of shapes, breathing their lungs full of the fine dust, and doomed to die, every one of them, within a certain definite time. Here they made the blood into albumen, and made other foulsmelling things into things still more foulsmelling. In the corridors and caverns where it was done you might lose yourself as in the great caves of Kentucky. In the dust and the steam the electric lights would shine like far-off twinkling stars—red and blue, green and purple stars, according to the color of the mist and the brew from which it came. For the odors in these ghastly charnel-houses there may be words in Lithuanian, but there are none in English. The person entering would have to summon his courage as for a cold-water plunge. He would go on like a man swimming under water; he would put his handkerchief over his face, and begin to cough and choke; and then, if he were still obstinate, he would find his head beginning to ring, and the veins in his forehead to throb, until finally he would be assailed by an overpowering blast of ammonia fumes, and would turn and run for his life, and come out half-dazed.

On top of this were the rooms where they dried the "tankage," the mass of brown stringy stuff that was left after the waste portions of the carcasses had had the lard and tallow tried out of them. This dried material they would then grind to a fine powder, and after they had mixed it up well with a mysterious but inoffensive brown rock which they brought in and ground up by the hundreds of carloads for that purpose, the substance was ready to be put into bags and sent out to the world as any one of a hundred different brands of standard bone-phosphate. And then the farmer in Maine or California or Texas would buy this, at say twenty-five dollars a ton, and plant it with his corn; and for several days after the operation the fields would have a strong odor, and the farmer and his wagon and the very horses that had hauled it would all have it too. In Packingtown the fertilizer is pure, instead of being a flavoring, and instead of a ton or so spread on several acres under the open sky, there are hundreds and thousands of tons of it in one building, heaped here and there in haystack piles, covering the floor several inches deep, and filling the air with a choking dust that becomes a blinding sand-storm when the wind stirs.

It was to this building that Jurgis came daily, as if dragged by an unseen hand. The month of May was an exceptionally cool one, and his secret prayers were granted; but early in June there came a record-breaking hot spell, and after that there were men wanted in the fertilizer-mill.

The boss of the grinding room had come to know Jurgis by this time, and had marked him for a likely man; and so when he came to the door about two o'clock this breathless hot day, he felt a sudden spasm of pain shoot through him—the boss beckoned to him. In ten minutes more Jurgis had pulled off his coat and overshirt, and set his teeth together and gone to work. Here was one more difficulty for him to meet and conquer!

His labor took him about one minute to learn. Before him was one of the vents of the mill in which the fertilizer was being ground—rushing forth in a great brown river, with a spray of the finest dust flung forth in clouds. Jurgis was given a shovel, and along with half a dozen others it was his task to shovel this fertilizer into carts. That others were at work he knew by the sound, and by the fact that he sometimes collided with them; otherwise they might as well not have been there, for in the blinding dust-storm a man could not see six feet in front of his face. When he had filled one cart he had to grope around him until another came, and if there was none on hand he continued to grope till one arrived. In five minutes he was, of course, a mass of fertilizer from head to feet; they gave him a sponge to tie over his mouth, so that he could breathe, but the sponge did not prevent his lips and eyelids from caking up with it and his ears from filling solid. He looked like a brown ghost at twilight—from hair to shoes he became the color of the building and of everything in it, and for that matter a hundred yards outside it. The building had to be left open, and when the wind blew Durham and Company lost a great deal of fertilizer.

Working in his shirt-sleeves, and with the thermometer at over a hundred, the phosphates soaked in through every pore of Jurgis's skin, and in five minutes he had a headache, and in fifteen was almost dazed. The blood was pounding his brain like an engine's throbbing; there was a frightful pain in the top of his skull and he could hardly control his hands. Still, with the memory of his four months' siege behind him, he fought on, in a frenzy of determination; and half an hour later he began to vomit—he vomited until it seemed as if his innards must be torn to shreds. A man could get used to the fertilizer mill, the boss had said, if he would only make up his mind to it; but Jurgis now began to see that it was a question of making up his stomach. At the end of that day of horror, he could scarcely stand. He had to catch himself now and then, and lean against a building and get his bearings. Most of the men, when they came out, made straight for a saloon—they seemed to place fertilizer and rattlesnake poison in one class. But Jurgis was too ill to think of drinking—he could only make his way to the street and stagger on to a car. He had a sense of humor, and later on, when he became an old hand, he used to think it fun to board a street-car and see what happened. Now, however, he was too ill to notice it—how the people in the car began to gasp and sputter, to put their handkerchiefs to their noses, and transfix him with furious glances. Jurgis only knew that a man in front of him immediately got up and gave him a seat; and that half a minute later the two people on each side of him got up; and that in a full minute the crowded car was nearly empty—those passengers who could not get room on the platform having gotten out to walk.

Of course Jurgis had made his home a miniature fertilizer-mill a minute after entering. The stuff was half an inch deep in his skin—his whole system was full of it, and it would have taken a week not merely of scrubbing, but of vigorous exercise, to get it out of him. As it was, he could be compared with nothing known to men, save that newest discovery of the savants, a substance which emits energy for an unlimited time, without being itself in the least diminished in power. He smelt so that he made all food at the table taste, and set the whole family to vomiting; for himself it was three days before he could keep anything upon his stomach—he might wash his hands, and use a knife and fork, but were not his mouth and throat filled with the poison?

And still Jurgis stuck it out! In spite of splitting headaches he would stagger down to the plant and take up his stand once more, and begin to shovel in the blinding clouds of dust. And so at the end of the week he was a fertilizer-man for life—he was able to eat again, and though his head never stopped aching, it ceased to be so bad that he could not work.

So there passed another summer. It was a summer of prosperity, all over the country, and the country ate generously of packing-house products, and there was plenty of work for all the family, in spite of the packers' efforts to keep a superfluity of labor. They were again able to pay their debts and to begin to save a little sum; but there were one or two sacrifices they considered too heavy to be made for long—it was too bad that the boys should have to sell papers at their age. It was utterly useless to caution them and plead with them; quite without knowing it, they were taking on the tone of their new environment. They were learning to swear in voluble English; they were learning to pick up cigar-stumps and smoke them, to pass hours of their time gambling with pennies and dice and cigarette-cards; they were learning the location of all the houses of prostitution on the "Levee," and the names of the "madames" who kept them, and the days when they gave their state banquets, which the police captains and the big politicians all attended. If a visiting "country customer" were to ask them, they could show him which was "Hinkydink's" famous saloon, and could even point out to him by name the different gamblers and thugs and "hold-up men" who made the place their headquarters. And worse yet, the boys were getting out of the habit of coming home at night. What was the use, they would ask, of wasting time and energy and a possible car-fare riding out to the stockyards every night when the weather was pleasant and they could crawl under a truck or into an empty doorway and sleep exactly as well? So long as they brought home a half dollar for each day, what mattered it when they brought it? But Jurgis declared that from this to ceasing to come at all would not be a very long step, and so it was decided that Vilimas and Nikalojus should return to school in the fall, and that instead Elzbieta should go out and get some work, her place at home being taken by her younger daughter.

Little Kotrina was like most children of the poor, prematurely made old; she had to take care of her little brother, who was a cripple, and also of the baby; she had to cook the meals and wash the dishes and clean house, and have supper ready when the workers came home in the evening. She was only thirteen, and small for her age, but she did all this without a murmur; and her mother went out, and after trudging a couple of days about the yards, settled down as a servant of a "sausage-machine."

Elzbieta was used to working, but she found this change a hard one, for the reason that she had to stand motionless upon her feet from seven o'clock in the morning till half-past twelve, and again from one till half-past five. For the first days it seemed to her that she could not stand it—she suffered almost as much as Jurgis had from the fertilizer—and would come out at sundown with her head fairly reeling. Besides this, she was working in one of the dark holes, by electric light, and the dampness, too, was deadly—there were always puddles of water on the floor, and a sickening odor of moist flesh in the room. . . .

The sausage-room was an interesting place to visit, for two or three minutes, and provided that you did not look at the people; the machines were perhaps the most wonderful things in the entire plant. Presumably sausages were once chopped and stuffed by hand, and if so it would be interesting to know how many workers had been displaced by these inventions. On one side of the room were the hoppers, into which men shovelled loads of meat and wheelbarrows full of spices; in these great bowls were whirling knives that made two thousand revolutions a minute, and when the meat was ground fine and adulterated with potato-flour, and well mixed with water, it was forced to the stuffing-machines on the other side of the room. The latter were tended by women; there was a sort of spout, like the nozzle of a hose, and one of the women would take a long string of "casing" and put the end over the nozzle and then work the whole thing on, as one works on the finger of a tight glove. This string would be twenty or thirty feet long, but the woman would have it all on in a jiffy; and when she had several on, she would press a lever, and a stream of sausage-meat would be shot out, taking the casing with it as it came. Thus one might stand and see appear, miraculously born from the machine, a wriggling snake of sausage of incredible length. In front was a big pan which caught these creatures, and two more women who seized them as fast as they appeared and twisted them into links. This was for the uninitiated the most perplexing work of all; for all that the woman had to give was a single turn of the wrist; and in some way she contrived to give it so that instead of an endless chain of sausages, one after another, there grew under her hands a bunch of strings, all dangling from a single center. It was quite like the feat of a prestidigitator—for the woman worked so fast that the eye could literally not follow her, and there was only a mist of motion, and tangle after tangle of sausages appearing. In the midst of the mist, however, the visitor would suddenly notice the tense set face, with the two wrinkles graven in the forehead, and the ghastly pallor of the cheeks; and then he would suddenly recollect that it was time he was going on. The woman did not go on; she stayed right there—hour after hour, day after day, year after year, twisting sausage-links and racing with death. It was piece-work, and she was apt to have a family to keep alive; and stern and ruthless economic laws had arranged it that she could only do this by working just as she did, with all her soul upon her work, and with never an instant for a glance at the well-dressed ladies and gentlemen who came to stare at her, as at some wild beast in a menagerie.

With one member trimming beef in a cannery, and another working in a sausage factory, the family had a first-hand knowledge of the great majority of Packingtown swindles. For it was the custom, as they found, whenever meat was so spoiled that it could not be used for anything else, either to can it or else to chop it up into sausage. With what had been told them by Jonas, who had worked in the pickle-rooms, they could now study the whole of the spoiled meat industry on the inside, and read a new and grim meaning into that old Packingtown jest—that they use everything of the pig except the squeal.

Jonas had told them how the meat that was taken out of pickle would often be found sour, and how they would rub it up with soda to take away the smell, and sell it to be eaten on free-lunch counters; also of all the miracles of chemistry which they performed, giving to any sort of meat, fresh or salted, whole or chopped, any color and any flavor and any odor they chose. In the pickling of hams they had an ingenious apparatus, by which they saved time and increased the capacity of the plant—a machine consisting of a hollow needle attached to a pump; by plunging this needle into the meat and working with his foot, a man could fill a ham with pickle in a few seconds. And yet, in spite of this, there would be hams found spoiled, some of them with an odor so bad that a man could hardly bear to be in the room with them. To pump into these the packers had a second and much stronger pickle which destroyed the odor—a process known to the workers as "giving them thirty percent." Also, after the hams had been smoked, there would be found some that had gone to the bad. Formerly these had been sold as "Number Three Grade," but later on some ingenious person had hit upon a new device, and now they would extract the bone, about which the bad part generally lay, and insert in the hole a white-hot iron. After this invention there was no longer Number One, Two, and Three Grade—there was only Number One Grade. The packers were always originating such schemes—they had what they called "boneless hams," which were all the odds and ends of pork stuffed into casings; and "California hams," which were the shoulders, with big knuckle joints, and nearly all the meat cut out; and fancy "skinned hams," which were made of the oldest hogs, whose skins were so heavy and coarse that no one would buy them—that is, until they had been cooked and chopped fine and labelled "head cheese"!

It was only when the whole ham was spoiled that it came into the department of Elzbieta. Cut up by the two-thousand-revolutions-a-minute flyers, and mixed with half a ton of other meat, no odor that ever was in a ham could make any difference. There was never the least attention paid to what was cut up for sausage; there would come all the way back from Europe old sausage that had been rejected, and that was mouldy and white—it would be dosed with borax and glycerine, and dumped into the hoppers, and made over again for home consumption. There would be meat that had tumbled out on the floor, in the dirt and sawdust, where the workers had tramped and spit uncounted billions of consumption germs. There would be meat stored in great piles in rooms; and the water from leaky roofs would drip over it, and thousands of rats would race about on it. It was too dark in these storage places to see well, but a man could run his hand over these piles of meat and sweep off handfuls of the dried dung of rats. These rats were nuisances, and the packers would put poisoned bread out for them, they would die, and then rats, bread, and meat would go into the hoppers together. This is no fairy story and no joke; the meat would be shovelled into carts, and the man who did the shovelling would not trouble to lift out a rat even when he saw one—there were things that went into the sausage in comparison with which a poisoned rat was a tidbit. There was no place for the men to wash their hands before they ate their dinner, and so they made a practice of washing them in the water that was to be ladled into the sausage. There were the butt-ends of smoked meat, and the scraps of corned beef, and all the odds and ends of the waste of the plants, that would be dumped into old barrels in the cellar and left there. Under the system of rigid economy which the packers enforced, there were some jobs that it only paid to do once in a long time, and among these was the cleaning out of the waste-barrels. Every spring they did it; and in the barrels would be dirt and rust and old nails and stale water—and cart load after cart load of it would be taken up and dumped into the hoppers with fresh meat, and sent out to the public's breakfast. Some of it they would make into "smoked" sausage—but as the smoking took time, and was therefore expensive, they would call upon their chemistry department, and preserve it with borax and color it with gelatine to make it brown. All of their sausage came out of the same bowl, but when they came to wrap it they would stamp some of it "special," and for this they would charge two cents more a pound.

Such were the new surroundings in which Elzbieta was placed, and such was the work she was compelled to do. It was stupefying, brutalizing work; it left her no time to think, no strength for anything. She was part of the machine she tended, and every faculty that was not needed for the machine was doomed to be crushed out of existence. There was only one mercy about the cruel grind—that it gave her the gift of insensibility. Little by little she sank into a torpor—she fell silent. She would meet Jurgis and Ona in the evening, and the three would walk home together, often without saying a word. Ona, too, was falling into the habit of silence—Ona, who had once gone about singing like a bird. She was sick and miserable, and often she would barely have strength enough to drag herself home. And there they would eat what they had to eat, and afterwards, because there was only their misery to talk of, they would crawl into bed and fall into a stupor and never stir until it was time to get up again, and dress by candle-light, and go back to the machines. They were so numbed that they did not even suffer much from hunger, now; only the children continued to fret when the food ran short.

Yet the soul of Ona was not dead—the souls of none of them were dead, but only sleeping; and now and then they would waken, and these were cruel times. The gates of memory would roll open—old joys would stretch out their arms to them, old hopes and dreams would call to them, and they would stir beneath the burden that lay upon them, and feel its forever immeasurable weight. They could not even cry out beneath it; but anguish would seize them, more dreadful than the agony of death. It was a thing scarcely to be spoken—a thing never spoken by all the world, that will not know its own defeat.

They were beaten; they had lost the game; they were swept aside. It was not less tragic because it was so sordid, because that it had to do with wages and grocery bills and rents. They had dreamed of freedom; of a chance to look about them and learn something; to be decent and clean, to see their child grow up to be strong. And now it was all gone—it would never be! They had played the game and they had lost. Six years more of toil they had to face before they could expect the least respite, the cessation of the payments upon the house; and how cruelly certain it was that they could never stand six years of such a life as they were living! They were lost, they were going down—and there was no deliverance for them, no hope; for all the help it gave them the vast city in which they lived might have been an ocean waste, a wilderness, a desert, a tomb. So often this mood would come to Ona, in the night-time, when something wakened her; she would lie, afraid of the beating of her own heart, fronting the blood-red eyes of the old primeval terror of life. Once she cried aloud, and woke Jurgis, who was tired and cross. After that she learned to weep silently—their moods so seldom came together now! It was as if their hopes were buried in separate graves.

Jurgis, being a man, had troubles of his own. There was another spectre following him. He had never spoken of it, nor would he allow anyone else to speak of it—he had never acknowledged its existence to himself. Yet the battle with it took all the manhood that he had—and once or twice, alas, a little more. Jurgis had discovered drink.

He was working in the steaming pit of hell; day after day, week after week—until now there was not an organ of his body that did its work without pain, until the sound of ocean breakers echoed in his head day and night, and the buildings swayed and danced before him as he went down the street. And from all the unending horror of this there was a respite, a deliverance—he could drink! He could forget the pain, he could slip off the burden; he would see clearly again, he would be master of his brain, of this thoughts, of his will. His dead self would stir in him, and he would find himself laughing and cracking jokes with his companions—he would be a man again, and master of his life.

It was not an easy thing for Jurgis to take more than two or three drinks. With the first drink he could eat a meal, and he could persuade himself that that was economy; with the second he could eat another meal—but there would come a time when he could eat no more, and then to pay for a drink was an unthinkable extravagance, a defiance of the age-long instincts of his hunger-haunted class. One day, however, he took the plunge, and drank up all that he had in his pockets, and went home half "piped," as the men phrase it. He was happier than he had been in a year; and yet, because he knew that the happiness would not last, he was savage, too—with those who would wreck it, and with the world, and with his life; and then again, beneath this, he was sick with the shame of himself. After-ward, when he saw the despair of his family, and reckoned up the money he had spent, the tears came into his eyes, and he began the long battle with the spectre.

It was a battle that had no end, that never could have one. But Jurgis did not realize that very clearly; he was not given much time for reflection. He simply knew that he was always fighting. Steeped in misery and despair as he was, merely to walk down the street was to be put upon the rack. There was surely a saloon on the corner—perhaps on all four corners, and some in the middle of the block as well; and each one stretched out a hand to him—each one had a personality of its own, allurements unlike any other. Going and coming—before sunrise and after dark—there was warmth and a glow of light, and the steam of hot food, and perhaps music, or a friendly face, and a word of good cheer. Jurgis developed a fondness for having Ona on his arm whenever he went out on the street, and he would hold her tightly, and walk fast. It was pitiful to have Ona know of this—it drove him wild to think of it; the thing was not fair, for Ona had never tasted drink, and so could not understand. Sometimes, in desperate hours, he would find himself wishing that she might learn what it was, so that he need not be ashamed in her presence. They might drink together, and escape from the horror—escape for a while, come what would.

So there came a time when nearly all the conscious life of Jurgis consisted of a struggle with the craving for liquor. He would have ugly moods, when he hated Ona and the whole family, because they stood in his way. He was a fool to have married; he had tied himself down, and made himself a slave. It was all because he was a married man that he was compelled to stay in the yards; if it had not been for that he might have gone off like Jonas, and to hell with the packers. There were few single men in the fertilizer-mill—and those few were working only for a chance to escape. Meantime, too, they had something to think about while they worked—they had the memory of the last time they had been drunk, and the hope of the time when they would be drunk again. As for Jurgis, he was expected to bring home every penny; he could not even go with the men at noontime—he was supposed to sit down and eat his dinner on a pile of fertilizer dust.

This was not always his mood, of course; he still loved his family. But just now was a time of trial. Poor little Antanas, for instance—who had never failed to win him with a smile—little Antanas was not smiling just now, being a mass of fiery red pimples. He had had all the diseases that babies are heir to, in quick succession—scarlet fever, mumps, and whooping cough in the first year, and now he was down with the measles. There was no one to attend him but Kotrina; there was no doctor to help him, because they were too poor, and children did not die of the measles—at least not often. Now and then Kotrina would find time to sob over his woes, but for the greater part of the time he had to be left alone, barricaded upon the bed. The floor was full of drafts, and if he caught cold he would die. At night he was tied down, lest he should kick the covers off him, while the family lay in their stupor of exhaustion. He would lie and scream for hours, almost in convulsions; and then when he was worn out, he would lie whimpering and wailing in his torment. He was burning up with fever, and his eyes were running sores; in the daytime he was a thing uncanny and impish to behold, a plaster of pimples and sweat, a great purple lump of misery. Yet all this was not really as cruel as it sounds, for, sick as he was, little Antanas was the least unfortunate member of that family. He was quite able to bear his sufferings—it was as if he had all these complaints to show what a prodigy of health he was. He was the child of his parents' youth and joy; he grew up like the conjurer's rose bush, and all the world was his oyster. In general, he toddled around the kitchen all day with a lean and hungry look—the portion of the family's allowance that fell to him was not enough, and he was unrestrainable in his demand for more. Antanas was but little over a year old, and already no one but his father could manage him.

It seemed as if he had taken all of his mother's strength—had left nothing for those that might come after him. Ona was with child again now, and it was a dreadful thing to contemplate; even Jurgis, dumb and despairing as he was, could not but understand that yet other agonies were on the way, and shudder at the thought of them.

For Ona was visibly going to pieces. In the first place she was developing a cough, like the one that had killed old Dede Antanas. She had had a trace of it ever since that fatal morning when the greedy street-car corporation had turned her out into the rain; but now it was beginning to grow serious, and to wake her up at night. Even worse than that was the fearful nervousness from which she suffered; she would have frightful headaches and fits of aimless weeping; and sometimes she would come home at night shuddering and moaning, and would fling herself down upon the bed and burst into tears. Several times she was quite beside herself and hysterical; and then Jurgis would go half mad with fright. Elzbieta would explain to him that it could not be helped, that woman was subject to such things when she was pregnant; but he was hardly to be persuaded, and would beg and plead to know what had happened. She had never been like this before, he would argue—it was monstrous and unthinkable. It was the life she had to live, the accursed work she had to do, that was killing her by inches. She was not fitted for it—no woman was fitted for it, no woman ought to be allowed to do such work; if the world could not keep them alive any other way it ought to kill them at once and be done with it. They ought not to marry, to have children; no working-man ought to marry—if he, Jurgis, had known what a woman was like, he would have had his eyes torn out first. So he would carry on, becoming half hysterical himself, which was an unbearable thing to see in a big man; Ona would pull herself together and fling herself into his arms, begging him to stop, to be still, that she would be better, it would be all right. So she would lie and sob out her grief upon his shoulder, while he gazed at her, as helpless as a wounded animal, the target of unseen enemies.

4. Rose Schneiderman and the Triangle Shirtwaist Fire

BONNIE MITELMAN

On the surface, the Progressive Era seemed to promote the betterment of the people. Productivity and real income rose steadily between 1900 and 1920, and government policies were aimed, usually successfully, at ensuring efficiency, stability, economic growth, and order. Farm prices emerged from their nineteenth-century slump and rural America seemed increasingly prosperous. The United States was on the rise as a global power, with the rest of the world taking note of its increasing population and economic clout.

But for some Americans, there was not much "progress" to the Progressive Era. Life in the working-class neighborhoods of large cities left much to be desired, especially for poor immigrants who had recently arrived in the United States. They labored for numbingly long hours performing repetitive tasks on assembly lines. The work was monotonous and often dangerous, with factory owners interested in nothing but productivity. Appalling working conditions and criminally low pay were the lot of the urban poor. Labor unions, still in their infancy, could do little to improve their lives. In 1911, when 146 women died in the Triangle shirtwaist fire, large numbers of Americans first learned of the misery in the sweatshops of New York City. In the following essay, Bonnie Mitelman describes the tragedy.

On Saturday afternoon, March 25, 1911, in New York City's Greenwich Village, a small fire broke out in the Triangle Waist Company, just as the 500 shirtwaist employees were quitting for the day. People rushed about, trying to get out, but they found exits blocked and windows to the fire escape rusted shut. They panicked.

As the fire spread and more and more were trapped, some began to jump, their hair and clothing afire, from the eighth and ninth floor windows. Nets that firemen held for them tore apart at the impact of the falling bodies. By the time it was over, 146 workers had died, most of them young Jewish women.

A United Press reporter, William Shepherd, witnessed the tragedy and reported, "I looked upon the heap of dead bodies and I remembered these girls were the shirtwaist makers. I remembered their great strike of last year in which these same girls had demanded more sanitary conditions and more safety precautions in the shops. These dead bodies were the answer."

The horror of that fire touched the entire Lower East Side ghetto community, and there was a profuse outpouring of sympathy. But it was Rose Schneiderman, an immigrant worker with a spirit of social justice and a powerful way with words, who is largely credited with translating the ghetto's emotional reaction into meaningful, widespread action. Six weeks following the tragedy, and after years of solid groundwork, with one brilliant, well-timed speech, she was able to inspire the support of wealthy uptown New Yorkers and to swing public opinion to the side of the labor movement, enabling concerned civic, religious, and labor leaders to mobilize their efforts for desperately needed safety and industrial reforms.

The Triangle fire, and the deaths of so many helpless workers, seemed to trigger in Rose Schneiderman an intense realization that there was absolutely nothing or no one to help working women except a strong union movement. With fierce determination and the dedication, influence, and funding of many other people as well, she battled to regulate hours, wages, and safety standards and to abolish the sweatshop system. In so doing, she brought dignity and human rights to all workers.

The dramatic "uprising of the 20,000" of 1909–10, in which thousands of immigrant girls and women in the shirtwaist industry had endured three long winter months of a general strike to protest deplorable working conditions, had produced some immediate gains for working women. There had been agreements for shorter working hours, increased wages, and even safety reforms, but there had not been formal recognition of their union. At Triangle, for example, the girls had gained a 52 hour week, a 12–15 percent wage increase, and promises to end the grueling subcontracting system. But they had not gained the only instrument on which they could depend for lasting change: a viable trade union. This was to have disastrous results, for in spite of the few gains that they seemed to have made, the workers won no rights or bargaining power at all. In fact, "The company dealt only with its contractors. It felt no responsibility for the girls."

There were groups as well as individuals who realized the workers' impotence, but their attempts to change the situation accomplished little despite long years of hard work. The Women's Trade Union League and the International Ladies Garment Workers' Union, through the efforts of Mary Dreier, Helen Marot, Leonora O'Reilly, Pauline Newman, and Rose Schneiderman had struggled unsuccessfully for improved conditions: the futility that the union organizers were feeling in late 1910 is reflected in the WTUL minutes of December 5 of that year.

A scant eight months after their historic waistmakers' strike, and three months before the deadly Triangle fire, a Mrs. Malkiel (no doubt Theresa Serber Malkiel, who wrote the legendary account of the strike, *The Diary of a Shirtwaist Striker: A Story of the Shirtwaist Makers' Strike in New York*) is reported to have come before the League to urge action after a devastating fire in Newark, New Jersey killed twenty-five working women. Mrs. Malkiel attributed their loss to the greed and negligence of the owners and the proper authorities. The WTUL subsequently demanded an investigation of all factory buildings and it elected an investigation committee from the League to cooperate with similar committees from other organizations.

The files of the WTUL contain complaint after complaint about unsafe factory conditions; many were filled out by workers afraid to sign their names for fear of being fired had their employers seen the forms. They describe factories with locked doors, no fire escapes, and barred windows. The *New York Times* carried an article which reported that fourteen factories were found to have no fire escapes, twenty-three that had locked doors, and seventy-eight that had obstructed fire escapes. In all, according to the article, 99 percent of the factories investigated in New York were found to have serious fire hazards.

Yet no action was taken.

It was the Triangle fire that emphasized, spectacularly and tragically, the deplorable safety and sanitary conditions of the garment workers. The tragedy focused attention upon the ghastly factories in which most immigrants worked; there was no longer any question about what the strikers had meant when they talked about safety and sanitary reform, and about social and economic justice.

The grief and frustration of the shirtwaist strikers were expressed by one of them, Rose Safran, after the fire: "If the union had won we would have been safe. Two of our demands were for adequate fire escapes and for open doors from the factories to the street. But the bosses defeated us and we didn't get the open doors or the better fire escapes. So our friends are dead."

The families of the fire victims were heartbroken and hysterical, the ghetto's *Jewish Daily Forward* was understandably melodramatic, and the immigrant community was completely enraged. Their Jewish heritage had taught them an emphasis on individual human life and worth; their shared background in the *shtetl* and common experiences in the ghetto had given them a sense of fellowship. They were, in a sense, a family—and some of the most helpless among them had died needlessly.

The senseless deaths of so many young Jewish women sparked within these Eastern Europeans a new determination and dedication. The fire had made reform absolutely essential. Workers' rights were no longer just socialist jargon: They were a matter of life and death.

The Triangle Waist Company was located on the three floors of the Asch Building, a 10-story, 135-foot-high structure at the corner of Greene Street and Washington Place in Greenwich Village. One of the largest shirtwaist manufacturers, Triangle employed up to 900 people at times, but on the day of the fire, only about 500 were working.

Leon Stein's brilliant and fascinating account of the fire, entitled simply *The Triangle Fire,* develops and documents the way in which the physical facilities, company procedures, and human behavior interacted to cause this great tragedy. Much of what occurred was ironic, some was cruel, some stupid, some pathetic. It is a dramatic portrayal of the eternal confrontation of the "haves" and the "have-nots," told in large part by those who survived.

Fire broke out at the Triangle Company at approximately 4:45 P.M. (because time clocks were reportedly set back to stretch the day, and because other records give differing times of the first fire alarm, it is uncertain exactly what time the fire started), just after pay envelopes had been distributed and employees were leaving their work posts. It was a small fire at first, and there was a calm, controlled effort to extinguish it. But the fire began to spread, jumping from one pile of debris to another, engulfing the combustible shirtwaist fabric. It became obvious that the fire could not be snuffed out, and workers tried to reach the elevators or stairway. Those who reached the one open stairway raced down eight flights of stairs to safety; those who managed to climb onto the available passenger elevators also got out. But not everyone could reach the available exits. Some tried to open the door to a stairway and found it locked. Others were trapped between long working tables or behind the hordes of people trying to get into the elevators or out through the one open door.

Under the work tables, rags were burning; the wooden floors, trim, and window frames were also afire. Frantically, workers fought their way to the elevators, to the fire escape, and to the windows—to any place that might lead to safety.

Fire whistles and bells sounded as the fire department raced to the building. But equipment proved inadequate, as the fire ladders reached only to the seventh floor. And by the time the firemen connected their hoses to douse the flames, the crowded eighth floor was completely ablaze.

For those who reached the windows, there seemed to be a chance for safety. The *New York World* describes people balancing on window sills, nine stories up, with flames scorching them from behind, until firemen arrived: "The nets were spread below with all promptness. Citizens were commandeered into service, as the firemen necessarily gave their attention to the one engine and hose of the force that first arrived. The catapult force that the bodies gathered in the long plunges made the nets utterly without avail. Screaming girls and men, as they fell, tore the nets from the grasp of the holders, and the bodies struck the sidewalks and lay just as they fell. Some of the bodies ripped big holes through the life nets."

One reporter who witnessed the fire remembered how,

A young man helped a girl to the window sill on the ninth floor. Then he held her out deliberately, away from the building, and let her drop. He held out a second girl the same way and let her drop. He held out a third girl who did not resist. They were all as unresisting as if he were helping them into a street car instead of into eternity. He saw that a terrible death awaited them in the flames and his was only a terrible chivalry. He brought around another girl to the window. I saw her put her arms around him and kiss him. Then he held her into space—and dropped her. Quick as a flash, he was on the window sill himself. His coat fluttered upwards—the air filled his trouser legs as he came down. I could see he wore tan shoes.

Those who had rushed to the fire escape found the window openings rusted shut. Several precious minutes were lost in releasing them. The fire escape itself ended at the second floor, in an airshaft between the Asch Building and the building next door. But too frantic to notice where it ended, workers climbed onto the fire escape, one after another until, in one terrifying moment, it collapsed from the weight, pitching the workers to their death.

Those who had made their way to the elevators found crowds pushing to get into the cars. When it became obvious that the elevators could no longer run, workers jumped down the elevator shaft, landing on the top of the cars, or grabbing for cables to ease their descent. Several died, but incredibly, some did manage to save themselves in this way. One man was found, hours after the fire, beneath an elevator car in the basement of the building, nearly drowned by the rapidly rising water from the firemen's hoses.

Several people, among them Triangle's two owners, raced to the roof, and from there were led to safety. Others never had that chance. "When Fire Chief Croker could make his way into the [top] three floors," states one account of the fire, "he found sights that utterly staggered him . . . he saw as the smoke drifted away bodies burned to bare bones. There were skeletons bending over sewing machines."

The day after the fire, the *New York Times* announced that "the building was fireproof. It shows hardly any signs of the disaster that overtook it. The walls are as good as ever, as are the floors: nothing is worse for the fire except the furniture and 141 [*sic*] of the 600 men and girls that were employed in its upper three stories."

The building *was* fireproof. But there had never been a fire drill in the factory, even though the management had been warned about the possible hazard of fire on the top three floors. Owners Max Blanck and Isaac Harris had chosen to ignore these warnings in spite of the fact that many of their employees were immigrants who could barely speak English, which would surely mean panic in the event of a crisis.

The *New York Times* also noted that Leonora O'Reilly of the League had reported Max Blanck's visit to the WTUL during the shirtwaist strike, and his plea that the girls return to work. He claimed a business reputation to maintain and told the Union leaders he would make the necessary improvements right way. Because he was the largest manufacturer in the business, the League reported, they trusted him and let the girls return.

But the improvements were never made. And there was nothing that anybody could or would do about it. Factory doors continued to open in instead of out, in violation of fire regulations. The doors remained bolted during working hours, apparently to prevent workers from getting past the inspectors with stolen merchandise. Triangle had only two staircases where there should have been three, and those two were very narrow. Despite the fact that the building was deemed fireproof, it had wooden window frames, floors, and trim. There was no sprinkler system. It was not legally required.

These were the same kinds of conditions which existed in factories throughout the garment industry; they had been cited repeatedly in the complaints filed with the WTUL. They were not unusual nor restricted to Triangle; in fact, Triangle was not as bad as many other factories.

But it was at Triangle that the fire took place.

The *Jewish Daily Forward* mourned the dead with sorrowful stories, and its headlines talked of "funerals instead of weddings" for the dead young girls. The entire Jewish immigrant community was affected, for it seemed there was scarcely a person who was not in some way touched by the fire. Nearly everyone had either been employed at Triangle themselves, or had a friend or relative who had worked there at some time or another. Most worked in factories with similar conditions, and so everyone identified with the victims and their families.

Many of the dead, burned beyond recognition, remained unidentified for days, as searching family members returned again and again to wait in long lines to look for their loved ones. Many survivors were unable to identify their mothers, sisters, or wives; the confusion of handling so many victims and so many survivors who did not understand what was happening to them and to their dead led to even more anguish for the community. Some of the victims were identified by the names on the pay envelopes handed to them at quitting time and stuffed deeply into pockets or stockings just before the fire. But many bodies remained unclaimed for days, with bewildered and bereaved survivors wandering among them, trying to find some identifying mark.

Charges of first- and second-degree manslaughter were brought against the two men who owned Triangle, and Leon Stein's book artfully depicts the subtle psychological and sociological implications of the powerful against the oppressed, and of the Westernized, German–Jewish immigrants against those still living their old-world, Eastern European heritage. Ultimately, Triangle owners Blanck and Harris were acquitted of the charges against them, and in due time they collected their rather sizable insurance.

The shirtwaist, popularized by Gibson girls, had come to represent the new-found freedom of females in America. After the fire, it symbolized death. The reaction of the grief-stricken Lower East Side was articulated by socialist lawyer Morris Hillquit:

The girls who went on strike last year were trying to readjust the conditions under which they were obliged to work. I wonder if there is not some connection between the fire and that strike. I wonder if the magistrates who sent to jail the girls who did picket duty in front of the Triangle shop realized last Sunday that some of the responsibility may be theirs. Had the strike been successful, these girls might have been alive today and the citizenry of New York would have less of a burden upon its conscience.

For the first time in the history of New York's garment industry there were indications that the public was beginning to accept responsibility for the exploitation of the immigrants. For the first time, the establishment seemed to understand that these were human beings asking for their rights, not merely trouble-making anarchists.

The day after the Triangle fire a protest meeting was held at the Women's Trade Union League, with representatives from twenty leading labor and civic organizations. They formed "a relief committee to cooperate with the Red Cross in its work among the families of the victims, and another committee . . . to broaden the investigation and research on fire hazards in New York factories which was already being carried on by the League."

The minutes of the League recount the deep indignation that members felt at the indifference of a public which had ignored their pleas for safety after the Newark fire. In an attempt to translate their anger into constructive action, the League drew up a list of forceful resolutions that included a plan to gather delegates from all of the city's unions to make a concerted effort to force safety changes in factories. In addition, the League called upon all workers to inspect factories and then report any violations to the proper city authorities and to the WTUL. They called upon the city to immediately appoint organized workers as unofficial inspectors. They resolved to submit the following fire regulations suggestions: compulsory fire drills, fireproof exits, unlocked doors, fire alarms, automatic sprinklers, and regular inspections. The League called upon the legislature to create the Bureau of Fire Projection and finally, the League underscored the absolute need for all workers to organize themselves at once into trade unions so that they would never again be powerless.

The League also voted to participate in the funeral procession for the unidentified dead of the Triangle fire.

The city held a funeral for the dead who were unclaimed. "More than 120,000 of us were in the funeral procession that miserable rainy April day," remembered Rose Schneiderman. "From ten in the morning until four in the afternoon we of the Women's Trade Union League marched in the procession with other trade-union men and women, all of us filled with anguish and regret that we had never been able to organize the Triangle workers."

Schneiderman, along with many others, was absolutely determined that this kind of tragedy would never happen again. With single-minded dedication, they devoted themselves to unionizing the workers. The searing example of the Triangle fire provided them with the impetus they needed to gain public support for their efforts.

They dramatized and emphasized and capitalized on the scandalous working conditions of the immigrants. From all segments of the community came cries for labor reform. Stephen S. Wise, the prestigious reform rabbi, called for the formation of a citizens' committee. Jacob H. Schiff, Bishop David H. Greer, Governor John A. Dix, Anne Morgan (of *the* Morgans) and other leading civic and religious leaders collaborated in a mass meeting at the Metropolitan Opera House on May 2 to protest factory conditions and to show support for the workers.

Several people spoke at that meeting on May 2, and many in the audience began to grow restless and antagonistic. Finally, 29-year-old Rose Schneiderman stepped up to the podium.

In a whisper barely audible, she began to address the crowd.

I would be a traitor to these poor burned bodies, if I came here to talk good fellowship. We have tried you good people of the public and we have found you wanting. The old Inquisition had its rack and its thumbscrews and its instruments of torture with iron teeth. We know what these things are today: the iron teeth are our necessities, the thumbscrews the high-powered and swift machinery close to which we must work, and the rack is here in the fire-proof structures that will destroy us the minute they catch on fire.

This is not the first time girls have burned alive in the city. Every week I must learn of the untimely death of one of my sister workers. Every year thousands of us are maimed. The life of men and women is so cheap and property is so sacred. There are so many of us for one job it matters little if 140-odd are burned to death.

We have tried you, citizens; we are trying you now, and you have a couple of dollars for the sorrowing mothers and daughters and sisters by way of a charity gift. But every time the workers come out in the only way they know to protest against conditions which are unbearable, the strong hand of the law is allowed to press down heavily upon us.

Public officials have only words of warning to us—warning that we must be intensely orderly and must be intensely peaceable, and they have the workhouse just back of all their warnings. The strong hand of the law beats us back when we rise into the conditions that make life bearable.

I can't talk fellowship to you who are gathered here. Too much blood has been spilled. I know from my experience it is up to the working people to save themselves. The only way they can save themselves is by a strong working-class movement.

Her speech has become a classic. It is more than just an emotional picture of persecution; it reflects the pervasive sadness and profound understanding that comes from knowing, finally, the cruel realities of life, the perspective of history, and the nature of human beings.

The devastation of that fire and the futility of the seemingly successful strike that had preceded it seemed to impart an undeniable truth to Rose Schneiderman: They could not fail again. The events of 1911 seemed to have made her, and many others, more keenly aware than they had ever been that the workers' fight for reform was absolutely essential. If they did not do it, it would not be done.

In a sense, the fire touched off in Schneiderman an awareness of her own responsibility in the battle for industrial reform. This fiery socialist worker had been transformed into a highly effective labor leader.

The influential speech she gave did help swing public opinion to the side of the trade unions, and the fire itself had made the workers more aware of the crucial need to unionize. Widespread support for labor reform and unionization emerged. Pressure from individuals, such as Rose Schneiderman, as well as from groups like the Women's Trade Union League and the International Ladies Garment Workers' Union, helped form the New York State Factory Investigating Commission, the New York Citizens' Committee on Safety, and other regulatory and investigatory bodies. The League and Local 25 (the Shirtwaist Makers' Union of the ILGWU) were especially instrumental in attaining a new Industrial Code for New York State, which became "the most outstanding instrument for safeguarding the lives, health, and welfare of the millions of wage earners in New York State and . . . in the nation at large."

It took years for these changes to occur, and labor reform did not rise majestically, Phoenix-like, from the ashes of the Triangle fire. But that fire, and Rose Schneiderman's whispered plea for a strong working-class movement, had indeed become the loud, clear call for action.

PART TWO

THE NEW WORLD POWER, 1900–1920

In the 1890s, although Europeans noticed with some amazement the extraordinary growth of the American economy, they still viewed the United States as a second-rate military power, a distant backwater in world affairs. Historically, the United States had been absorbed with internal affairs, concentrating on domination of North America and insisting, in such foreign policy statements as the Monroe Doctrine, that Europeans recognize the continent as an American sphere of influence. The United States contributed to its image as a provincial, second-rate power by worshipping at the altar of isolationism, hiding behind the two oceans and preaching a continuing message of American virtue and European vice.

By 1920, all that had changed. The United States declared war on Spain in 1898, and the subsequent overwhelming American victory announced to the world that a new power had appeared. As an immediate result of the war, the United States established its own empire, imposing a virtual protectorate in Cuba and acquiring sovereignty over Puerto Rico, Guam, Hawaii, and the Philippines. Those acquisitions gave the United States an enormous stake in the Pacific, requiring a two-ocean navy and rapid access to much of the world. To facilitate naval mobility and international trade, President Theodore Roosevelt seized what became the Panama Canal Zone from Colombia in 1903 and began construction of the waterway. The United States completed its formal territorial acquisitions by purchasing the Virgin Islands in 1917 from Denmark. Along with these new territorial entities came the challenges of governance, protection, and economic development. The old isolationist philosophy would not be able to survive the new responsibilities.

But the Spanish–American War was only a sideshow, at least compared to World War I, in the emergence of the United States as the premier power on earth. When Great Britain, France, and Russia went to war with Germany, Italy, Austria–Hungary, and Turkey in 1914, President Woodrow Wilson initially adopted a position of neutrality, hoping to stay out of the conflict. But Germany made that impossible. Submarine warfare against American merchant vessels cost American lives and forced the president's hand. In 1917, the United States declared war, and Wilson soon turned the conflict into a crusade for democracy. The American army provided the Allies with the resources they needed to defeat Germany, and the American economy supplied enormous, unprecedented volumes of war goods. When the armistice was signed in November 1918, there was no doubt anymore about the relative position of the United States in the world. The American economy was by far the largest and healthiest on earth and the American army and navy the most powerful. The world financial center had shifted from London to Wall Street. The American century had begun.

5. Fighting Life in the Philippines

HENRY C. ROWLAND

During the Spanish–American War, Filipino nationalists, led by Emilio Aguinaldo, readily cooperated with the United States, hoping a Spanish defeat would bring about the independence of the Philippines. Much to Aguinaldo's disappointment, the American victory only ushered in a new era of subjugation. When the United States refused Filipino demands for independence and imposed its own colonial administration, Aguinaldo launched a guerrilla campaign against the Americans. It was a bloody conflict, characterized by atrocities on both sides. General Jacob H. Smith urged his troops to "kill and burn and take no prisoners . . . the more you kill and burn the better it will please me. I want all persons killed who are capable of bearing arms in actual hostilities in the United States."

And kill and burn they did. Between 1899 and 1902, U.S. soldiers killed more than 20,000 Filipino troops and saw to the deaths of more than 200,000 Filipino civilians because of famine, disease, and war-related events. The extent of the slaughter created a backlash of antiwar criticism. Philosopher William James wondered, "Could there be a more damning indictment of that whole ideal termed 'modern civilization' than this amounts to?" When news surfaced of American soldiers cold-bloodedly murdering large numbers of Filipino women and children, the public brooded about how such events could ever happen. In the following essay, written at the height of the Filipino–American War, Henry C. Rowland describes how and why they occurred.

A primary consideration of the tales of cruelty proceeding from the Philippines must naturally first evoke the query, "Are they true?" "Is it actually the case that commissioned officers of the United States Army have summarily ordered the execution of natives without trial; have ordered the torture of others; and that these orders have been unquestioningly obeyed by non-coms, and privates?" If so, how can it be explained? How can the average American citizen of education and enlightened civilization, who, on the way to his office, reads in a creditable newspaper an account of these atrocities committed by other American citizens of very possibly his own type and associations; how can this well-ordered, well-regulated, modern-minded individual conceive such horrors?

He cannot.

For him to try to deduce from his own observation and experiences the psychic reversion or avatism by which, in a few weeks' time, a civilized individual can hark back to a primitive state of savagery, would be as difficult as it would for him to follow the chemical diatheses by which a few minutes' incineration of his physical self might cause it to be resolved into its original elements.

To presume that these reports of atrocities are wholly or partially untrue, would be to eliminate the necessity of this argument, for the sake of which we will grant the following:

(1) That United States commissioned officers have ordered the execution without trial of natives; (2) that United States commissioned officers have ordered the torture of natives; and (3) that these orders have been carried out without protest, by subordinates; i.e., non-commissioned officers and private soldiers.

It is easy to understand a monomania of blood-thirstiness existing in the individual as the result of heat, fever, exposure, and other climatic conditions. History is full of such cases. The difficult task for us is the conception of an obedient fulfillment of cruel and savage orders by exactly such men as we see about us every day. If our troops were bound by such infrangible ties of discipline as characterize the rank and file of certain continental armies, whose soldiers have sucked in a martial atmosphere from infancy, and to whom the obedience of an order is as much of an unconscious reflex as the act of closing the eyes at the report of a gun, the matter would be clearer.

This, however, is by no means the case. The average American soldier is a comparatively recent production, and although in an all-round military capacity we refuse to admit the existence of his superior, it is true that a blind, implicit obedience to orders is not his highest qualification. On receiving an order, his first instinct is to analyze its reason, not with any idea of questioning it, but in order that he may carry it out with the greatest individual intelligence. He presupposes that the order is a proper one, but if by any chance it was not, he would be very apt to discover the fact at once.

He is supposed to think. It is required of him. The result is that where three orders would be necessary to obtain a certain result with a platoon of Russian peasants, the American soldier would require but one; that one suggesting to his mind the other two. When he is advancing in open order or on the skirmish line he is often trusted to fight his own fight in his own way; that is, he is expected to use his head. We know of one regiment, which, during its service in Luzon, was able to take entire charge of the repairing and running of the Manila and Dagupan Railroad. In the ranks were to be found experienced civil and mechanical engineers, train-crews, linemen, telegraphic operators, train dispatchers, switchmen; in fact, all of the component parts of a complete railroad system. The start of one of these trains was a cure for nostalgia. The engine-driver in the customary blue jean overalls and leather artisan's cap would lean from the window of the diminutive cab; the fireman would loll back with the bell-rope in his hand, and some wit from the ranks, who was playing the *rôle* of conductor, with 200 rounds swung from his waist and a revolver in the place of a ticket punch, would wave his arm and cry, "All aboard for the Northern Limited, stopping at Malolos and Calumpit, junction of the railroad and the dirt road!"

When a man of this sort is ordered to shoot at some one, he is apt to know that it is not a saluting charge! If he was ordered to shoot his brother, or a "bunkie," we fear that he would not act with the lofty, martial self-sacrifice to duty chronicled in history. The chances are that he would shoot high, or perhaps toss his piece into the culprit's hands with an admonition to "hike for the woods"!

A knowledge of these conditions forces us to admit that in the case of the trialless, wholesale executions of which we read, the orders to kill are carried out by the men, not in blind obedience, but because such orders seem to them good. The factors in the production of such a state of mind cannot be distinguished at a range of 12,000 miles. An intelligent comprehension of them demands either a personal experience or an accurate reproduction. Reading in his morning paper of the torture and wholesale extermination of helpless Filipinos, the average New Yorker or Philadelphian thinks at once of the Tom, Dick, or Harry whom he happens to know in the Philippines, and is assured that if only all of the men were of the type of this particular acquaintance there would be no such disgraceful blots on the pages of our nation's recent history!

Now, as a matter of fact, it is just some such Tom, Dick, or Harry who has done these things. Let us try to follow the military career of these three types, and see if we can throw some light upon the casuistry producing such results.

Tom is an intelligent young Irish-American born in New York City. His father is a sub-contractor, fairly prosperous and respected. Tom has a good public-school education, and has held a position as shipping clerk in a wholesale house, but has lost it through being a trifle wild in his habits. This has brought down the ire of his parent. They have quarreled, and Tom, in pique and despondency, has enlisted in the United States Regular Infantry.

Dick has been "raised" in Gainesville, Georgia. He is a high-spirited boy, and the fireside reminiscences of Civil War veterans have roused his martial ardor. A quarrel with his sweetheart leaves him with the conviction that he is destined for a hero's death—or proud return.

Harry is a clerk in his uncle's store, the only one in a middle Western village. He has watched the trainloads of troops rushing through on their way to the Pacific Coast, and being Anglo-Saxon, and therefore adventurous, he has been unable to resist the temptation of following them.

Tom, Dick, and Harry meet in the Presidio at San Francisco. There they are physically reexamined, and assigned to the same company of the same regiment.

Tom was once a "boss" of one of his father's gangs of men, and has a natural capacity for sub-leadership; that is, for inducing other men to carry out the orders of some one in authority. This faculty, with the tactics learned in a militia regiment to which he had once belonged, soon secures for him the rank of "lance corporal."

The regiment embarks on one of the big transports, and as the Farallones slowly merge into the haze below the sky-line, the trio experience the first real pangs of homesickness, which are not alleviated by the month's voyage to Manila.

On landing in Luzon the regiment is sent immediately to the front. At this time almost any direction is the front, and they have not far to go. At first the excitement of the firing-line, and their interest in strange, new surroundings, sweep away the nostalgia. Later, when the glamour of the novelty has worn off, it returns again, but in the sub-acute and chronic form which is much more insidious. With it they run the usual gamut of heat, fever, dhobie itch, and dysentery, but they are a hardy trio, and all of these elements are but factors in the tempering process. At the end of their first year they find themselves practically immune from petty tropical disorders, but deep down under the chromic tan and the lean, sinewy muscles the sluggish ulcer of discontent gnaws at their hearts.

When the regimental surgeon writes "Nostalgia" as the diagnosis of a patient, he is apt to hesitate for a moment to decide whether the more fitting term might not be "Malingering." At any rate, patients with the former malady do not receive any extra amount of care and attention. Yet this condition, this chronic homesickness, is one of the most dangerous disorders which we have to treat. It represents the solution from which may crystallize insanity. It is the more dangerous in that it is so often unsuspected, and will smolder along until it finally bursts into a flame of suicidal, or homicidal, mania. It accounts for more dementia than sun or fever.

Tom, Dick, and Harry see cases of this kind before they have been long in the islands. They were sent to garrison a town on the Laguna de Bay. The place had already been twice taken by American troops, but their regiment took it a third time, and then occupied it. It is not the capture of a place that endangers a regiment; it is the subsequent inertia of garrison duty. The excitement of campaigning had by this time entirely worn off. Even the prospect of a fight failed to give them the former thrills. They were forced to rotate in a very limited orbit, as there were only two companies of them, and the insurgents were entrenched all about the place.

When a man is herded with a body of other men for awhile, he begins, to a certain extent, to lose his individuality. When there is not one single familiar feature in all of his environment, this loss of a former identity is much enhanced. He begins to cease to think of himself as Jones or Brown or some one else, of such and such a place. He is simply a unit of a certain whole, and the discharge of his duties in this capacity grows more and more automatic. He is no longer influenced by the conditions under which he was born and bred. He ceases to be governed by his former code of ethics. There is nothing around him to remind him that he is himself. His principles unconsciously adjust themselves to surrounding conditions and circumstances. What young Mr. Brown, of Greenfield, Illinois, might have done if offered an indignity by any one, has nothing to do with what Sergeant Brown,—th United States Infantry, might do if, when half-sick and thoroughly disgusted at the end of a long day's march, he is fired on by a native from a Nipa hut.

One day while on guard duty a second sergeant of one of the companies was suddenly seized with an acute dementia. The worst feature of his case lay in the fact that at the time his belt was full of ammunition, and his Krag-Jörgensen was in his hands. He had strayed a few yards from the outposts, "shack," when suddenly and without the slightest warning he threw up his piece and opened a hot, though deliberate fire upon his comrades. The others, recognizing the situation, promptly took to cover. The cover was full of Filipinos, but that was an unimportant item: the Filipinos were poor shots, the sergeant known to be a fine one.

Seeing no one in sight, the madman started for the enemy's trenches at a slow run, and as he ran he howled. The last that was seen of him was as he disappeared in an intervening clump of bamboos. Two days later he returned unharmed, with but five rounds left in his belt. The dementia had passed, leaving him confused and a trifle depressed. Why he was not killed was never definitely learned. His comrades told the surgeon that for several weeks he had been moody and uncommunicative. Once or twice he had remarked that unless they went on a "hike" before long he would lose his mind. His diagnosis was entered in the hospital records as "acute mania," and there being no return of the disorder, he was in due time recorded as "recovered."

A few days later a corporal suddenly leaped from the window of a Nipa hut where he was quartered, and without the slightest discoverable cause, sprang upon a passing native, threw him to the ground, and began to beat him unmercifully. It took ten men to take the soldier to the hospital, where for two hours he raved, suffering apparently from the delusion that he was in action. The surgeon did not give him any sedative, wishing to observe the case. This man had formerly belonged to the signal corps, and in his delirium he sent and received messages, and went through all the technicalities of an advance under fire. Before long he became quiet and slept all night. The following morning he had no recollection of the incident, but was very depressed, rather ashamed of his being in hospital, and requested to be returned to duty as he "felt all right." This man bore an excellent reputation, was popular with his officers and comrades, and had never been known to drink or in any way badly comport himself.

There were two other men in the company who were known to be suffering from chronic nostalgia. The resulting depression of spirits had made them negligent of their duties to the extent of being several times reprimanded, and once or twice sent to the guard-house. Soon there developed the profound conviction that every one was leagued against them. This in one case produced a morbid mental condition that resulted in an attempted suicide by jumping into the river. The other was found by an officer and a squad of men deliberately attempting the murder of a native. It was impossible to discover any motive for the act. One of these men returned to San Francisco under the care of the author, the other was lost sight of. The man who was sent home made a perfect recovery before the Golden Gate was reached.

There was another case of a commissioned officer whose health was such that he was ordered by the commanding medical officer to remain in hospital. This order produced a state of irritation in the patient entirely disproportionate to the cause. Upon his attempting to leave the officers' ward he was forcibly detained, at which his rage knew no bounds, even reaching the point of his loudly threatening to kill the medical officer upon the next opportunity that offered. The recovery of this patient was, as far as we know, complete. Indeed, he could hardly have been described as demented at any time. He was really no more insane than is the man who becomes wildly infuriated at some inanimate object, after the manner of a child who attacks a door against which it has knocked its head.

Quantities of such cases might be cited, all going to prove conclusively that under certain unaccustomed conditions it is possible for men to behave in a manner entirely foreign to all prehabitual impulse as the result of unusual influences upon which they have no gauge. This would, of course, only apply to those whose lives have formerly run in more or less of a groove or track, and usually upon scheduled time. When a machine of this sort gets derailed the wheels continue to revolve, and the result is apt to be disastrous to surrounding objects as well as to the machine.

Tom, Dick, and Harry observe these things with sympathy. Although they have never run off their own track, they are able to understand how it would feel. They do not know the meaning of the word "psychology"; a dissertation on nervous physiology would be lost upon them; nevertheless they are clearly able to follow the cause and effect. Often when on outpost duty through the long, soft, mysterious tropic night, they have felt the gnawing pain of a heartaching homesickness, though they would not have described it as such, so faint and dim has the thought of home become. One by one their letters have ceased to arrive. The last transport brought no tidings, and at their lack, the cold chill of disappointment has proved as hardening as a pail of water on glowing steel. They have long since ceased to look upon friendly natives with a kindly toleration; no longer do they play with the brown babies and chat with the soft-eyed mothers in the market-place. They have found comrades who had grown to trust these furtive islanders, cold and stark, hacked and dismembered in the bananas. They look aslant at the "Amigos" who wish them a smiling, guttural greeting as they pass. A native's life assumes in their eyes an equal value to that of a sheep-killing collie. The sight of a trench full of dead insurgents awakens no more feeling than the wreck of a cattle train. They ponder among themselves, and decide that the only chance of pacification lies in a wholesale cataclysm; an inundation of human blood that will purge the islands of treachery.

So it is with their hard-faced company commander, who has fought his men on both sides of the same trenches. When he plans an advance, the slippery foe rise and scatter like a covey of partridges, to return later and stealthily cut up the outposts. A town or village is taken; let it be three days abandoned, and it is all to do again. No base is necessary for this guerrilla foe who mobilize by a smoke on the mountain side, and can make a long day's march upon a handful of bananas and a gourd of ditch water. The captain despairs of accomplishing his work upon any preconceived system of tactics. His enemy refuse either to fight or to surrender. The Filipino soldier is only to be trusted when a Krag has crashed through his vitals. The officers can see ahead of them neither victory nor defeat. They begin to regard the insurrectos as vermin only to be ridded by extermination. They are rats who refuse either to leave the house or to enter the traps. Partial relief comes at last when the batallion is ordered to the southern islands, and here we see them in still another setting. This is the picture:

The scene, a mountainous island in the Sulu Sea. Palms fringe a gleaming beach in a broad belt of glistening green. Above it, higher on the slope, is a stretch of sun-scorched meadowland. Over this a dark green wall, before which rise the bald trunks of mighty trees, marking the fringe of the forest.

A column of men winds out of the long cool avenue of cocoa palms, pauses a moment, and strikes across the furnace of open meadow beyond which lies the forest. In single file they take the native wood-cutters' winding path, which lies twisting and turning up the incline where the merciless rays of the afternoon sun beat vertically, to be thrown quivering back in shimmering heat waves that mask the outline of the dark green wall beyond. Here and there they dip into a gully where a month ago a spring had been; now dry and parched. The flaming rays have seared the vivid green till it blends with the desiccated meadow grass.

Heat! Heat! Heat! Hot noises, hot smells, dry hot baking vegetation that rustles crisply against their thighs. In the impalpable powder beneath their feet creep creatures stifling to see; lizards breathing dust, insects whose lurid glow is like an ember. Hot smells of dust and scorched weeds burn their throats and nostrils. Over their head comes the droning hum of insects that sounds like an overdose of quinine, and might be. From a dead tree a bell-bug strikes his clear, ringing note.

The contents of canteens are filtered through their hides in the first 500 yards; after that they slake their thirst with thoughts of the cool springs in the woods above. Faster they climb, with the nervous energy which protests more against the thought of up-hill work than at the hill itself. They go through the heat like salamanders, their tough, wiry muscles carrying them along reflexly. They have learned to numb their minds; to avoid translating the effects of discomforts until the cause lies behind. They breathe the dust without a murmur, sweep up the slope, and with a sigh of relief, plunge into the cool dark shadows where never a wanton ray of sunlight strikes the dark, damp mold. An order is given; with one accord canteens and haversacks are unslung, and they throw themselves dog-like and panting, full length upon the fresh green moss. None is tired, none is sick. This is part of their pay—God knows slight enough!—and they take it as they take the heat. These are the survival of the fittest; the volunteer-regulars, the hardy remnants of half a score of regiments tempered to the last degree of martial tropic fitness.

The spring is found and canteens filled; then up they come fresh as flowers after a shower, tough as the lianas that catch their ankles. A sing-song order, and they are under way again, twisting and turning, in and out, trampling the ferns that never before have felt the tread of a white man's foot. Somewhere in front of them lies the sea; somewhere behind them skirting its shores is the other company; between them insurrectos who have broken their faith. Their path is the winding track of the native wood-cutters until they strike the big teak timber; then they make their own. Their guide is the raw-boned company commander, whose grim features following the great law of nature that blends the creature with its environment, are as rough, furrowed, and sun-baked as the arid plains from which he comes. His compass is in his head; the compass of the gull and prairie wolf. Their objective point is the far shore of the island, where the sparkling waves of the Sulu Sea beat on a gleaming sand.

Up they go, saving their breath to drive the rod, while overhead the noisy forest population chatters and screams with loud expressions of wonder and contempt. The tuneful note of a bell-bird comes tolling worshipfully with note subdued through the deep, dark forest aisles.

Great trumpet-shaped orchids, whose vivid colors pierce the shadows like a flame, swing lazily to the breath of the forest. Insects sparkle in the ferns like jewels, and luscious poisonous fruit half hidden tempts them seductively.

Late in the day they dip into a ravine and cross a cascade where the water, strange to say, is clear and cold. Here they camp.

While it is still light, two privates stray away; curious, investigating, comparing Filipino ferns with Pennsylvanian; teak with hemlock timber; admiring greatly. They poke and peer, cut open a nut, whittle a stick, and wonder at the play of colors in the grain, and finally they find upon a small bush a handsome fruit, and because it much resembles a persimmon, they promptly eat. Then within easy earshot of the company they stretch out upon the moss and sleep, nor dream of the furtive, stealthy steps that encircle them as they lie.

The day comes crawling crimsonly down the lofty Pampyan boles accompanied by a maddening chorus of chirping and song, as the tropic woods awake. A blaze of yellow light, and it is broad day. The sleeping company rises stiffly; pipes are lit, and the drowsy mess cooks kindle tiny fires here and there. Coffee is quickly over, and at roll-call two of the company are missing.

Unanswered shoutings reëcho in eerie calls from the shadowy gorge below. Louder cries are mocked in the high whispers over their heads. A purposeless noise in an awesome place vibrates the nerves that carry fear, so the clamor is stopped, and hurrying squads are sent to beat the near-by thickets. The brother of one of the missing men, and an old chum of the other are in the party that finds them—finds *part* of them—headless, weltering in a pool of blood beneath a fern tree. There are other things about them that are strange, things that are missing, for aborigines are queer collectors.

The men of the searching squad look at them for a moment in silence, a silence observant of every detail. One curses softly, another bursts into tears, not of sorrow and sympathy, but the tears that are displaced by an underlying load of homesickness and past fever. Another man longs to grasp an object that is lying near, and dance and shriek and rave. The corporal says no word, but soon he shakes his head and smiles, a smile to jar the reason of those that see.

Suddenly he whips his revolver from the holster and fires straight into the air. A man questions the act, and says that it is contrary to orders, for the evening before smokes were sighted.

"D——n the orders. I want the others to see!"

The others come—and see. The hard-faced captain gives some sharp-toned orders, and the mutilated corpses are quickly interred where they lie. At the conclusion a man has a chill, and after the chill he raves. Two men carry him bound to a stretcher until he is able to walk again.

They cross the divide that rises between them and the sea beyond, then down they go, following the watercourse which tumbles in their line of march. Fresh water leads to salt; their destination is the sea, and the beach is easier to travel than tangled forest. Besides, they have a horror of the place, and because there is so much room for noise they travel in silence and whispers. Men who laugh at the spit of a Mauser, leap at the hoarse croak of a Toucan. Swarthy cheeks that defied the slanting rays of the tropic sun, blanch at the rustle of a jungle monkey.

They trip on slippery boulders and coast down slanting rocks upon their heels. Their eyes are all about them, watching for the Unknown.

Down they go, slipping and falling, bruising their bodies on roots and stones, stung by insects and poisonous plants, choking with thirst (for they have left the stream), and haunted by the shadows now creeping in from the west. Then suddenly they plunge from the tangle into a beaten path and see far below them a vista of sparkling waves.

The head of the column halts while the stragglers come in. Down the slope beneath them a smoke rises straight into the breathless air. They see it without heed, for the town below is friendly, and it is at the earnest supplication of its Presidente that they have come.

On they swing in column of fours, strongly but in silence, for their spirits are as low as the sun that is dropping in the sea beneath. At the bottom of the hill the path turn sharply and winds between cane and bananas. Here the captain calls another halt, while his keen and restless eye roves searchingly over the thicket in the line of march.

Far ahead some roofs of Nipa thatch grow golden in the sunset. Above them towers the spire of a cathedral, from whose high belfry no angelus is heard. Quiet is on every hand, but they will find it busy in the market-place. Still, something is lacking, something is in excess. It is the feeling of oppression in the air—the low barometric unrest that affects the nerves of the skillful mariner before the glass begins to fall.

A sharp, quick order, and the company is divided. Another order, and the first platoon halts, while a squad quickly deploys as skirmishers in advance of the column.

The cultivated fields are passed, then the road dips through a thicket before coming out upon the town. Here the jungle advances impenetrably, thick as a fog, darker than the forest, for the light that they have just left.

The last squad has entered, when a rustling arises from the creepers on both sides—the rustling of an anaconda as it uncoils; the rustling of the king cobra, as, with sibilant hiss, it raises its head to strike. It smites first the ears of the captain.

"Lie down!"

Many have obeyed before they hear the order. The jungle spouts flame. There follow parabolic flashes of light and the glint of spear and barong, kris and bolo, as the thicket swarms with life; a foul, festering life, such as only a tropic sun can spawn.

Nimbly the slant-eyed prowlers slip though the bamboo stalks, and heavy knife in hand leap agilely into the road to complete the massacre begun, never thinking that one of the weary-footed foe can have withstood the shock of the unexpected onslaught.

The corporal, who is bunkie to the murdered man of the night before, laughs for the second time that day as he parries a bolo thrust, wrenches the weapon from the claw-like hand that wields it, and sends it crashing through the dome-shaped skull. He laughs again as he picks a long spear from the ground, and digs it into the bowels of a native who has thrust a Remington against his breast. He is still laughing as the piece goes off, and blows his heart out.

A child to-day is the same as a child of three thousand years ago; yet see the difference in the man. That is to say, a civilized, educated man lives three thousand years in thirty. Truly we are very old!

Yet sometimes we hark back along the trail until we reach a point that coincides with our environment—a point where the treatment of a primitive condition will not be warped by a misapplied modernism.

So it is with the company. Each man thinks of the headless corpses on the mountain side; each man is living in the glamor of late impression. They have seen savage sights; they have eaten the food of savages; they have thought savage thoughts; the cries of savages are ringing in their brains. In all their surroundings there is not one single object to remind them that they belong to an era of civilization. Their lust of slaughter is reflected from the faces of those around them. They crave slaughter more than food and sleep.

Homesickness and fever, sun and treachery, have broken down their few centuries of civilization.

The fight is over. A score of dead men lie grotesquely as they fell. A score of prisoners stand sullenly, surrounded by their captors. The captain gazes on them moodily and tugs his long mustache. The men, panting and dripping sweat and blood, watch the captives as terriers surround a rat-trap. A beardless boy with the bar of a lieutenant pinned to the collar of his flannel shirt steps to his commanding officer.

"What shall we do with them?" he asks, nodding to the scowling group of natives.

The captain looks at his dead and wounded. New lines seem to furrow his care-worn face.

"Bring them along. Make them carry the dead and wounded."

The column is again in motion, slower than before. In silence they enter the silent village, now deserted. They reach the market-place.

"Halt!"

"Line those niggers up against that wall."

Scowling and sullen, muttering and watchful of a chance, the bolomen are jostled into place.

"Fall in!"

The weary men shuffle to their places.

"In two ranks! Form compan-i-e! March!"

"Front rank—kneel!"

"Load!"

The boyish lieutenant turns to his captain. Both men's faces are pale beneath their tan.

"Are you going to shoot them, sir? Will it ——"

"Oh, my God—what's the use—what else is there to do?"

One of the wounded men upon a bamboo stretcher groans, grips his abdomen, shrieks, and drops back dead.

A change comes over the face of the lieutenant. He falls back to his place.

"Load!" The order is superfluous.

"Aim! Pick the man facing you!"

"Fire!"

A roar reëchoes from the mountain side. The brown line wavers and wilts, groveling in the dust. Three men of the prisoners scramble to their knees.

Tom, now a sergeant, walks to the first, and places the muzzle of his revolver to his head.

"This is for Dick!" A sharp report. He walks to the second.

"This is for Harry!" The scream of the victim mingles with the crash. The third man leaps to his feet. The pistol covers him.

"This is for *me!*"

6. Terrorism in the Age of Roosevelt: The Miss Stone Affair, 1901–1902

RANDALL B. WOODS

One of the risks of global power status in the twentieth century has been the problem of international terrorism. The reach of U.S. economic power and popular culture is enormous, and smaller, disinherited political groups and religious fundamentalists around the world frequently attempt to promote their own agendas, or bring about the withdrawal of American influence, by targeting the United States or its citizens for terrorist attacks. The 1989 bombing of a Pan American flight over Scotland by Libyan terrorists and the 1993 bombing of the World Trade Center by Islamic fundamentalists are only the most recent examples of this phenomenon.

Periodically, the State Department must issue travel advisories, warning Americans about which parts of the world to avoid because of terrorist threats. Occasionally, the State Department will also urge American nationals to leave certain parts of the world because terrorist risks are too high. Not coincidentally, the first modern terrorist attack on the United States came in 1901, soon after the establishment of the American empire. In September 1901, the Internal Macedonian Revolutionary Organization kidnapped and held Ellen M. Stone, a Congregationalist missionary, for ransom. In the following essay, Randall B. Woods describes the incident.

During the eighteenth and nineteenth centuries, American diplomatic, religious and commercial representatives abroad lived and worked relatively free from the threat of revolutionary terrorism. This was true in part because there were few Americans living overseas and because the United States was a third-rate power, considered to have little influence in the councils of the world. By the turn of the century, however, various forces and events had converged to thrust the United States into the international limelight. Throughout the latter half of the 1880s evangelists and exporters vied with strategic expansionists such as Alfred Thayer Mahan in demanding that the United States play a larger role in world affairs and, specifically, that it enter the race for overseas colonies. To the delight of American imperialists, the McKinley administration declared war on Spain in 1898 and a year later forced that thoroughly defeated nation to hand over Guam and the Philippines in the Pacific and Puerto Rico in the Caribbean. Clearly, the Spanish–American War marked America's arrival as a world power, but not all agreed that the nation's new status would prove beneficial. During the opening weeks of 1899 anti-imperialists argued that empire would force the United States to assimilate subordinate peoples, create the need for a much larger defense establishment, and involve the nation in the colonial rivalries of the great powers. They could have added, had they foreseen it, that America's newly won prestige would attract the attention not only of the established members of the international community but of the militant, have-not groups as well. In short, notoriety brought the

Republic influence and power, but it also transformed its citizens abroad into potential hostages for those groups wanting to enlist American money and might in their cause.

In September 1901 one of those groups, the Internal Macedonian Revolutionary Organization, seized and held for ransom Ellen M. Stone, a Congregationalist missionary. During the six months of her captivity, the Roosevelt administration, the American public, and her superiors on the American Board Commissioners for Foreign Missions struggled with the now-familiar issues connected with acts of international terrorism. Was Stone to be regarded as an individual who had merely fallen prey to one of the hazards of her profession, or should she be viewed as a personification of the nation and defended to the last? What role should the federal government play in the matter? Should the ransom be paid? Would not accession to the demands of the terrorists invite further kidnappings? Could the administration afford politically to abandon the hostage, especially given the fact that she was a woman and a missionary? How were the missionary authorities to resolve the conflict between the practical need to protect their agents from further acts of terrorism and the moral need to do everything in their power to free Stone? If the money was to be used by the kidnappers for revolutionary purposes, would the government against whom the revolution was to be directed permit ransoming? To what extent should diplomatic factors be allowed to outweigh humanitarian considerations? If and when the hostages were freed, who should be held responsible and what measures should be taken to prevent a repetition? The "Miss Stone Affair," as the incident came to be called, introduced the United States to twentieth-century international terrorism and in so doing provided the Republic with one of its first lessons in the limitations of great power status.

The site of the Miss Stone Affair was Macedonia, one of the most volatile areas in the world at the turn of the century. Lying just south of the Rilo, or Balkan, Mountains, Macedonia in 1901 was the sole remaining European possession of the Ottoman Empire. Historically important because it commanded the mountain corridor route leading from Central Europe to the Mediterranean, Macedonia had been subjected to countless invasions. As of 1900 the threat of war hung over the province once again as Bulgarian irredentists and Macedonian nationalists sought to overthrow Turkish rule.

Throughout the latter half of the nineteenth century, Russia, hoping to acquire a warm water port on the Mediterranean, pressured Turkey to recognize the national aspirations of various Balkan peoples. St. Petersburg, of course, expected the resulting Slavic Christian states to be Russian satellites. Increasingly, Tsarist diplomacy focused on Bulgaria and in 1878 Nicholas II went to war with the Sultan in order to set the Bulgars free. The conflict consisted of a series of lopsided defeats for Turkey, and in late 1878 the Sultan signed the Treaty of San Stefano which created a huge independent Bulgaria stretching from the Danube to the Aegean to the Black Sea and including all of Macedonia. The great powers, feeling that San Stefano threatened the balance of power not only in the Balkans but in Europe as well, intervened and forced Russia and Bulgaria to accept the Treaty of Berlin, which returned Macedonia to Turkey, in its stead.

Not surprisingly, after 1878 both Bulgars and Macedonians labored unceasingly to free Macedonia from Turkish rule. To this end Prince Ferdinand, Bulgaria's expansionist ruler, established in 1895 the External Organization—known also as the Supreme Macedonian–Adrianopolitan Committee. Dedicated to armed revolution, the External Organization actually advocated "either way" to Macedonian redemption—autonomy or incorporation into the Bulgarian state. In intermittent and uneasy alliance with the Sofia-based group was a collection of militant Macedonian autonomists who in 1893 had organized themselves into the Internal Macedonian Revolutionary Organization. Between 1893 and 1897 IMRO concentrated on gathering arms and perfecting its organization. Each Turkish *kaza,* or county, became a revolutionary district complete with IMRO *cheta,* or militia. IMRO agents, who were fond of comparing themselves to the *haidositi,* Macedonian Robin Hoods who had for years protected Christians from the "barbarous Turk," levied taxes on the Macedonian peasantry, compelled the natives to conceal members of the *chetas,* and generally sought to establish a shadow government able to assume immediate control once the forces of the Sultan were defeated. In 1897 the Turks discovered the existence of IMRO when they unearthed a cache of revolutionary arms hidden in the Macedonian village of Vinitza. The incident touched off a general war between IMRO and the Turkish military establishment which lasted from 1898 through 1903.

By 1900 several of IMRO's leaders had come to the conclusion that expulsion of the Turks and attainment of Macedonian independence would require not only continued direct action but foreign intervention as well. Although the western Europeans were sympathetic to the cause of Macedonian independence, the chances in 1900 that one or more of the Powers would force the Turks to relinquish Macedonia appeared remote. Consequently the revolutionaries looked increasingly to the New World for sympathy and aid. In cities from Boston to Oakland literally hundreds of Macedonian immigrants-turned-propagandists worked to persuade the United States to intervene in the Balkans and oust Turkey from her last European stronghold. "Some of the powers are going so far as to openly encourage the Turk to go on in the extermination of the defenseless Christians while the rest of them are playing the part of lukewarm spectators," declared one IMRO circular which was widely distributed in the United States. "American interference . . . is the only effective measure against the present slaughter and the only means of producing peace, order, and good government." And, in fact, American public opinion was well aware of the situation in the Balkans and sympathetic to the victims of Turkish oppression. Nonetheless, the Republic's tradition of noninvolvement in European affairs proved stronger than its desire to crush the Turk, and the support given Macedonia by the United States continued to be largely verbal and moral.

A deterioration in relations between IMRO and the External Organization in 1901, during which the latter attempted to exterminate the former, persuaded the IMRO leaders to seek American aid by a more direct means. The close working relationship that existed between IMRO and the External Organization between 1895 and 1901 had been maintained largely through the efforts of Boris Saraffof, head of the Organization as well as officer in the Bulgarian army. The alliance crumbled, however, when in 1902 Saraffof temporarily fell from grace and was imprisoned by Bulgarian authorities. With Saraffof languishing in the royal dungeon Ferdinand selected a successor to head the External Organization. With the Prince's blessing, the new president, a Bulgarian general named Tsoncheff, proceeded to rid by force when necessary the revolutionary movement of its autonomist elements. Thus, by the fall of 1901, those within the External Organization and IMRO who refused to see annexation as the only solution to the Macedonian question were having to fight a two-front war, one against the Turks and the other against Tsoncheff.

Two IMRO members who refused to abandon the cause of Macedonian independence were Yani Sandanski, a former school teacher, a socialist, and a veteran revolutionary, and Hristo Tchernopeef, a rugged *chetnik* chieftain. Both were charter members of IMRO, district committee representatives, and fanatical autonomists. By late September 1901 pressure on the two men and their followers in northern Macedonia had become intense. "Tsoncheff's rank impudence was backed by Ferdinand's gold," Tchernopeef later wrote, "and with the pretense of revolution he began sending big, armed bands across the frontier to oust us out of our rayons [fortified camps]." At this point Sandanski and Tchernopeef decided to capture an American living in Macedonia, collect a large ransom from the United States, and blame the whole affair on Turkey. Such a bold stroke, they believed, would provoke the United States into demanding an end to Turkish misrule in Macedonia while in the meantime providing them with the ready cash necessary to defeat the Bulgarian annexationists.

In searching for a victim, IMRO inevitably turned to the American missionary community in the Balkans. The Protestant evangelists living in Bulgaria and Macedonia constituted one of the largest and most active proselytizing bodies in the world, and although there was some United States commercial activity in that area, the missionaries comprised America's most important link to European Turkey. American missionary activity in the Balkans dated back to 1810, the year a group of Presbyterian and Congregationalist clerics founded the American Board Commissioners for Foreign Missions. By 1903 the Board had 140 workers in the field operating out of over 70 mission stations spread throughout Bulgaria and Macedonia.

Between 1878 and 1903 the American missionaries living in the Balkans became increasingly anti-Turkish and openly sympathetic to the cause of Macedonian liberation. The Turkish government, which viewed the ABCFM representatives as purveyors of such dangerous concepts as democracy and nationalism, and Moslem religious leaders, who perceived the missionaries as spiritual threats to the nation of Islam, vied with each other in harassing Protestant clergy and layworkers in Macedonia. Such persecution tended to create a desire within the American community to see Macedonia under a new political authority. In addition, the missionaries absorbed anti-establishment ideas from the people among whom they lived and worked. Literally, dozens of high-ranking Macedonian–Bulgarian officials were graduates of Robert College in Constantinople. Both George Washburn, president of Robert College, and William W. Peet, American Board treasurer for Turkey, cultivated former students of the institution, and as a result they both influenced and were influenced by the irredentists in Sofia. In addition, as the Sublime Porte had repeatedly pointed out, the large Protestant congregations in Strumitza, Salonica, Razlog, Bansko, and other towns along the Macedonian–Bulgarian border were hotbeds of nationalism. Not a few members of the IMRO *chetas* were graduates of local missionary schools. In March 1902 J. F. Clarke, head of the American Collegiate and Theological Seminary in Bulgaria, reported to Boston that the Protestant pastor at Bansko had been a revolutionary leader until the previous spring and that twenty of the mission students in that community were part of a band planning an attack on the Turks. It was not difficult for the missionaries to view the members of the IMRO and the External Organization as Christian soldiers fighting against the forces of tyranny and heathenism. "I respected them," Clarke confessed in his report on the student revolutionaries in Bansko, "and my heart was with them." In December 1902 E. B. Haskell complained to his superiors in Boston: "The general situation of the country is the worst in the nine years of my residence in Macedonia. The Turkish government is the same old reactionary, tyrannical, heartless monstrosity it has always been . . . I suppose it is useless to dwell longer on the Unspeakable Turk." By the turn of the century a number of ABCFM representatives were even going so far as to urge United States intervention to oust the "unspeakable Turk" from Europe. "Macedonia ought to be free," proclaimed Clarke in 1904. "If it is possible for America to do ought for their freedom, it will be like the act of freeing Cuba and the Philippine Islands."

Whether Macedonia was to be a part of Bulgaria or an independent nation was far less important to the missionaries than expulsion of the Turks; they were convinced that law and order would return to the Balkans only after the Sultan's minions were driven from Europe. Peace and social order, in turn, were essential to the expansion of Christianity. In September 1902 Ellen M. Stone, ABCFM representative in charge of the "Bible women" of Macedonia and Bulgaria, wrote United States Consul General in Bulgaria, Charles Dickinson, urging immediate action by the Roosevelt administration to dislodge the Turks. "The indispensible thing," she concluded, "is to have Turkey (Macedonia) a safe place for anyone to live in." E. B. Haskell concurred: "I don't see where this anarchy is to end. . . . You can imagine that under these circumstances people's minds are largely occupied and religious work makes little headway."

Ironically, one of the factors that persuaded Sandanski and Tchernopeef to seize a missionary for ransom was the sympathy of the American religious community for their cause. The revolutionaries anticipated that the Americans would direct their hostility toward Turkey rather than IMRO and that the missionaries might even prove to be cooperative during the course of the kidnapping.

On September 3, 1901 Sandanski, Tchernopeef, and 20 IMRO *chetniks* captured Ellen Stone as she and several native companions returned from conducting a training school at Bansko. With a view to public opinion, Stone's abductors, whom the missionaries thereafter referred to as "brigands," made the capture as dramatic as possible, swooping down on the party as it wound its way through a narrow defile in the rugged Perim Mountains in northern Macedonia. The brigands, whom Stone described in her ransom letters as "bearded, fierce of face, wild of dress . . . all athletic and heavily armed," spoke only Turkish and attempted to portray themselves as bandits with simple monetary motives. In order to terrorize the party more completely, the revolutionaries brained a Turkish soldier who inadvertently wandered on the scene. On September 4, Sandanski and Tchernopeef released all of the party except Stone and Mrs. Katerina Tsilka, a native co-worker of Stone's whom the brigands decided to retain as "chaperon," and then fled with the two women northward into the mountains. On September 26, H. C. Haskell, station chief at Samokov (Bulgaria) received a note from Miss Stone indicating that she and Mrs. Tsilka, who was then seven months pregnant, would be shot unless a ransom of 25,000 Turkish pounds ($110,000) was delivered to their captors within twenty days.

Stone and Tsilka's kidnapping threw the American missionary community and the State Department into momentary disarray. Despite a half-century of missionary activity in the Balkans, no ABCFM representative had ever been captured and held for ransom. Officials involved in the case were hampered both by lack of precedent and the knowledge that every decision they made would constitute a precedent that would either plague or enlighten future generations.

The immediate reaction in both Boston and Washington was to follow the path of least resistance and seek release of the captives through application of direct pressure on the Turks. On September 6, Dr. Charles Daniels, one of the corresponding secretaries of the Board, notified Secretary of State John Hay of Stone's and Tsilka's plight and requested that United States representatives in Constantinople demand of the Porte that Turkish authorities secure Stone's release immediately. Both Consul-General Charles Dickinson and Minister John G. A. Leishman complied, but the results were hardly what the Board expected or desired. On September 20 a Macedonian messenger delivered another beseeching message from Miss Stone to Treasurer Peet in Constantinople. "The men who captured us first showed courtesy . . . towards us. . . . But now since Turkish soldiers and Bashi-Bazouks [Moslem irregulars] have begun to pursue us . . . our condition is altogether changed. . . . Therefore I beg you to hasten the sending of the sum and that you will insist before the Turkish government that it stop the pursuit of us by the soldiers . . . otherwise we will be killed." At the same time the Turkish authorities in Bansko, Razlog, and other north Macedonian communities began to harass local Protestants, claiming that they and the missionaries, including Miss Stone, had engineered a fake kidnapping in order to raise funds for the Macedonian revolutionaries. Throughout late September and early October, the various stations in Macedonia flooded the "Rooms," as the Board's headquarters in Boston were called, with reports of beatings and torture of local Protestant clerics and laymen. As a result Minister Leishman, at the Board's urgent request, reversed field and directed the Porte to call off his troops.

At this point the Board decided to go ahead and pay the ransom and on September 23 it so directed Treasurer Peet in Constantinople. The ABCFM's decision was largely the product of pressure applied by the captive's relatives and friends. Especially vociferous in Stone's behalf was *The Christian Herald,* for which she had worked. "No sum of money, be it ever so large, can ever be named as a true standard of value for a human life," proclaimed the *Herald*. "There are gradations also of value, some lives ranking far higher than others in the service of their country and in the Kingdom of our Lord Jesus Christ. . . . We hesitate not to say, *Miss Stone must be ransomed with gold, cost what it may!*" Hard-heartedness, the Board realized, was a label it could ill-afford. Too, Boston was certain that sooner or later Turkey could be made to pay.

The Board's decision to pay up, however, soon came under attack from field workers in Macedonia and Bulgaria. Whether or not they sympathized with the Macedonian cause, most of Stone's colleagues were reluctant to support any action that would encourage further acts of terrorism. "What is paid will be a price on our heads," warned Reverend J. W. Baird. "If I should be so taken," declared the Reverend James Clarke, who like Baird, was situated at Samokov, "I do not think I should wish ransom to be paid for me whatsoever the result might be." Consequently, on September 28 Smith, enclosing a copy of Clarke's letter, notified Secretary of State Hay that the Board would, after all, not ransom Miss Stone; rejection of the brigands' demands was "indispensible to the security of the American missionaries now resident in European Turkey."

Although it had decided not to accede to the terrorists' demands, the Board was equally determined to avoid the blame for Miss Stone's death if that should be the result of its refusal to pay. Consequently, at its October 4 meeting the committee, after reaffirming its decision not to pay the ransom, resolved to place management of the affair squarely in the hands of the Roosevelt administration. To this end, the Board cabled Washington and arranged an audience with the new President to acquaint him with the position of the missionary community. Shortly after the committee adjourned, Smith wrote Peet: "Tonight Mr. Capen [Dr. Samuel Capen, President of the ABCFM] and I go to Washington to urge the government to do whatever is necessary to secure Stone's release. . . . I tremble to think of the alternatives."

By the time the American Board met on October 4, the Roosevelt administration had had a chance to consider its options and work out a course of action. Initially the State Department had acquiesced in Boston's demands and attempted to secure the captives' release through pressure on Turkey. By the middle of the month, however, American officials realized that those who had kidnapped Stone and Tsilka were not simple mountain bandits. On September 20, Leishman wrote Hay that Miss Stone's captors were not Turks, but agents of the "Bulgarian Committee" who had seized the two women in hopes of making money for their cause, or provoking foreign intervention, or both. On September 24, the Department requested Consul-General Dickinson, then in Salonica interviewing missionaries in connection with the Stone affair, to go to Sofia and persuade the Bulgarian government to lend all possible aid in forcing the brigands to release Stone and Tsilka.

Actually, despite its instructions to Dickinson, the State Department had decided that a diplomatic approach to the Stone problem, whether through Turkey or Bulgaria, had little chance of success. If the United States allowed the Turks to force a confrontation with the brigands there was a good chance, as Miss Stone had warned, that the captives would be killed. Indeed, such had been the case in a number of previous incidents involving Europeans held for ransom when the Turks had been allowed a free hand. Nor could the Ottoman government reasonably be expected to pay the ransom for in so doing it would be contributing to a movement whose sole purpose was to overthrow Turkish rule in Europe. Attempts to force the Bulgarian government to accept responsibility and secure Stone's release would be pointless as well. Washington assumed that the outrage had been perpetrated by Bulgarian irredentists controlled by Ferdinand, and thus the Bulgarian government could not logically be expected to bring them to justice. Moreover, because the outrage had occurred on Turkish soil, the Bulgars could legitimately disclaim all responsibility. Finally, the Roosevelt administration could not afford to become too aggressive with Sofia lest it alienate Russia.

If government to government pressure was not likely to secure Miss Stone's release, what then? There was always the practical approach: Miss Stone could be left to her own devices. And at one point, Roosevelt favored just such a course. On October 2, the President wrote First Assistant Secretary of State Alvey Adee that the United States government should not be expected to rescue Miss Stone from her predicament: "Every missionary, every trader in wild lands should know and is inexcusable for not knowing that the American government had no power to pay the ransom of anyone who is captured by brigands or savages."

Yet, there were a number of reasons why the administration could not abandon the beleaguered Bible worker to the wilds of Macedonia. The American Board, the State Department, and the White House were subjected to almost daily pleas and demands from Stone's family that the government effect her rescue. As time passed with no apparent progress in negotiations, her relatives sought to embarrass the administration by giving press interviews in which they pondered the possible dire circumstances of her imprisonment. In addition, if Miss Stone were to meet an untimely end, Roosevelt and Hay feared, the yellow press was sure to demand war with the responsible parties, whoever Hearst, Pulitzer, and other molders of popular opinion decided they might be. But in the end it was the Victorian morality of the age that prevented abandonment of Miss Stone. "Women have no earthly business to go out as missionaries in these wild countries," Roosevelt confided to Adee. "They do very little good but it is impossible not to feel differently about them than men. If a man goes out as a missionary he has no kind of business to venture to wild lands with the expectation that somehow the government will protect him as well as if he stayed at home. If he is fit for his work he has no more right to complain of what may befall him than a soldier has in getting shot. But it is impossible to adopt this standard about women."

With the diplomatic and "practical" approaches discredited, the only alternative left to Roosevelt and Hay was payment of the ransom. The Rough Rider, however, was reluctant even to consider this option. Most obviously, if Washington even agreed to negotiate directly with the brigands, much less capitulate to their demands, it would be setting a dangerous precedent. Moreover, after all of Roosevelt's rhetoric about stronger nations displaying firmness and the "right stuff" in their dealings with the "uncivilized," it would have been unseemly, to say the least, for the administration to have knuckled under to the terrorists.

After due deliberation, Washington decided that the only solution that could even begin to satisfy the multiple exigencies of the situation was for the missionaries themselves to raise and pay the ransom. Thus, when Capen and Smith called at the White House on October 5, Roosevelt declared that under no circumstances could the government finance Miss Stone's deliverance and then in the same breath insisted that it was "imperative" that the ransom be raised. When the Board members protested that the Prudential Committee had voted unanimously not to pay, the President suggested that the amount be collected through a popular subscription. Although Capen and Smith complained that the abduction was a national affair and that it ought to be the responsibility of the federal government, they agreed. As a sop to the disgruntled missionaries, Roosevelt promised finally that if after Stone's release the sum could not be extracted from Turkey, then he would go to Congress and request compensation.

In choosing ransom by popular subscription as a solution to the Stone affair, the Roosevelt administration and the American Board hoped simultaneously to deflect charges that they had appeased the forces of international political terrorism and to avoid responsibility for any harm that should come to Miss Stone. The private donation approach, however, contained an unforeseen pitfall. All concerned hoped to bargain with the brigands in order to hold the amount paid to an absolute minimum, their reasoning being the higher the ransom, the greater the inducement to future brigandage. Unfortunately, to be successful, a popular subscription required, above all else, publicity. Papers ranging from the *New York World* to the *Oakland Enquirer* not only urged their readers to contribute but printed almost daily the amounts raised. Sandanski and Tchernopeef learned through IMRO operatives in the United States that a fund-raising drive was underway and in the days that followed how much had been collected on any given date. Thus, attempts by United States representatives to persuade the revolutionaries to accept less than had been collected were doomed to failure.

Efforts to secure Miss Stone and Mrs. Tsilka's early release were hampered by a prolonged misunderstanding between Washington and its representative in Sofia, Consul-General Charles Dickinson. From the first Dickinson assumed that the abduction was the work of the "Bulgarian revolutionary committee" and that the *komitate* was controlled directly by the Bulgarian government. He was, moreover, adamantly opposed to the payment of any ransom at all. Capitulation, he was convinced, would subject American business and religious interests in the Balkans to perpetual peril, and, in all likelihood, lead to the execution of the captives. As a result, although Roosevelt, Capen, and Smith had decided on the 5th that the ransom should be paid, responsibility to be affixed and punishment extracted at a later date, the Consul-General, supported by a coterie of missionaries in Macedonia, continued well into November to seek to resolve the kidnapping through political pressure. Specifically, he attempted to compel the Bulgarian government and the Russian ambassador, whom Dickinson believed to be the driving force behind Bulgarian irredentism, to force their hirelings, the brigands, to release Stone and Tsilka. He got nowhere.

By late November, Stone's family and friends were frantic. American and European papers were filled daily with reports of the captives' demise. "Miss Stone and Madame Tsilka cut to pieces by brigands and buried on the spot," ran a typical report in the *New York World*. Led by Charles Stone, a brother and an influential Boston businessman, acquaintances and relatives had by November become openly critical of Dickinson and the hardliners among the missionaries. Particularly obnoxious to them was J. W. Baird who viewed the abductors as "Socialists" and "Anarchists," who believed the whole matter could be rectified by a "surprise armed attack" on the brigands, and who said as much to any reporter that would listen. On November 23 the Congregationalist published an article blasting Dickinson for violating his instructions and needlessly endangering the lives of the prisoners. Shortly thereafter Stone wrote both Hay and Judson Smith demanding that the Consul-General and his cohorts be brought to heel. "Coercing Bulgaria means inevitable conflict with Russia, Macedonian expectations realized, American mission imperiled, our hopes blasted," Stone warned the Secretary of State on December 2.

Thus, the State Department and American Board seemed to be back precisely where they had started. Hay, Adee, Smith, and Barton were sure of only two things: Stone and Tsilka must be ransomed as quickly as possible, and Dickinson must be excluded from the negotiating process. The answers to the all-important questions of how and who were provided by Dr. George Washburn, head of Robert College in Constantinople and a man considered by many to be the most influential American in the Balkans. Washburn enjoyed particularly close ties with the Bulgarian government. Robert College had graduated a generation of Bulgarian leaders, including several current members of Ferdinand's cabinet, and Washburn, called by some "the father of Bulgaria," made it a practice to keep in touch with his former students. Dickinson's handling of the Stone affair, especially his attempts to coerce the Bulgarian government, appalled the prominent Congregationalist. Convinced that both the Bulgarian government and the Russian representative in Sofia had done everything in their power to secure Stone's release, Washburn advised Hay and Roosevelt by cable on December 15 that there was no alternative except to come to terms with the brigands and pay the ransom. As the negotiations would be difficult and dangerous, they should be "confided to trusty men who know the people and language."

Well aware that the report would confirm existing assumptions in the State Department and tend to support a policy previously decided upon, Washburn in consultation with the United States Chargé d'Affaires in Constantinople, Spencer Eddy, took it upon himself to appoint and instruct the "trusty men." On December 13 the two persuaded W. W. Peet, Bible House Treasurer at Constantinople, and Alexander Garguilo, first dragoman (interpreter) at the American legation, to undertake the mission. Peet and Garguilo were to proceed to Salonica where, armed with letters from the Turkish minister of the interior, they would secure the full assistance of the Vali (governor). From Salonica they were to proceed to Djumabala near the Bulgarian border, there to make contact with the brigands and convince them to accept the $66,000 that had so far been raised. The two men departed Constantinople the evening of December 16, 1901.

The Peet–Garguilo mission proved to be a dramatic, cloak-and-dagger affair. The Turkish authorities, while pretending to cooperate, were determined to prevent payment of the ransom and hoped to use the "committee" to locate and destroy the brigands. As a result, for nearly a month Peet and Garguilo traipsed around Macedonia followed by a large contingent of Turkish troops. Eventually the two men, using a third party intermediary, not only established contact with Stone's abductors but actually conducted negotiations. On February 2, in the Macedonian village of Bansko under the very noses of 200 Turkish troops, the committee turned over 230 pounds ($66,000) of gold to the brigands in return for a promise to release Stone and Tsilka within ten days. Peet deceived the Turks by smuggling the ransom out of his closely watched cottage sixty pounds at a time, and then replacing it with an equal weight of lead shot.

Although the committee had no guarantee whatever that the brigands would fulfill their part of the bargain, they need not have worried, for Sandanski and Tchernopeef had been anxious to release their captives for months. Mrs. Tsilka had given birth to a baby girl in November and as a result the brigands were forced to deal not only with the unspeakable Turk, the treacherous General Tsoncheff, and a group of seemingly indecisive American negotiators, but to care for the needs of an infant as well. Moreover, Stone and Tsilka were hardly the helpless, breathless creatures depicted by the newspapers. Indeed, it is possible that the brigands suffered more from their act of terrorism than did the missionaries. As Tchernopeef put it several years later during an interview with an American reporter: "Have you ever found yourself in a position of strong opposition to a middle-aged woman with a determined will all her own? She assuming the attitude that you are a brute and you feeling it?" The revolutionaries, moreover, had to endure almost daily attempts to convert them to Protestant Christianity. Nevertheless, because of the intensity of Turkish patrol activity, three weeks passed before the brigands felt it was safe to part with their captives. Finally, to the relief of both captives and captors, Tchernopeef and Sandanski deposited Miss Stone and Mrs. Tsilka beneath a pear tree near the Macedonian town of Strumitza. It was 4 A.M. on February 23, 1902.

Aside from its obvious melodramatic qualities, the Stone affair is noteworthy for a number of reasons. The 66,000 *Miss-Stonki,* as the revolutionaries called the ransom money, were used to finance the Macedonian uprising of 1903. Shortly after Stone and Tsilka's release, a series of events and forces combined to heal the breach between the External Committee and IMRO. In the spring of 1902 the Turks released a group of IMRO leaders captured in Salonica in the summer of 1901. Simultaneously, Boris Saraffof returned from exile to resume direction of the External Committee and IMRO. During the last days of March a secret Congress of revolutionary leaders representing all factions convened in Sofia. Hristo Tchernopeef attended and tuned the Stone ransom money over to the general body for its disposition. The funds were subsequently spent to purchase arms and ammunition preparatory to a general uprising scheduled for the fall. The rebellion was temporarily delayed but then, in August 1903, some 50,000 Macedonians and Bulgars rose in revolt, not a few of whom were armed with Manlicher and Mauser rifles purchased with *Miss-Stonki.* Although the rebels succeeded in seizing most of the Monastir *vilayet,* where they organized a revolutionary council and attempted to liberate the rest of Macedonia, the revolution was quickly and brutally suppressed.

As far as the United States was concerned, the Miss Stone affair constituted a particularly thorny introduction to one of the burdens of major power status. Many Americans who during the Spanish–American War had glorified in anticipation of empire and enhanced prestige that victory over a European power would bring failed to perceive that once the United States took its place among the international elite that it would become a suitable object of political terrorism. The abduction was an intensely frustrating affair for the country. The honor of the nation demanded that Stone be released immediately, the guilty parties apprehended and punished, and the responsible government chastised. The fact that the victim was a missionary and a woman served to make the populace particularly sensitive to considerations of honor. The seizure was, in a way, a challenge to America's nationhood. Yet, as in all such situations there was the possibility that hasty action might bring about the death of the prisoners. Also serving to hold the Big Stick in check was the fact that the brigands were Macedonians struggling against the hated Turk, freedom fighters who had enjoyed widespread sympathy in the United States for a number of years. Thus, it was particularly difficult in this case to differentiate between good and evil. Nearly everyone wanted to blame Turkey, and some did, despite the facts of the case, but in the end there was no clear consensus about what course the authorities should take.

For the Roosevelt administration, the Stone affair was an education in the diplomacy of terrorism. Although the stakes were relatively low, no incident more vividly demonstrated to the new President the importance of circumstance in policy formation. The United States could not officially pay the ransom. That would be cowardly, dishonorable, and a bad precedent. Yet, prevailing morality would not permit the sacrifice of Stone's life. Even if T. R. had not shared conventional attitudes toward the "weaker sex," there was the election of 1904 to consider. Despite Roosevelt's statement in 1898 that Turkey was one of the two countries in the world he would most like to smash, bludgeoning the Sultan would in this case serve no useful purpose. Coercion of Constantinople would have endangered Miss Stone's life, produced further Turkish outrages against the native population, and thereby provoked not only the Turks but the Macedonians against United States interests in the Balkans. Pressure on Bulgaria was out of the question. With Russia posing as Ferdinand's protector, Roosevelt, Hay, and Adee believed there was simply no chance that Washington could compel Sofia to bring the brigands to heel. (The State Department never clearly understood the political situation in the Balkans; i.e., that from September 1901 through March 1902 the External Committee and IMRO were at war.) Moreover, alienation of the Russian government, as attempts to coerce Bulgaria would surely accomplish, would hardly serve America's long-range interests in Europe. Roosevelt labored throughout his administration to maintain the balance of power in Europe and prevent a clash over the Balkans, goals that necessitated cooperation rather than confrontation with St. Petersburg.

In short, the Stone affair served to introduce T. R. and twentieth-century America to international political terrorism. While all too familiar to contemporary governments, the complicated negotiations that inevitably follow such kidnappings were novel to Roosevelt and his advisors. Appropriately enough, Alvey Adee, the career diplomat who had been in the State Department for nearly a generation, summed up the administration's reaction to the Stone affair. "This has been a hard week for me," he wrote John Hay after a particularly harrowing round of negotiations, "and my mind is black and blue all over with the coming of the beloved Saturday afternoon. . . . I have been worse off than Stephen,—I have been Stoned all the time with a continuous but unfatal result."

7. The Anti-German Crusade, 1917-1918

MUNROE SMITH

In April 1917, when President Woodrow Wilson sent his war message to Congress and asked for a declaration of war against Germany, the United States began its twentieth-century role as the most powerful nation in the world. World War I had already become, by far, the bloodiest in human history. Millions of people died in the senseless slaughter, and as a result of the conflict philosophers abandoned their beliefs in inevitable progress. In order to participate in such a conflict, and to inflict a similar slaughter on Germany, the United States painted the enemy in particularly inhuman terms. Only by convincing Americans that Germans were uniquely brutal would the public countenance such a death toll. The federal government, led by the Committee on Public Information, launched an anti-German propaganda crusade that painted Germany in the worst light and cast German-Americans in the role of traitors. Superpatriots harassed German-Americans, outlawed the teaching of German in public school, and prevented the performance of music by German composers. Hollywood studios produced such anti-German films as The Prussian Cur, The Claws of the Hun, *and* To Hell with the Kaiser. *The following essays appeared in 1917 and 1918 in the* North American Review *and provide a good description of how Americans perceived Germany at the height of World War I.*

THE GERMAN THEORY OF WARFARE

In the present war Germany has shown a disregard of humane instincts and of international rules and customs that is unprecedented in modern warfare between civilized States. She has introduced into land warfare the use of poisonous gases and of liquid fire. Also the bombardment by aircraft, without the preliminary notice required by custom, not only of "fortresses" but also of open villages and cities. In some of the places bombarded there were no constructions of military importance nor any appliances of war except anti-aircraft guns. That German officers have at times used civilian enemies as fire-screens, and that German troops have in some instances been instructed to give no quarter, even to wounded enemies, is established by German testimony.

Germany has introduced into sea warfare the use of submarines, not only against war vessels but against merchantmen, and not only against enemy ships but against those of neutrals. Of late Germany is avowedly sinking hospital ships, on the plea—denied and unproven—that such ships have been used to carry soldiers and munitions of war.

In Belgium and in other occupied territories the German authorities have subjected the civil population to a reign of terror unexampled in modern war. They have repressed "sniping," the destruction of railroads and telegraphs, and other hostile acts, by burning villages and towns and by killing the inhabitants; that is, by indiscriminate punishment of possible offenders, whose guilt was not established, and of much larger numbers of men, women and children who were undoubtedly innocent. To prevent offenses and to ensure order, the German authorities have seized civilian hostages, to be shot if any hostile act or transgression of military orders should occur in the locality.

The German army has secured from civilian enemies services of direct or indirect military value, not only by threats and by imprisonment but also by depriving them of food. Finally, Germany has deported at least a quarter of a million Belgian and French men and women to German factories and to labor camps, where they are subjected to similar if not greater duress. General von Bissing claimed that many Belgian workmen "voluntarily" signed labor contracts; but he admitted that those who refused to sign were deported and received a lower rate of pay.

Violation of private property rights has been frequent and flagrant. The districts occupied by German troops have suffered not a little from irresponsible private looting and destruction. They have suffered much more from organized official looting in the form of excessive requisitions, indemnities and contributions. In some instances, not only the local authorities but prominent citizens also have been made responsible for prompt payment; in other instances the levy has been secured by house-to-house search and distraint of goods. In their retirement from occupied French territory, not only have the Germans destroyed everything that could be of use to the armed forces following their retreat, but they have endeavored also to destroy everything that could be of use to the civil population.

Official pleas of justification for those acts which are admitted fall into two classes. Either they invoke "necessity" or they allege prior breaches of law by Germany's enemies which have forced the German Government to exercise the right of retaliation. Each of these pleas implies a recognition that the German acts were at least irregular. In view of this attitude, it is pertinent to show that for nearly a century German military writers have specifically recognized many of these acts as regular and normal incidents of war, and have developed general theories of warfare which justify all the others.*

Terrorism, defended in the present war largely on the ground of atrocities alleged (but not proved) to have been committed by civilians, was advocated by Hartmann forty years ago:

Terror seems relatively the milder method of holding in subjection masses of people who have been thrown out of the normal and regular conditions of peace. . . . Bluntschli, Jacquemyns and others . . . object to imposing upon towns in which offenses have been committed fines which exceed the amount of damage that has been done; they condemn the burning of villages from which civilians have attacked troops; they refuse their assent to the taking of hostages, whose arrest is to

---

*The German military writings cited in the following pages are: Gen. Carl von Clausewitz, *On War* (1832), translated by Col. F. N. Maude (3 vols., 1911); Gen. Julius von Hartmann, *Militärische Notwendigkeit und Humanität*, in the *Deutsche Rundschau*, vols. xiii, xiv (1877–1878); *The German War Book*, published under the auspices of the German General Staff, translated by J. H. Morgan (1915).

prevent illegal acts on the part of the population. . . . Military realism in listening to such utterances silently shrugs its shoulders.

Hartmann and the War Book justify also the harshest measures needed to secure services from civilian enemies, even services of military value:

When the law of peace [Hartmann argues] is supplanted by the law of war . . . it does not abandon its claim to continued authority. All paragraphs of the domestic code threatening punishment for treason remain in force; only extreme duress imposed by the invader can protect the inhabitants, in case these render services to the invading army, against subsequent accountability to their own courts in case of a change in the fortunes of war or after the conclusion of peace. Here interest and fear must silence patriotism and the sense of right in the hostile population. This is certainly far from moral, but it is a military necessity and the inevitable result of military invasion.

The summoning of the inhabitants to supply vehicles and perform works [the War Book explains] has also been stigmatized as an unjustifiable compulsion upon the inhabitants to participate in "military operations." But it is clear that an officer can never allow such a far-reaching extension of this conception. . . . The argument of war must decide.

The War Book follows Hartmann in justifying the taking of hostages— a policy adopted, but more sparingly practiced, in the war of 1870:

Since the lives of peaceable inhabitants were without any fault on their part thereby exposed to grave danger, every writer outside Germany has stigmatized this measure as contrary to the law of nations and as unjustified towards the inhabitants of the country. As against this unfavorable criticism it must be pointed out that this measure, which was also recognized on the German side as harsh and cruel, was only resorted to after declarations and instructions of the occupying authorities had proved ineffective, and that in the particular circumstance it was the only method which promised to be effective. . . .

As regards requisitions the War Book quietly brushes away all limitations of international law and custom:

Article 40 of the Declaration of Brussels requires that the requisitions (being written out) shall bear a direct relation to the capacity and resources of a country, and, indeed, the justification for this condition would be willingly recognized by everyone in theory, but it will scarcely ever be observed in practice. In cases of necessity the needs of the army will alone decide. . . .

This leaves the door wide open to unlimited spoliation, without resort to indemnities or contributions. By both Clausewitz and Hartmann the right of requisition is in fact treated as one of several possible methods of crippling the enemy. The former writes:

Invasion is the occupation of the enemy's territory, not with a view to keeping it, but in order to levy contributions upon it or to devastate it. The immediate object here is neither the conquest of the enemy's territory nor the defeat of his armed force, but merely to do him damage in a general way.

The right of requisition, Clausewitz asserts, "has no limits except those of the exhaustion, impoverishment and devastation of the country." And in the light of experience he suggests to his successors:

Whatever method of providing subsistence may be chosen, it is but natural that it would be more easily carried out in rich and well-peopled countries, than in the midst of a poor and scanty population. . . . There is infinitely less difficulty in supporting an army in Flanders than in Poland.

The system of requisitions [Hartmann explains] goes far beyond the taking of means of subsistence from the country in which war is being conducted; it includes the entire exploitation of that country. . . . This implies that military necessity can make no distinction between public and private property, that it is entitled to take what it needs wherever and however it can. . . . The fundamental principle of all warfare must not be ignored; the hostile State is not to be spared the suffering and privations of warfare; these are particularly adapted to break its energy and to coerce its will. . . . The State at war must spare its own means for conducting war and must injure and destroy those of the enemy.

The foregoing utterances are corollaries of a broader general theory. In German military philosophy, war is normally and properly a struggle, not solely between the armed forces of the contending States, nor solely between their Governments, but between their populations. The contrary theory, that war is a contest between the armed forces of the belligerent States, is a temporary aberration. It is comparatively modern, and it is already antiquated. It took form, according to Clausewitz, in the time of Louis XIV, when the universal military service of primitive peoples and of early States had been replaced by the hired services of professional soldiers. With the reappearance of universal military duty, with the substitution of great popular armies for small mercenary armies, war reverted to what Clausewitz terms "its true nature" and "its absolute perfection." The sustenance of these popular armies, as he already perceived, had made victory more largely than before a question of economic resources, and war more largely a struggle between the belligerent nations as economic organizations. Since his time, with the rapid development of the natural sciences and the mechanical arts, new and enormously costly instruments and munitions of war have been devised, and, in order to secure an adequate provision of the means of war, all the material resources, all the brains and all the labor power available in the warring nations is drawn into some sort of war work. It seems a logical inference that distinctions between combatants and non-combatants and between public and private property have lost their justification. In modern war every member of a nation, without regard to age and sex, is at least a potential combatant, and all property is potentially State property.

With war thus widened—or thus restored to "its absolute perfection"—the interests at stake, ideal and material alike, are vastly greater and more general. Defeat in the dynastic wars of the 17th and 18th centuries meant chiefly loss of princely power and prestige. Defeat in a modern national war means not only national humiliation but possible national ruin. Besides defraying the enormous cost of the war, the defeated nation may be compelled to pay a crushing indemnity. If it cannot pay at once, it may be forced to pay gradually. In the present war, as soon as the German hope of a speedy triumph was dissipated, German writers pointed out that the districts occupied by their armies, if not annexed, could be held until they were ransomed. A distinguished economist, Professor Schumacher, indicated that Germany's defeated enemies might be forced to accept commercial treaties and to submit to tariff discriminations that would enrich Germany at their expense. Here again we have a reversion to primitive warfare. Defeat of a tribe meant the destruction or enslavement of all its members. Defeat of a nation today may mean indefinite economic servitude.

It may be added that, in a war for naval supremacy, it is widely believed that victory may give control of the markets of the world and that defeat may mean practical exclusion from overseas trade.

With such ideal and material issues at stake, a modern nation at war will inevitably develop a "will to victory" as intense as that of a savage tribe, and will care little more than a savage tribe how victory is won. What degree of regard can be expected for sentiments of humanity, or for a formal law that is substantially antiquated? The nation must win—honorably, if it can, but by all means it must win. . . .

The ultimate test of right and wrong conduct, therefore, is to be found in its military outcome. Is this pragmatic test to be applied to the commanding officer who violates a law or custom of civilized warfare? Is he to be disavowed and cashiered if his action does not prove successful? Certainly not, for this would lame initiative. "It is quite immaterial," says Hartmann, "whether the anticipated effect can actually be attained; the question is only whether the person responsible for the action was entitled to expect a successful result." This dictum enables us to grasp the full meaning of a pregnant sentence in the War Book—the very next sentence after that last cited:

It follows from these universally valid principles that wide limits are given to the subjective freedom and arbitrary judgment of the commanding officer.

This German theory of warfare is undeniably logical and consistent. The only question is whether all the factors that enter into the problem have received adequate consideration.

We note, first, that natural human feelings, the instinctive reactions of sentiment and of conscience, are considered only to be set aside. They are to be suppressed because they tend to impair the efficient conduct of a war. We note next that these reactions appear to be deemed important only in the case of officers. It is conceivable, however, that the reactions of conscience may have some effect upon the morale of privates, and that a nation in arms may fight better with a good conscience than with a bad one. In the diaries and letters of German soldiers we see that some at least have felt qualms. In one case where, because of alleged sniping, "eight houses were destroyed with their inmates," and "out of one house alone two men with their wives and an eighteen-year-old girl were bayoneted," the diarist writes: "The girl made me feel bad, she gave such an innocent look." After describing the looting and destruction of working-men's houses, another diarist writes: "Atrocious! After all there is something in what is said about German barbarians." And in a letter describing the devastation of a district abandoned by the German troops, the writer says: "We can scarcely be looked upon as soldiers—when we are at the front it is as if we were the greatest criminals."

This point, of course, is not to be overstressed. Most of the German soldier diarists seem to have become quickly hardened to every form of brutality. Few show enjoyment of atrocities, but nearly all accept ruthlessness as necessary. "The women were a sight," one of them writes, and adds: "but there is no other way." At the same time, the spiritual revolt of the finer natures cannot be regarded as a wholly negligible factor, even as regards the successful prosecution of a war.

Of the effect of ruthless warfare upon the minds of their adversaries German military writers have much to say. They recognize, however, but one possible effect. Merciless conduct of war will break the energy and coerce the will of the enemy nation. It will shake the morale of the combatants and will make the oppressed civil population clamorous for peace. That breaches of the laws and customs of war and acts of unusual inhumanity may have the opposite result; that these may steel the will and increase the energy of the hostile nation; that soldiers may meet "dirty fighting" with double fury, and that oppressed civilians may protest against any peace that does not bring redress for wrongs endured and afford some security against like injuries in the future—all this is left out of the German calculations. Even military writers must know what everyone knows, that in time of peace nothing so spurs men to resistance as a sense of wrong; but they seem to assume that this reaction will not take place in war.

Of neutral reactions to lawlessness and inhumanity German military writers say nothing. What is on the whole most significant is that they speak of all restrictions upon the "War Power" as "self-imposed." They refuse to recognize the laws and customs of war as imposed by "any external authority." In this they follow the theory accepted by the majority of German writers on politics and on jurisprudence. These hold that international law binds a State only in so far as a State consents to be bound by it.

The reason why the Germans, and those who accept the German theory, can not see that the rules of international law are imposed upon the single State by the society of States, is because this society is not politically organized and has no machinery for the enforcement of its rules. A powerful State may therefore, with apparent impunity, set these rules aside and take such action as its peculiar immediate interests seem to require. A weak State, indeed, can not do this; but the Germans courageously extricate themselves from this logical difficulty by denying that weak States are really States. They call such States "tolerated communities."

The fallacy of the German reasoning lies in the assumption that a society can not act upon its members otherwise than through political organization. They forget that even in politically organized societies men are coerced through other than political agencies and by other than political methods—for example, by ostracism. They ignore the fact that societies wholly destitute of political organization may extemporize economic and even physical coercion, by boycotting or "running out" or lynching those who disregard the interests and the sentiments of the group. To say that the restrictions which the society of civilized nations has developed by custom or by convention are "self-imposed" upon each State, is as if one should say that in a frontier mining camp, into which no sheriff has yet made his way, the custom that prohibits "claim-jumping" is imposed upon each prospector by himself, not by the group in which he is living.

In treating international law as negligible; in ignoring the opinions,

the sentiments and the conscience of neutral nations, which express material and spiritual interests that are superior to the selfish interests of any
single State and are the reservoir from which new international law is
steadily drawn—the German theory of warfare leaves out of its calculations
no less a factor than the World. The nation at war is to proceed as if it and
its antagonist were fighting on Mars. What is more, it is to proceed as if,
after the war, it were not obliged to come back into the World.

From one point of view, of course, neutral nations must be included in
military calculations. They also may migrate to Mars. To avert their hostility,
to secure, if possible, their support, is of no slight importance; but this is
the business, not of the General Staff, but of the Foreign Office. It seems,
however, to be the general belief of military men that the action or inaction
of neutrals will be determined chiefly, if not wholly, by the progress of the
war. A neutral nation will presumably wish to be on the winning side. It will
certainly avoid entanglement with belligerents who seem to be losing.
These considerations enhance the importance of rapid victory and reinforce the demand for ruthless warfare.

The political authorities of a State, unless their minds are hopelessly
militarized, see the other side. They know that sentiment counts, and they
hesitate to antagonize neutral sentiment. They realize that a great modern
war disturbs the economy of the world, and they are loth to increase the
disturbance by extending the scope and the destructiveness of warfare.

At the outbreak of the World War, the Teutonic diplomatists made
some effort to avoid the appearance of aggression. They were overridden
by the military authorities, to whom the first blow seemed all important,
and Germany declared war on Russia and France. The German Foreign
Office appreciated the political risks involved in the invasion of Belgium.
Here again the diplomatists were overridden by the military chiefs. The
immediate result was a British declaration of war. The entry of Great Britain into the war made it possible for Japan and Italy to join the coalition
against the Central Empires.

So far as we can judge from the news that has been permitted to
emerge from Germany or has leaked out, in spite of the censorship, during
the past three years, the difference between the military and the political
point of view has continued to manifest itself in conflicts between the
military and political authorities. There seem to have been differences of
opinion regarding air raids upon French and British cities. There seem to
have been conflicts in the matter of civilian deportations. In the matter of
submarine warfare against merchant vessels it is notorious that there was
not only conflict but a series of political crises. After the "war zone" procla-
mation issued by the German Admiralty in February, 1915, Germany
backed and filled on this issue for nearly two years, until in January, 1917,
the navalists won a complete triumph.

This issue outranked all others, because in unrestricted and indiscriminate submarine warfare on commerce the German military authorities saw the best chance of crippling Great Britain, if not the only chance of
winning the war; while the German political authorities rightly feared energetic and widespread neutral reactions.

Warfare upon enemy commerce, as previously conducted, rarely involved the destruction of captured vessels. In the great majority of cases

this was unnecessary, and it was contrary to the interest of the captor State. Normally, therefore, captured vessels continued to minister to the needs of the world. In submarine warfare, on the other hand, even in so called "cruiser warfare," the destruction of the captured vessel is almost always necessary. Destruction ceases to be the exception and becomes the rule. The resulting diminution of sea tonnage is a serious injury to the whole world. Unrestricted submarine warfare against enemy vessels increases the injury; indiscriminate submarine warfare against all merchant vessels, enemy and neutral, makes the injury intolerable. If Germany had deliberately sought an issue that would array the world against her, she could hardly have found one more certain to accomplish this result. Unrestricted and indiscriminate warfare against sea trade is not only illegal and barbarous, it not only shocks the sense of right and the conscience of humanity, but it also menaces the welfare of the world because of the extent to which civilization rests upon ocean carriage.

In the conduct as in the inception of this war the German military authorities have had their way. Never in the history of the world has the militarist theory had a fairer or more crucial test. What has been the result of the experiment? The Central Empires expected to fight two Powers and two or three small States. They were victorious at the outset; they say that they are still victorious—what allies has victory brought them? Turkey and Bulgaria. What of the rest of the world? In coalition against them are six Powers—without including Brazil, which is virtually at war with Germany—and ten small States. They have enemies today in every continent and in the islands of all the seas. Germany has learned that the world, although politically unorganized, is capable in an emergency of collective action against an offending State, just as the mining camp, although destitute of constituted authority, is capable of collective action against a claim jumper. The World is organizing itself into something that looks very like a Vigilance Committee.

In the conduct as in the inception of this war, not only has Germany disregarded Bismarck's "imponderables"; she has also left out of account world factors of seemingly obvious weight. Her military authorities have manifested in a most striking way the defects of the single-track mind, and they have drawn Germany into dire peril. . . .

WE MUST KILL TO SAVE

For three years and a half Europe has been drenched in blood. For three years and a half the manhood of Europe—youth in the glory of its gallantry, in the splendor of its promise—has been fed to the furnace of war. Europe is a temple of sorrow, and Rachel mourns for her children because they are not.

Soon, all too soon, France, hitherto the playground of the western world, will be sacred soil to Americans. There our dead will rest. Rude wooden crosses will dot the shell scarred battlefields, each simple cross marking the grave of an American soldier who died in France in defense of the America he loved and those dear to him. America has yet to suffer her spiritual agony, but she cannot be spared. She, like Europe, must toil painfully the weary road to Calvary.

Has not the time come for America to take stock, to ask itself if it knows the meaning of this war, to face facts instead of feeding on illusion? Millions of men have been slaughtered, more millions have gone forth in the pride of their strength to come back broken. Shall America swell the ever-mounting toll, giving and yet giving the youth on whom its future centers, or shall the guiding hand of America lead the world to peace?

Rhetoric is a spiritual stimulant, and like its grosser counterpart often valuable when a sudden burst of moral or physical energy is required, but after the effect wears off there comes reaction, exaltation gives way to depression, reality takes the place of imagination, and truth is grim. It is unfortunate that the American people entered this war with two alluring rhetorical phrases ringing in their ears—unfortunate because it has obscured the real meaning of the war and diminished its importance to them.

We were told that we went to war to make the world safe for Democracy. If this were all there is of it, clearly in the long catalogue of immoral and wanton wars that blackens the page of history there would be no war more immoral or more wanton than this. We believe in Democracy, we know its blessings, in the strength of our conviction we see that through Democracy the world marches to progress, but if we should try by force of arms to make peoples embrace Democracy who are wedded to autocracy, morally we should be as guilty as Louis XVI, who slew his thousands in the name of the gentle Christ who taught charity and love. It is what every bigot and zealot has done. Believing with sincerity that there was only one way to gain salvation, that every other way led to eternal damnation, with clear conscience and the frenzy of the fanatic he consigned to the rack and the stake the misguided, because better for them death or torture than torment without end. Our boasted civilization is back in the middle ages if in this enlightened day we are willing to make war to spread the political system of which we approve.

But, as we have said over and over again, what we are fighting for is not to make the world safe for Democracy but to make the world safe for us. Forced into war by Germany, who violated our rights as ruthlessly as she did those of Belgium, we are fighting a war of self defense. We are today in peril. To avert that peril we have taken up arms. We are fighting to defend our wives and children from the defiling hand of the German. We are fighting to protect our homes from a beast who knows no mercy, a beast whose lust is destruction; we are fighting to preserve the institutions we love, the liberty we cherish, the freedom dear to us. We are fighting in France because it is there we can strike the enemy, but if we are defeated in France we shall be conquered in America; no longer shall we be freemen but the slaves of the most merciless and brutal taskmaster the world has known. Our danger is great, and only our courage and our determination can avert it.

Nor is it true, rhetoric again to the contrary, that we are fighting not the German people but only the German Emperor and the German Government, and for the German people we have no feeling of hate. You can no more separate the German Government from the German people than you can separate the bite of the mad dog from his blood. The wickedness and infamy of the German people is in their blood; it is the corruption and poison of their blood that have made the German people—not a small class or a caste, not their rulers alone, but the whole people—a nation of savages. Nor is it true that the Prussian alone is guilty. The brutality of the Prussian cannot be exceeded, for that were impossible, by Bavarian or Saxon, but in the refinement of their cruelty, their beastliness, their inhumanity, between North and South German there is little choice.

With this premise established our duty lies clear before us.

Our duty is to kill Germans. To the killing of Germans we must bend all our energies. We must think in terms of German dead, killed by rifles in American hands, by bombs thrown by American youths, by shells fired by American gunners. The more Germans we kill, the fewer American graves there will be in France; the more Germans we kill, the less danger to our wives and daughters; the more Germans we kill, the sooner we shall welcome home our gallant lads. Nothing else now counts. There is no thought other than this, no activity apart from the duty forced upon us by Germany. The most highly civilized nations are united as they never were before, actuated by the same impulse. In England, France and Italy, among the English speaking peoples of the new world, under the southern cross and on the torrid plains, they like us see their duty clear. It is, we repeat, to kill Germans.

We have no apologies to make, no excuses to offer, no regret for having unclothed the masquerade of rhetoric and put the case in stark and naked words. Doubtless we shall offend the over nice sensibilities of those well meaning but unbalanced persons who waste their sympathies over the sufferings of the lobster as his complexion turns from dirty blue into delicate pink while they are unmoved by the knowledge of the misery and distress of the poor and unfortunate. We hope so. We are endeavoring to arouse the millions of easy going, complacent Americans, unctuously flattering themselves they are good Christians because they feel no hate, to whom the war has as yet no meaning, to a realization of what this war means, not only to them but also to their men; that it is the lives of their men against the lives of Germans.

We do not know how many Germans we have yet to kill, whether it is 500,000 or 5,000,000, but we do know that when the necessary number has been killed, when the German people lose heart and rebel against being led to the slaughter, this war will end, but that is the only way it will end. We may play at war and pay the cost in the toll of blood, or we can make war with courage, resolution and intelligence and our reward shall be fewer of those pathetic crosses on the wayside of France. . . .

When we speak of winning the war we do not mean a stalemate peace. We can have peace tomorrow on the basis of the map of August 1, 1914, but that would be no real peace, it would be simply a temporary truce; it would be a breathing spell to enable the exhausted belligerents to recuperate and feverishly prepare for a renewal of hostilities on an even greater scale; and in reality it would be a German victory. Peace, a perdurable peace, will come only when the fangs of the mad beast of Europe have been drawn, when the military power of Germany is broken; when the German people are under the harrow, sweating to pay the indemnity that is the price of their crime, in their poverty and suffering made to realize the suffering they have brought to the world.

8. Doughboys at Cantigny

JAMES HALLAS

In the summer of 1917, General John J. "Black Jack" Pershing led the American Expeditionary Force to Europe, where it was to join British and French forces in defeating the German and Austro–Hungarian armies. One of Pershing's first stops was a Paris cemetery, where he placed a wreath on the grave of the Marquis de Lafayette, who 140 years earlier had come to America to assist the Continental Army in its struggle with Great Britain during the American Revolution. In doing so, Pershing symbolically thanked the French and remarked that the "United States was now returning the favor." For the first time ever, United States troops were fighting on European soil in a war the Europeans had started. The tradition of foreign policy isolationism, first announced when President George Washington warned Americans to avoid "entangling alliances," was over. But Pershing insisted on maintaining his troops as an independent fighting force, even though the Europeans wanted to integrate American units as replacements into British and French regiments.

On July 4, 1917, the First Division of the United States Army marched through the streets of Paris, the French mobs cheering them on. The real fighting did not begin until two months later, and when it started, the Americans more than proved themselves. The United States tipped the scales in favor of the Allied powers. It was not, however, without a price. During the sixteen months of intense battle between August 1917 and November 1918, more than 125,000 American soldiers—"doughboys"—were dead. In the following essay, James Hallas described how they fought at the Battle of Cantigny in 1918.

When doughboys of the U.S. First Division arrived in the Picardy region toward the end of April 1918, they little suspected they were about to make history. They were more occupied with sore feet and aching backs than with a tiny fly-blown French village named Cantigny. But, unlikely as it seemed, it was Cantigny that was to be the scene of the first significant offensive by American arms in World War I.

The situation on the western front was grim in spring 1918. Indeed, the presence of American troops in Picardy was a measure of just how grim. Though the United States had entered the war more than a year before, there were only six U.S. divisions in France, and of these, only four could be considered ready for combat. The Allies, bled white by nearly four years of war, could only hope they would be able to contain the German army until enough American troops could be trained and fielded to tip the balance in their favor.

Struggling to make up for prewar unpreparedness, the American Expeditionary Force commander, General John "Black Jack" Pershing, hoped to acquaint his troops with modern warfare by gradually exposing them to more active fronts, while building up an independent army organization. Pessimists in French and British military circles believed the situation on the western front would create serious obstacles to this plan. They were right.

On March 21 the German army, stiffened with new reserves following

Russia's collapse in late 1917, struck Allied forces in northern France. The first rush virtually destroyed the British Fifth Army at St. Quentin and gained an astonishing thirty miles in six days. As disaster loomed, Pershing discarded his master plan. On March 28 he offered his doughboys to the soon-to-be-appointed Allied supreme commander, General Ferdinand Foch. Despite their lack of experience, the Americans were sorely needed. They were also willing to fight. "Well, we came over here to get killed," one high-ranking American officer told Foch bluntly. "Where do you want to use us?"

Foch selected Pershing's most experienced division, the First, later dubbed the "Big Red One" after its distinctive shoulder patch. It was a good choice. The First Division had arrived in France the year before and, after the initial hoopla, buckled down to serious training under French tutelage. In autumn 1917, the division had done its first stint in a quiet part of the line in Lorraine. After a break for further training, it had returned to the same region in January and was still in the line when the German offensive broke in northern France.

Though still untried, the division's officers were to prove first rate. Of those who were to participate in the attack at Cantigny, division commander Robert L. Bullard would later head an army; two of the other officers would later command corps; four would command divisions; and two, including a soft-spoken Virginian by the name of George Catlett Marshall, Jr., were destined to become chiefs of staff of corps.

All were still an unknown quantity on April 5 when the Big Red One received the call. The enemy offensive in Picardy had been blunted, but Foch needed the doughboys to reinforce General Marie Eugène Debeney's French First Army, who were exhausted after heavy fighting. The division would go into the line opposite German-held Cantigny, located about three miles west of Montdidier and fifty-five miles northeast of Paris.

During the last week in April, the French 45th and 162nd divisions sidestepped to give the Big Red One its two and one-half miles of front opposite Cantigny. The doughboys came in on foot. "Our socks were worn out," recalled Sergeant Dan Edwards, who later won the Congressional Medal of Honor at Soissons. "Most of us were barefoot in our boots. . . . We carried full packs, our clothes were crawling with cooties; we were so dirty you could smell us a mile. . . . " The French were in worse shape. In one battalion only two officers had survived the previous ten days of fighting, an indication of the power of the enemy offensives launched in March and April.

The Montdidier sector was the scene of the deepest German penetration during the March offensive. By the time the First Division arrived, the enemy had struck the British with another attack farther north, but the area around Cantigny—once inhabited by some 200 French civilians—remained fairly active. The village had changed hands twice in the recent fighting and was now held by elements of the German 30th Division.

The doughboys immediately realized they had inherited a hot spot. From a tactical standpoint, Cantigny sat on gently rising ground that had the advantage of overlooking American positions less than 1,000 yards away. The French had done little to organize their defenses. When the 16th and 18th infantry regiments went forward, the poilus turned over a front line of shell holes and rifle pits blown or scraped into the chalky soil.

By contrast, the enemy was present in force. The deceptively pretty forests dotting the region were stiff with German artillery—at least ninety batteries by intelligence estimates—and judging by the number of shells coming over, they had ammunition to burn. All roads and trails were under constant artillery fire; enemy aircraft and observers on the high ground directed fire on American battery positions; mustard gas made woods and ravines untenable. In one "shoot" all four guns of an American artillery battery were destroyed within minutes.

Attempts to suppress the enemy artillery with counterbattery fire met with little success, and American casualties mounted at an alarming rate. The worst incident occurred on the night of May 3–4 when an estimated 15,000 high explosive and gas shells fell on doughboys of the 18th Infantry. Two hundred men were killed; another 600 were wounded or gassed.

Day after day the German artillery combed the American line. One officer compared his tour of the sector to "living in a room where some one was eternally beating the carpet." Cowering in their shallow holes, some doughboys lost their nerve. A sergeant in Lieutenant Jeremiah Evart's platoon approached him about one man who went to pieces every time a shell burst anywhere in the area—which was frequently. The other men in the squad had threatened to shoot the man if he did not control himself. The sergeant believed they were serious. "You can't really blame them, can you, Lieutenant?" he inquired anxiously.

On the other hand, there was ample evidence that the Germans were suffering too. American artillery was dumping some 10,000 shells a day on enemy positions, and though the German guns seemed unscathed, the enemy infantry was feeling the gaff. Letters taken from prisoners and enemy dead complained bitterly of the constant fire. POWs told American intelligence officers that the tour of duty in the line had been cut to four days because of the severe artillery activity. Each man had to bring his four days of rations in with him, they revealed, because resupply had become virtually impossible.

General Bullard attributed the First Division's high casualty rate— more than 2,000 men between April 28 and May 27—to laxity in the field. He pointed out that French outfits on the flanks were losing less than half as many men as the Big Red One and scolded his platoon leaders for carelessness. In truth, the reason for the disparity between French and American casualties went deeper than Bullard suspected. The German High Command, deeply concerned about the potential impact of American troops on the war, had issued orders that the newcomers were to be punished with all available force whenever and wherever they appeared in the line. This tactic was designed to sap American morale and show that the presence of U.S. troops in the field was no guarantee of an eventual Allied victory.

The activity in the sector was also due to Cantigny's location. The enemy High Command hoped to dupe General Foch into believing they would resume the offensive in Picardy, when in fact the next drive was scheduled to take place between Rheims and Soissons in late May. Cantigny and the surrounding high ground masked the German rear areas from Allied observation and allowed for considerable deception. As long as the Germans held Cantigny and maintained a high level of activity, they had every reason to believe the Allies would focus their attention on the sector, while preparations for the real drive farther south went unhindered.

As it happened, the Allies had their own ideas about Cantigny. Anticipating renewed enemy attacks in the region, Foch originally planned to counter with an offensive of his own on the Montdidier front. The First Division's role in this drive would be to straighten the line by capturing the bulge at Cantigny. General Foch ultimately dropped his plans for an offensive at Montdidier. However, the First Division's orders, slightly modified, remained in force. The doughboys were to execute a local attack to capture and hold Cantigny, thereby straightening the line.

By World War I standards, the proposed assault on Cantigny—involving a single American regiment—would be little more than a skirmish. But because the operation would also be the first offensive action of the war by American troops, it gained an importance which far outstripped its size. Beyond any tactical advantage to be gained from taking Cantigny, the attack was also designed to show that Pershing's Americans were finally in the war in earnest. Success would lift Allied spirits and prove that the United States was a force to be reckoned with. By the same token, failure would discourage the Allies—already in low spirits following recent German advances—and raise enemy morale. Consequently, the operation was planned in meticulous detail. Failure was unthinkable.

Bullard decided to use the 28th Infantry Regiment in the attack. His decision was prompted as much by the regimental commander as it was by the fact that the outfit was reasonably fresh. Colonel Hanson E. Ely, described by a contemporary as "tougher than an alligator steak" and "as hard-boiled as a picnic egg," had been grumbling for action for some time. Bullard decided to accommodate him.

On May 23–24, four days before the attack, the 28th Infantry moved to a position twelve miles behind the lines where the terrain resembled the objective at Cantigny. Enemy trenches and strongholds were reproduced from airplane photographs of Cantigny. The doughboys rehearsed the assault right down to the approach on specific dugouts and machine gun nests.

The plan was fairly simple. Attacking behind a rolling barrage, one battalion would drive directly on the village while the regiment's other two battalions advanced on either flank. The objective, an imaginary line fifty-five yards north of Cantigny, curved back to the original positions, forming an arc of slightly more than a mile. The total attack force, including support troops and engineers, would number approximately 4,000 men.

Intelligence had determined that the enemy lines were held by the German 82nd and 25th reserve divisions (the former had recently relieved the German 30th Division), backed by an estimated ninety batteries of artillery. To ensure the doughboys received adequate support, the French brought up an additional 346 guns and 40 trench mortars. Approximately 200,000 rounds of ammunition were trucked forward for the preliminary barrage and supporting fire. The French also provided twelve light tanks and a number of flame thrower detachments, the latter to pry diehard defenders out of the rubble. Meanwhile, American engineers constructed dummy trenches to divert enemy artillery from the real jump-off point.

The preparations suffered at least two unexpected setbacks. First, as the attack date drew near, an enemy shell blew up a large dump of pyrotechnics and small arms ammunition destined for the attack force. Second, and worse still, an engineer detachment on its way to dig the jump-off trenches wandered into no man's land one night and promptly came under attack. The engineers escaped, minus their tools, but the lieutenant in command of the detachment vanished along with a map pinpointing the trenches and supply dumps being readied for the attack (his grave was located beyond Cantigny after the war). Suspicious of this activity, the Germans mounted a raid to take prisoners and gather information in the early hours of May 27. The raid was also intended as a feint to cover the renewed German offensive which jumped off that same day between Soissons and Rheims.

The enemy attacked in two groups after a barrage lasting an hour and a half. The group on the right attempted to penetrate the 28th Infantry's positions in Bois St. Éloi, but was repulsed. The group on the left, trying to hit positions near Bois de Fontaine and Belle Assise Farm, had more success. The raiders overran the front line before doughboys rushed up from the rear and drove them back. One group of enemy soldiers tried to drag off a stunned American prisoner, but were wiped out when some doughboys sprinted after them and freed their comrade. Some of the Americans pursued the raiders right into their trenches in Bois Allonge before retiring to their own lines.

Three other doughboys, wounded and yanked out of listening posts, were less fortunate and ended up facing German intelligence officers. Not one of the Americans mentioned the pending attack on Cantigny. The doughboys captured three Germans in return and killed many more, but their own casualties were also high. One engineer company alone lost thirty-three officers and men. The toll of dead and wounded was also steep among the 26th Infantry, who had taken the brunt of the attack on Bois de Fontaine and Belle Assise Farm.

Indirectly, the German raid could be viewed as something of an asset. When one side raided the other it was customary to return the compliment. There was reason to hope the Germans would view the opening of the attack on Cantigny as merely a retaliatory raid.

More serious implications were created by the massive German attack launched that same day near Soissons. Caught by surprise, the Franco–British front along the Chemin des Dames crumbled. By noon the enemy was pouring across the Aisne River and driving toward the Marne. The Big Red One was informed that the French artillery support brought up for the Cantigny attack would be forced to leave for the main front as soon as the village had been seized. Their departure would leave the division with only its three artillery regiments to deal with the concentration of enemy guns around Cantigny. There was little choice, but the imbalance would be sorely felt in the days ahead.

The night of May 27–28 was clear, but the early morning hours brought the usual haze. Firing during the night remained normal on both sides. The attacking infantry was supposed to get some sleep in the hours before the 6:45 A.M. jump-off, but few men had either the nerves or the experience to get any rest. Huddled in their waist-deep trenches, the doughboys waited as dawn began to streak the sky. Suddenly, at 5:45 A.M., the preparatory barrage opened up.

"Cantigny just began to boil up," recalled one of the doughboys. "In a short time we couldn't see it at all, we couldn't see the ground anywheres. The air was full of trees, stones, timber, equipment, bodies, everything you can imagine, all smashed up and whirling around with the dirt. The shells kept on going overhead in one steady screeching yowl, without a let-up." The noise was deafening. No less than two heavy guns pounded each known German battery position; howitzers concentrated on the village itself, while the lighter guns blasted trenches, machine gun positions, and roads.

Platoon leaders moved along the assault line, gesturing and checking equipment. Each man carried 220 rounds of rifle ammunition, two hand grenades, a rifle grenade, two full canteens, one shelter half, a flare, four sandbags, a shovel or pick, and rations for two days. Now, as the clock wound down, some of the men consulted khaki-covered bibles or blew sand from cartridge clips.

At 6:45 A.M. the artillery slammed down a rolling barrage in front of the attack force. Platoon leaders beckoned and the doughboys climbed out of the trenches. Cantigny, now screened by a cloud of dust, lay across the fields less than 1,000 yards away. A forward artillery observer later recalled that the village "seemed not more than a good golf-ball drive away from me."

Watching from observation posts, division officers could see the barrage —like a wall of whitish smoke mixed with the flash of explosions and showers of chalky soil—rolling toward the village. Fifty yards behind, the attack wave advanced with the tanks. Two hundred yards farther back was the second wave, and five hundred yards behind them came the third. The soldiers plodded forward, skirting shell holes and trying to keep the proper interval at a rate of about 110 yards every two minutes. Stunned by the artillery barrage and the sight of tanks, the Germans reacted weakly. Only a few enemy machine guns went into action, and there were few American casualties.

"Nothing could have been less romantic seeming," wrote Lieutenant Daniel Sargent, a former volunteer ambulance driver with the French. "The tanks looked like haycarts (horseless); the infantry looked like hay-makers that carried rifles instead of pitchforks. Nobody was running, or I should say no American soldier was running, for some Germans had come running out of Cantigny toward the tanks with their arms raised in surrender. But the advance was wonderfully steady, and no one was falling dead, insofar as I could see. If a soldier did fall, it seemed as if he had merely stumbled."

Within fifteen minutes the center battalion had entered the village. Working in small groups, the doughboys flushed dazed Germans from cellars and shell holes. French flame thrower squads moved methodically from dugout to dugout, sending thirty-foot streams of flame down the steps. An American lieutenant never forgot the sight of one German who emerged "just as I had seen rabbits in Kansas come out of burning straw-stacks [he] ran ten to fifteen yards then fell over singed to death."

The village was quickly secured, and the doughboys moved up to the objective line, but not before an enemy detachment, overlooked in trenches off to the right, opened up on the advance. Caught by surprise, a doughboy platoon was shot to ribbons before the German stronghold was cleaned out.

The attack also went well for the flank battalions. The battalion on the left advanced straight to its objective and tied in with the center battalion. The battalion on the right overcame resistance centered in a small ravine, then it too linked up with the center battalion. By 7:20 A.M. all objectives had been taken. Division artillery slapped a protective box barrage around the new position, and the doughboys started to dig in. German prisoners trickled to the rear. In the village and its environs, Colonel Ely's men had captured five officers and 225 men. Enemy dead numbered in the hundreds. American casualties were negligible.

The blow had been so abrupt that German reserves in the woods to the north of the village did not realize exactly what had happened. Just before 8 A.M. an enemy force numbering about fifty men tried to move in on the village. The doughboys dropped their shovels and drove the Germans off in a hail of rifle fire. At 9:30 A.M. another enemy force of about 100 men attempted a second probe. Again the effort lacked vigor and was easily beaten off. Despite its lackluster execution, the second probe confirmed enemy suspicions that Cantigny had been lost. Planning began immediately for a counterattack in force. Through the rest of the day German reserves trickled forward to the woods north of the village.

The German reinforcements were poor material from a military point of view. Both the 82nd and 25th reserve divisions contained large numbers of middle-aged men and young boys made sedentary by long stints in defense-oriented sectors. But Lieutenant General Baron von St. Ange, commander of the 82nd Division, had little choice but to throw them into the battle. The high ground around Cantigny gave the Americans a clear view of German positions along the Aisne River, an advantage St. Ange preferred to deny the Big Red One if at all possible.

As of 10 A.M. the situation appeared stable from the American point of view. Colonel Ely phoned brigade headquarters to report that losses had been small and the position was well in hand. Lieutenant Colonel George Marshall, assistant operations officer, reconnoitered the front and reported some 300 American casualties. German dead numbered about 800 by his estimates. Counterattacks were viewed as inevitable. French aircraft were already dropping notes pinpointing enemy concentrations. Marshall presumed the attacks would be launched from Bois de Framicourt and its ravine; from Fontainesous-Montdidier, a town to the east; and from the park of Château de Jenlis to the south. U.S. artillery received orders to pound all three approaches during the night.

Meanwhile, the German artillery had recovered from the first shock and began to take the village under heavy fire. American casualties mounted steadily. Colonel Ely requested counterbattery work, but the French guns had pulled out for the fighting on the Marne just ninety minutes after the capture of Cantigny. The division attempted to silence the German batteries with its heavy howitzers, but results were minimal. The tanks, most of which had broken down during the attack, had been repaired and immediately hustled back to the reserve areas, so no support was available from that quarter.

By 2 P.M. Ely reported more losses from mop-up operations in the ravine south of Cantigny. One company had lost all its officers and a third of its men. A battalion commander had been mortally wounded. Meanwhile, German reinforcements from the 272nd Reserve Infantry Regiment were pulling together for a counterattack in force. They had few doubts that the village would be retaken. A major was chosen to lead the first wave "with calmness and certainty."

At 5:10 P.M. a small enemy counterattack broke up under artillery fire. Twenty minutes later the main assault got under way as the German first wave emerged into the open from Bois de Framicourt. Ignoring heavy mortar and artillery fire, the doughboys blasted holes in the enemy ranks with machine guns, automatics, and rifles. The survivors kept coming, preceded by pioneers who blasted gaps in the newly-strung American wire. Some made it to the American front line.

Sergeant Dan Edwards, a hard-bitten professional soldier, had considered the previous enemy counterattacks "a picnic." Now, with his two flank guards dead, he looked up from his machine gun to see a German soldier standing over him with a bayonet. The enemy soldier, his face shining "like a boy scout that's doing his good deed for the day," responded to Edwards' attempt to surrender by stabbing him four times. As he gathered for a final lunge, Edwards rolled away in desperation, yanked out his pistol, and shot him through the midsection. The German "looked surprised, and then disappointed, and then, just as he keeled over, he looked completely hopeless," Edwards recalled years later.

The German first wave quickly shattered on the American position. The second wave was shot to pieces in no man's land. The third was aborted before it could press the attack. But the doughboys had also taken heavy casualties, and any elation they might have felt over their victory was soon dampened as the German artillery resumed the intense fire on the village. Ely informed the brigade: "Two officers left in one battalion. All men in one company gone but twelve. He will stay but should be allowed to reinforce." The division machine gun officer reported: "Line in front [of] Cantigny probably lost. Our troops to counterattack when [the] barrage starts."

The situation was not quite that serious, but it was bad. As darkness fell, ambulance detachments struggled under heavy fire to evacuate the scores of American casualties. The 28th Infantry had lost 522 men dead or wounded out of a total strength of about 3,150. Casualties in other Big Red One units totaled 302. Division command ordered three companies of reserves from the 18th and 26th infantry regiments into the line. A company of engineers was also sent forward to reinforce the line south of Cantigny. And two battalions from the 18th Infantry were alerted for possible action.

The village came to the public's attention the next day by way of an Allied communiqué which read: "The Americans, in a brilliant local action, have taken Cantigny and held it despite repeated determined counterattacks." The phrasing insinuated that the victory was secure. It was not. That same morning the enemy launched two more fruitless counterattacks against the village. German artillery and machine guns raked the American lines throughout the day. "Front line pounded to hell and gone," Ely informed his superiors in the afternoon, "and [the] entire front line must be relieved [by] tomorrow night or I will not be held responsible."

At 5:45 P.M. the Germans mounted another counterattack against Ely's thinned line. American artillery, machine gunners, and riflemen broke up the attack, but elements of the 28th Infantry, located on the left, were forced back to the old line. Ely, with his reserves gone, reported he might have to pull the whole regiment back. Division command sent up reinforcements from support and began arrangements to relieve Ely's exhausted outfit with the 16th Infantry.

Though showing signs of strain, Ely's men remained determined. Returning from Cantigny where he had been directing artillery fire, Lieutenant Daniel Sargent encountered a very tough-looking, but strangely agitated infantry officer who rambled on about his experiences in the village. "Too bad that we got driven back out of Cantigny after all," he muttered. "Those Germans are too strong for us, too strong for anyone." Sargent told him the doughboys were still holding the village. The officer accompanied him for a few more steps, then turned abruptly on his heels and headed back toward Cantigny.

Still not reconciled to defeat, St. Ange tried again on the evening of May 30. Like a scene from a recurring nightmare, the Americans crouched under a deluge of enemy shells, then watched as two waves of German infantry charged out of Bois de l'Alval. Numb with fatigue, the doughboys stood to their guns and managed to break up the attack. It was the enemy's last effort. Cantigny belonged to the Americans.

On the night of May 30–31, the 16th Infantry came in to relieve the remaining 28th Infantrymen. Despite an easy beginning, Cantigny had come at high costs. The 28th Infantry took the bulk of the casualties with 187 killed and 636 wounded. In the end, the division lost 1,033 officers and men killed and 4,197 wounded between April 19 when it took over the sector and July 13 when it finally left.

At home, the Cantigny fight inspired banner headlines. The Allies, despite their preoccupation with the German offensive near Soissons, also found encouragement in the American success. Nevertheless, the tactical gain, while of some importance, hardly measured up to the amount of hoopla greeting the American victory. German tacticians observed with some accuracy that their troops had been second rate. Had the timing and organization of the counterattacks been better, they noted, the doughboys would not have been able to hold Cantigny. Ely himself advised American Expeditionary Force headquarters that his opponents had not been of the highest caliber; and despite the number of doughboy casualties (most apparently inflicted by artillery fire), the enemy had not attacked with marked enthusiasm.

As a symbol of American determination, however, Cantigny was beyond price. This determination was recognized by the enemy corps commander in the region, Lieutenant General Baron von Watters. He told his superiors in polite parlance that the doughboys should be butchered the next time around or there would be trouble in the future. Watters saw Cantigny for what it was—not a major battle or a significant disaster, but an ominous beginning. Events were to prove it the beginning of the end.

PART THREE

RACE AND ETHNICITY IN THE NEW CENTURY, 1900–1920

During the first decades of the twentieth century, the United States found itself facing a number of new challenges, not the least of which was a bewildering ethnic diversity. During the eighteenth and early nineteenth centuries, the vast majority of immigrants arriving in the United States came from the countries of northern and western Europe—Great Britain, Germany, Norway, Sweden, and Denmark. Except for the Irish Catholics, most of the immigrants were Protestants. They were also white, which made their assimilation into the larger culture relatively easy, at least compared to the immigrant groups coming later. Also, except for the Irish, large numbers of the early immigrants settled on farms in rural areas, where they were less visible to the dominant culture.

After the Civil War, the traditional demographic profile changed. The factors driving people out of northern and western Europe—rapid population growth, the commercialization of agriculture, and industrialization— made their way into eastern and southern Europe, disrupting traditional economic systems and creating a permanent, migrant proletariat looking for work on large farms and in cities. Several million Europeans roamed the continent looking for jobs in cities and on commercial farms. Some of them looked across the Atlantic Ocean as the answer to their hopes and dreams. Because of new developments in shipping technology, the trans-Atlantic journey was quicker, safer, and cheaper than ever before, and by the 1880s large numbers of Poles, Italians, Russian Jews, Czechs, Slovaks, Greeks, Hungarians, Lithuanians, Romanians, Croatians, and Serbians were arriving in the United States, where they hoped to improve their economic circumstances. Unlike the early generations of immigrants, they were Roman Catholic, Eastern Orthodox, and Jewish in their religious persuasion—very different from the Protestant majority. They often had darker complexions. And they tended to settle in the cities of the North and Northeast where jobs in factories, mines, mills, and packinghouses were readily available. In these urban settings, the "new immigrants" were more visible than their earlier counterparts and encountered more discrimination. The number of incidents of anti-Semitism and anti-Catholicism increased dramatically, and calls for immigration restriction became more urgent and intense. Many people wondered whether the long-term American commitment to egalitarianism and democracy would survive the mass immigration from southern and eastern Europe.

The new, ethnically diverse cities were also attracting native-born Americans looking for industrial jobs. American agriculture underwent commercialization as well in the nineteenth century, and marginal producers who could not make a living on small farms sold out and headed for the cities. In the South, the attacks of the boll weevil in 1913 destroyed substantial portions of the cotton crop and sent hundreds of thousands of African Americans to cities in the North. A year later, when World War I erupted in Europe, American industrial production boomed and there were jobs available for the incoming black workers. The presence of rural whites, new immigrants, and African Americans precipitated a series of cultural clashes, race riots, and political demagoguery throughout the North in the early 1900s. Once again Americans had to decide whether egalitarianism applied to everyone. Time and time again, from the rise of Jim Crow laws in the 1880s to the incarceration of Japanese Americans in the 1940s, they failed the test, but the ideological commitment survived. Most Americans tried to work out their dream amidst the traumas of war, economic collapse, and social change—to discover "America" and interpret its mission. Pluralism and equality remained the American vision in 1945.

9. Dinner at the White House

In February 1993, just a few weeks after his inauguration as president of the United States, Bill Clinton hosted a meeting at the White House for a dozen leaders of the gay and lesbian communities. Gay rights was a movement Clinton had long embraced, and gays and lesbians overwhelmingly supported his candidacy in the election of 1992. The meeting was relatively short; they discussed such problems as AIDS, civil rights, and antigay violence. By that time, however, President Clinton was in the middle of the political firestorm created by his plan to end discrimination against gay men and women in the military. News of his meeting with gay leaders was a major story in both the broadcasting and print media the next day, and a huge chorus of protest erupted among some religious fundamentalists and conservatives. Religious broadcasters were shrill in their denunciations, accusing Clinton of leading the nation down the path to immorality and the destruction of the family. Ninety-two years earlier, President Theodore Roosevelt encountered similar protests for his decision on October 16, 1901, to invite Booker T. Washington, the famous African-American educator and president of Tuskegee Institute, to dine with him at the White House. The following selections, taken from The New York Times, *the Atlanta* Constitution, *the Mobile* Weekly Press, *and the Booker T. Washington Papers, illustrate how vehemently southern racists objected to the president's decision to have dinner with a black man.*

SOUTHERN DEMOCRATS BERATE THE PRESIDENT

Dispatches from many points in the South contain opinions of the press and politicians on President Roosevelt's action in entertaining Booker T. Washington at dinner. Democrats condemn the President and Republicans say that his action will rebound to the credit of the party. The opinions expressed are as follows:

NEW ORLEANS—The President assumes to do officially that which he would not dream of in the way of violating accepted social usages.

The Times Democrat—White men of the South, how do you like it? White women of the South, how do you like it? When Mr. Roosevelt sits down to dinner with a negro, he declares that the negro is the social equal of the white man.

The Daily States—In the face of the facts it cannot but be apparent that the President's action was little less than a studied insult to the South, adopted at the outset of his Administration for the purpose of showing his contempt for the sentiments and prejudices of this section, and of forcing upon the country social customs which are utterly repugnant to the entire South. In addition to all this, he is revivifying a most dangerous problem, one that has brought untold evil upon the whole country in the past, but which was hoped, and believed, had been removed by the firmness and wisdom of the South.

The Daily Item, the only Republican paper in the city, says in the course of a long apology for the action of the President: The *Item* does not believe that the courtesy shown Booker T. Washington by the President is an attempt to break down the barriers that society has erected between the races. Society is abundantly able to take care of itself, but politics demand the use of many and various means for obtaining information and arriving at beneficent results.

MONTGOMERY, ALA.—Editor Hood: "Roosevelt has destroyed the threatened Republican boom in the South." Ex-Gov. Oates: "No respectable white man in Alabama would ask Washington to dinner or go to dinner with him."

NASHVILLE, TENN.—*The Nashville Banner:* It was a mistake which will be deplored by a strong public sentiment.

CHARLOTTE, N.C.—Editor Smith of *The News:* "Roosevelt is the only consistent Republican, so far as the race question is concerned, who has been in public office since the war." Ex-Mayor McCall: "The President's attempt to make the negro equal to the white man socially is an insult to Southern people."

RALEIGH, N.C.—Josephus Daniels, National Democratic Committeeman: "It is not a precedent that will encourage Southern men to join hands with Mr. Roosevelt." Dr. Priest, Republican: "It will have the effect of inspiring the Republican Party all over the South."

LOUISVILLE—C. F. Grainger, Democratic candidate for Mayor: "I can't believe the President did that."

ATLANTA, GEO.—Gov. Candler: "No self-respecting Southern man can ally himself with the President after what has occurred."

AUGUSTA, GEO.—Mayor Phinisey: "It will hurt his influence, not only in the South, but will be condemned in the North." State Senator Sullivan: "It is a serious blunder." P. M. Mulherin: "No President can force social equality." Lieut. Gov. Tillman of South Carolina, in Augusta today: "Social equality with the negro means decadence and damnation."

LITTLE ROCK, ARK.—President Fletcher of the First National Bank: "I think the President has made a serious and grave mistake."

APPROVAL IN BOSTON

BOSTON, Oct. 18—Judging from a score or more of interviews with representative Bostonians, which are published here this evening, President Roosevelt's course in entertaining Booker T. Washington is approved in this city.

William Lloyd Garrison said: "It was a fine object lesson and most encouraging. It was the act of a gentleman, an act of unconscious, natural simplicity."

Major Henry L. Higginson said: "I have invited Booker T. Washington to my house. He has been my guest at my table. When he comes to Boston, I shall be glad to do it again."

Col. Thomas Wentworth Higginson: "I heartily approve of President Roosevelt's course."

The Rev. Dr. George A. Gordon: "Every good citizen of the country admires President Roosevelt and every good citizen admires his guest."

President Eliot of Harvard: "Harvard dined Booker T. Washington at her table last commencement. Harvard conferred an honorary degree on him. This ought to show what Harvard thinks about the matter."

Professor Charles E. Norton: "I uphold the President in the bold stand that he has taken."

Professor N. S. Shaler: "If I were in Roosevelt's place I would do the same thing myself."

Moorfield Storey: "The President is just right. I applaud him in that position every time."

Col. N. P. Hollowell: "I think it is altogether admirable on the part of the President."

Henry B. Blackwell: "I think the action of President Roosevelt in entertaining Booker T. Washington at the Executive Mansion was eminently wise, timely, and proper."

THE DINNER INCIDENT

Washington, Oct. 19—Quite the most exciting subject of conversation here for a day or two has been the entertainment at dinner on Wednesday by the President of Booker T. Washington. The news got out just as other announcements have been made of the guests of the President to dine, Mr. Roosevelt having adopted that method of meeting persons with whom he desired to have extended conversation.

The response that was flashed back from the South, where it was learned with something of a shock that a negro had sat at table with the President and his family, was the first intimation to the President that he had transgressed. The subject has been dealt with here by the newspapers with delicacy. The critical reports from the South have been printed, and there has been some deprecatory comment upon the resentful tone of Southern criticism.

Among public men there is manifest a distinct aversion to be quoted about the matter. But the general tone of conversation points to a pretty general disagreement with the President as to the propriety of the departure from a traditionary avoidance of just such events. The President has heard some of the criticisms upon him, and has told his visitors that he has been surprised at the intemperate language applied to him for inviting Mr. Washington to dine at the White House.

To one of his callers today, a friend who did not introduce the subject, the President is reported to have said, in referring to the dinner incident: "I do not need to give you an explanation of the Booker Washington affair, do I?" The visitor made a reply of inquiry. Then the President went on to say that he was amazed that he could be so misunderstood by those who had criticized him.

When he had declared that he did not intend to have anything to do with the white or black "scalawags" in the South, and followed that declaration by avoiding some appointments that he believed should not be made, and appointed some Democrats because he believed it to be for the best interests of the public service, he was applauded. But he considered that he had a perfect right, and that it was his duty in order to accomplish what he desired to do, to consult with white and black men who are not "scalawags."

He admired him for his character, his devotion to a cause, and for what he has accomplished.

The President does not pretend to defend himself from his assailants by entering upon a discussion of the color question. That seems to have had no weight with him in considering whether he should or should not invite Mr. Washington. The idea of a violation of Southern prejudice and tradition with the purpose of provoking and alienating his Southern friends never entered his mind.

That does not palliate the offense in the estimation of hosts of people in Washington. They are disposed to believe and say, as many do, that the President did not reflect before asking Mr. Washington to be the first negro to dine at the White House. Over and over again today attention has been directed to the fact that while President McKinley was extremely kind to all colored visitors, that he made many appointments of colored men to office, that he provoked some bitter criticism at the South by putting colored men in Post Offices against the determined opposition of white people in the towns where the negroes were to collect and distribute the mails, he never went to the extremity of asking any negro to dine with him.

When he visited Tuskegee Institute he was the guest of Mr. Washington but did not, it is said, dine with him. This was commented upon as thoughtful regard for local opinion against social association between whites and blacks. It cannot be truthfully said that the President regards the incident and the subsequent comment as humorous, although it has been said that he did and that he proposed to get more fun out of it by asking Mr. Washington to dine with him again.

No such reckless story is believed by those who know Mr. Roosevelt. That it is regretted by many Republicans is plain enough. Maryland Democrats have seized upon the incident to turn it to account in the pending State campaign, and Republicans have admitted that it may give the State to the Democrats. The prosecution of Rear Admiral Schley has been a pretty hard load to carry, it is admitted, and would have handicapped the Republicans, and now this negro-at-dinner incident is being advertised in campaign fashion in all the leading papers of the State.

In Virginia, where a rather brave boast of Republican success has been put forth, the Booker Washington incident is proclaimed by some of the politicians as settling any doubt about Democratic victory. It does not appear that the President took counsel with anybody before inviting Mr. Washington, or that he cared to know whether he had departed from tradition or not. No man knows better what the traditions of this country are than the President.

It is probably a matter of indifference to him that he was the first President to entertain a colored man at table. When Mr. Cleveland was President he was hotly condemned by many persons for having Frederick Douglass and his white wife at one of the White House receptions. The

Democrats and some Republicans who saw the couple there were horrified. But it was not the black man and his white wife who were invited. The invitation received by the Douglasses was received because all the officers of the District of Columbia were invited and without discrimination.

There were other colored officers there but the others did not accept the invitations. In that respect they were like the late colored Senator Bruce, who was repeatedly invited as a Senator, but never responded by attending. A writer to *The Star* says that President Lincoln once had Douglass at the White House at tea. He had it from Mr. Douglass.

The President's offense to the South does not appear to have estranged all his former friends in that section, for he had many calls from Southern men yesterday and today, among his callers today being Representative Livingston of Georgia, Gen. J. Wheeler of Alabama, and Gen. Fitzhugh Lee. Senator McLaurin, in whom the President is interested and from whom he acknowledges he has received excellent advice, also called.

THE PRESIDENT'S DINNER TO BOOKER T. WASHINGTON

TO THE EDITOR OF *The New York Times:*

I was surprised at your last Sunday's editorial entitled "Two Friends of the South." One thing all should know, and none better than those who conduct *The Times,* and that is that the political–social entity called "The South" has been for thirty-five years waging a holy, though at times a desperate, war against bitter, relentless, and sometimes selfish and willfully blind adversaries, in order to maintain inviolate the purity, the integrity, the manliness, the womanliness of the Anglo-Saxon race in that part of God's green earth (I use the term Anglo-Saxon in its broad sense).

In this life-and-death contest, the end of which evidently is not yet a while, the people of the South have exhibited a patience, a heroism, a constancy, a devotion, a loyalty, a dignity, a just and reasonable pride of race, which should command respect, the sympathy, and the understanding of the world, particularly of those of their own race in their own country.

The effect of this contest will not be confined to the South, nor to this country alone. Upon the result of it will depend the perpetuation of the dominant qualities of the Anglo-Saxon race. And the Southern people believe that that man is an enemy to his race, and ipso facto, an enemy to God and mankind, who in this day and generation will do anything by example, precept, or argument to lessen the social barrier between the Anglo-Saxon and the negro races in this country.

That is the meaning of the Southern criticism of President Roosevelt for entertaining a negro at a private dinner at the White House. To his critics it did not appear to be a mere personal matter between Mr. Roosevelt and his guest, but a quasi-public affair, in which their President saw fit to take such action as would, if carried on and on to its legitimate conclusion, bring to naught the bitter trials and tribulations and labors of a generation gone.

Believe me, in this contest of many years with the negro, the Southern people have not walked "as fools, but as wise." A tremendous problem was forced upon them which they were obliged to solve, though it were to the exclusion of all other matters. They yet have their shoulders to the wheels of this same problem, and are moving it slowly toward solution.

The people and newspapers of the North should help and not obstruct; they should try to think and understand, and not hastily misjudge. They should know that this is with the people of the South, a racial, not a personal matter; that goodness, kindness, and humanity prevail in the South between the individuals of the two races; that they are mutually interdependent and exceedingly well disposed toward one another, and that, finally, the best friends (I am inclined to say the only true friends) the negro has on earth are among the white people of his own section.

The Anglo-Saxon and the negro must reach their destinies in this country along parallel lines, let us trust, but with the lines never approaching to social unity. It will be better for both races if this be so.

—*Englewood, N.J., Oct. 22, 1901*

MR. ROOSEVELT'S INDEPENDENCE

To those who know and appreciate the independent fearlessness of his character and his faithfulness to conviction it is decidedly amusing to learn of President Roosevelt's absolute indifference to the antediluvian comment and senile protests that seem to have been stirred up in the South, because the President of the United States, in his private capacity of citizen, saw fit to entertain at dinner a man whom any nation might and would be proud to claim for its own; one who has been honored by social recognition even in exclusive England.

Certainly no one who has the faintest conception of our "Teddy's" character imagined for a moment that the thought of apologizing to any one for sitting at table with Mr. Booker Washington could enter his head, and the writer little doubts that President Roosevelt does not consider the honors were unevenly divided on that occasion.

The South, and, for that matter, the East, West, and North, might as well realize the fact that we have as President something new—a man with a backbone; and that in spite of the unhappy circumstances leading to his occupation of the Executive Chair, he is as truly President of the United States as though placed there directly by the votes of the people.

The South especially needs to be told some plain truths. For example: That while thinking people of the North fully appreciate certain phases of the color question in the South, that section may expect to remain just where it is—a goodly proportion of a century behind other parts of the country—so long as the petty, narrow-minded sentiments to which its public men are giving utterance in regard to President Roosevelt's action pass there for truth.

The sentiment that, under our form of government, denies recognition to true merit, social or otherwise, because that merit is covered by a colored skin, is foreign to all republican principles, and the word patriotism is a mockery in the man who holds such views, for patriotism can never justify itself by a willingness to uphold one moral principle while denying another. Nor is the spirit that undertakes to dictate to another what guests he shall entertain at his private table that of a gentleman.

—Alexander Doyle

NEGRO GUEST ENTERTAINED BY ROOSEVELT

Booker T. Washington, the well known negro educator, president of the Tuskegee, Ala., institute, was a guest of President and Mrs. Roosevelt at dinner at the white house tonight. Washington is probably the first American negro to dine with a president of the United States and his family, although it was reported that President Cleveland once entertained a negro friend at the white house board.

Since President Roosevelt occupied the white house there has hardly been a dinner or luncheon without its guests, and as the president has been so free with his invitations no special list of guests is prepared and the ushers do not know who the guests will be until they arrive. Tonight, just before 8 o'clock, a negro in evening dress presented himself at the white house door, and giving his name, said that he was to dine with the president. Booker Washington has made several visits to the white house and his face is known there, so he was at once admitted into the private apartments and the president notified of his arrival. No other guest arrived and the dinner was soon served.

Dinner at the white house since the Roosevelts have occupied the mansion has been a family affair, Mrs. Roosevelt and the two children appearing at the table with father, mother and guests. After dinner the president takes his guests to the library, and there, over cigars, things political and otherwise are discussed.

Tonight the usual order of affairs was not disturbed on account of the color of the guest of honor, and Washington left the white house about 10 o'clock, apparently very much pleased with his dinner and his chat with the president.

WILL YOU WALK INTO MY PARLOR

"Will you walk into my parlor
And my guest this evening be?"
'Twas the President inviting
The distinguished "Booker T,"
"Oh, yes thanks your Excellency,
I will take a tea and chat,
For the world will scarcely notice
While I rest my coat and hat."

But alas for good intentions,
And such democratic ways!

For there came a cry from Dixie,
And a fire was set ablaze.
"You insult us, you outrage us!
You commit an awful sin!
When you welcome to your table
That—er—man with a dark skin!

"Matters not that he is learned,
That he talks with fluent grace,
And might help to solve the "problem"
For, Sir, that is not "his place."
Foreign rulers have him honored
Statesmen, scholars make him welcome
Call him eloquent—refined,

"But alas! all goes for nothing—
This outrageous, social sin!
What can ever soothe our feelings
Or can make the White House clean?
Forthwith every hungry Negro
Will demand the same high fare;
We must take them to our parlors,
Entertain them nicely there.

"Nay! By all the traditions,
By the memory of our sires,
By the help of Ancient Woden
They shall not see our hearth fires!
Down with Roosevelt! out with Booker!
At the kitchen fill your mouth,
And beware how you shall tamper
With the feelings of the South!"

TEDDY'S MISTAKE OR BOOKER'S RECEPTION

The Lyrics to a Song by Keith and Christian

[Petersburg, Va., ca. November 1901]

TEDDY'S MISTAKE OR BOOKER'S RECEPTION
BY KEITH & CHRISTIAN

SUNG TO THE MUSIC OF COON, COON, COON

Rough Rider, Mr. Roosevelt, was searching out for fame,
Invited one black gent to dine, Booker Washington was his name;
He took him to the dining hall where a sumptuous lunch was spread,
The paramount issues of the day were then in order read.
Next came the negro problem; they agreed it must be solved:
Now Ted, said he, come let me see the amount that is involved;
'Tis not a money question, but a social thing with me,
I'll show these white folks in the South who shall dine with me.

CHORUS—For he is a coon, coon, coon, and Booker is his name,
Coon, coon, coon, I need him in the game.
Coon, coon, coon, now I am not to blame
For being born a white man instead of a coon, coon, coon.

Teddy is good at shooting lions and riding a vicious horse,
He made a dandy soldier, but, he can't be a negro's boss,
For he stands on a social basis with the whole of the African race;
Now isn't he a nice gentleman to fill McKinley's place.
He is thinking of taking a Southern tour, but he must forget it soon,
For the South don't like a President that dines at home with a coon;
He had better go West and show himself no more,
Because his finish we can see in nineteen hundred and four.

CHORUS—Caused by a coon, coon, coon, and this coon has lots of fame,
Coon, coon, coon, he is not to blame.
If Ted could change his color he would be the same;
He loves Booker Washington cause he is a coon, coon, coon.

Jeff Davis was our President, a noble man was he,
Abe Lincoln was the Yankey that set the coons all free;
McKinley was a hero, he left us all too soon,
And Roosevelt, now our President, takes pride to dine a coon.
No doubt he thought 'twould bring him fame, but his job will be the price,
Before he dines again with him he had better think twice,
For he must remember he is still on American ground,
And the South will say to him, go way back and sit down.

CHORUS—He loves a coon, coon, coon, now do you think it's fair,
Coon, coon, coon, sitting in Teddy's chair;
From a coon, coon, coon, such things we must bear,
Just because this Rough Rider loves a coon, coon, coon.

10. The Brownsville Affray

RICHARD YOUNG

The Civil War ended in 1865, but the South had a long memory, and during the forty years after Appomattox, southerners became convinced that the North had engaged in an unjust war of extermination with the goal of destroying slavery and imposing African-American rule on the states of the former Confederacy. They created a mythology about Reconstruction, condemning the twelve years of northern rule in which the Union army occupied the South, northern "carpetbaggers" and southern "scalawags" exploited the economy, and illiterate former slaves controlled local governments. The white ruling class, which had controlled southern society and politics before the Civil War, returned to power after Reconstruction, condemning African Americans to a life of agricultural toil with no hope of economic improvement. White southerners remembered the years of Reconstruction with an exaggerated horror. In July 1906, when the federal government announced that the 26th Infantry Regiment at Fort Brown in Brownsville, Texas, would be replaced by the three companies of the 25th Infantry Regiment, an African-American unit, white Texans reacted with self-righteous indignation, conjuring up Reconstruction-like images of military occupation and black rule. Racial tensions ran high in Brownsville on July 28, 1906, when the African-American soldiers arrived by rail. In the following essay, Richard Young describes what later became known as "The Brownsville Affray."

August 13, 1906: It was just past midnight on a sultry summer night. Fred Combe, the mayor of Brownsville, Texas, was falling asleep on his back porch. Army Major Charles Penrose, the commanding officer of nearby Fort Brown, was preparing for bed. A late birthday party was breaking up at the Cowen residence near the fort. Downtown, players anted up in a poker game at the Crixell Saloon. It was, from all appearances, a typical Sunday night in the sleepy Texas border town.

But someone had no intention of letting the town rest. A group of armed men—perhaps ten, perhaps as many as twenty—had quietly gathered in Cowen Alley, near a low fence that separated Fort Brown from the town.

Suddenly the silence was shattered as the men began moving rapidly up the alley toward the center of town, firing at windows as they ran. As bullets peppered the houses, startled residents dropped to the floors next to their beds. Downtown, police lieutenant M. Y. Dominguez ran out of a saloon and mounted his horse to investigate the disturbance. When he suddenly rode into range of the shadowy figures firing weapons, Dominguez wheeled his horse to escape, but he was shot just as he made the turn. (His arm would later be amputated.) Minutes later the men loosed a volley into the Ruby Saloon, killing barkeeper Frank Natus, who was reaching out to close the alley door.

After the shooting at the saloon, the killers melted back into the night, leaving chaos in their wake. Mayor Combe ran out of his house to investigate the explosion of gunfire and was told that "the Negroes are shooting up the town."

The firing in Brownsville ended after just ten minutes, but repercussions from the incident were destined to continue for many years afterward. Because of the racial implications involved, such eminent leaders as then-Secretary of War William Howard Taft, U.S. Senator Joseph B. Foraker, black leader Booker T. Washington, and President Theodore Roosevelt would become ensnared in a mystery that has never really been solved and in a controversy that has never fully been laid to rest.

It had all started when the government announced that the all-white Twenty-sixth Infantry Regiment at Fort Brown would be replaced by three companies of the all-black Twenty-fifth Infantry Regiment, then stationed at Fort Niobara, Nebraska. The black troopers had compiled a long and honorable tradition of service in the Indian wars, in the Spanish-American War, and in the Philippines. To the citizens of Brownsville, however, the service record of the men of the Twenty-fifth meant far less than the color of their skin.

The news of the transfer of the Twenty-fifth to Fort Brown was met immediately with angry talk and threats. First Sergeant Nelson Huron of the departing Twenty-sixth overheard a resident say, "The people of Brownsville don't want them damned niggers here and they won't have them." Victorio Fernandez, one of Brownsville's Mexican police officers, reportedly said, "I want to kill a couple of them when they get here." At a rail station in San Antonio, a man heard some Brownsville residents say they would "shoot over the barracks" of the Negro troops to frighten them.

The black soldiers arrived by rail on Saturday, July 28, and marched to Fort Brown past sullen townspeople. Situated at the mouth of the Rio Grande near the Gulf of Mexico, Brownsville had seen its heyday around the time of the Civil War, when it had been one of the principal seaports of the Confederacy. The end of the war and the coming of the railroad had spelled the end for Brownsville as a center of commerce. In 1906, Brownsville was a small town awash with racial hatred. Some businesses and drinking establishments refused to serve the black soldiers. Certain saloons opened up segregated back rooms for the blacks, Jim-Crow fashion.

In the most serious of several incidents that took place following the arrival of the black soldiers, Privates James W. Newton and Frank J. Lipscomb were taking a Sunday evening stroll through Brownsville on August 5. As they walked down Elizabeth Street they approached a group of whites on the sidewalk—among them U.S. customs inspector Fred Tate and his wife, who were conversing with a half-dozen women. Tate later claimed that the two black soldiers had continued walking straight down the sidewalk, plowing right through the ladies congregated there. The soldiers claimed that they had stepped aside into the street and that Tate had come after them. In any case, what followed was not in dispute. Tate pulled out a .45-caliber Colt six-shooter and shouted, "I will learn you how to get off the sidewalk when you see a party of white ladies standing there." He proceeded to pistol-whip Newton.

The soldiers were paid on Saturday, August 11, and passed what many in town considered the most peaceful soldiers' payday ever seen in Brownsville. Not one soldier was arrested, and there were no cases of excessive drunkenness. But later that weekend, a Mrs. Lon Evans reported that a soldier tried to crawl through a window in her home. The next day, the headlines in the *Brownsville Daily Herald* trumpeted:

INFAMOUS OUTRAGE
Negro Soldiers Invaded Private Premises Last Night
and Tried to Seize a White Lady

That night, a climate of rumor and hysteria gripped Brownsville. Several men from the town were ready to go to the fort with weapons to precipitate a fight. Because of the excitement, Mayor Combe rode out to talk to Major Penrose. The mayor requested that the black soldiers be confined to quarters for the evening because of "a great deal of danger in town."

Major Penrose prudently decided to order his men in, setting a curfew of 8:00 P.M. Captain Macklin sent out patrols to fetch the men still in town. Sergeant Taliafero, one of the soldiers on patrol, later reported that a townsman called out to him, "It is a good thing your C.O. has ordered you all in tonight because some of you were going to get killed."

The soldiers spent the remainder of the evening on the post, fishing in a lagoon, talking on the barracks porches, and playing cards and billiards in the dayroom. The moon was down when "Taps" sounded at 11:00 P.M., and all was quiet.

At midnight, Major Penrose heard two shots that he thought were pistol shots, then six or seven reports that he knew were from high-powered rifles. The attack had begun—and confusion reigned. Ambrose Littlefield, who was at the corner of Cowen Alley and Thirteenth Street, saw the raiders standing under a streetlamp on the corner of Washington and Thirteenth. He later identified them as black soldiers. However, George Thomas Porter, who lived at Thirteenth and Washington, looked out of his window and did not see anyone turn out of Thirteenth, nor did he see anyone under the streetlamp.

Police Lieutenant Dominguez said that from his vantage point at Washington and Fourteenth he looked toward Cowen Alley and saw eight men cross Fourteenth in the dark. Another policeman, Officer Padron, said he met Dominguez in a different place at that time.

Paulino Preciado, who was drinking in the Ruby Saloon when the shots killed the barman, said that he saw soldiers in the alley. But he later recanted, saying that "I could not see anybody in the alley, as it was dark out there, and I was in the light."

At Fort Brown, according to the testimony of Captain Macklin, the chain of sentinels stationed along the wall were unable to see men just ten to fifteen feet away in the dark because "everything was a blank." Major Penrose assumed that someone was firing on the fort and ordered his men into emergency formation.

According to the noncommissioned officers, all the men were in formation and accounted for—*while* the firing could still be heard in town. Later that night, Penrose sent a patrol to town under the command of Captain Samuel Lyon. Lyon reported back, to the surprise of Penrose, that the townspeople thought the soldiers had done the firing. The next morning, Penrose ordered a check of the weapons and ammunition. All rifles were clean and all ammunition accounted for.

On August 13, that same Monday morning, the town began an investigation. The major himself retraced the line of attack and found fifty to sixty expended Army shells along the way. He appointed an investigating committee composed of leading citizens of the town. They heard the testimony of twenty-two witnesses, eight of whom implicated the black soldiers as the raiders. Five of those witnesses said they actually saw blacks; three others said they recognized that the men were black from the sound of their voices. The tenor of the investigation can be surmised from one typical question:

Q. "We know that this outrage was committed by Negro soldiers. We want any information that will lead to a discovery of who did it."

On August 15, after two days of investigation, the citizens' committee sent a telegraph message to President Theodore Roosevelt in Washington, in which they informed him that the town was terrorized and under constant alarm. They asked "to have the troops at once removed and replaced by white soldiers." The War Department complied, sending the Twenty-fifth Infantry from Fort Brown to Fort Reno, Oklahoma.

Meanwhile, Texas authorities were conducting their own investigation: on August 23, warrants were issued for the arrest of twelve members of the black battalion for murder and conspiracy to commit murder. The twelve were selected by Texas Rangers after questioning. Although the investigation uncovered no solid allegations against the twelve and no witnesses could conclusively put them at the scene of the crime, they were removed to Fort Sam Houston in San Antonio.

Army General William S. McCaskey, Commanding General of the Department of Texas, said that the "manner by which their names were procured is a mystery. As far as is known there is no evidence that the majority of them were in any way directly connected with the affair."

The Army's investigation of the incident hit a brick wall. President Roosevelt sent Major August P. Blackson, Inspector General of the Southwest Division, to check into the matter. Blackson reported that the involvement of the men of the Twenty-fifth "cannot be doubted" but that the men of the battalion would not testify against their comrades.

Blackson contended that those who refused to "peach" or "squeal" on their comrades should "be made to suffer with the others more guilty, as far as the law will permit" because of their "conspiracy of silence." He recommended that "all of the enlisted men of the three companies present on the night of August 13 be discharged from service and be debarred from reenlistment." It appears that almost no one involved in the official Army investigation seriously addressed the notion that the men might actually be innocent and that they were saying nothing because they had nothing to say.

President Roosevelt ordered General Ernest A. Garlington to get information from the twelve soldiers incarcerated at Fort Sam Houston and from the rest of the men of the Twenty-fifth at Fort Reno. Garlington reported that each man "assumed a wooden, stolid look [and] denied any knowledge of the affair," which confirmed his belief that "the secretive nature of the race, where crimes charged to members of their color are made, is well known." Garlington wrote that he knew that many men without direct knowledge would suffer, but that they had stood together during the investigation and so should "stand together when the penalty falls."

On November 5, Roosevelt instructed Secretary of War William H. Taft to carry out the recommendation. Taft waited until after the November 9 congressional elections, then began discharge proceedings against all of the men of the three companies. The process was completed within ten days—without a court-martial or a hearing. Many of the men wept as they turned in their weapons and equipment. In all, 167 men, including many who had served with honor on the frontier, in Cuba, and in the Philippines were released, making this the largest mass punishment in U.S. Army history. One of the discharged men was a twenty-six-year veteran, and thirteen of the soldiers had been decorated for bravery in the Spanish–American War. Six men were Medal of Honor recipients.

The pro-Roosevelt *Outlook* editorialized that there was "no doubt" that some of the soldiers of the Twenty-fifth Regiment were guilty of murder in the first degree, and that the president's decision had been "both wise and just, notwithstanding the fact that some who are innocent suffer with the guilty." The *Outlook* concluded that there was "no reason whatever for regarding this action as having any relation to the race issue."

But blacks throughout the land saw it differently. Many felt betrayed by Roosevelt, whom they had perceived to be a friend of the black people. He was, after all, the leader of the party of Lincoln—and most black people still voted for the Republicans in 1906. Beyond that, during the Spanish–American War Roosevelt had fought with black troopers on his flank, and they had rescued him on more than one occasion. He had always spoken highly of their courage and ability as soldiers, which made it particularly galling when he contended that this case should convince black people not to "band together to shelter their own criminals."

Debate in the black community grew so heated that the nation's foremost black leader, Booker T. Washington, urged his people to tone down their attacks on the president. Because Washington had never spoken in defense of the soldiers, his stand was perceived to be justification of Roosevelt's action at the expense of the Negro movement. Other black leaders, most notably W. E. B. DuBois, were quick to capitalize on the issue—and they gained power in their community as Washington fell from favor.

The Constitutional League (a civil rights organization and precursor to the National Association for the Advancement of Colored People) lodged an official protest over the dismissal of the black soldiers on December 10, 1906. More importantly, the U.S. Senate began its own investigation. The hearings lasted from February 4 through June 14, 1907, and were resumed on November 18, 1907, and continued through March 10, 1908.

The Senate listened to the testimony of more than one hundred and sixty witnesses. The Majority Report concluded that the shooting had been done by some eight to twenty soldiers, who were never identified. The guns used had been 1903 Springfield rifles, according to the report, and the ammunition had been government issue. Of the witnesses, fifteen said they saw the attackers clad in soldiers' uniforms.

During the hearings the black soldiers acquired a powerful champion, Senator Joseph B. Foraker of Ohio, a politician from within Roosevelt's own Republican party and a long-time foe of the president. Senator Foraker and three other senators wrote the minority opinion. They pointed out that there had been no indictments, despite the administration's desperate measures to secure them. This was no small matter, as the *New York Evening Post* pointed out in an editorial: "When a Texas grand jury cannot find an indictment against a hated 'nigger' it looks as if the President of the United States had a pretty poor case when he discharged those men."

The dissenters also wrote that if anyone had a motive to shoot up the town of Brownsville, it was the white gambling-house owners, not the black soldiers. Their reason was financial: the houses were segregated, and the owners were losing most of the revenue they would have been taking in if Fort Brown had been manned by white soldiers. It was the contention of Foraker and the other dissenters that the owners had probably staged the incident in order to effect the removal of the black troops.

Foraker and the others charged that the black soldiers had been punished without access to their right to a fair public trial. They further stated that the soldiers had been loyal for years and that even if some were guilty, all should not have been discharged. Furthermore, no conspiracy had been proven, and much of the testimony had been contradictory and unreliable.

These new investigations brought prior assumptions into question and raised new questions that would never be satisfactorily answered. An editorial in the March 19, 1908, *Independent* stated: "The investigation by the Senate leaves it somewhat doubtful whether the shooting was actually done by the soldiers."

Many of the witnesses claimed to have identified the attackers as black soldiers from a distance of thirty to one hundred feet, but in a firing conducted at night by the Army under conditions similar to those of the night of August 13, witnesses as close as fifty feet could see only the flash of weapons and nothing of the person firing. At a distance of just two paces on such a night, it was not possible to distinguish the race of men standing quietly in a line.

The forty Government-Issue shells found immediately outside the fort wall had been piled neatly in a circle approximately ten inches in diameter. Because a Springfield rifle ejects expended cartridges a distance of ten feet, it would have been necessary for the men firing the rifles to find and retrieve the spent shells in the dark and neatly pile them, an action that would have been not only bizarre but nearly impossible on a moonless night. The piles of cartridges suggest that they were left there as "evidence" —scattered by someone who wanted to make it look as if the soldiers had fired them.

According to the dissenters, the rounds *had* been fired by the men of the Twenty-fifth—but on the range at Fort Niobara, sometime prior to their transfer to Fort Brown. A microscopic study conducted at the Springfield Armory proved that all of the expended cartridges had been fired by the same four rifles, all of which belonged to members of Company B. In the check of weapons ordered by Major Penrose on Monday morning, three of the four rifles were found to be clean and covered with cosmoline, a thick lubricant that would have rendered it nearly impossible to fire them. It is possible that these three rifles could have been fired and then cleaned and oiled during the night, but it is almost certain that the fourth rifle was not fired on the night of August 13. It was found buried deep in a footlocker in the locked supply room. In order to retrieve the weapon, the investigators had to remove bunks and baggage that had been piled on the locker after the move from Fort Niobara.

The dissenters theorized that the empty shells were policed up at Fort Niobara and put into boxes, and then were transported along with other equipment to Fort Brown. The boxes containing the empty shells were left unguarded on the porches of the barracks there. It would have been easy for a civilian who worked on post to pocket these rounds without anyone noticing.

The live military rounds fired into the houses could be explained by the fact that the departing Twenty-sixth Infantry had often bartered with civilians, trading ammunition for whiskey and other items. The Twenty-sixth had also left a great deal of used equipment, including old uniforms, in the barracks when they left camp. Scavengers from town were frequent visitors to the post in the time between the departure of the Twenty-sixth and the arrival of the Twenty-fifth. It was not uncommon to see townspeople wearing articles of military clothing, and it certainly would not have been difficult to put together "uniforms" for the raiders.

All of these possible contradictions to the official version of the incident came to light after the men had been discharged. The mystery was never solved. No one was ever tried for the murder of Frank Natus. But the Roosevelt administration remained adamant in insisting that it had followed the right course in dismissing the men, and neither Theodore Roosevelt nor his successor, William Howard Taft, wanted anything to do with reopening the investigation.

An Army Court of Inquiry did convene to hear evidence on the issue of reinstatement of the 167 men, but the hearings were not public. On May 4, 1909, for reasons never disclosed, the Court of Inquiry reinstated fourteen of the soldiers to full honors and rank. The other 153 accused men remained pariahs, discharged without honor or chance of redemption. They had never been convicted of a crime, nor was any evidence produced against them—yet they remained outcasts.

Sixty-six years after the Brownsville incident, in 1972, U.S. Representative Augustus Hawkins initiated legislation to restore honor to the men of the Twenty-fifth Infantry. Senator Hubert H. Humphrey backed the motion in the Senate, saying, "We in government have a duty to demonstrate that we can admit an error and can correct a terrible wrong." Eventually, Secretary of the Army Robert F. Kroehlke issued an executive order that gave the 153 men honorable discharges, albeit without back pay or allowance. Congress in turn authorized a twenty-five-thousand-dollar pension for any of the discharged men still living and ten thousand dollars to any surviving spouse.

Only one of the men, eighty-six-year-old Dorsey Willis, lived to collect the money. Willis claimed that the dishonorable discharge had ruined his life, saying, "To take a persons's rights from them is bad, you know. They had no right to eliminate me without trying me and finding me guilty, but they did . . . None of us said anything because we didn't have anything to say. It was a frame-up through and through."

11. The Passing of the Great Race

MADISON GRANT

Industrialization, the rise of the cities, and the new immigration precipitated a series of cultural crises in the United States. The old faith in a political and economic system blessed by God no longer seemed so certain. In 1890 the Department of the Interior announced the closing of the frontier, and many Americans wondered where discontented people could go to release pent-up frustrations. The depression of 1893 left millions hungry and out of work; Jacob Coxey's army of the unemployed was marching on Washington; Eugene Debs and the American Railway Union had struck the Pullman Company; the Populists were up in arms in the South and West; and all this came in the wake of the Homestead Strike at the Carnegie Steel Works and the Haymarket Riot in Chicago. People feared revolution. And the cities—full of Catholics and Jews, strange languages, exotic foods, and crowded tenements— seemed breeding grounds for political and social unrest. An atmosphere of crisis— first in the 1890s and again during World War I, the 1920s, the Great Depression, and World War II—precipitated nativist fears throughout the country and demands for immigration restriction.

These tensions first appeared just when racist theories were becoming popular. Many whites accepted implicitly the inferiority of African Americans, Native Americans, and Mexican Americans, and late in the 1800s these theories reached fruition in Jim Crow laws, the reservation system and Dawes Act for the Indians, the acquisition of Mexican-American land, and even in the decision of the McKinley adminis- tration to take possession of the Philippine Islands in 1898. Racism was a fact of life. But it gained new intellectual adherents, and some argued that there were fixed racial differences among white Europeans. Historians George Bancroft and Herbert Baxter Adams, political scientists Francis Lieber and John W. Burgess, biologist Robert Knox, and classicist William F. Allen began promoting the theory of Teutonic origins, arguing that the Anglo-Saxon, Nordic, and Germanic peoples were the superior "race," responsible for free-enterprise capitalism, technology, and political liberty. They also claimed that Jews, Slavs, Italians, and Greeks, though racially "above" black and brown people, were markedly inferior to Germans, English, and Scandinavians in intellectual capacity, ambition, and social organization. The following essay, written by Madison Grant in 1916, is an example of such racist thinking.

RACE AND DEMOCRACY

Failure to recognize the clear distinction between race and nationality and the still greater distinction between race and language, the easy assump- tion that the one is indicative of the other, has been in the past a serious impediment to an understanding of racial values. Historians and philolo- gists have approached the subject from the view-point of linguistics, and as a result we have been burdened with a group of mythical races, such as the

105

Latin, the Aryan, the Caucasian, and, perhaps, most inconsistent of all, the "Celtic" race.

Man is an animal differing from his fellow inhabitants of the globe, not in kind but only in degree of development, and an intelligent study of the human species must be preceded by an extended knowledge of other mammals, especially the primates. Instead of such essential training, anthropologists often seek to qualify by research in linguistics, religion, or marriage customs, or in designs of pottery or blanket weaving, all of which relate to ethnology alone.

The question of race has been further complicated by the effort of old-fashioned theologians to cramp all mankind into the scant six thousand years of Hebrew chronology, as expounded by Archbishop Usher. Religious teachers have also maintained the proposition not only that man is something fundamentally distinct from other living creatures, but that there are no inherited differences in humanity that cannot be obliterated by education and environment.

It is, therefore, necessary at the outset for the reader to thoroughly appreciate that race, language, and nationality are three separate and distinct things, and that in Europe these three elements are only occasionally found persisting in combination, as in the Scandinavian nations.

To realize the transitory nature of political boundaries, one has only to consider the changes of the past century, to say nothing of those which may occur at the end of the present war. As to language, here in America we daily hear the English language spoken by many men who possess not one drop of English blood, and who, a few years since, knew not one word of Saxon speech.

As a result of certain religious and social doctrines, now happily becoming obsolete, race consciousness has been greatly impaired among civilized nations, but in the beginning all differences of class, of caste, and of color, marked actual lines of race cleavage.

In many countries the existing classes represent races that were once distinct. In the city of New York, and elsewhere in the United States, there is a native American aristocracy resting upon layer after layer of immigrants of lower races, and the native American, while, of course, disclaiming the distinction of a patrician class, nevertheless has, up to this time, supplied the leaders of thought and the control of capital, of education, and of the religious ideals and altruistic bias of the community.

In the democratic forms of government the operation of universal suffrage tends toward the selection of the average man for public office rather than the man qualified by birth, education, and integrity. How this scheme of administration will ultimately work out remains to be seen, but from a racial point of view, it will inevitably increase the preponderance of the lower types and cause a corresponding loss of efficiency in the community as a whole.

The tendency in a democracy is toward a standardization of type and a diminution of the influence of genius. A majority must of necessity be inferior to a picked minority, and it always resents specializations in which it cannot share. In the French Revolution the majority, calling itself "the people," deliberately endeavored to destroy the higher type, and something of the same sort was, in a measure, done after the American Revolution by the expulsion of the Loyalists and the confiscation of their lands.

In America we have nearly succeeded in destroying the privilege of birth; that is, the intellectual and moral advantage a man of good stock brings into the world with him. We are now engaged in destroying the privilege of wealth; that is, the reward of successful intelligence and industry, and in some quarters there is developing a tendency to attack the privilege of intellect and to deprive a man of the advantages of an early and thorough education. Simplified spelling is a step in this direction. Ignorance of English grammar or classic learning must not be held up as a reproach to the political and social aspirant.

Mankind emerged from savagery and barbarism under the leadership of selected individuals whose personal prowess, capacity, or wisdom gave them the right to lead and the power to compel obedience. Such leaders have always been a minute fraction of the whole, but as long as the tradition of their predominance persisted they were able to use the brute strength of the unthinking herd as part of their own force, and were able to direct at will the blind dynamic impulse of the slaves, peasants, or lower classes. Such a despot had an enormous power at his disposal which, if he were benevolent or even intelligent, could be used, and most frequently was used, for the general uplift of the race. Even those rulers who most abused this power put down with merciless rigor the antisocial elements, such as pirates, brigands, or anarchists, which impair the progress of a community, as disease or wounds cripple an individual.

True aristocracy is government by the wisest and best, always a small minority in any population. Human society is like a serpent dragging its long body on the ground, but with the head always thrust a little in advance and a little elevated above the earth. The serpent's tail, in human society represented by the antisocial forces, was in the past dragged by sheer force along the path of progress. Such has been the organization of mankind from the beginning, and such it still is in older communities than ours. What progress humanity can make under the control of universal suffrage, or the rule of the average, may find a further analogy in the habits of certain snakes which wiggle sideways and disregard the head with its brains and eyes. Such serpents, however, are not noted for their ability to make rapid progress.

To use another simile, in an aristocratic as distinguished from a plutocratic, or democratic organization, the intellectual and talented classes form the point of the lance, while the massive shaft represents the body of the population and adds by its bulk and weight to the penetrative impact of the tip. In a democratic system this concentrated force at the top is dispersed throughout the mass, supplying, to be sure, a certain amount of leaven, but in the long run the force and genius of the small minority is dissipated, if not wholly lost. *Vox populi,* so far from being *Vox Dei,* thus becomes an unending wail for rights, and never a chant of duty.

Where a conquering race is imposed on another race the institution of slavery often arises to compel the servient race to work, and to introduce it forcibly to a higher form of civilization. As soon as men can be induced to labor to supply their own needs slavery becomes wasteful and tends to vanish. Slaves are often more fortunate than freemen when treated with reasonable humanity, and when their elemental wants of food, clothing, and shelter are supplied.

The Indians around the fur posts in northern Canada were formerly the virtual bond slaves of the Hudson Bay Company, each Indian and his squaw and pappoose being adequately supplied with simple food and equipment. He was protected as well against the white man's rum as the red man's scalping parties, and in return gave the Company all his peltries—the whole product of his year's work. From an Indian's point of view this was nearly an ideal condition, but was to all intents serfdom or slavery. When, through the opening up of the country, the continuance of such an archaic system became an impossibility, the Indian sold his furs to the highest bidder, received a large price in cash, and then wasted the proceeds in trinkets instead of blankets, and in rum instead of flour, with the result that he is now gloriously free, but is on the highroad to becoming a diseased outcast. In this case of the Hudson Bay Indian the advantages of the upward step from serfdom to freedom are not altogether clear. A very similar condition of vassalage existed until recently among the peons of Mexico, but without the compensation of an intelligent and provident ruling class.

In the same way serfdom in mediaeval Europe apparently was a device through which the landowners overcame the nomadic instincts of their tenantry. Years are required to bring land to its highest productivity, and agriculture cannot be successfully practiced even in well-watered and fertile districts by farmers who continually drift from one locality to another. The serf or villein was, therefore, tied by law to the land, and could not leave except with his master's consent. As soon as these nomadic instincts ceased to exist serfdom vanished. One has only to read the severe laws against vagrancy in England, just before the Reformation, to realize how widespread and serious was this nomadic instinct. Here in America we have not yet forgotten the wandering instincts of our Western pioneers, which in that case proved to be beneficial to everyone except the migrants.

THE PHYSICAL BASIS OF RACE

In the modern and scientific study of race we have long discarded the Adamic theory that man is descended from a single pair, created a few thousand years ago in a mythical Garden of Eden somewhere in Asia, to spread later over the earth in successive waves.

Many of the races of Europe, both living and extinct, did come from the East through Asia Minor or by way of the African littoral, but most of the direct ancestors of existing populations have inhabited Europe for many thousands of years. During that time numerous races of men have passed over the scene. Some undoubtedly have utterly vanished, and some have left their blood behind them in the Europeans of to-day.

It is a fact, however, that Asia was the chief area of evolution and differentiation of man, and that the various groups had their main development there, and not on the peninsula we call Europe.

We now know, since the elaboration of the Mendelian Laws of Inheritance, that certain bodily characters, the so-called unit characters, such as skull shape, stature, eye color, hair color, and nose form, are transmitted in accordance with fixed mathematical laws, and, further, that various unit characters which are normally correlated, or belong together, may, after prolonged admixture with another race, pass down separately, and form what is known as disharmonic combinations. Such disharmonic combinations are, for example, a tall brunet, or a short blond; blue eyes associated with brunet hair, or brown eyes with blond hair. In modern science the meaning of the word "character" is now limited to physical instead of mental and spiritual traits as in popular usage. . . .

There exists to-day a widespread and fatuous belief in the power of environment, as well as of education and opportunity to alter heredity, which arises from the dogma of the brotherhood of man, derived in turn from the loose thinkers of the French Revolution and their American mimics. Such beliefs have done much damage in the past, and if allowed to go uncontradicted, may do much more serious damage in the future. Thus the view that the negro slave was an unfortunate cousin of the white man, deeply tanned by the tropic sun, and denied the blessings of Christianity and civilization, played no small part with the sentimentalists of the Civil War period, and it has taken us fifty years to learn that speaking English, wearing good clothes, and going to school and to church, does not transform a negro into a white man. Nor was a Syrian or Egyptian freedman transformed into a Roman by wearing a toga, and applauding his favorite gladiator in the amphitheatre. We shall have a similar experience with the Polish Jew, whose dwarf stature, peculiar mentality, and ruthless concentration on self-interest are being engrafted upon the stock of the nation.

Recent attempts have been made in the interest of inferior races among our immigrants to show that the shape of the skull does change, not merely in a century, but in a single generation. In 1910, the report of the anthropological expert of the Congressional Immigration Commission, gravely declared that a round skull Jew on his way across the Atlantic might and did have a round skull child, but that a few years later, in response to the subtle elixir of American institutions, as exemplified in an East Side tenement, might and did have a child whose skull was appreciably longer; and that a long skull south Italian, breeding freely, would have precisely the same experience in the reverse direction. In other words, the Melting Pot was acting instantly under the influence of a changed environment.

What the Melting Pot actually does in practice, can be seen in Mexico, where the absorption of the blood of the original Spanish conquerors by the native Indian population has produced the racial mixture which we call Mexican, and which is now engaged in demonstrating its incapacity for self-government. The world has seen many such mixtures of races, and the character of a mongrel race is only just beginning to be understood at its true value.

It must be borne in mind that the specializations which characterize the higher races are of relatively recent development, are highly unstable and when mixed with generalized or primitive characters, tend to disappear. Whether we like to admit it or not, the result of the mixture of two races, in the long run, gives us a race reverting to the more ancient, generalized and lower type. The cross between a white man and an Indian is an Indian; the cross between a white man and a negro is a negro; the cross between a white man and a Hindu is a Hindu; and the cross between any of the three European races and a Jew is a Jew. . . .

One subspecies of man, and one alone, specialized in light colored eyes. This same subspecies also evolved light or blond hair, a character far less deeply rooted than eye color, as blond children tend to grow darker with advancing years, and populations largely of Nordic extraction, such as those of Lombardy, upon admixture with darker races, lose their blond hair more readily than their light colored eyes.

Blond hair also comes everywhere from the Nordic species, and from nowhere else. Whenever we find blondness among the darker races of the earth we may be sure some Nordic wanderer has passed that way. When individuals of perfect blond type occur, as sometimes in Greek islands, we may suspect a recent visit of sailors from a passing ship, but when only single characters remain spread thinly, but widely, over considerable areas, like the blondness of the Atlas Berbers or of the Albanian mountaineers, we must search in the dim past for the origin of these blurred traits of early invaders.

The range of blond hair color in pure Nordic peoples runs from flaxen and red to shades of chestnut and brown. The darker shades may indicate crossing in some cases, but absolutely black hair certainly does mean an ancestral cross with a dark race—in England with the Mediterranean race.

In Nordic populations the women are, in general, lighter haired than the men, a fact which points to a blond past and a darker future for those populations. Women in all human races, as the females among all mammals, tend to exhibit the older, more generalized and primitive traits of the race's past. The male in his individual development indicates the direction in which the race is tending under the influence of variation and selection.

It is interesting to note in connection with the more primitive physique of the female, that in the spiritual sphere also, women retain the ancient and intuitive knowledge that the great mass of mankind is not free and equal, but bond and unequal.

The color of the skin is a character of importance, but one that is exceedingly hard to measure as the range of variation in Europe between skins of extreme fairness and those that are exceedingly swarthy, is almost complete. In general the Nordic race in its purity has an absolutely fair skin, and is consequently the *Homo albus,* the white man par excellence.

Many members of the Nordic race otherwise apparently pure have skins, as well as hair, more or less dark, so that the determinative value of this character is uncertain. There can be no doubt that the quality of the skin and the extreme range of its variation in color from black, brown, red, yellow to ivory-white are excellent measures of the specific or subgeneric distinctions between the larger groups of mankind, but in dealing with European populations it is sometimes difficult to correlate shades of fairness with other physical characters.

It often happens that an individual with all the Nordic characters in great purity, has a skin of an olive or dark tint, and it much more frequently happens that we find an individual with absolutely pure brunet traits in possession of a skin of almost ivory whiteness and of great clarity. This last combination is very frequent among the brunets of the British Isles. That these are, to some extent, disharmonic combinations we may be certain, but beyond that our knowledge does not lead. Owners, however, of a fair skin have always been, and still are, the objects of keen envy by those whose skins are black, yellow, or red.

Stature is another unit character of greater value than skin color, and perhaps than hair color, and is one of much importance in European classification because on that continent we have the most extreme variations of human height.

Exceedingly adverse economic conditions may inhibit a race from attaining the full measure of its growth, and to this extent environment plays its part in determining stature, but fundamentally it is race, always race, that sets the limit. The tall Scot and the dwarfed Sardinian owe their respective sizes to race, and not to oatmeal or olive oil. It is probable that the fact that the stature of the Irish is, on the average, shorter than that of the Scotch, is due partly to economic conditions, and partly to the depressing effect of a considerable population of primitive short stock.

Mountaineers all over the world tend to be tall and vigorous, a fact probably due to the rigid elimination of defectives by the unfavorable environment. In this case altitude would operate like latitude, and produce the severe conditions which seem essential to human vigor. The short stature of the Lapps and the Esquimaux may have been originally attributable to the trying conditions of an Arctic habitat, but in any event it has long since become a racial character.

So far as the main species of Europe are concerned, stature is a very valuable measure of race. . . .

THE COMPETITION OF RACES

Where two races occupy a country side by side, it is not correct to speak of one type as changing into the other. Even if present in equal numbers one of the two contrasted types will have some small advantage or capacity which the other lacks toward a perfect adjustment to surroundings. Those possessing these favorable variations will flourish at the expense of their rivals, and their offspring will not only be more numerous, but will also tend to inherit such variations. In this way one type gradually breeds the other out. In this sense, and in this sense only, do races change.

Man continuously undergoes selection through social environment. Among native Americans of the Colonial period a large family was an asset, and social pressure and economic advantage both counselled early marriage and numerous children. Two hundred years of continuous political expansion and material prosperity changed these conditions and children, instead of being an asset to till the fields and guard the cattle, became an expensive liability. They now require support, education, and endowment from their parents, and a large family is regarded by some as a serious handicap in the social struggle.

These conditions do not obtain at first among immigrants, and large families among the newly arrived population are still the rule, precisely as they were in Colonial America, and are to-day in French Canada, where backwoods conditions still prevail.

The result is that one class or type in a population expands more rapidly than another, and ultimately replaces it. This process of replacement of one type by another does not mean that the race changes, or is transformed into another. It is a replacement pure and simple and not a transformation.

The lowering of the birth rate among the most valuable classes, while the birth rate of the lower classes remains unaffected, is a frequent phenomenon of prosperity. Such a change becomes extremely injurious to the race if unchecked, unless nature is allowed to maintain by her own cruel devices the relative numbers of the different classes in their due proportions. To attack race suicide by encouraging indiscriminate breeding is not only futile, but is dangerous if it leads to an increase in the undesirable elements. What is needed in the community most of all, is an increase in the desirable classes, which are of superior type physically, intellectually, and morally, and not merely an increase in the absolute numbers of the population.

The value and efficiency of a population are not numbered by what the newspapers call souls, but by the proportion of men of physical and intellectual vigor. The small Colonial population of America was, man for man, far superior to the average of the present inhabitants, although the latter are twenty-five times more numerous. The ideal in eugenics toward which statesmanship should be directed, is, of course, improvement in quality rather than quantity. This, however, is at present a counsel of perfection, and we must face conditions as they are.

The small birth rate in the upper classes is, to some extent, offset by the care received by such children as are born, and the better chance they have to become adult and breed in their turn. The large birth rate of the lower classes is, under normal conditions, offset by a heavy infant mortality, which eliminates the weaker children.

Where altruism, philanthropy, or sentimentalism intervene with the noblest purpose, and forbid nature to penalize the unfortunate victims of reckless breeding, the multiplication of inferior types is encouraged and fostered. Efforts to indiscriminately preserve babies among the lower classes often result in serious injury to the race.

Mistaken regard for what are believed to be divine laws and a sentimental belief in the sanctity of human life, tend to prevent both the elimination of defective infants and the sterilization of such adults as are themselves of no value to the community. The laws of nature require the obliteration of the unfit, and human life is valuable only when it is of use to the community or race.

It is highly unjust that a minute minority should be called upon to supply brains for the unthinking mass of the community, but it is even worse to burden the responsible and larger, but still overworked, elements in the community with an ever increasing number of moral perverts, mental defectives, and hereditary cripples.

The church assumes a serious responsibility toward the future of the race whenever it steps in and preserves a defective strain. The marriage of deaf mutes was hailed a generation ago as a triumph of humanity. Now it is recognized as an absolute crime against the race. A great injury is done to the community by the perpetuation of worthless types. These strains are apt to be meek and lowly, and as such make a strong appeal to the sympathies of the successful. Before eugenics were understood much could be said from a Christian and humane view-point in favor of indiscriminate charity for the benefit of the individual. The societies for charity, altruism, or extension of rights, should have, however, in these days, in their management some small modicum of brains, otherwise they may continue to do, as they have sometimes done in the past, more injury to the race than black death or smallpox.

As long as such charitable organizations confine themselves to the relief of suffering individuals, no matter how criminal or diseased they may be, no harm is done except to our own generation, and if modern society recognizes a duty to the humblest malefactors or imbeciles, that duty can be harmlessly performed in full, provided they be deprived of the capacity to procreate their defective strain.

Those who read these pages will feel that there is little hope for humanity, but the remedy has been found, and can be quickly and mercifully applied. A rigid system of selection through the elimination of those who are weak or unfit—in other words, social failures—would solve the whole question in one hundred years, as well as enable us to get rid of the undesirables who crowd our jails, hospitals, and insane asylums. The individual himself can be nourished, educated, and protected by the community during his lifetime, but the state through sterilization must see to it that his line stops with him, or else future generations will be cursed with an ever increasing load of victims of misguided sentimentalism. This is a practical, merciful, and inevitable solution of the whole problem, and can be applied to an ever widening circle of social discards, beginning always with the criminal, the diseased, and the insane, and extending gradually to types which may be called weaklings rather than defectives, and perhaps ultimately to worthless race types.

Efforts to increase the birth rate of the genius producing classes of the community, while most desirable, encounter great difficulties. In such efforts we encounter social conditions over which we have as yet no control. It was tried two thousand years ago by Augustus, and his efforts to avert race suicide and the extinction of the old Roman breed were singularly prophetic of what some far seeing men are attempting in order to preserve the race of native Americans of Colonial descent.

Man has the choice of two methods of race improvement. He can breed from the best, or he can eliminate the worst by segregation or sterilization. The first method was adopted by the Spartans, who had for their national ideals, military efficiency and the virtues of self control, and along these lines the results were completely successful. Under modern social conditions it would be extremely difficult in the first instance to determine which were the most desirable types, except in the most general way, and even if a satisfactory selection were finally made, it would be, in a democracy, a virtual impossibility to limit by law the right to breed to a privileged and chosen few.

Experiments in limiting breeding to the undesirable classes were unconsciously made in mediaeval Europe under the guidance of the church. After the fall of Rome, social conditions were such that all those who loved a studious and quiet life, were compelled to seek refuge from the violence of the times in monastic institutions, and upon such the church imposed the obligation of celibacy, and thus deprived the world of offspring from these desirable classes.

In the Middle Ages, through persecution resulting in actual death, life imprisonment, and banishment, the free thinking, progressive, and intellectual elements were persistently eliminated over large areas, leaving the perpetuation of the race to be carried on by the brutal, the servile, and the stupid. It is now impossible to say to what extent the Roman Church by these methods has impaired the brain capacity of Europe, but in Spain alone, for a period of over three centuries, from the year 1471 to 1781, the Inquisition condemned to the stake or imprisonment an average of 1,000 persons annually. During these three centuries no less than 32,000 were burned alive, and 291,000 were condemned to various terms of imprisonment and other penalties, and 7,000 persons were burned in effigy, representing men who had died in prison or had fled the country.

No better method of eliminating the genius producing strains of a nation could be devised, and if such were its purpose the result was eminently satisfactory, as is demonstrated by the superstitious and unintelligent Spaniard of to-day. A similar elimination of brains and ability took place in northern Italy and in France, and in the Low Countries, where hundreds of thousands of Huguenots were murdered or driven into exile.

Under existing conditions the most practical and hopeful method of race improvement is through the elimination of the least desirable elements in the nation by depriving them of the power to contribute to future generations. It is well known to stock breeders that the color of a herd of cattle can be modified by continuous elimination of worthless shades, and of course this is true of other characters. Black sheep, for instance, have been practically destroyed by cutting out generation after generation all animals that show this color phase, until in carefully maintained flocks a black individual only appears as a rare sport.

In mankind it would not be a matter of great difficulty to secure a general consensus of public opinion as to the least desirable, let us say, ten per cent of the community. When this unemployed and unemployable human residuum has been eliminated, together with the great mass of crime, poverty, alcoholism, and feeblemindedness associated therewith, it would be easy to consider the advisability of further restricting the perpetuation of the then remaining least valuable types. By this method mankind might ultimately become sufficiently intelligent to deliberately choose the most vital and intellectual strains to carry on the race. . . .

The Nordics are, all over the world, a race of soldiers, sailors, adventurers, and explorers, but above all, of rulers, organizers, and aristocrats in sharp contrast to the essentially peasant character of the Alpines. Chivalry and knighthood, and their still surviving but greatly impaired counterparts, are peculiarly Nordic traits, and feudalism, class distinctions, and race pride among Europeans are traceable for the most part to the north. . . .

12. Italian Exodus to America

ALEXANDER DeCONDE

Between 1880 and 1924, more than two million Italian immigrants permanently settled in the United States, most of them in Boston, New York City, Philadelphia, Chicago, New Orleans, and San Francisco. They became targets of the most violent nativist crusades in the country. Calling them "black dagos" and "wops," many Americans considered them ignorant, inferior, and superstitious, lacking ambition and social taste. The size of the Italian migration alarmed them, as did Italian Catholicism and their concentration in urban ghettos. Italian immigrants often became scapegoats for the problems of crime, slums, and poverty. Rumors of organized crime circulated wherever Italians settled. In the 1890s the "Black Hand" conspiracy, imported from Italy, was supposedly responsible for the increase of crime in America. Some people blamed the "Mafia" for social problems in the 1920s and 1930s, and as late as the 1950s and 1960s people were worrying about the "Cosa Nostra."

Violence against Italian immigrants began as early as the 1870s. In 1874 four Italian strikebreakers were killed by union mine workers in Buena Vista, Pennsylvania, and in 1886 a mob in Vicksburg, Mississippi, lynched an Italian American. When an Italian immigrant was murdered in Buffalo in 1888, the police summarily arrested 325 other Italians as suspects. The worst incident occurred in 1891. In New Orleans, Irish police chief David Hennessey had built a political reputation investigating Sicilian crime. In 1891 he was murdered, and an outraged public decided the Mafia was responsible. Nine Italians were arrested, but a jury acquitted six of them and declared mistrials for the others. An outraged mob entered the parish jail and lynched eleven Italian inmates, three of whom were Italian nationals.

There were hundreds of other serious incidents of anti-Italian discrimination in America. Lynchings occurred in West Virginia in 1891 and 1906; Altoona, Pennsylvania, in 1894; Erwin, Massachusetts, in 1901; Marion, North Carolina, in 1906; Tampa, Florida, in 1910; Wilksville, Illinois, in 1914; and Johnson City, Illinois, in 1915. And in 1920 marauders invaded the Italian neighborhood of West Frankfurt, Illinois, and systematically burned the community to the ground. Actually, the Italian immigrants were a hardworking, law-abiding community. In the following essay, Alexander DeConde describes the Italian migration to America.

The United States is home to more people of Italian origin than any other country in the world except Italy herself. Italian-Americans, one of the nation's largest ethnic groups, are part of America's bone and flesh. Although Italians experienced what was common to millions of other Europeans who migrated, they also contributed to a unique aspect of American history. They made up, from the 1880s until the 1920s when restrictive laws cut off the flow, the only truly great proletarian immigration to this country.

The first Italians to migrate to North America were not proletarians; nor were they people of distinction who made an impression on colonial society. The largest group consisted of 200 Protestants, "Waldensians" from the valleys of Piedmont who arrived in New Amsterdam in the spring of 1657. Other Italians who migrated in the colonial era did so as individuals, not in groups. There were, of course, exceptions. In 1768 about 100 indentured Italian laborers were among those who failed to establish an agricultural colony at New Smyrna in Florida. Italians who came to the English colonies were generally artists, musicians, or adventurers who settled in cities along the Atlantic seaboard.

In Italy the few intellectuals who concerned themselves at all about the New World lamented the absence of Italian settlements there. Italians did not go to North America in the 17th and 18th centuries because Italy was not united and had no colonies there, and because the laws of the various petty Italian states barred emigration.

Unlike the English, Italians at this time were not considered a migrating people. The *contadini,* or peasants, worked the soil and seemed unwilling to leave it.

Early in the 19th century the idea of immigrating to the United States became attractive to Italians. In September 1816 the American consul at Livorno reported that "the number of applicants to go to the United States has become incalculable; from professors of the highest services to the labouring peasant; and had they the means, as they have the will, Italy would be half depopulated." In coffee houses in Milan and elsewhere America was "the common subject of conversation."

Yet little is known about the flow of Italian immigrants to the United States in these years. Each state dealt on its own with foreigners who entered its ports. Not until 1820 did the Federal Government begin keeping records on immigration. Although Federal statistics were better than the state records, they did not for many years give a reliable account of Italian immigration. According to Federal records, only thirty Italians arrived in 1820, but more probably came.

Elsewhere Italians were already on the move in search of economic betterment. In that year nearly half of all immigrants who entered Brazil were Italian. After that date a few hundred Italians trickled into the United States each year.

Slowly small pockets of Italian settlements grew in various parts of the United States. A number of Italian missionaries, seamen, and travelers went to the Pacific Coast before 1830, but it took the gold rush of 1849 in California to attract Italians in substantial numbers. Many were merchants rather than prospectors. "The miners mined the mines, and the Italians mined the miners," according to immigrant folklore. In any case, enough Italians came so that the Kingdom of Sardinia opened a consulate in San Francisco in 1850.

Although few in number, the immigrants who were laying the foundation for Italian community life in American cities encountered various prejudices. Poor and friendless, they clung together in slums, fearing to settle in the hostile countryside. Contrary to the views of many historians, discrimination against Italians did not coincide with the massive immigration of later decades; they felt the cruelty of bigotry almost as soon as they appeared on the American scene. In New York City in 1857, for example, when an Italian was charged with murdering a police officer, mobs attacked and insulted all the Italians they could find.

These early immigrants, about 14,000 between 1820 and 1860 according to official records, but probably more, came mostly from the central and northern regions of the Italian peninsula. Most of them settled in Eastern cities, though California attracted more Italians than did New York. Many were small shopkeepers, street vendors, entertainers, and truck gardeners. Those with an education often taught languages—Italian, French, and Spanish. Some were political refugees, men with university degrees but without a trade or technical knowledge that could help them earn a living.

During most of the 19th century, and especially before Italy's unification in 1870, the great mass of Italians who chose to go overseas immigrated to South rather than to North America. Most were from northern Italy and most went to Argentina and Brazil. Before unification emigration from southern Italy, often prohibited by law, had been slight. With unification and the establishment of a stronger national government, legal restrictions either disappeared or became ineffective; southern Italians began an exodus, much of it to the United States.

In 1870 a population of 27 million placed an almost intolerable strain on the resources of the new Italian nation. It had too many people trying to make a living off the scant soil. Everywhere in the industrial countries, where technology had broken down old patterns of living, people were moving from farms to cities seeking a richer life. In Italy, too, this movement from the land swelled the cities, but unlike the cities in more advanced industrial nations, those in Italy could not absorb the swarming, hungry *contadini*.

Within a century, or from the time of the American Revolution, Italy's population had doubled, producing unemployment and widespread unrest. Emigration worked as a kind of social safety valve. Italy became an exporter of strong human bodies to other regions that needed labor and could offer food. New, relatively cheap, easy to obtain, and what was then considered swift transportation also stimulated a mass overseas migration. Despite improvements in travel, for most Italian peasants the voyage through the Mediterranean and across the Atlantic, taking from two to three weeks, was an agonizing experience. They were packed in steerage in row after row of dirty bunks, like herring in a barrel. There they ate, slept, inadequately took care of toilet functions, and often huddled in fright.

When the exhausted immigrants landed in the United States, exploiters swarmed around them. Runners who spoke Italian, or one of its various dialects, piloted the newcomers to boarding houses where they were cheated and robbed. Employment agents also swindled the immigrants, as did railroad representatives who sold them counterfeit or worthless railroad tickets.

Aware of these indignities, some of the leaders of the new Italy urged the people not to emigrate. In more than one instance the *contadini* answered, explaining why they were forced to abandon their country. "We plant and we reap, but never do we taste white bread," they said. "We cultivate the grape but we drink no wine. We raise animals for food but we eat no meat. We are clothed in rags. . . ."

Most of the Italians who stepped off the trans-Atlantic steamers in the 'seventies settled in the large industrial centers of the East and Middle West. Their first homes were in the deteriorating sections of those cities. There, as around Mulberry Street in New York City, they formed "Little

Italies." In Philadelphia and elsewhere newspapers were already carrying stories of squalor, drunken brawls, and crime in the Italian neighborhoods.

By the end of the 'seventies the character of Italian immigration had changed. Now instead of northern Italians the great majority of newcomers were swarthy, illiterate *contadini* from the south. They seemed particularly strange because Americans had not previously encountered Italians of this kind in large numbers. Earlier immigrants had experienced prejudice, but these newcomers met almost instant hostility. As early as 1872 the *New York Times* reported that in the city's "business community there is an almost unanimous refusal to hire Italians." In 1874 the Armstrong Coal Works in western Pennsylvania brought in a group of Italian laborers to break a strike. Immediately, hatred of strikebreakers and prejudice against Italians produced violence. The other workers rioted, attacked, and killed several of the Italians. Even the earlier northern Italian immigrants, concerned about damage to their own precarious status, looked with contempt on the Sicilians, Neopolitans, and other southerners.

With these peasants came something seemingly new, the worker who took seasonal employment to earn a little money and then return to Italy, "as a bird in springtime repairs to its old nest." Although others, such as Irishmen, Poles, and French Canadians, came seasonally, and migratory workers were familiar to Europe, no previous immigrants had brought with them as many temporary laborers as did the Italians. These "birds of passage" angered old-stock Americans who considered them flighty and lacking in character. Actually, the relative swiftness of the steamship and the cheapness of steerage accommodations did more to stimulate temporary immigration than did Italian traits.

Disliking the seasonal job hunter and Italians in general, native Americans grumbled about this large ethnic group, which could not be fitted into what they considered the desirable pattern of American life. Nativists began to talk about an unpleasant change from an "old" to a less desirable "new" immigration, and to concern themselves with the nation's "unguarded" gates.

Ironically, the formative years of Italian immigration ended and massive immigration began at a time when a reborn nativism was on the rise in the United States. The coming of the southern Italian intensified this nativism, leading to demands by old-stock Americans for some kind of Federal control—really restriction—over immigration. Despite this hostility the *contadini* kept coming.

The year that marked the beginning of Italian immigration to the United States as a massive proletarian movement was 1880. Census figures for that year claim that 44,000 Italians were in the country, with 12,000 of them in New York, the area of heaviest concentration. Other thousands spread over America yearly thereafter, at least 10,000 pouring out of steerage in 1900. In that year the country contained more than 480,000 Italians, or nearly three times as many as a decade earlier.

Now the Latin peasant tide swelled to huge proportions. From 1900 to 1910, well over two million Italians hustled through American ports. Nearly three times as many arrived in this decade as had in the preceding ten years. In 1907 alone as many as 285,000 poured in, and they kept coming. In 1900 Italians comprised fewer than 5 percent of the foreign-born population. At the end of the decade they made up about 10 percent of the foreigners, even though the census enumerated slightly more than 1,300,000, or just about 60 percent of those who had arrived in that decade alone. In these ten years, when European immigration into the United States rose to its highest level, the Italian inundation reached a crest higher than that from any other nation. The flood from Italy, which peaked in 1913, had turned into one of mankind's great voluntary movements of population, the largest overseas movement of people in Europe's history.

Many more Italians came than stayed permanently, and more arrived than official sources indicate. Thousands entered the country illegally. Throughout the 'eighties and 'nineties a third or more who came returned to Italy. In the 'eighties the new pattern of Italian emigration became clear. As many Italians were pulling up roots to go overseas as were migrating to neighboring countries, such as France or Switzerland. In the 'nineties the United States became their favorite goal.

Like that from other countries, this southern Italian migration followed a pattern. Most immigrants were young men between the ages of 14 and 45. Italy sent a higher proportion of males to the United States than did any other European country. So the average Italian immigrant was a young, robust male, uneducated and unskilled, but in the most productive years of his life. When he became reasonably settled and acquired enough money for the passage he sent for his family in Italy.

In the first years of the 20th century fewer immigrants returned to Italy than in the past. Many visited their old homes briefly, but few stayed. Most returned to America and what they regarded as home.

This outpouring of humanity from the Italian peninsula surprised Americans. Italian immigrants had, the sociologist Edward A. Ross said, "shot up like Jonah's gourd." Since their arrival contributed noticeably to the changing character of immigration to the United States, and of the ethnic composition of the population, though not as abruptly as nativists maintained, old-stock Americans became increasingly critical. Why, they asked, did Italians keep rushing to a strange and often hostile land?

Italians kept coming in greater numbers than anticipated for the same reasons that caused other peoples to emigrate, and for unique reasons also. The United States had the reputation of a land of plenty with an expanding economy that required workers. The inexperienced and unlettered could find jobs quickly in mines or factories because technology had eliminated the need for skills.

This economic attraction, as well as the improvements in travel, was not enough in itself to force conservative *contadini,* for whom emigration amounted to an admission of failure at home, to desert the soil. Students of emigration believe that few people leave home by true free choice, or according to an Italian proverb, *chi sta bene non si muove,* or "he who is well off doesn't move." The Italians also came because, as in the 'seventies, their homeland virtually expelled them; they left in a mass act of protest against intolerable conditions. For the *Mezzogiorno,* or southern Italy, the last decades of the 19th century were a time of economic stagnation. Agriculture, the nation's main economic activity, suffered a severe depression, much of it resulting from competition with other countries. The new national government did little to help alleviate the economic distress. Its leaders talked about agricultural reform in the *Mezzogiorno* but poured resources into industrialization of the north.

More peasants than ever from Calabria, the Abruzzi, or Sicily came to feel that they could not do worse in other lands than in their own. Even though they may never have ventured beyond their native village, more and more responded to the posters of emigration agents giving the prices and dates of voyages to America and became willing to encounter the perils of a strange environment. They borrowed money for the voyage, sometimes paying as high as 50 percent interest.

Most of the emigrants from southern Italy might have followed the northerners who had in earlier decades converged on South America except that conditions there, temporarily at least, seemed uninviting. An outbreak of yellow fever in Brazil claimed some 9,000 Italian victims and led the Italian Government temporarily to ban immigration to that country. In Argentina political disturbances, financial crises, and a war with Paraguay crippled economic life and caused prospective immigrants to think twice about going there.

Once the south Italian emigration had set its course for the United States it rapidly gained momentum. Periodic crises at home also maintained its flow. Between 1884 and 1887 cholera epidemics that killed 55,000 people set many on the move. Ten years later a poor harvest deepened peasant unrest, and touched off bread riots and other violence in cities.

At first the government of the new Italy deplored or ignored the exodus. Slowly, despite the influence of land-owners in parliament who opposed emigration, the attitude of the government changed. Seeing advantages in emigration, officials even encouraged it. In emigrating to a richer land, such as the United States, Italians often helped themselves and their country by relieving the economic pressure at home. Immigrants continued to help by sending home some of the money they earned. These remittances gave the Italian Government badly needed cash and became important in Italy's effort to balance her economy. Immigrants in the United States, like those in South America, bought Italian foods and other products. By creating a demand for Italian goods they also helped in building Italy's foreign markets.

Emigration also had negative aspects. In the *Mezzogiorno* it thinned out the population, emptying whole villages of able-bodied men, and leaving streets choked with grass and weeds. The cry *Ci manca la mano d'opera* ("We lack the working hand") could be heard through the countryside. "The young men have all gone to America," one villager explained in 1908. "We are rearing good strong men to spend their strength in America."

"America letters" from relatives and friends who had emigrated to the United States often awakened desires in *contadini* for a better life. Even though sometimes stained with tears these letters, and the cash or money orders they often contained, told of the material advancement available in the New World for those who were prepared to bend and strain in a strange land. If you are willing to sweat, the American letters said, come and join us.

This message appealed to the *contadini* whose main assets were strong arms and a willingness to work. On the average, southern Italians brought with them about half as much money as did northerners, who carried into the United States slightly more cash than the average immigrant of any other nationality. The southerner usually had so little capital and education that he could work only with pick and shovel, or at some other job requiring no skills, such as hod carrier or mortar mixer. "Whenever you see a shovel, a steamroller, or a dredging machine," one observer noted in 1909, "there also you see Italians."

Two characteristics that Italians brought with them, although often criticized, helped them in facing life in the jungles of strange cities—tightly knit family ties and loyalty to their *paese*, or "home village." "Italy for me," immigrants would say, "is the little village where I was raised." In New York, Boston, Chicago, and elsewhere Italians congregated in deteriorating neighborhoods with their *paesani* (others from the same region) recreating what sociologists call urban villages, or the Italian country town in a city environment. Such settlements were often divided into almost as many groups as there were sections of Italy represented. Few were exclusively Italian, and the make-up of all was in a state of flux.

It was logical for immigrants who could speak no English to want to seek familiar faces, to be near relatives or those whose language and customs they understood. *Paesani* could assist in finding a job or place to live, and could help in emergencies. By custom and tradition Italians expected aid from relatives. Their family cohesiveness and provincial clannishness was not unusual. Earlier immigrants—the English, the Irish, the Germans, and others—had also settled among relatives or countrymen from the same region, and they too had created urban villages. But the Italian, who often continued to think of himself as a Calabrese, a Veneziano, an Abruzzese, or a Siciliano, seemed stranger, more conspicuous, less capable of national feeling, and more clannish than earlier immigrants.

Density of population was usually greater in the Little Italies than elsewhere. In 1904 a tenement-house inspector described Philadelphia's Little Italy as thirty-five blocks of tightly packed humanity. Under such conditions life could be tolerable only when people appreciated each other's customs. In California social conditions differed from those in the East. Little Italies were less crowded there, less provincial, and more prosperous.

The narrow loyalties of the Italians also brought disadvantages. Along with illiteracy, they hampered the development of Italians into a cohesive ethnic group capable of exerting pressure on a statewide or national level for the advantage of all. Italians often did not work together as effectively as immigrants in other ethnic groups; differences in dialect and the lack of widespread written communication kept them apart.

Like the Poles, Ukranians, Jews, and other immigrants, Italians banded together in fraternal organizations, especially in mutual aid societies similar to those they had known in the homeland. These societies provided a kind of group-benefit insurance for workmen, small shopkeepers, and others. Here Italians showed a capacity to help each other in meeting the problems of America's industrial society. In New York City alone, in 1910, there were more than 2,000 Italian mutual-benefit societies.

In time, out of the experience of living together within American communities, immigrants discovered the larger ethnic bond—that they were Italians, not just *paesani,* with a common heritage and common interests. Italian newspapers, magazines, and other publications, despite shortcomings, contributed to the growth of this ethnic identity.

So concerned were most immigrants with the steady pressure of earning daily bread that at first they had little interest in, or time for, even the most meager of cultural pursuits. Contrary to his reputation for being hot-tempered and pleasure-loving, the average Italian was sober, frugal, and hard-working. He usually drank less alcohol and worked longer hours and harder than immigrants of other nationalities. When he drank, it was usually wine in the home, not hard liquor in the saloon. He was so eager to save that he frequently injured his health. He skipped meals, worked in perilous, congested ,and unsanitary mines and factories, and exposed himself to all kinds of harsh weather to earn a little money. Industrialists employed Italians because they were readily available, and in many kinds of work they produced good results. Even though the percentage of skilled workers among them was lower than among other immigrants from Western Europe (but higher than those from Eastern Europe), the skilled Italians ranked high as stonecutters, mechanics, mariners, barbers, seamstresses, shoemakers, and as blue-collar workers in general.

Italian workers, like Greeks, Austrians, Syrians, Mexicans, and other new immigrants, made use of a form of bossism called the *padrone* system. It was not really a system, but more a vehicle used by Italian workers to adjust to American conditions. A *padrone* was frequently a boss who recruited and often exploited laborers. He supplied *contadini* to employers at rates that gave him a solid profit. In this form the *padrone* system flourished only in the formative stages of Italian immigration. In the 1890s the *padrone* shifted from being a recruiter to acting as a special kind of employment agency.

Newly arrived Italians, ignorant of American conditions, were pleased to be able to place themselves in the hands of a *padrone*, often a leader from their own *paese* or someone who could speak their dialect as well as English. They relied on him for jobs and food and lodging. In a land of strangers he provided an anchor, a sense of security.

In 1897, according to one estimate, *padroni* controlled about two thirds of the Italian labor in New York. Working through *padroni*, Italians largely succeeded the Irish in the rough labor required to build and maintain railroads, highways, and other construction projects. In time, as immigrants learned to make their own way, they dispensed with the services of *padroni*.

Italian immigrants improved themselves by slowly expanding their business and other economic activities. In New York City they were particularly active in the manufacture of men's and women's clothing. Until about 1890 Jews dominated that industry. Italians invaded the garment district and within a few years were second only to the Jews in the numbers employed there. Despite their peasant background and educational limitations, Italian immigrants showed an impressive business ability. Even though they had to start on a shoestring, often as pushcart peddlers, they owned thousands of stores, restaurants, wholesale food concerns, small contracting businesses, trucking and moving companies, brickmaking firms, and the like. The business spirit, according to some sociologists, appeared stronger among Italians than among other immigrants such as the Irish.

Italians found success mostly in small businesses. Rarely did immigrants, or their sons, claw their way to the top in the world of big business.

In their business ventures many enjoyed a feeling of independence they had not known in Italy. In the United States even simple peasants learned that if they worked faithfully and behaved themselves they could get ahead. This idea, even if its reality often eluded them, appealed to their manhood.

Italians most often discovered the better life in America's cities rather than on her farms. Although Italian agricultural workers could be found throughout the country, with a considerable number of them in California and Louisiana, the immigrants who became independent farmers were few in relation to their numbers. Only scattered groups of Italians settled in the farm states of the Middle West and South. The immigrants at flood tide made their homes mostly in the cities of the Middle Atlantic states and New England, with large groups around Chicago, New Orleans, and in California. The census of 1910 classed about 80 percent of all Italians as urban, a percentage of city dwellers about twice that of the population as a whole. Only in New Orleans did Italians exceed all other foreigners. In no other large city, except New York, did they rank either first or second among immigrant groups.

Critics and reformers, at a time of shortage in farm hands, deplored the urban concentration of Italians. Yet by 1910 students of population distribution could find no statistical "evidence of a tendency to city life distinguishing the Italians either from the native population or from other classes of the foreign-born." In other words, *contadini* showed no greater fondness for urban life than did anyone else. When Italians started arriving in great numbers America's cities were exploding, not just growing. Everywhere native Americans were deserting farms for jobs and bright lights in the cities. These same attractions, not love for the crowded tenement, lured Italians to the cities.

It took capital to buy land and farm equipment; *contadini* usually had none. In the United States these former peasants could earn more money as industrial workers than as farm hands. To succeed as a farmer the Italian came too late. By 1890 the frontier, with its cheap or free farmland, had practically disappeared. Land became expensive, capital scarce, and competition among farmers intense.

When Italian immigrants turned to the soil they took up truck farming in New York and New Jersey, vine-growing in California, and cultivation and fruit-growing in Louisiana and Texas. These farmers, often skillful and successful, were usually northern Italians who had enough money to buy land.

Success in agriculture came most readily to Italians in California. In the early years of the 20th century they came to comprise the second largest foreign group in the state. While Italians elsewhere were hustling for jobs in industry, about half or more of those in California worked in agriculture. Many owned fruit orchards, dairies, and vineyards, as well as truck farms.

Italian immigrants generally avoided the South, mainly because of low wages, the plantation–tenant system, and the religious and ethnic bigotry common there.

The southern experience was unusual only because it was extreme; almost everywhere Italians found themselves culturally isolated. Even in their crowded urban villages many, especially the unmarried males, were overcome by dreadful loneliness. The long separation of the sexes produced an unwholesome situation, but Italians were probably no worse off than other immigrants, many of whom had also come as single men. Loneliness did not seem to spur assimilation; Italians and old-stock Americans seldom intermarried. Since Italian women were relatively scarce, the male was the one who usually married outside his ethnic group.

Outsiders considered Italian women passive; they were not. When men could not obtain jobs or earned wages too low to maintain the family, the wives worked. Some, like native Americans, took jobs just to get ahead. So eager were Italian women to earn that at the turn of the century they gained the reputation of accepting lower wages than any other women in the United States. Few birds of passage could be found among them. Once settled with husband and family, they usually had no intention of returning to Italy. The women were the churchgoers. Far more than the men they kept alive the traditional Italian adherence to the Catholic faith. This clinging to the church was significant, for one of the striking changes in life for Italians in the United States occurred in religion.

Contadini were as ignorant in religion as in other matters. They found the Catholic churches in the United States different from anything they had known in the old country. "The fact is," an Irish Catholic observed, "the Catholic Church in America is to the mass of Italians almost like a new religion." Italians considered the American Catholic church cold and uncongenial, mainly because the Irish dominated it and infused it with a harsh militancy. *Contadini* could not speak intimately with Irish priests as they did with their own clergy in Italy. At first they had little choice; they had to use the Irish priests or dispense with religion. Some chose to abandon Catholicism; most remained loyal, or nominally so, but in their own way. The church dilemma of the Italians was aggravated by the fact that they were the first Catholic people to come to the United States in large numbers without bringing their own religious leaders with them.

Even though Franciscans and Servites, or servants of Mary, had been ministering to Italians in the United States since the Civil War, they did not have to deal with large numbers of unlettered *contadini*. The Franciscans opened the first Catholic church dedicated to the service of Italians in New York City, but not until 1867. Other churches of that kind followed, but slowly. In the 'eighties, as Italian immigration approached flood stage, American Catholic leaders became concerned about the shortage of churches for the newcomers.

In 1888, with the arrival of Scalabrinian Fathers, immigrants finally got priests of their own from Italy who came with the sole purpose of ministering to their spiritual needs. In 1897 the first Salesian priests arrived in San Francisco, and in the next year in New York City also to care for local Italians.

Some Italians drifted to atheism or Protestantism. In the 'nineties several Protestant denominations established mission churches in Italian neighborhoods of Eastern cities. They proselyted on the assumption that the Catholic Church was socially backward and was failing to meet the needs of the *contadini*. By 1916 more than 50,000 Italians had joined American Protestant churches.

As soon as finances permitted, those Italians who took their Catholicism seriously helped to stem the flow to Protestantism. These laymen set up their own parishes and built churches like those in Italy. Although such efforts to make immigrants feel comfortable in American Catholicism brought Italian control of a number of neighborhood churches, they made no dent in the Irish dominance of the hierarchy. Moreover, most of the churches in Little Italies remained under Irish priests, carryovers from the days when these neighborhoods had been Irish. As in Boston's North End and Milwaukee's Third Ward, Italians moved into neighborhoods the Irish had vacated. Frequently they had to fight the Irish parish by parish to take over the churches in their own neighborhoods. This religious rivalry paralleled that in the streets where Italian and Irish workers had battled since the 1870s, and where the youths still fought.

Conflict did not always mar the relationship; often the Irish helped Italian newcomers. Knowing English well and having arrived earlier, the Irish built a powerful church hierarchy. Italians used this institution in their struggle for a place in American life.

In politics, too, the Italian found himself dependent on Irish leadership, mainly on the network of Irish political machines in the cities. Since Italians arrived later and were slower than members of other ethnic groups, such as Jews, to become naturalized Americans, they lagged in political activity. They needed Irish help. Like other ghetto immigrants most of them became Democrats. By 1892 Chicago had an Italian alderman, and two years later Italians were sitting in the Illinois legislature. New York elected its first Italian to public office in 1897.

Italians brought with them little that they could contribute to American politics. Most *contadini* also contributed no more to the refined cultural life of their adopted land than they had to that of their old country, which was little. They were usually so backward that they could not even appreciate what meager culture the big cities offered the poor. As Jane Addams has pointed out, in Chicago they rarely knew of the existence of public art galleries. They made their most immediate contribution to American life with back-breaking labor.

The experience of the *contadini* in a new culture often awakened in them a spirit that had been dormant, not dead. It expressed itself in one of the distinguishing characteristics of the Italian immigrant—his adaptability. Wherever these peasants went, to North or South America, or elsewhere, they made the best of their new situation, no matter how onerous, and adjusted fairly rapidly. While retaining their own traits, they reconciled themselves to the customs of their country of settlement and worked for its welfare as well as for their own. Even though suffering from persistent discrimination, they did not fester as a disaffected minority. This adaptability amounted to a considerable achievement in a country where the people were particularly hostile to cultural diversity. But in 1921, when the era of massive immigration ended and Italians were becoming part of the national fiber, they still had a long way to go to rise above their proletarian origins to achieve sweet success, American style.

PART FOUR

SCHIZOPHRENIC DECADE, 1920-1929

World War I ended in 1918 and the Great Depression began in 1929. Sandwiched between those two cataclysmic events was the decade of the 1920s, a curious period in American history, a time when the United States left behind its rural, agrarian past and entered the era of the urban industrial society. There was a veneer of power and prosperity to the decade. The United States was widely admired as the major political and military power in world affairs, and the economy seemed to be booming; the stock market reached unprecedented levels and money was being readily made. Between 1920 and 1929, Americans purchased tens of millions of radios, and national broadcasters distributed sports, news, and entertainment programs nationwide. In Hollywood, the film industry marketed movies nationwide. Because of the increasing number of radios and films, and the advertising associated with them, Americans for the first time were listening to the same programs, reacting to the same images and symbols, enjoying the same heroes. The fact that the automobile became a mass consumer product in the 1920s provided millions of people with unprecedented mobility, contributing even more to the emergence of a national culture. For many historians, modern America was born in the 1920s.

But it was a difficult transition. The Department of Commerce announced in 1924 that for the first time in history, more Americans lived in cities than in rural villages and more worked in factories than on farms. Ever since the colonial period, Americans had associated cities with crime, pollution, immorality, and corruption, and the fact that most people now lived there seemed to threaten the traditional conviction that strength and stability came from life on the land. Americans were not living on the land anymore; they were on the concrete, and it worried traditionalists. The cities were also filling up with new immigrants from eastern and southern Europe and with African Americans from southern farms and plantations —people who appeared to be very different from the white Protestant majorities of the past.

Urban life and ethnic diversity found expression in religious fundamentalism, racial and ethnic conflict, and right-wing political agitation. Rural Protestants, especially in the South, were alarmed about the secular theologies emerging from northern seminaries and universities, and they focused their resentment on the theory of evolution. School districts passed legislation prohibiting the teaching of evolution, and the ensuing controversies were symbolized by the famous Scopes trial in Dayton, Tennessee, in 1925. Rural Protestants also supported the Prohibition movement. The United States suffered as well from ethnic stress. The Ku Klux Klan grew dramatically in the 1920s, especially in the North, targeting Catholics, Jews, and African Americans for its wrath. Race riots erupted in a number of cities, and demands for immigration restriction became more strident. The Red Scare targeted liberals, socialists, and communists for special persecution.

Concerns about changing moral values were reflected in the scandals of the decade. When Americans learned that several baseball players on the Chicago White Sox had conspired to lose the 1919 World Series in return for gambling bribes, an acute sense of disillusionment settled on the country. If baseball was corrupt, what could Americans trust? In Washington, D.C., the scandals of the Harding administration—Teapot Dome, the Veterans' Bureau, and the Alien Property Custodian Office—deepened the fundamental American suspicion regarding politicians. Sexual scandals in Hollywood outraged more traditionally minded Americans in the Midwest and South. When historians compare the 1920s with the 1990s—two periods of ethnic diversity, racial conflict, nativist pressures, sports delirium, and the pervasive power of the broadcast media—they see more similarities than differences and locate the beginnings of modern society there.

13. The President under Fire

RICHARD K. MURRAY

The United States has had some good presidents and some not so good. None were better than George Washington, Abraham Lincoln, and Franklin D. Roosevelt, and not one was worse than Warren G. Harding. A Republican U.S. Senator from Ohio, Harding won the presidency in 1920 when the United States rejected the Democratic Party in hopes of returning to "normalcy," ostensibly the normalcy of Republican presidents from Ulysses S. Grant to Theodore Roosevelt. Harding was unsuited for the White House. Intellectual limitations prevented him from fully grasping the economic and diplomatic challenges facing the country; indolence kept him from applying himself to any of those problems; and poor judgment led him to appoint a series of scoundrels to prominent positions in the administration. Harding wanted to spend his time playing cards with White House cronies and frequenting prostitutes in Washington, D.C., brothels, both of which he did on a regular basis. Excessive eating and drinking were additional vices.

Three years into his presidency, Warren Harding had not returned the country to normalcy. Quite the contrary. He was embroiled in a series of political scandals, all involving graft and corruption on the part of his subordinates. The president was personally free of scandal, but his political reputation was ruined. Mercifully, he died of a stroke in 1923 before the full effects of the scandals had ruined him emotionally. In the following essay, Richard K. Murray describes the fall of the Harding administration.

On November 2, 1920, while playing golf at a Columbus, Ohio country club with his campaign manager Harry M. Daugherty, Warren G. Harding was elected President of the United States. Receiving the largest popular mandate to that time of any presidential candidate since the Civil War, this 55-year-old Republican senator, known mainly for his loyalty, his friendliness, and his malleability, stepped into the most demanding job in the world.

Harding succeeded Woodrow Wilson, World War I leader and liberal Democratic President, whose final two years in office had turned into a disaster. Not only had Wilson sustained a humiliating defeat at the hands of the Senate on the question of the League of Nations in 1919, but in the midst of that battle he had suffered a paralyzing stroke which thereafter drastically reduced his effectiveness. For the remainder of his term, 1919–1921, Mrs. Edith Bolling Wilson, the President's second wife, was some say the closest thing that the nation had to a chief executive. During these two years labor unrest, inflation, a sharp economic recession, and an anti-radical "red scare" disrupted the domestic scene. The Democratic party meanwhile fell to internal squabbling and entered the election of 1920 badly disorganized.

Harding and the Republicans took advantage of this situation by capitalizing on the postwar public desire for stability and tranquility. Harding promised the nation a "return to normalcy," and upon his election he pursued that goal. For help he appointed some outstanding men to his cabinet—Charles Evans Hughes (Secretary of State), Andrew W. Mellon

(Secretary of Treasury), Henry C. Wallace (Secretary of Agriculture), and Herbert C. Hoover (Secretary of Commerce). With their advice and counsel he stabilized a disintegrating executive system, brought efficiency into government operations, pacified an angry and divided society, lowered taxes, reduced the national debt, restored confidence to business, underwrote a return to prosperity, and sponsored the most important international peace conference of the post-war era—the Washington Naval Disarmament Conference of 1922.

By early 1923, despite the claims of Democrats and some dissident Republicans representing farm elements, political conditions were in Harding's favor. There was no doubt about his re-nomination in 1924 and there was growing confidence about his re-election. Then the unexpected happened. Late in December 1922, while undergoing a routine physical checkup (Harding had a history of heart disease), the President was told by Dr. Charles E. Sawyer, his physician and longtime Marion (Ohio) friend, that Charles Forbes, director of the Veterans' Bureau, was engaged in corrupt activities. Dr. Sawyer urged the President to look into the matter immediately.

Forbes had been a Congressional Medal of Honor winner in World War I and had served as a regional campaign manager for Harding in the Pacific Northwest in 1920. After the election Harding had appointed him to the Veterans' Bureau post largely on a whim—Forbes was an excellent raconteur and a skilled card player. Neither Harry Daugherty (currently Attorney General) nor Will H. Hays (presently Postmaster General and former chairman of the Republican National Committee) had endorsed this appointment. Responsible for dispensing patronage, these two men had earlier passed over Forbes as being unreliable, Daugherty telling the President that his selection would be a mistake.

Sawyer's warning caused Harding only minor concern, and he offhandedly requested his private secretary, George B. Christian, to "ask around" about any suspicious Forbes activities. Christian later reported that he could find nothing, and the President forgot about it. But in late January 1923 Dr. Sawyer again warned the President that something was wrong in the Veterans' Bureau and suggested that he order Attorney General Daugherty to investigate the situation. Exhibiting more concern, Harding did so and at the same time called Forbes to the White House, asking him directly whether his actions would stand scrutiny. Forbes assured the President that they would because he had nothing to hide.

However, Daugherty's investigation showed differently and in a private report to the President in February he disclosed that Forbes was illegally selling surplus government hospital and drug supplies to private firms and was also buying and then reselling hospital sites to the government at exorbitant prices. Confronted by this evidence, Harding alternated between despondency and rage, finally summoning Forbes back to the White House and, as one eyewitness later claimed, grabbed Forbes by the throat, shook him "as a dog would a rat," smashed him against the wall with such force that "his teeth rattled," and shouted at him, "You double-crossing bastard!" Surprised and bewildered, Forbes seized Harding's legs, begged for clemency, and a still-angry President finally agreed that he could sail for

Europe immediately and resign his post upon arriving there. This Forbes did on February 15.

It was an unwise move by Harding. He should have turned Forbes over to the proper legal authorities; at least he should have sought congressional help in exposing Forbes's crimes. But loyalty, concern for his own renomination and re-election, anxiety over what a further investigation might uncover, and compassion for the culprit were among the motives which prompted Harding to do otherwise. In any case, Forbes's resignation did not quell rising rumors of corruption within the administration or forestall budding demands for a congressional investigation into the Veterans' Bureau.

Such demands crescendoed when on March 14, less than a month after Forbes's resignation, Charles F. Cramer, chief counsel to the Veterans' Bureau and Forbes's close confidant, stood in front of the bathroom mirror in his Washington home and fired a .45 caliber bullet into his right temple. The press clamored for answers but the White House responded by announcing that Cramer was despondent over some "recent severe financial reverses," and for that reason had shot himself. The White House knew better. Cramer had helped Forbes arrange the fraudulent buying and selling of hospital sites.

These were only the first drops of a torrent of troubles for Warren Harding. Prophetically Florence Harding, the President's wife, had inserted a brief typed note in her household account book for February 1923:

The President is coming under some very powerful influence and needs to safeguard his health. . . . The opposition of the Moon to the Sun and Saturn in his horoscope shows that he cannot depend upon his friends. He would be suspicious of the ones he *should* trust and *trust* those he *should* be suspicious of.

Whatever the merits of astrology, in this instance Mrs. Harding was not far from the truth, for even before the Cramer suicide Harding had been told, this time by several friendly senators, that Jesse ("Jess") W. Smith, Harry Daugherty's personal secretary and general factotum, was also engaged in corrupt activities. Allegedly Smith was peddling liquor patents and other government favors as the leader of a small group of petty grafters who operated out of a "little green house on K Street."

Already shaken by the Forbes incident, Harding immediately ordered Daugherty to talk to Smith. Daugherty reported back to Harding that the rumors of corruption about Smith were unfounded but that Smith was "indiscreet" in some of his personal contacts. Since Harding knew Smith intimately from their Ohio days and had often had him as a guest in the White House the President was willing to believe only the best about him. However, when rumors concerning Smith's corruption persisted, Harding ordered Daugherty to "get him out of Washington" and return him to Ohio.

No record remains of Daugherty's final conversations with Smith. We only know that in mid-May Smith's name was removed from the presidential entourage which was scheduled to make a trip to Alaska in mid-June. Moreover, Jess Smith turned up in his hometown of Washington Court

House (Ohio) on May 27, sought out his divorced wife, Roxy Stinson, and confided to her that he was afraid for his life, that he did not intend to be made a scapegoat, and that "they are out to get me." Harry Daugherty was also in Washington Court House at the same time, returning to Washington, D.C. on May 29 and going directly to the White House where he remained for the next several days. Smith returned to the Capital on May 28, spent the following day seeking out old friends and mumbled something about them all "having to hang together for Harding's sake." Sometime during that day he also went to the White House and had a brief talk with Harding. Then on the morning of May 30, still dressed in his pajamas and sitting on the bed in his room in Harry Daugherty's Wardman Park Hotel apartment, Smith put a bullet through his brain and pitched forward into a metal wastebasket.

The body was found shortly afterward by a special assistant to the Attorney General, Warren F. Martin. He quickly notified William J. Burns, founder of the Burns Detective Agency and head of the FBI, who occupied the apartment directly below Daugherty's. Burns and Martin then called the White House, which hurriedly dispatched Dr. Joel T. Boone, assistant White House physician, to the death scene. After examining the body Dr. Boone left it in the custody of Burns who shipped it off to Washington Court House for burial. No autopsy was performed nor were any kind of records, papers, or accounts ever found.

The effect on the White House was staggering. It immediately gave out the story that Smith had severe diabetes (which was true), that he had not fully recovered from a recent appendectomy (which was also true), and that he had killed himself in a fit of despondency over his ill health (only a partial truth at best). Harding himself had received Burns's call from the Wardman Park apartment and had issued the order that had sent Dr. Boone on his way. The Smith suicide gave the President final irrefutable proof that his administration was riddled with corruption and opened the possibility that even his closest friend, Attorney General Daugherty, might also be involved.

Unable to give voice to this latter suspicion, and even more fearful of taking decisive action, Harding attempted to maintain "business as usual." The very night of Smith's suicide, May 30, a couple was invited to the White House to provide relief from the tension and signify presidential calmness. Daugherty, however, was still there because he could not bring himself to return to his Wardman Park apartment. Mrs. Harding was obviously nervous the entire evening. At dinner the President spoke only a few words, creating frequent awkward pauses. Afterward there was a private showing of a motion picture in the upstairs hall, but even this offered no diversion. From time to time Daugherty could be heard uttering a long, low "O-o-o-o-o-o-o," while the President remained silent. Sensing that something was wrong, the two guests quickly departed from the movie, leaving the occupants of the White House alone with their apprehensions.

It was a worried President who left Washington on June 20, 1923 on his trip to Alaska. He had been living with the knowledge of corruption for six months and this had sapped both his mental and physical vitality. Reporters who covered the departure noted several things. Daugherty was conspicuous by his absence; other advisers, not known as presidential cronies, made up the presidential party. Also, Harding seemed to have aged; he looked ill, and both Mrs. Harding and Dr. Sawyer were engaged in an abnormal amount of fussing over him.

By now the Senate, acting on the previous rumors concerning Forbes, had voted for an investigation into the Veterans' Bureau. At the same time it had also decided to examine certain oil leasing procedures of the Department of Interior whose secretary, presidential confidant and ex-senator Albert B. Fall, was bitterly detested by conservationists. The primary purpose of this latter investigation was not to uncover corruption but merely to provide a brake on the private exploitation of conservation lands. In 1921 the Interior Department had secured from the Navy Department jurisdiction over certain oil reserve lands which Fall desired to have developed by private companies under terms of the General Leasing Act of 1920. Although such action was not approved by conservationists, it was legal so long as all bids were open and competitive.

There is no evidence that Harding knew of the impropriety of Secretary Fall's leasing activities when he left Washington. Forbes, Cramer, and Smith were on his mind. At the moment the press and the public had heard only rumors concerning even these men. There were still no hard facts and the White House continued to maintain its silence and at least an outward appearance of imperturbability.

From the outset the Alaskan trip was filled with drama. Some reporters noted that when the presidential train stopped at Kansas City Harding had a private conference with Mrs. Emma Fall, wife of the Interior secretary, at her request and came away from the conversation visibly upset. Not long after, Harding made his famous statement to newspaperman William Allen White: "My God, this is a hell of a job! I have no trouble with my enemies. I can take care of my enemies all right. But my damn friends, my God-damn friends, White, they're the ones that keep me walking the floor nights!" Later, at Juneau, it was said that a seaplane arrived with a special message from Washington which Harding read with trembling hands and thereafter sank into a deep depression. As the presidential party moved farther north Harding's sleeping habits became increasingly irregular and twice he played bridge all night, much to the discomfort of his partners, among them Herbert Hoover. Hoover later claimed that the President was once on the verge of telling him "something dreadful," but asked him instead, "Hoover, if you knew there was a scandal brewing, what would you do?" Hoover replied, "Publish it, and at least get credit for integrity on your side." When Hoover asked for particulars, Harding said that he had discovered some irregularities in the Justice Department involving Jess Smith, but that before he could act Smith had killed himself. When Hoover asked whether Attorney General Daugherty was also involved, Harding "abruptly dried up and never raised the question again."

When the presidential party arrived on July 26 at Vancouver on the way back home, reporters were shocked at the appearance of the President, one of them remarking that he was "not just tired or worn out. He is an entirely exhausted man. . . ." Others noticed his sallow complexion and the stoop to his frame. All commented on the breaks in his voice when delivering a speech the next day in Seattle. That night, July 27, while en route by train to San Francisco, the President suffered a heart attack, and upon his arrival in the Golden Gate city was put to bed in the Palace Hotel. There, apparently on his way to recovery, he suddenly succumbed to a massive cerebral hemorrhage on the evening of August 2.

President Harding was barely in his grave when the Senate's various investigations began. Starting in October, the Veterans' Bureau probe quickly uncovered Forbes's and Cramer's malfeasance, connected it with a few corrupt businessmen, but with no one higher in the administration. The oil leasing investigation proved more sensational. Centering on the leasing contracts issued for the development of oil reserve lands at Salt Creek (Teapot Dome), Wyoming, and Elk Hills, California, this investigation, under the chairmanship of Democratic Senator Thomas Walsh, at first discovered nothing unusual and by January 1924 was prepared to close. Then, through information supplied by Carl C. Magee, editor of the *New Mexico State Tribune* and an old political enemy of Fall, it was learned that the Interior secretary had recently built an irrigation reservoir and a hydroelectric plant on his New Mexico Three Rivers ranch at a cost of $40,000. It was also discovered that Fall had recently purchased neighboring land for over $100,000. Other suspicious activities were soon brought to light, with Fall refusing to testify under oath but claiming that his leasing actions had been taken in the interests of national security and with no benefit to himself. In the end it was revealed that Fall had not allowed open and competitive bidding on the oil reserve contracts but had awarded them arbitrarily to two oilmen, Edward L. Doheny and Harry F. Sinclair, in exchange for a $100,000 "loan" and almost $300,000 in Liberty Bonds.

Meanwhile a third and even more sensational investigation began— this one into the various activities of the Justice Department. By now (February 1924) investigation mania was in full cry and the orderly process of government came to complete standstill. The press engaged in a Roman holiday of sensationalism while gleeful Democrats predicted the demise of the Republican party. Presidential hopefuls suddenly appeared everywhere. Congress in turn, anxious to reassert its authority following the accumulation of presidential power during the war years, considered the executive branch fair game.

While the Veterans' Bureau and oil investigations were judiciously handled, the one involving the Justice Department was messy. In charge of this probe was Democratic Senator Burton K. Wheeler, an ambitious upstart who from the beginning promised the public "great revelations." He paraded before the country a succession of dramatic witnesses, many of whom were self-confessed liars, bootleggers, swindlers, prison inmates, and ex-FBI agents. Daugherty in turn committed the colossal blunder of trying to stop this investigation by threatening witnesses, seizing documents, eavesdropping, intercepting mail, burglarizing senators' offices, and using FBI agents for various extra-legal jobs.

The testimony, meanwhile, portrayed an administration burdened with scoundrels and gross wrongdoing, and charged that Attorney General Daugherty was the mastermind behind it all. It was said that Daugherty was Harding's Svengali, that Jess Smith had been murdered to keep him from talking, and that Mrs. Harding had killed the President to spare him impeachment. Harding, it was claimed, had regularly attended bacchanalian orgies complete with booze and lewd women at the "little green house on K

Street." All this was allegedly tied in with a gigantic plot to barter away the nation's resources to big business which would reap huge profits.

These charges were nonsense. In the end the only ones that stuck were relatively unsensational. Smith and his small group of obscure confederates (the so-called "Ohio gang") had sold liquor licenses and other government favors for pay-offs. Smith had also arranged with Thomas W. Miller, the Alien Property Custodian, for the transfer of a German-owned firm to private American hands, and some of this bribe money ($50,000) had made its way into a bank account held jointly by Smith and Daugherty.

These were the infamous Harding scandals which rocked the nation in 1923–24. In time, all of them—the Veterans' Bureau scandal, the Smith–Justice Department deals, and the Fall oil leases—became blurred in the public mind and were labelled with the misnomer "Teapot Dome." For approximately four months during the height of these investigations, rumor fed rumor and untruths obliterated the truth as parties and politicians jockeyed for safety and position. In the process reputations were tarnished, careers ruined, lives blighted—not by proof but by innuendo and guilt by association. Almost no high government official was immune. The innocent were placed in the same category as the guilty and for a time not only Fall and Daugherty, but Hoover, Hughes, Mellon, and even Coolidge were suspect.

Upon becoming President, Coolidge attempted to soothe public furor by maintaining an image of rectitude and by appointing a two-man bipartisan panel (Republican Philadelphia lawyer Owen J. Roberts and Ohio Democratic ex-Senator Atlee Pomerene) to initiate the necessary criminal proceedings. As a result of their work and that of several grand juries, indictments were finally handed down against Forbes, Miller, Fall, and Daugherty. Forbes was convicted and spent two years in jail, Miller ultimately served thirteen months, and Secretary Fall twelve. Daugherty was tried twice. His first trial resulted in a hung jury and his second in an acquittal because of insufficient evidence.

The political consequences of the Harding scandals proved in the long run to be even less important than these relatively minor legal ones. In the end, Coolidge weathered the storm by appearing to be pure and by backing full disclosure. The Republican party suffered no lasting hurt, retaining both houses of Congress as well as the White House in 1924. Even the public quickly rebounded, eventually viewing the *exposure* of Teapot Dome as being far more significant than its *existence*. Indeed, the public rapidly lost interest in the scandals, only a few spectators attending the conclusion of the Wheeler circus and none being present at the oil investigation. Some even turned on Wheeler and Walsh for creating such a fuss and for finding so few culprits. One editor met Walsh's final report, which implicated only Fall, with the comment: "After the thunder and the earthquake, the still small voice. . . ." Another grumbled, "If this is all that Senator Walsh had to recommend, we might as well not have undertaken the investigation at all."

Harding, on the other hand, even though he was dead and had taken no part in the scandals other than to attempt to hide them, continued to suffer. His gentleness and compassion, as well as his foreign and domestic successes, were quickly forgotten. Only the scandals remained. Even today that is what he is remembered for. Residing along with Grant at the bottom of the presidential pile, Harding has not had posterity deal with him any kindlier than the press of his own day which, in the hyperbole common to the 1920's, nicknamed him "the King of Scandals."

On June 6, 1931 President Herbert Hoover stood before a battery of microphones on the outskirts of Marion, Ohio, to dedicate the beautiful colonnaded Harding Memorial and ended his brief eulogy with the following words:

Here was a man whose soul was seared by a great disillusionment. We saw him gradually weaken not only from physical exhaustion but also from mental anxiety. Warren Harding had a dim realization that he had been betrayed by a few of the men whom he had trusted, by men whom he had believed were his devoted friends. It was later proved in the courts of the land that these men had betrayed not only the friendship and trust of their staunch and loyal friend but they had betrayed their country. That was the tragedy of the life of Warren Harding.

Thus, to the end, attested to by no less than a subsequent President of his own party, Warren Harding remained the *major* victim of Teapot Dome.

14. "Big Bill" Tilden: Superstar of the 1920s

JAMES S. OLSON

A European news commentator recently remarked, "You don't have to be an American to be famous, but you must be famous in America to be truly famous around the world." Historians who assess the impact of the United States on the world in the twentieth century will no doubt have to deal with the appearance of a global popular culture revolving around music, television, film, and sport, and it is the United States that has largely created the modern world of celebrities and superstars. The wedding of popular culture and the mass media took place during the 1920s, when radio and movies first distributed images and messages on a national scale. Movie stars and sports heroes became household names as Americans fell in love with actors like Theda Bara, Clara Bow, Douglas Fairbanks, and Rudolph Valentino, adventurers like Charles Lindbergh, and sports heroes like Babe Ruth and Red Grange.

But beneath the glitter and superficial prosperity of the 1920s, there was a dark side to American life. The economy was lurching toward the Great Depression, and racial, religious, and ethnic tensions ran deep in the society. Historians often use the term "schizophrenic" in describing the 1920s because the decade seemed possessed of so many dual meanings. Bill Tilden, the greatest tennis player in the world in the 1920s and early 1930s, had a dual personality that reflected the ambiguities of the decade. In the following essay, James S. Olson describes the life of Bill Tilden and how it symbolized the decade of the 1920s. The essay is based on Frank DeFord's biography: Big Bill Tilden: The Triumphs and the Tragedy.

He was the best in the world, the best that ever was, an elite of one in the most elitist of games. Tall and thin, William "Big Bill" Tilden was blessed with strength, grace, and unimaginably quick reflexes. He had a million-dollar smile and, as one sportswriter remarked years later, "legs Betty Grable should have had." When he was still a teenager, Tilden's hairline started to recede, but the shift stopped abruptly in his mid-twenties, leaving him with a most distinguished profile. Decked out in the court fashion of the day—a white sweater, crisp white slacks, and white tennis shoes—Bill Tilden cut a superstar figure in the image-conscious 1920s. He was a golden boy, a legend in the making, an idol of the rich and famous.

Tilden was a complex man, not unlike the decade that made him famous. The 1920s in the United States was a schizophrenic era, a time of mixed images. On the surface, it was a time of prosperity and gaiety—fabulous stock market gains, dance marathons, bathing beauties, flag-pole sitters, flappers, movies, radio soap operas, fan magazines, and sports, lots of sports. But there was an underside to America in the 1920s, a darker side, an economy hurtling toward the Great Depression and a society troubled over racial tension, organized crime, anti-Catholicism, anti-Semitism, and political fanaticism. Tilden was a perfect symbol of the 1920s, a rich, handsome man who parlayed athletic prowess into superstardom but who harbored a deep, dark, ugly secret.

Unlike today's tennis heroes, Tilden achieved superstar status a little late. He was twenty-seven years old when he won his first major championship—Wimbledon in 1920—but he did not lose a major tournament for the next seven years, reigning as the acknowledged king of the sport. Born to a wealthy family in Germantown, Pennsylvania, in 1894, Tilden got an Ivy League education at the University of Pennsylvania and had the money and the leisure to indulge his God-given talents. He grew up on tennis courts and country clubs, acquiring a competitive spirit tempered only by the desire to be a gentleman, to win but to do it with dignity and style, with the good manners befitting his position in society. Nor did Tilden want to humiliate his opponents. Simple victory was enough. In major tournaments, he also wanted to make sure that the crowd got its money's worth, that the games went to advantage, the sets to the limit, the matches to five sets. More often than not, when playing a lesser opponent, Tilden intentionally lost points and games, and sometimes even sets, to make the score look good and the match a thriller. He was so talented that spectators never knew what he was doing. Sometimes his lobs were a few inches too long, his backhands just an inch or two wide of the line, his serves a fraction too low, slamming into the very top of the net and giving the point away. But he never sacrificed matches. Big Bill loved being the best, loved winning, feeling the adulation of spectators and the awe of other tennis players.

He was also obsessed with winning gracefully and fairly. Tilden never threw temper tantrums over poor officiating, never complained about a bad call, never even did a double take at a linesman or a referee. Such behavior was unbecoming his patrician manners. Tilden preferred being above it all, letting his style and talent speak for themselves. Nor did he ever want to win a point or game or set or match on a bad call. At a 1923 tournament in New York City, Tilden was playing in the finals. The match was tied at two sets apiece, with Tilden up seven games to six in the final set. He was serving with the score at forty-forty. Tilden hit a blistering serve and expected an ace, but his opponent slammed a backhand that just barely hit the line to Tilden's left. The linesman called it out, awarding Tilden the point and the opportunity to serve for the match. Tilden's opponent protested the call and Tilden publicly agreed, telling the referee that the return had hit the line and was good. When the official refused to reverse the decision, Tilden intentionally double-faulted his next serve, evening the match and negating the effect of the bad call. He then served two aces for the win.

During the 1920s, America was searching for heroes, new heroes consistent with a new America. The people of the United States underwent a collective identity crisis in the 1920s. World War I had started out as a great crusade to "make the world safe for democracy," but it had ended up in the cynicism of the Versailles Treaty and the refusal of the United States to join the new League of Nations. Many Americans felt betrayed. Their own country also seemed to be changing. Ever since the early 1600s, Americans had viewed themselves as a rural, "country" people whose lives revolved around the land and the open spaces and whose economy was based on farming. But in 1920, the Bureau of the Census announced that for the first time in United States history, more Americans lived in cities than in the country. For the first time, less than half the country made their living as farmers. A vast immigration was also under way, but this time the new-comers were primarily Catholics and Jews from southern and eastern Europe, people who seemed strange and different. The heroes of the 1700s and 1800s had been real people who had real accomplishments—soldiers, cowboys, explorers, mountain men, Indians and Indian fighters like Kit Carson, Cochise, Sitting Bull, Buffalo Bill Cody, Davy Crockett, Robert E. Lee, or Jim Bridger.

Because of the industrialization and urbanization that had changed the country so dramatically, the older heroes seemed increasingly irrelevant. What America needed in the 1920s was new heroes, superstars more in tune with an increasingly urban society instead of the western, frontier icons so common to the nineteenth century. But it was difficult to find real heroes in a mass urban society. During the 1920s there was only one real hero, one person who did something really heroic. On May 20, 1927, Charles Lindbergh came to the attention of the world when he flew a single-engine airplane, *The Spirit of St. Louis,* from New York to Paris. His success in making the solo flight across the Atlantic made him a global hero. In the United States, Lindbergh's feat struck an extraordinarily responsive chord, a great act of individual courage in an age of cities, factories, and bureaucracies. He became the most famous—and admired—person in the country because what he had done seemed a throwback to an earlier era when real people used raw courage to achieve the impossible.

But there was only one Charles Lindbergh, and Americans needed to constantly replenish their supply of heroes, so they invented superstars, manufactured them out of whole cloth, found in the worlds of movies and sports the superstars they needed. Rudolph Valentino surfaced as the film star of the decade. He worked as an extra in a number of films until he was finally featured in two enormous 1921 hits—*The Four Horsemen of the Apocalypse* and *The Sheik.* With those successes, Hollywood made Valentino into the country's greatest male sex star. Women by the millions consumed news of his stage and private life, and in the process Valentino assumed larger-than-life dimensions. Several later films were also huge hits, especially *Blood and Sand* in 1922 and *Monsieur Beaucaire* in 1924. Ironically, it was Valentino's death from peritonitis on August 23, 1926, that guaranteed his status in the history of Hollywood. He was hardly a great actor, and most film historians suspect that his popularity would not have survived the transition to sound films, but in death Valentino achieved a legendary stardom. His funeral was really the first one for a major screen star, and tens of thousands of people showed up at the cemetery, creating a traffic jam of unprecedented proportions. The funeral marked the birth of a national pop culture in the United States. He was the first of America's twentieth-century celebrity superstars.

The greatest sports hero of the 1920s was Babe Ruth. Before Babe Ruth, baseball had been a game of base hits, stolen bases, excellent pitching, and fine defense. But Ruth electrified New York Yankee fans in 1920 by hitting fifty-four home runs and batting .376. It was an extraordinary achievement, since all the rest of the American League teams combined hit only fifty home runs in 1920. In 1921 Ruth came back and hit fifty-nine home runs with 170 runs batted in. In the process, he became a larger-than-life figure, a genuine American hero, despite the fact that he was a known womanizer and a prodigious drinker. But America needed a hero and Ruth fit the bill. He was gregarious, charismatic, and enormously talented. In 1930, with America sinking into the Great Depression, the Yankees signed Ruth to a contract of $80,000 a year, more money than President Herbert Hoover made. When a journalist asked Ruth what he thought about making more money than the president, the Babe replied: "I had a better year than he did."

Bill Tilden did not have the same superstar status as Ruth or Valentino, but he was still one of the pantheon of American heroes in the 1920s. He liked being around the rich and the famous, keeping friends in the country club world of tennis as well as in the glittery world of Hollywood. Big Bill went to all the parties and frequently had bit parts in movies. Actually, he was more comfortable around the stars and starlets of Hollywood than he was in the company of people like Babe Ruth or Red Grange, the great running back for the University of Illinois and the Chicago Bears. Hollywood was more tolerant of his secret, more willing to let people pursue their sexual objectives in peace, whatever those objectives happened to be.

Big Bill Tilden was a superstar in the 1920s, but he was also a homosexual. The people closest to Tilden were aware of his sexual orientation, but they kept his confidence. He never married and was rarely seen in the company of women, and only on ceremonial occasions so the press could attest to his "normal" instincts. Toward the end of his life, Tilden recalled that he had had only one heterosexual experience in his life, back when he was twenty-five years old. "The experience was so repulsive to me," he said, "that I puked all over when it was finished." There was an effeminate charm to Tilden, so much so that in an age of television he probably would not have been able to sustain a superstar image. His voice and mannerisms would have been too obvious for a homophobic public to accept. Ty Cobb, the great baseball player for the Detroit Tigers, had never met Tilden, only hearing of his exploits on the tennis court. At a party in Chicago in 1926, Cobb looked over at Tilden who was on the other side of the room, leaned to a friend, and said, "Who's the fruit over there?" When his friend told him it was Bill Tilden, Cobb's jaw dropped and he said: "Jesus Christ, he's a real queer."

Rumors followed Tilden wherever he went, and close observers noticed his glances. Big Bill never, ever, took a second look at an attractive woman, but his eyes often tracked handsome male passersby, especially younger men. Occasionally during the 1920s, enterprising journalists desperate for a story tried to entrap Big Bill. They would hire young bellhops at fancy hotels to entice Tilden into a homosexual tryst, or send known younger homosexuals to courts where Tilden was practicing to see if a liaison could be set up. But they never succeeded. Tilden was careful during his heyday—extremely discreet. In fact, he was probably a celibate homosexual during his most successful playing years in the 1920s. It was almost as if tennis was the only gratification he needed, tournament victories the only orgasms in his life. He once even remarked that "Sex has never been very important in my life; I have had an outlet through athletics."

Later in his life, when he wrote his autobiography, Tilden hinted at his tastes:

Throughout all history there has been a record of occasional relationships some-what away from the normal. One knows that this condition exists, that it is more or less prevalent and always will be. History further demonstrates that in frequent instances, creative, useful and even great human beings have known such relationships.

The condition may or may not call for some action in individual cases, but if it does, it calls for more psychiatric than legal or punitive measures. The list of celebrated people in this age and previous ones who have deviated from the norm makes it obvious that this is not a sign of "degeneracy" in the usual sense.

It is, if anything, an illness; in most cases, a psychological illness. . . . Greater toler-ance and wider education on the part of the general public concerning this form of sex relationship is one of the crying needs of our times, if only for the support which thereby would result for serious studies of the problem.

By that time, however, Bill Tilden's homosexuality was no longer an abstrac-tion or a state of mind. Late in the 1920s and early 1930s, Tilden lost some of the edge on his game. He turned thirty-six years old in 1930, and it was more and more difficult for him to compete with the best of the younger players. Like all world-class athletes, Tilden began to witness the unraveling of his skills and the inevitable loss of status that implied. Without the adulation of millions and the sweetness of victory to satisfy his private urges, Tilden's sexual appetites became more overt and the rumors more ominous.

Big Bill Tilden also had a secret within a secret. In the cultural atmo-sphere of the 1920s and 1930s, homosexuality was not discussed much in public circles and only whispered about in private circles. Those in the sports world who knew about Tilden's appetites were content to leave him be, as long as he kept winning and as long as he was discreet. But even many of them fretted over the other rumors. Throughout his career, Big Bill had always enjoyed the company of boys. He was extremely friendly and touchy with the ball boys on the tennis courts, often taking them to dinner and to movies after the matches, visiting them at home, going to their schools to put on clinics, taking them on weekend trips, and giving them free tennis lessons. He seemed especially friendly with pre-adolescent boys, particularly those who were a little overweight and had a cherubic counte-nance. Friends remembered how easily boys could distract Bill. He gawked at them. At tournament clinics, Tilden insisted on coaching the cutest boys around, rather than the most talented. Big Bill Tilden was a pedophile, a "chicken queen" or "chicken hawk" in modern parlance, a lover of young boys.

Tilden loved the company of boys, and for the vast majority of those he befriended, his affections were more paternal than sexual. He would much rather spend the afternoon with a twelve-year-old boy than with a beautiful adult, female or male, even when there was no sex involved at all. Tilden managed to keep his pedophilia a secret for much of his life because he was careful and because it did not usually become physical. But in his late thirties, just when the male sex drive begins to level out before its decline, Tilden's libido went into overdrive. He was becoming a sexual predator. During a train trip from Southampton, England, to London in 1938, a young tennis pro told Bill that he had a date in the city that night. Tilden replied: "Well, I have a date, too, although, of course, things are a little different with me. Dickie boy has just come over from the States to see me. Those of us who have my way of thinking, well, we look upon ourselves as the chosen few. I think it's my responsibility to convert young boys. We are the exceptional. God has smiled upon us."

Even then, Tilden managed to keep his attitudes and activities out of the press. During World War II he toured the country putting on tennis exhibitions for servicemen and appeared in a number of films and plays. Ironically, his best reviews came from his role in Lillian Hellman's *The Children's Hour,* a play about homosexuality. He hobnobbed with Hollywood's best, including Errol Flynn, Charlie Chaplin, Katherine Hepburn, and David Selznick. After the war, he was the leading figure in the establishment of the Professional Tennis Players Association, even though many younger players now despised him. To them, he was no longer "Big Bill." William Tilden was now known as "The Old Bitch," "The Pervert," and "Queenie." They needed his name and his fame—Tilden had put tennis on the cultural map in America—but they did not want to spend a minute with him off court.

Soon the rest of America felt the same way. Big Bill Tilden's luck ran out on November 23, 1946. Two Los Angeles police officers spotted a 1942 Packard weaving somewhat precariously down Sunset Boulevard, with a young boy at the wheel. Next to the boy, with his left arm around his shoulders and his right arm in the boy's lap, was an older man. The police stopped the car, noticed that the boy's pants were undone, and quickly arrested Bill Tilden. They booked him on misdemeanor charges of "lewd and lascivious behavior with a minor." Tilden humbly signed a confession. He expected to be given probation.

But Tilden was going to have a string of bad luck. Judge A. A. Scott, a man with conservative political leanings, presided over the trial. Los Angeles was already abuzz with rumors that Charlie Chaplin, the silent film star and close friend of Bill Tilden, was facing charges of lewd conduct with underage girls, and Scott had no tolerance for it. He even conjured up images of orgies at Chaplin's Hollywood home, with Charlie victimizing little girls and Big Bill having his way with little boys. Even though Tilden entered a guilty plea, Scott gave him a chance to explain his behavior, asking Bill if he had ever been sexually intimate with a minor before. Tilden lied. He said, "No." Judge Scott was not an idiot; he knew that older pedophiles were once younger pedophiles and that the likelihood of Tilden's having committed the crime just one time was extremely remote. He threw the book at Big Bill, sentencing him to one year in prison, the maximum for the misdemeanor. Big Bill Tilden, superstar of the 1920s, had become the pervert of 1947.

He proved to be a model prisoner, accepting work assignments without complaint, obeying prison rules, and treating guards with the requisite deference. Tilden spent nine months in prison before winning parole. The condition of his release was quite clear: He was to avoid contact, all contact, with children and adolescents. That put Tilden in a financial bind, since it cut off all of his coaching opportunities. He had been dipping into his inheritance for years, slowly dissipating it, and the expenses of his trial had cut into it even more. When he got out of prison at the end of 1947, Bill Tilden was broke.

He scratched out a living with the help of a few friends who stood by him through it all, but the miserable turnaround in his life sent Tilden into a depression, and in that depression the monster in him went on the prowl again. The greatest tennis player in the history of the world was now cruising high school parking lots, junior high school bus stops, city parks, and YMCAs, looking for little boys and young teenagers. On January 28, 1949, the Los Angeles police arrested Tilden again, this time for trying to seduce a sixteen-year-old young man. Judge Scott heard the case, telling Tilden, "You're just an old degenerate." Big Bill replied: "Judge, I just can't help myself." Scott revoked his parole and sent Tilden back to prison.

Tilden was released from prison on December 18, 1949, but his life was over. Two days later the Associated Press, in its assessment of the greatest athletes of the twentieth century, voted Tilden superstar status, along with people like Babe Ruth and Jack Dempsey. But the rest of America was not so kind. The University of Pennsylvania expelled him from its alumni association, and tennis clubs around the country removed his picture from their galleries of heroes. The Los Angeles Tennis Club declared him a *persona non grata*, banning him from its courts, and the major tournament sponsors politely, and not so politely, told Tilden not even to show up as a spectator. On June 5, 1953, the misery came to an end for one of America's greatest sports heroes. Big Bill Tilden had a heart attack and died alone in a one-room apartment near Hollywood and Vine in Los Angeles.

15. Bruce Barton's *The Man Nobody Knows:* A Popular Advertising Illusion

EDRENE S. MONTGOMERY

The publication of Bruce Barton's The Man Nobody Knows *in 1924 sparked a bitter religious debate in the United States. Historians have often used Barton's writings as an example of how big business values affected American popular culture in the 1920s. Barton described Jesus Christ as a very successful businessman, an executive who "picked up twelve men from the bottom ranks and forged them into an organization which conquered the world." His portrait of Jesus was essentially secular, ignoring any dimension of deity and painting the founder of Christianity as the most successful "organization man" in history.*

Businessmen were amused with Barton's idea, but fundamentalist Christians were outraged. They were on edge anyway. During the 1920s America was caught up in a huge struggle for cultural power. Conservative, fundamentalist religious groups were alarmed at the triumph of secular consumerism in the United States, and they engaged in a crusade to return America to its Christian roots. The controversies over the teaching of evolution in the schools and prohibiting the production and distribution of alcoholic beverages were visible examples of cultural conflict, as was the debate over The Man Nobody Knows. *Barton managed to do what nobody else did in the 1920s—bring Protestants and Catholics together on the same issue. Clerics from all denominations denounced the book with equal passion. At the same time, however, the book was a best seller, appealing to millions of people who bought the volume or read it in serial form in the* Woman's Home Companion. *In the following essay, Edrene S. Montgomery discusses the controversy and the appeal of* The Man Nobody Knows.*

When the *Woman's Home Companion* published the first installment of Bruce Barton's *The Man Nobody Knows* in December, 1924, it was aware that the series would spark controversy. Scribner's had already refused to publish the book because it was "too advanced" for their readers. While the publishers acknowledged the intrinsic value of Barton's "Discovery of the Real Jesus," they nevertheless feared that it would shock a public accustomed to traditional religious literature and give the impression of irreverence. In an effort to stem the tide of adverse criticism, the editors of the *Woman's Home Companion* took the precaution of eliminating certain phrases which might incur the wrath of the religious community.

Barton's conception of Jesus was, indeed, controversial. The young advertising executive, son of a Congregational minister, portrayed Christ as the founder of modern business—a strong, vigorous outdoor man who "picked up twelve men from the bottom ranks" of society and, with the force of his personal conviction, "forged them into an organization which conquered the world." The message he proclaimed was simple. "There is a success which is greater than wealth or titles," he said. "It comes through making your work an instrument of greater service, and larger living to your fellow men and women. *This* is my Father's business and he needs your help." With the characteristics of a modern executive—the voice and manner of a leader, the personal magnetism which inspires loyalty and commands respect, the abilities to select men and to cultivate their hidden talents, and unlimited patience—he built "so solidly and well that death was only the beginning of his influence." His was the greatest success story of all time.

This unconventional portrait, emphasizing the human character of Jesus, was of little comfort to those who found refuge in traditional expressions of religion. Unprecedented prosperity, smug isolationism, and an expanding consumer economy which made the radio, refrigerator and automobile household necessities were insufficient to shake them from their safe moorings. Even the darker side of the twenties, harboring in its shadows provincialism, fundamentalist modernist warfare over evolution, and racial, ethnic and class conflicts, served only to enhance the safety of their certitude by contrast. These Americans made clear their objections to Barton's portrait of Christ.

The avalanche of criticism began soon after the appearance of the second installment describing Christ as an "Outdoor Man." Roman Catholics immediately took issue with Barton's dismissal of the Virgin Birth and bitterly resented his contention that Jesus had brothers and sisters. Indignant letters, accompanied by subscription cancellations, poured into the offices of the *Woman's Home Companion*. Statements to the effect that Barton was "venturing upon very thin ice" and "wandering from the facts of Christian consciousness" were supplemented by the official Catholic position: "We believe that Mary was a virgin before, during and after the birth of Jesus." The reaction was so intense that Barton felt compelled to take action. After consulting with Protestant religious authorities to insure that apologies were not in order, he prepared a letter which could be used to answer complaints. Although he refused to enter into a doctrinal dispute, he assured Catholics that he had written the articles "in a spirit of reverence and with a genuine desire to help." From the number of favorable responses, it was apparent to him that the series was "making Jesus more real to many people, to whom he was hardly more than a myth." And this had been his intention.

As the series continued, many Protestants discovered that Barton was emphasizing the humanity of Christ at the expense of his divinity. Insulted by this affront to their personal Savior, pious Christians quickly joined the ranks of his detractors. Cries of "blasphemy," "sacrilege," and "false teaching" came from all denominations and regions of the country. An Episcopalian minister from Roxburg, Pennsylvania, denounced him in an eight-page letter as a foolish modernist "who sets himself up as a young god." A Sunday school teacher from Jefferson City, Missouri, said hearing Jesus described as a "good *man*" was sacrilege to her Presbyterian ears. And a Congregationalist from Fairburg, Nebraska, simply urged him to repent. But the Methodist housewife from New York City expressed the sentiment best: "Mr. Barton discusses Jesus as casually as he would a candidate for Sheriff." Such discussion had the effect of reducing him "from the ineffable to the commonplace" and she, along with many other devout Christians, would have nothing to do with such heresy.

But aside from these criticisms, the popularity of the work was undeniable. Barton appeared to strike a responsive chord in the hearts of many middle class Americans who were cast adrift, without the anchor of assurance provided by traditional religion, amidst a series of changes which were so rapid they were deeply disturbing. Trends accelerated by World War I, including industrialization, urbanization, and advanced technology, brought rapid changes in values and behavior patterns. The ideals of an older, more individualistic America—thrift, industry and restraint coupled with Victorian moral standards—no longer seemed relevant to a twentieth century mass culture characterized by installment buying, speculation, instant gratification and sexual permissiveness. Many middle class Americans, caught up in this conflict of cultures without the certitude of a traditional creed, found that Barton's portrayal of Christ addressed itself to their deepest religious needs. A mechanical engineer from Anderson, Indiana, expressed it well: "Your work answers the call of my heart and reason. I have spent years as a worker in the Methodist Church. I have observed her failure to feed the people. The church creeds are not, as you say, representative of God and his fatherhood, his love, and Jesus and his work." This sentiment was echoed by men, women and children all over the country.

When Bobbs-Merrill published the book in 1925 and a newspaper syndicate picked up the series in 1926, enthusiasm for the work continued to be widespread. A general merchant from Water Valley, Mississippi, said he had gotten more good out of the book than any other he had read. "It has given me an entirely different conception of my Savior, and has made me closer to Him than I have ever been in my life," he reported. A Toronto businessman remarked that the book was to him what the Rosetta stone had been to Egyptologists, "a key that unlocked great treasures of knowledge and came at a time when I was discouraged in my work." And an elderly Congregational minister, recovering from illness in Forest Hills, Massachusetts, found that the book "fitted perfectly into the deep yearning of my heart in these twilight years." Barton had touched the hearts of these and other middle class Americans, fulfilling spiritual needs where the churches had failed.

One of the aspects of Barton's work which appealed to readers most was his physical description of Christ. "A physical weakling!" he had said. "Where did they get that idea? Jesus pushed a plane and swung an adze; he was a successful carpenter. He slept outdoors and spent his days walking around his favorite lake. His muscles were so strong that when he drove the money-changers out, nobody dared oppose him!" This description appealed to readers who had rejected what they termed "the squeamish, whimpering, weak-kneed God Jesus of the churches" and "the washed out, faded, effeminate" portraits of the artists. As a minister of a Christ Reformed Church in Altoona, Pennsylvania, pointed out, Barton's description was more in keeping with the portrait of the Gospels: "a rugged man of action." It was also similar to the way many middle class Americans themselves pictured Christ. "All my life I have loved to picture Christ as the manliest of men," said a reader from Santa Rita, New Mexico, who gave a description which bore a striking resemblance to Barton's own: "A great powerful, robust, open-countenanced fellow, whose noble soul shone in His handsome featured face." Not unexpectedly, Barton's portrait was es-

Was Jesus a Physical Weakling?

The painters have made Him look so—but He swung an adze and pushed a saw until He was thirty years old. He walked miles every day in the open air. He drove a crowd of hard-faced men out of the Temple. He faced Jewish hatred and Roman power without a tremor.

BRUCE BARTON brings Christ within the range of a reasonable faith. He paints a new picture of Him—a sincere, reverent, constructive picture of the personality that H. G. Wells names first on the list of the greatest figures in history.

If there is a young man in college or in business to whom you would like to make a gift that will give him a thrill, send him these remarkable books.

That is why we felt it consistent to offer these two great books in conjunction with the Review of Reviews. They show you that it is not what you *profess* on Sundays that counts—but what you LIVE on week-days. That religion is not a matter of forms or ceremonies—but LIFE ITSELF.

So what more appropriate books could we bring to you with the magazine that gives you the record of all that is worth while in the life of today? That takes the scattered items of daily news, ties them together, gives you a clear, connected picture of the real events of the month?

pecially appealing to women. As a woman from Newcastle, California, explained, "It makes him the strong vigorous character I like." Even the president of Yale University, James R. Angell, addressed himself to this point in a letter for which Barton was especially grateful. He concluded that a description of Jesus as a rugged masculine character had been greatly needed and thanked Barton for rendering "a great service in secularizing . . . the portrait of the Christ."

Another aspect of the work which appealed to readers was Barton's emphasis on Christ's humanity. The overwhelming majority of those who liked the book were pleased that Barton had described Jesus in human terms, with doubts and uncertainties as well as triumphs and successes. They were delighted that he had cut through the mystical, transcendent qualities preached by the clergy and saw fit to portray Christ in concrete, material terms. Appreciative letters, discussing this point, poured in from all parts of the country. "Like thousands of others I am grateful for the human Jesus you have so wonderfully provided," said a man from Little Rock, Arkansas. "I have been searching for years for a book which would talk about Jesus the man and not Jesus the son of God," reported a New York City health instructor. "Thank you for the 'Man,'" said a woman from Lorain, Ohio. But the best expression of this sentiment came from an eighteen-year-old girl whose prize book review on *The Man Nobody Knows* appeared in the *Detroit Free Press*. "The book points out to us how very human Jesus was," she began. "Mr. Barton awakens the dormant minds and hearts of those who read this book to the fact that Jesus was a leader of men, a meek but powerful human being and a just judge of humanity."

So dramatically had Barton awakened "the dormant minds and hearts" of those who read the book that a number of readers, acquainted with spiritualism, believed that he had been divinely inspired. A seventy-year-old woman from Pottstown, Pennsylvania, wrote Barton, "I feel the Great Ones have inspired you at just this critical time to give people a more rational idea of the Man." Another woman from Hinsdale, Illinois, believed that Barton had such an understanding of the "Principle" behind Jesus' words and actions that he was performing "as a Channel for the expression of that Spirit, not as a person." And a woman from Minneapolis told Barton, "I have a very strong feeling Jesus dictated that book to you." As if to lend credence to these thoughts, a private medium from Brooklyn, New York, reported that she had received a communication in 1923 informing her that "A picture of Christ more wonderful than any ever painted which will convert many souls, will be given to the world by a medium unacquainted with art or letters." She was certain that this message prophesied *The Man Nobody Knows*.

A final aspect of the work which appealed to readers was Barton's modern perspective on Christ's life. His failure to emphasize the miraculous aspects of Christianity—the Virgin Birth, the Resurrection, the Second Coming—appealed to readers who had discarded the traditional creeds, what they termed "the hypothetical, imaginative, cloistered" truth of the clergy, in favor of the interpretations of modern scholarship. Advancements in science, comparative religion, and higher criticism of the Bible had challenged the prevailing world view affirming God's supernatural intervention in history. The controversial theory of evolution—by asserting a constantly changing universe, substituting the ascent of man for the doctrine of Original Sin, relating humanity to the rest of the animal kingdom, and elevating chance to a new position of authority—was by far the most unsettling scientific pronouncement. The emphasis placed on this issue during the twenties tends to obscure the fact that there were other points of religious contention as well. Discoveries in comparative religion challenged the uniqueness of Christianity by revealing similar religious beliefs and practices all over the world. The higher criticism, by analyzing how ancient peoples explained their spiritual experiences, removed much of the mystery surrounding Christian belief. It was now possible to regard the Bible as a progressive unfolding of God's truth, rather than an inerrant document containing "scientific opinions, medical theories, historical judgments, and spiritual insights" beyond the realm of dispute.

While conservative Christians rejected this modern approach, liberal Christians, endeavoring to achieve intellectual and spiritual integrity, tried to incorporate this knowledge in their Christian faith. Barton's modern treatment of Christ's life, unencumbered by questionable doctrines and supernatural interpretations, addressed itself to their specific needs. As one reader put it: "Having tried for years to swallow the dogmas of Protestantism and a belief in the so-called miracles of the Bible, I finally have found a belief, I feel, is sound and satisfactory." Readers also appreciated the modern role which Barton assigned to Jesus and the modern setting in which he dramatized Christ's life. "He has shown us . . . the figure and character of Jesus . . . moving at home among the common enterprises of life; touching the lives of men and women . . . in their social fellowships, in their intellectual habits, in their businesses," said a minister from Scranton, Pennsylvania. Barton's portrait had brought the character of Jesus within the grasp of the modern man.

The cumulative effect of these attractive features of the book—Barton's physical description of Christ, his emphasis on Christ's humanity, and his modern perspective on Christ's life—was that many readers perceived his image of Christ as "real." Statements to the effect that Barton had captured the "real character" or the "real personality" of Jesus and had portrayed the "real facts" of his life were frequent reminders of the effectiveness of his technique. A naval officer, stationed at Camp Endicott, Rhode Island, thought the book was "the truest picture of the Master" to be found. A woman from New Rochelle, New York, said Barton portrayed "the Nazarene as he really was . . ." not as people wanted him to be. And a minister from Cambridge, Massachusetts, found that Barton "made the Son of Man *real* to people, and not merely a conventional figure in a stained glass window or an actor in a theological drama."

. . . Experiencing the strains of that tension between modern and traditional patterns of thought and behavior which distressed their parents, young people, in the words of one observer of the twenties, had "thrown religion overboard." The conservative churches, ill-suited to their needs because of rigid, authoritarian attitudes and practices, were incapable of holding their allegiance. And the liberal churches, predicated on the inevitability of progress and the perfectability of the human race, had been shattered by World War I. While many college students were regular or semi-regular churchgoers, religion did not play an important part in their lives. Some of the more serious-minded turned, instead, to politics and social reform. But most merely transferred their allegiance from religion to leisure, sports, and jazz. Those who experienced a feeling of spiritual loss would find in Barton's strong, heroic figure of Christ, a person capable of inspiring their loyalties and commanding their respect. As one young man put it: "the Jesus whom Barton discussed . . . would probably have been Captain of the Princeton Football Team, and just the man that we would 'root' for."

Appreciative letters, challenging the stereotype image of youth in the twenties as "iconoclastic, irreverent, and frivolous," revealed how popular Barton's work had become. Tired of the weekly "this-is-the-formative-period-of-your-lives, now-is-the-time-for-you-to-determine-what-sort-of-men-you-will-be" kind of sermon, a Princeton undergraduate suggested that every clergyman in the country be sent a copy of *The Man Nobody Knows*. A college sophomore from Waterville, Maine, who had just passed through that period "in which every creed of the college student is torn to bits," found Barton's work extremely helpful. And a nineteen-year-old boy from Kingston, Pennsylvania, reported that he had placed a sign, with one of Barton's quotations, high up on the wall of his room, between a tennis racket and an Indian tomahawk, for inspiration. "I know Jesus Christ thanks to you," he said, "and not to the Sunday School teachers who taught me to stare at him from afar in mingled dread and admiration."

Jesus Preached in the Market Place

The modern market places are the advertising pages of newspapers eand magazines, where the sellers of the nation display their wares before the millions of buyers.

Every employer in the United States ought to send copies of these books to the ten most valuable men in his organization. They would give them a new thrilling conception of modern business.

For, as one newspaper put it—"Here is a story of Jesus that makes the modern man sit up and take notice." Barton gives you a Christ you can accept, regardless of your creed.

"I know that through the Review of Reviews views have been presented to me that I could not otherwise have had access to; because all earnest and thoughtful men, no matter how widely their ideas diverge, are given free utterance in its columns," said Roosevelt.

"Perhaps the most important book of the day," says George Barr Baker of *The Man Nobody Knows*. "The central character in Christian history has been made intimate and strong and lovable and thrilling."

In addition to being a source of personal inspiration, Barton's work became a familiar vehicle for popularizing religious thought. Business executives sent copies as gifts, especially at Christmas, to employees, associates and friends, and frequently used the book as an inspirational sales guide. Since it stimulated lively discussion, Sunday schools, Bible classes and discussion groups used it to inspire interest in religious topics; the Boy Scouts studied it as a guide to fellowship; and public lecturers included it in their programs to attract large audiences. Excerpts soon found their way into sermons, radio broadcasts and films. A man from Eaton, Indiana, even wrote a song which he had published under the title "Only the Man that Nobody Knows." And Cecil B. de Mille seriously considered making the book into a motion picture.

During its long publishing career, *The Man Nobody Knows* continued to stimulate widespread interest. When Bobbs-Merrill originally published the book in 1925, they anticipated that it would sell between 500 and 1,000 copies. Instead, it enjoyed tremendous sales, not only in cities but in towns and villages, many of which had no bookstores and few book buyers. It was fourth on the best seller list in the category of nonfiction in 1925, and climbed to the position of first in 1926. In that year, Grosset & Dunlap published an omnibus edition of *The Man Nobody Knows* and *The Book Nobody Knows*, Barton's work on the Bible. By 1956, these and subsequent editions had sold more than a million copies. In addition to the *Woman's Home Companion*, a number of newspaper syndicates published the book in serial form, and the *Reader's Digest* ran a condensed version in 1965. The book was also translated into almost every foreign language, including Scandinavian, and into braille for the blind.

An outstanding feature of the book's publishing career has been the longlasting impact it has had on its readers. Many years after first encountering the work, readers wrote to express their gratitude for the significant role it had played in their lives. "About fifteen years ago I had the pleasure of becoming acquainted with . . . *The Man Nobody Knows*," recalled a reader from Chicago. "Your fine understanding of human nature, and deep spiritual sense have helped me over many a rough spot in the years since then." This sentiment was echoed by enthusiastic readers many times over in the postwar years.

The popularity of the work cannot, as has often been done, be explained entirely in terms of the cult of success. The identification of the sacred and profane in the person of Jesus as the founder of modern business was not the aspect of the work which readers appreciated most. In fact, there is a noticeable absence, in the hundreds of letters they sent, of references to "business," Christ's role as a "modern executive," his use of modern advertising techniques, or any other indications that middle class Americans were using the book to elevate business to the status of a national religion or that they required religious justification for the secular pursuit of material wealth. Rather, they appeared to embrace, without guilt or remorse, the new economic and social status which the order of modern business produced. If they, along with many other middle class Americans, were not as "dynamic, expansive, and supremely confident" about building a new America, "a business civilization based . . . upon a whole new set of business values," as Arthur Link suggests, at least they expressed no misgivings about the task.

Another explanation for the popularity of the work may be found in the solution which Barton's portrait of Christ, cast in concrete, material terms, provided to a twentieth century American spiritual dilemma. The breakdown of the island community, which accompanied modernity, severed traditional community ties and left in its wake a "hunger for wholeness." Both fundamentalists and modernists sought to minister to this need by restoring a sense of community to modern society. Fundamentalists, by reaffirming the traditional tenets of Christian faith and emphasizing the supernatural aspects of Christ's life, erected a fortress around their subculture which made it possible "to ignore, explain away or distance themselves from others." Modernists, by adapting their Christian faith to current circumstances and describing God in abstract terms as the "Creative Reality," the "Directive Intelligence," or the "Power not Ourselves," constructed the larger, more flexible shelter of an all-inclusive ideological outlook. Neither approach was completely satisfactory. One was too constrictive for modern society and required the same conceptual framework in which traditional Christianity had flourished. The other was too expansive to restore the desired sense of community and demanded an abstract conceptual process which was unfamiliar to most Americans. Together they constituted a "tyranny of limited alternatives."

While middle class Americans sought to satisfy this "hunger for wholeness," many were no longer able to perceive the mystical, supernatural, other-worldly qualities of traditional Christian belief. The mystical portraits

Why Jesus Succeeded

In Founding the Greatest Enterprise on Earth
What is the greatest business ever built?
What is the oldest?
What is the one with the most workers?
What is the one with the widest market?

It is the Christian Church!

BRUCE BARTON, eminent business man and author, studied the life of Jesus in order to find out the qualities He had which made His business become the greatest of all time.

His study inspired him to write "THE MAN NOBODY KNOWS"

JESUS was a real executive, Barton found, with a magnetism that demanded respect. He selected men untrained in His field, saw their possibilities, developed and organized them. Jesus was a great advertising man. He knew how to make words effective. Barton concludes that the parables are the greatest advertisements of all time.

The principles of modern salesmanship are all brilliantly exemplified in Jesus' talk and work. To two fishermen whom he wanted, He said, "Come with me and I will make you fishers of men." No offer of a position teaching a new religion—that would not have aroused their interest.

Barton found that Jesus developed three rules for gaining success in any business. These principles have never been improved—and are as sound today as they were 1900 years ago.

He terms it the most exalted success story of all time.

Jesus he calls the "Great Companion," and goes on to say that "His great message was that religion is not a matter of forms or ceremonies, but life itself, the everyday business of daily work. All business is his Father's business, all honest work is worship, all productive labor is a spiritual service. For what is modern business but the machinery which God has set up for feeding and clothing and making happier His children, for finishing the unfinished task of creation?"

As President Coolidge put it—"The man who builds a factory builds a temple. And he who works there, worships there."

Reverently, respectfully, Bruce Barton brings the reader closer to "The Man Nobody Knows" BY A MEANS OF APPROACH NEVER BEFORE ATTEMPTED—WITH A BREADTH OF APPEAL NEVER BEFORE EQUALLED!

Barton's conception of Jesus will undoubtedly set everyone to intense thinking. It gives the business man, who usually walks by the church door, a Jesus that he can understand, that speaks the same language he does today. It opens to others a far deeper, far more intimate view of Him than they are likely to have had.

This book can be read in two hours—but it will be remembered a lifetime.

of Christ, so vivid to earlier generations of Christians who perceived a multidimensional reality encompassing both the supernatural and the natural, meant little to them. The luster of twentieth century material reality, viewed through a one-dimensional scientific lens which screened out all but natural causes, blurred the contours of the supersensible so that many Americans were blind to these other-worldly visions of Christ. Nor were they capable of finding emotional satisfaction in the abstract, intellectual portraits conceived by modern churchmen. When a leading psychologist conducted an investigation into the ways his students thought about God, some of the answers were startling. "I think of him as real, actual skin and blood and bones, something we shall see with our eyes some day," said one student. "I have always pictured him according to a description in *Paradise Lost* as seated upon a throne, while around are angels playing on harps and singing hymns," reported another. "I think of God as having bodily form and being much larger than the average man," said a third. These physical images of God are indicative of how one-dimensional modern perception of reality had become. Spiritual ideals, fashioned by the clergy in mystical or abstract forms, were no longer capable of capturing men's imaginations. There was a gap between the ideal and the real. Barton's portrait of Christ, cast in concrete, material terms, provided a new set of ideals which Americans could clearly perceive. As one reader put it: "Your brilliant handling of the life and character of Jesus has supplied the missing link in my grasping for a clear picture of my relationship to the whole." Barton had closed the gap between the ideal and the real. In so doing, he challenged the fundamentalist modernist "tyranny of limited alternatives" and restored a sense of community to modern society where the churches had failed.

The idea of secularizing Christ was, of course, not original with Barton. From the earliest days of industrial development, successful attempts were made to bring the spiritual ideals of the age into conformity with the realities of the environment. Notable examples include Mrs. Humphrey Ward's *Robert Elsmere* (1888), Charles Sheldon's *In His Steps* (1897), and Winston Churchill's *The Inside of the Cup* (1913)—popular secularizations of Christianity which were best sellers during previous decades. These earlier secularizing efforts, however, possessed a common flaw: they challenged the social and cultural values of the modern industrial system. While this characteristic was acceptable to earlier generations of Americans, who feared the monopolistic power of the giant "trusts" and experienced strong anxieties over their loss of independence, it posed a definite problem to Barton's generation.

During the twenties, the modern industrial system, reaching every aspect of life, molded the personality of the individual and established his goals. Economic activity, success and material gain became ends in themselves. An instrument in the hands of overwhelmingly strong forces outside himself, man became a servant to the very machine he had built. While he kept the illusion of being master of his own fate, he experienced the intense feeling of insignificance and powerlessness which his ancestors once felt for God. Nevertheless, conditions of modern life—the assurance of government protection, the benefits of advanced technology, and the continuing fact of prosperity—prevented him from lashing out at the giant corporations which were largely responsible for his fate. Instead, he trans-

Have You Ever Read

The World's Best Seller?

What book is the world's best seller?

What book is the most popular in the world?

What book is printed in millions of copies annually?

What book has been translated into five hundred tongues?

What book was distributed to over 9,000,000 people in 1925?

What book is in almost every home?

What book is it that everybody thinks he knows and understands?

What book is it that nobody knows?

"THE BOOK NOBODY KNOWS" IS THE BIBLE

THERE must be something in a book when it outlasts and outlives every other book that has ever been written. When it comes through fire and flood and earthquake, practically unscathed. There isn't a corner of the world where you won't find a copy of this book. There isn't a language or a dialect that hasn't its translation.

Are you interested in Evolution? Read the first chapter of Genesis. There it is, the whole story of creation, not at all at variance with the best scientific knowledge. Biology? Man's place at the top of the pyramid of life is the same in both Genesis and biology. Hygienics? Barton shows that much of our modern health regulation and medical practice were foreshadowed by centuries by the Mosaic Law. This it is that was responsible for the healthy sex life of the Jews from ancient times, which is the reason for their amazing racial continuity. Law? The Ten Commandments, simple, direct. The cornerstone upon which nations have erected their legal and ethical codes. Human Nature? Wm. L. Phelps says—"You can learn more about human nature by reading the Bible than by living in New York."

THE BOOK NOBODY KNOWS makes the Bible the most interesting piece of literature in all the world. Just as Barton has helped to put Jesus' name today on every man's tongue, so will the Bible be taken down now and dusted and READ.

The world needed someone to prove that the best seller of all time is not only a book for gray-beards to wrangle and fight over, but a book that everybody should read and enjoy.

THE BOOK NOBODY KNOWS is a sincere argument for the use of the Bible in all phases of human endeavor, for all men in every walk of life. There is no creed set forth, no dogmatism mars the direct simplicity of Barton's book. Every home that contains a copy of the Bible should have a copy of this personally conducted tour through the Bible. Everyone who reads the Bible should read Bruce Barton's book. Everyone who does *not* read the Bible *will start doing so*, once he has read THE BOOK NOBODY KNOWS.

formed the evil spirit of the "trusts," which the Populists and Progressives had tried to exorcise from their midst, into the benevolent god of modern business which he served. Fear changed to awe, distrust to confidence, skepticism to faith, and hostility to adoration. Standing before the vast economic machine, much as Henry Adams had stood before the dynamo at the turn of the century, he experienced an intense feeling of awe. "Before the end, one began to pray to it," Adams had said. "Inherited instinct taught the natural expression of man before silent and infinited force." Earlier secularizations, which discredited the benevolent god of modern business, were consequently unacceptable. Barton's secularized portrait of Christ, which reinforced the culturally sacred values of economic activity, success and material gain, satisfied the spiritual needs of his generation.

The significance of the public reaction to *The Man Nobody Knows* goes beyond what it reveals about middle class America's adjustment to the modern age. The widespread acceptance of Barton's portrait of Christ also sheds light on the social impact of modern advertising during its formative years. The same advertising genius which popularized Betty Crocker and projected the image of United States Steel as a public servant designed an image of Christ which many perceived as "real." Yet Barton's account was largely fictional. As one critic pointed out: "They crucified Jesus . . . because he was not pleasant, not popular, not successful, not an executive, not a winner, not a manager, not an advertiser, not a good business man." Barton's success in projecting his image as "real" suggests that modern Americans were receptive to other forms of advertising illusion as well.

The degree to which modern advertising plays with reality has been the subject of a small, but growing, body of recent literature. A notable example is Daniel Boorstin's *The Image: or What Happened to the American Dream* (1962). Evaluating our twentieth century experience, he identified a "peculiarly American menace" which was partially attributable to advertising. It was the "menace of unreality." He explained: "We risk being the first people to make their illusions so vivid, so persuasive, so 'realistic' that they . . . are the very house in which we live; they are our news, our heroes, our adventures, our forms of art, our very experience." It would seem that if advertising poses a threat, it is not so much in inducing consumption as it is in disguising reality.

The stage for this "menace of unreality" was already set in the twenties. While readers who corresponded with Barton sometimes objected to his portrait of Christ for doctrinal reasons, more often they accepted it as "real" because it satisfied their spiritual needs and cushioned the shock of change. Only one reader clearly perceived that he had substituted the ideal for the real. Recognizing the relationship between the book and art and advertising, she exclaimed: "I love it, but just the way I love the Lions in front of the Public Library. They must have been done by an American advertising man. It's the way we would like real lions to be. And Jesus in your story is the way you would like him to be, and I suppose the man who created the Wrigley Chewing Gum advertisement would like those who chew gum to feel the way the figures to on the electric sign. But, I love it all, because it's American." If Barton's portrait of Christ was an advertising illusion, it nevertheless claimed a necessary function. By closing the gap between the ideal and the real and restoring a sense of community to modern society, it facilitated middle class America's adjustment to the modern age. The twentieth century "menace of unreality," under these circumstances, was less a threat than a kindness.

16. The Glamorous Crowd: Hollywood Movie Premieres between the Wars

DAVID KARNES

The automobile, radio, and motion picture were the greatest cultural technological achievements of the 1920s. Of the three, movies did the most to create a mass culture in the United States. Between 1910 and 1920 the movie industry boomed. Major studios—Metro-Goldwyn-Meyer, Warner Brothers, Columbia, and RKO—began to produce full-length, high-budget motion pictures, appealing to more affluent audiences, and by 1920 there were more than 20,000 movie theaters in the country. That number grew to 28,000 in 1929. Many of the new theaters were huge "palaces" capable of seating 1,000 to 2,000 people in luxurious splendor. Actors and actresses like Charlie Chaplin, Buster Keaton, Fatty Arbuckle, William S. Hart, Rudolph Valentino, Clara Bow, and Theda Bara became popular culture superstars, instantly recognizable anywhere in the country.

The cultural impact of motion pictures was enormous. Before the movies, American culture was sharply divided along ethnic and regional lines. The ethnic theaters, ethnic language newspapers, regional and ethnic dialects, and local legends and heroes predominated. Movies changed all that. All over the country, across regional and ethnic lines, a new cultural currency appeared on film. Americans attended the same movies, watched the same stars, laughed at the same jokes, and listened to the same dialects and theater music. Vaudeville and the ethnic theaters rapidly declined, giving way to a new mass culture. In the motion pictures, the modern America of industrialization, secularism, sexuality, and urbanization was portrayed to the entire world. In the following essay, David Karnes describes the glamour and hype of Hollywood movie premieres between World War I and World War II.

The history of the movies is largely that of an ever more sophisticated medium through which fantasy is made to feel real. This encroachment of artifice on the everyday world is most strikingly presented in the 1939 novel that is still considered the classic account of Hollywood, Nathaniel West's *The Day of the Locust.* Although the tensions between glittering "screen" make believe and sobering "back lot" reality have long been a commonplace—indeed, the opposition around which most Hollywood exposés revolve—it was West's impressive achievement to reveal something quite different. Fantasy in *The Day of the Locust* consists not simply of false fronts; rather, it is lived experience. Hollywood is not so much a factory producing dreams as it is an edifice of illusions which West's characters, in their "need for beauty and romance," all too willingly accept as reality. In short, Hollywood succeeds not by obscuring the real by way of make believe, but instead by inextricably joining the two.

The fragility of this reality–illusion juxtaposition is revealed midway through the book when a huge, overbuilt set collapses under its own weight, dragging actors and extras down into the rubble. Yet the truly nightmarish edge to West's vision emerges in the novel's remarkable finish. The scene is a gala film opening on Hollywood Boulevard, which is overflowing with gathered, anxious fans. As celebrities arrive, the hopes, cravings, and frustrations of the crowd mount. Finally, the crudest spark ignites the multitude, transforming it into a crusading mob which runs riot along the Boulevard, first burning and destroying, then dancing "joyously in the red light of the flames." In this unforgettable climax, West showed how the emotionally volatile fusion of dream and reality which underlay moviedom's mystique might ultimately explode and bring Hollywood crashing down.

While melodramatic, West's selection of a gala film opening as the setting for his apocalyptic finale was the choice of an astute observer, one who well understood the importance of the movie premiere in Hollywood's network of power. The glamour which nourished movie culture depended upon the ways in which Hollywood's worldly realities and fantastic appeals so irresistibly reinforced one another, and it was around this linkage that early movie premieres developed. They occurred, first of all, in front of a palatial movie palace smack in the heart of real-life Hollywood, the geographic place where the "real world" movie industry resided and prospered. Moreover, these gala openings showcased the stars, figures who existed both on- and off-screen and who thereby tangibly embodied movie culture's capacity to bridge the two realms. Finally, the studios cleverly deployed an entire productive apparatus—microphones, cameras, radio announcers, and spotlights—to transform the premiere's Boulevard festivities into a brilliantly orchestrated scene of show business fantasy. If the event afforded a real-life glimpse of screen idols, it did so only amidst the instruments of movie make believe, and only in a setting which preserved movie culture's "larger-than-life" aura. With eyes typically riveted on the film, many commentators have missed these important dynamics occurring outside the theater auditorium. West, on the other hand, saw how the premiere skillfully transferred Hollywood's potent "magic" from the screen to the street. He thus detected at this crucial crossroads of reality and illusion an awesome power which might ultimately pull Hollywood apart.

Yet for all his keenness of vision, West's timing was a little late. The carefully manipulated titillations of early movie culture, servicing the lavish consumer capitalism of its day, did indeed arouse energies of growing volatility. And if events never reached the scale of those West imagined, hints of anarchic and potentially subversive force increasingly surfaced from the mid-to-late 1920s through the early Depression years. Premiere energies, however, were not inherently disorderly, and West, writing in 1939, failed to see how they had been shrewdly and successfully rechanneled by the late New Deal years. Over the course of the 1930s, Hollywood largely abandoned the wild, carnivalesque film debuts of the previous decade, adopting in their place a very different celebration of small town, all-American, and eventually, militarist values. However rambunctious their youth, the premieres, by the end of the Second World War, had been brought to heel by a new national political culture. The chronicle of Hollywood movie premieres between the wars is thus the tale of an exuberant emergence followed by an ultimate domestication. In this transformation across two decades, the premieres, so artfully constructed from a fusing of the real and the imagined, asserted their place in the developing politics of movie culture.

Hollywood movie premieres achieved their initial prominence both by capitalizing upon older cultural forms and by offering something qualitatively new. Structurally, the movie palace had descended from the opera house and the live stage or vaudeville theater, and film openings drew at least some cultural legitimation from first nights performed at these earlier, more established institutions. Similarly, the premiere's street festivities had such playful precursors as the circus and the amusement park with their carnivalesque, outdoor spirit. But while borrowing from many forerunners, the orchestrators of Hollywood movie premieres grafted on their own special features. By joining three key elements—stars, media technologies, and showmanship savvy—Hollywood's "new Barnums" created the unique dynamics out of which movie premiere glamour distinctively emerged.

"Hollywood Premiere is a Sight Worth Going Miles to See" headlined *Motion Picture* in 1928, alongside a photograph showing Hollywood Boulevard packed with "huge throngs." This attraction, not of the film but of the premiere as an event in itself, heralded a strange new phenomenon. Conceding that "film first nights in New York are but tame affairs compared with similar events in Hollywood," *The New York Times* in 1929 reported the most remarkable West Coast feature as "the impressive throng of young and old persons who have no admission tickets." Likewise, a 1931 *Saturday Evening Post* article contrasted the traditional "first-nighter" of the live stage, "one who attends the performance in evening clothes and chauffeur," with Hollywood premiere-goers, the "ten to twenty thousand habitual first-nighters who never see the inside of a theater." As *Collier's* put it in 1929, "the picture about to be shown for the first time may be just another seven thousand feet of film; the audience is the show."

This featured theater "audience," so spellbinding to curbside fans, consisted chiefly of motion picture stars. Film historians have dated the first movie "premieres" to 1913, when Carnegies, Lodges, and Vanderbilts began conferring "society" status on opening night events in New York. Yet premiere houses on Hollywood Boulevard accommodated Hollywood's very different style of elite: the stars who drew the crowds. These real-life movie idols sported the most luxurious apparel, arrived in the finest sedans, and displayed a worldly success every bit as enchanting as the romantic roles they acted out on the screen. Indeed, the premieres afforded vicarious access to a sumptuous realm of desire which somehow eluded daily life. As Hollywood director William de Mille insisted in 1933, "the real meaning of the premiere" must be sought in the psychological process of identification with the stars and in the public's wish to celebrate "those who have helped them find their dream-selves."

Trappings of genuine moviemaking heightened this enthralling celebration of dreamy make believe. Before batteries of microphones and flashing cameras, a master of ceremonies introduced arriving celebrities who invariably gushed, "Hello everybody! I'm sure this is going to be the greatest picture of the year." Instrumental to the rise of radio, Hollywood had its first three stations by 1922 and soon thereafter "the arrival of stars, directors, producers, and society leaders was broadcast in detail . . . to the home sitting public." Premiere-goers were thus all too aware of their role in a nationally broadcast entertainment. At least one 1928 opening advertised that a camera crew would actually film "motion pictures of arriving guests." Not coincidentally, Hollywood Boulevard on opening night resembled nothing so much as a sprawling outdoor movie set. Even before World War One, onlookers had been drawn to the then-dusty streets of Hollywood to witness and to experience live filmmaking. And as Carey McWilliams remarked, the original "circus and carnival" atmosphere fostered by Hollywood's outdoor filming survived by the mid-1920s "only in the gaudy premieres with their blazing klieg lights."

These bright premiere lights, perhaps like nothing else, generated the glamorous aura that transformed a Hollywood parade of the stars into near-fantasy. Director Mack Sennett remembered the earliest Hollywood as "a little, typical village. It wasn't glamorous. Glamour? No. They had no searchlights then. Oh, God, no . . . Searchlights!" Yet after World War One things began to change. The first act of the Hollywood Chamber of Commerce following its 1921 formation was a campaign to encourage the Boulevard merchants to keep their lights on after closing hours, and the lights of movie openings even more profoundly altered Hollywood's image. When *Photoplay* dubbed Hollywood Boulevard the "New Broadway" in 1929, and others began saluting it as the "Great White Way of the West," the geographically transplanted power was not simply electrical, but also psychological, deriving from Hollywood's growing capacity to capture and deploy the promise and fantasy radiated in blazing light.

This lighting of Hollywood and its premiers was largely the work of Otto K. Oleson, Danish immigrant, Hollywood Chamber of Commerce president, and founder of his own illuminating company. As the story is usually told, shortly after the First World War Oleson came across two abandoned military searchlights in a muddy San Diego field. Deemed obsolete by the government, they were easily acquired and by 1920 put to good use advertising Los Angeles automobile agencies. Oleson's new venture flourished more fully once brought to Hollywood. There, he pioneered lighting techniques that allowed for the indoor filming of movies, and more important to his legacy, innovated means for the outdoor lighting of premieres. "We light the world . . . ," proclaimed the motto of the Oleson enterprise. On a somewhat more modest scale, the new "klieg lights" of Otto K. Oleson, "King of Illumination," provided the "pencil of light" which "pierced the heavens" at Hollywood movie openings.

Pencils of light soon joined up with much greater quantities of simulated power, thereby providing an especially brilliant showcase for premiere glamour. "Hollywood Decks Itself in Light," proclaimed the *American City* of 1928, referring to an Oleson-engineered promotional display. Hailed as "one of the greatest electrical spectacles ever attempted outdoors," twenty-eight Army searchlights threw 4,200,000,000 candlepower "into the skies" over Hollywood Boulevard. Such energies shone forth with increasing magnitude at 1920s film openings. Theater rooftops glowed, spotlights greeted arriving guests, and "giant reflectors fluttered their broad, bright shafts against the dark hills and away over the illuminated plains of Los Angeles to the shores of the ocean." Indeed, the structure of a premiere was largely defined by its manipulation of light against dark, with the heaviest dose of all being reserved for the theater's fore-court, a threshold symbolically shared by the picture palace and the outside world. There, arc lamps from the lobby showered arriving luminaries in light. Every modern-day Hollywood picture book contains a profusion of photographs illustrating the fabled premiere lights. One shot of a 1927 opening is especially compelling. The awesome power of the picture de-rives not from the crowds, the cars, or the parade of arriving guests; the real force is contained in the streaks of light literally blasting out of the theater forecourt, as if from a veritable furnace of energy.

Mere show business? Perhaps. But blazing lights at Hollywood pre-mieres added a special dimension to movie culture, traditionally seen as something relegated to the domain of the theater and the dark. While movie-watching was couched in dreamy darkness, the potency of Holly-wood's outdoor premieres drew upon an opposite yet equally transporting atmosphere of heavenly brightness. As early as 1922, journalists wrote of the "floodlights of filmdom" turning "the night into brilliance brighter than noon-day." In 1928, "great studio lights" lit Hollywood Boulevard "far more brilliantly than a mere sun could have lighted it." And again, in 1930, premiere klieg lights made the night "brighter than midday." The images of the "star," that which shines bright amidst the night sky, captured well this notion of something more exotically luminous than ordinary daytime. By bringing together stars, microphones, cameras and lights, Hollywood movie premieres suggested to "the common herd—the ticketless tourists," the plain Americans who bought tens of millions of movie admissions each week during the 1920s, that they too could share in a bit of Hollywood fan-tasy. Not surprisingly, out-of-town vacationers soon planned trips around Hollywood openings, which by the end of the decade were "among the tourist sights of California."

Finally, in addition to stars and technologies, premiere glamour drew upon a clever showmanship acutely sensitive to the needs of the times. This it found in the person of Sidney Grauman, universally considered the father of the "gala" premiere. Born in the Midwest, the teen-aged Grauman journeyed with his father to the Alaskan Klondike, scene of the last great rousing nineteenth-century gold rushes. There, he staged talent shows for the miners. Grauman next moved to San Francisco, a more settled "rush" town, where, after the 1906 earthquake destroyed the movie houses, he exhibited films in a large circus tent. By the time he arrived in Los Angeles, he was well acquainted with the more bawdy and buoyant side of American popular culture. Grauman first staged premieres in downtown Los Angeles, but it was on Hollywood Boulevard that he engineered his "gala" celebrity parades by locating his theaters far back from the street, and erecting elaborate entries with carpeted, canopied walkways that afforded spectator viewing from both sides. But even more important than these structural enhancements were the new images and symbols Grauman supplied in such concentrated form. A Grauman premiere constituted nothing less than a grand spectacle of sensual, exotic splendor, and that was something American popular culture clearly craved during the return to "normalcy."

Arabian and Asiatic luxury offered an especially tantalizing stage for 1920s premiere fantasy. From P. T. Barnum's Great Asiatic Caravan, Mu-seum and Menagerie of the 1850s, to Coney Island's "Streets of Cairo" exhibits at the turn of the century, Americans had long been drawn to the mysteries of the East. Early Hollywood, with its opulent Babylonian sets and biblical epics, continued the flirtation. Sid Grauman consummated the affair. His Egyptian Theater, opened in 1922 as the original setting for "Hollywood-style" premieres, presented itself as an "artistic monument to Egypt's glory." Whereas earlier movie houses had used classical, Renaissance, or Rococo architecture, *Motion Picture News* likened the Egyptian entrance to "the gateways of Egyptian palaces during the days of Cleopatra." Hieroglyphs, sphinx-heads, and lush foliage adorned a grand entryway guarded by Arab sentries sporting rifles and desert robes. Grauman's showcase opened amidst a larger Egyptian craze sweeping both the United States and the film industry in 1922—the year King Tut's Tomb was discovered—and the new atmosphere drew the fire of many local conservatives, who complained of "the loathsome and degraded Orientalism that has oozed into Hollywood." But the public proved less moralizing, and in a favorite play on words, the Egyptian Theater soon became a most popular "Mecca" for tourists.

The growing tourist pilgrimage depended on Grauman's ability to ensure that the real-life action on the street matched the make-believe drama on the screen. "The public doesn't demand anything," preached Grauman, who insisted that "showmanship is like any other merchandising." As evidenced at *The Thief of Bagdad* premiere of 1924, Grauman knew his public well. Indeed, the opening transformed a "whole section of Hollywood into a sort of Arabian night's fantasy in itself." A "huge, sphinx-like sitting Egyptian god, eight feet high, flanked by great twenty-foot candles" protected the forecourt. Spectators marveled at large mechanical elephants and a "gorgeously arrayed Egyptian Prince." The *Los Angeles Times* declared: "Never has there been so much of the spirit of the carnival at Grauman's Egyptian Theater, so much of light and gaiety, so much free, flurrying spontaneous enthusiasm." This spirit filled "not only the playhouse itself, and the esplanade of the entrance way, but virtually all the boulevard in the immediate vicinity . . . everybody wanted to have some part in the event."

The talk of the town, movie premieres became central to Hollywood's rising fame in the 1920s. With the Egyptian's 1922 grand opening, the *Hollywood Daily-Citizen* foresaw an auspicious night marking "Hollywood's advent from the status of a small town to a city of metropolitan importance, where world premieres are shown. . . . as Hollywood has become the production center of the motion picture world, so it will become the center for the presentation of the great premiere showings of the world." Following the Egyptian's 1924 opening of Cecil B. De Mille's *The Ten Commandments,* the *Los Angeles Examiner* concluded: "A premiere of a motion picture of note rivals the opening of the Metropolitan grand opera if the brilliant assemblage and wealth of fine costumes are considered." Gala movie premieres thus complemented Hollywood's movie production role, and the two became intimately intermeshed. As Mae West recalled of one of her first Hollywood openings, "It was all glitter. . . . All of it is wonderful and full of a foolish magic which is the essence of motion picture making."

Supplying even more of this "essence," Grauman opened his second gala premiere movie house on Hollywood Boulevard in 1927, after five years of staging openings at the Egyptian. His new Chinese Theater soon became Hollywood's number one attraction, a success achieved by embracing as never before American notions of the luxuriously decadent Orient. The Chinese put forth an exotic rainbow of shape, color and light. Spectators confronted a ninety-foot-high bronze pagoda roof, "aged to the color of green jade," ornamented with iron masks, and supported by large coral red piers. The eaves tilted upward like "forked dragon tongues" in harmony with the "mammoth stone dragon" below. Towering minarets of burnished copper, a forty-foot wall surmounted by "four ornate obelisks," two "colossal fountain bowls catching the spray of bronzed gargoyles," stone dogs, drooping "Chinese vines and verdure," full grown cocoa palms, and a lush Oriental garden rounded out the decor. Embellishing the night-time scene were "jeweled lamps casting iridescent rays" and the flames of the "ever-burning fires."

Like the movie premieres which so heavily contributed to its fame, the Chinese Theater was intended to blur the border of the real and the imagined. Grauman wanted his "dream castle" forecourt to create the illusion of "entering another world." Theater stationery contained the Chinese legend, "Portals to the theater are the long-sought-for portals to paradise," and the building's style reportedly reflected "the most glorious period in architectural fantasy." American culture had long placed its sturdy virtue in opposition to the enervating vices of Asiatic despotism, luxury, and licentiousness. Yet amidst the 1920s celebration of consumer titillation and splendor, with vamps, sheiks, and Babylonian princesses dominating the movie screen, Sid Grauman thought the time clearly ripe to bring "all the mystery of the Orient" to the "very heart of the cinema capital of the world."

Cecil B. De Mille's *King of Kings,* the first film to play at the Chinese, served both to "dedicate and consecrate" the new "temple of the cinema," and to cement Grauman's marriage of screen fantasy and street reality. De Mille's film would be Hollywood's most lavish account of Christ's life, and the *Los Angeles Times* anticipated the event with a huge panorama of Christ on the Cross towering over Roman soldiers and masses of followers. Days later, the same paper displayed a large drawing of mobs and lights in front of Grauman's Chinese Theater. The mass imagery of the film spectacle neatly correlated with the mass energy being aroused for what was expected to be Hollywood's grandest movie premiere ever. Ranking the evening as "the most important event in recent Western theatrical history," the *Los Angeles Times* thought it appropriately located on Hollywood Boulevard, the "street of romance."

Romance, to be sure, but the *King of Kings* opening evinced a more complicated psychological dynamic. "Hundreds of Police Battle to Keep Crowds in Check," announced the next day's headlines. The mob, estimated at 25,000, jammed the Boulevard, stalled traffic, and forced arriving guests "to leave our cars several blocks away and fight our way to the theater. . . . Constantly the police would form in line with hands stretched in front of them, and at the word would charge the crowd, putting all their weight in the effort, and then forward would surge the people and the big officers would go sprawling backwards." Masses of spectators "clustered against the motor cars, peering in the windows," until forced back by charging police details. The *Los Angeles Examiner* reassuringly reported "no real scrapping, for most of the outfit were women, girls and children, but it was a bit tough at that, for such a huge mass was out of all control."

Assorted Hollywood legends have it that the "near riot" resulted in broken ribs, "one teenage boy being shoved under a car," and twenty-five cases of fainting. D. W. Griffith, father of the epic film, with all of its scenes of sensual, violent mass humanity, was dismayed. "Never in London, Paris or New York have I seen such a crowd," he exclaimed. Sid Grauman, father of the gala premiere, with all of its promotion of romantic and highly charged human energy, put events to their logical commercial advantage. "30,000 Persons Fought to gain admittance to the opening of the show-place of the world. . . . Never before has any box office turned away so many people," gloated the next day's movie ads. Indeed, the chaos merely enhanced the legend. "The greatest of all premieres," heralded the *Holly-wood Daily-Citizen,* and Will Hays, national guardian of movie morality, ex-ulted, "This man Grauman is the greatest showman the world has ever had." A lonely discordant voice came from one movie critic, who felt *King of Kings'* depiction of the Way of the Cross "deficient in the mob spirit. . . . One expected to see the surge of a vast infuriated mass of figures, but the action seems badly scattered. . . . That is not a mob, as mobs are known in history." The reviewer should have stepped through the exit doors. The spectacle on the Boulevard, perhaps more than the show on the screen, affirmed with epic proportions the new values and dramatic force of movie culture. The great age of the silent cinema was anything but silent.

Incorporating even "real-life" mob clamor into their alluring fantasy of crowd glamour, Hollywood movie premieres became an increasingly pow-erful and sometimes ominous presence during the late 1920s and early Depression years. By 1930, the Carthay Circle (1926), the Pantages (1930), and Warner Brothers' Hollywood Theater (1928) all competed with the Egyptian and Chinese as gala premiere houses, with the Carthay Circle especially prominent in staging major film openings. As activity intensified, spirits occasionally took a disorderly turn.

As early as 1925, Gloria Swanson made a forced mid-premiere escape from a downtown Los Angeles Grauman theater after police warned her that the crowds outside could no longer be contained. A 1928 gathering at the Carthay Circle opening of *Lilac Time* "mobbed the front door, ran the police force ragged, dislodged fragments of the stucco building, crashed through ropes, shattered windows and howled like wolves." The Chinese drew especially excitable mobs. The crowd at *Grand Hotel* (1932), seeking "a closer glimpse of the screen beauties . . . burst through the police lines" and forced officers "to throw up iron chains across the theater forecourt to prevent the great throng from swarming into the showhouse itself." Months later, a woman suffered a broken leg when crushed by the crowds at the Chinese opening of *Strange Interlude.* The *I'm No Angel* (1933) pre-miere reportedly came "very close to a dangerous street riot."

Offering a nearness to Hollywood glamour that both teased and eluded curbside fans, the premieres could be both enticing and pro-foundly frustrating. A participant in one early Depression premiere motor-cade recalled seeing the "faces pressed close to the windows on both sides," faces which turned from glee to a disconcerting "near-resentment" when the occupants proved unfamiliar. The fact that most spectators could not gain admittance to opening night showings compounded the tensions. Given the aggravated emotional setting, it is not surprising that some perceived a specter of danger on the horizon.

This threatening volatility appeared most alarmingly in May, 1930, when Sid Grauman, outshining the competition, staged Hollywood's biggest premiere spectacle at the Chinese. The film, Howard Hughes's air battle epic *Hell's Angels* boasted a record-breaking three years of production and an enormous advance publicity campaign. "Tonight the Sky's the Limit in Hollywood," promised opening day ads, encouraging fans to "Come to Hollywood Tonight to Join in the Mardi Gras Festivities." These "festivities" included thundering fireworks, parades of military units, and over 250 searchlights shining on overhead airplanes that dropped flares, screeched sirens, and executed mock battle maneuvers. An "apotheosis" of showmanship, rejoiced the *Los Angeles Evening Express,* while *The New York Times* applauded "an electrical display such as Hollywood has never before beheld." Such "electrical" energy also proved explosive on the solidly massed pavement below. Grauman arranged for police, Marines, firemen, and even Boy Scouts to handle the crowd, but extra reserves and 100 additional Marines were required. "At intervals," reported the *Los Angeles Evening Herald,* "officers drove motorcycles with back-firing exhausts down the hedging fringe of the crowds, shearing back the line like a reaper lays back standing wheat. This was necessary to keep the automobiles from being over-run." At the high water mark of Hollywood Boulevard movie openings, premiere energies could indeed seem on the verge of explosion.

If such "Pandemonium," as the *Hollywood Daily-Citizen* described it, might inspire the genius of a Nathaniel West, its more immediate effect was to draw the attention of Hollywood's critics. As early as 1927, the *New Republic* attacked Hollywood's "corruptly glamorous values," which the masses allegedly adopted from lack of "values and glamour of their own." And in 1930, Vincent Sheean, writing in *Commonweal,* found a new and more sharply focused target. Sheean recounted a disturbing recent trip to Hollywood. The most distressing experience of his stay was a visit to a Hollywood movie premiere. "There is no more remarkable spectacle in the United States," he declared, "than the sight of these mobs in the streets of Hollywood, drinking some mysterious increase of life, some exquisite high pleasure, out of the glimpsing of a stranger's passing." Sheean despaired of Hollywood's dangerous "magic," rooted in "the starved fancy of a people whose aesthetic life is so impoverished that it can find in the prettiness of these photographed faces all beauty, all romance." As a sort of "emotional capital of the country," Hollywood and its "sorcery" were said to represent all of "the violence and morbidity, the vast intensity, and childlike hysteria, of American itself." To its detractors, identification with the stars, the linchpin of premiere glamour, thus emerged as the root of Hollywood's evil.

Critics prayed that Hollywood had overplayed its hand, that economic crisis would bring the entire industry crashing down, but they underestimated the capacity of movie culture to adapt to changing times. In 1932 the *New Republic* gloatingly predicted that the studios, having "addicted the public to lavishness," would no longer be able to deliver the goods under Depression conditions. Little mourning was anticipated for the collapse of

Hollywood, an edifice reportedly built on the formulas of "glamour, romance, sex," and on the dollars of the bewitched, the people standing on soapboxes "for a better view of one's favorite movie queen as she attends opening night." To be sure, by 1933 nearly one-third of all American movie houses closed, including, for a short while, Grauman's Chinese Theater. But Hollywood hardly proved a Depression casualty. The 1930s were among Hollywood's most "golden" of years. And as historian Robert Sklar argues, this was the time when Hollywood helped reshape "the basic moral, social and economic tenets of traditional American culture."

While Sklar refers to film content, this new traditionalism was at least as visible in the transformation of Hollywood glamour outside the theater. If the times rendered Asiatic luxury and Hollywood Boulevard frivolity anachronistic, movie culture could deploy its talents in ways more appropriate to New Deal America. By the 1930s, noted Carey McWilliams, "Hollywood" was not a geographic place, but rather a "state of mind," to be found wherever the influence of motion pictures might go. The studios discovered that the feelings engendered by their movie premieres were similarly portable. By mobilizing these energies on a new nationwide scale, Hollywood could retain its potent glamour, while making it more acceptably and squarely all-American. And by exchanging their early image of carnival splendor for a Depression-era spirit of civic festival, Hollywood movie premieres not only overcame hard times, but set the stage for a new interplay between movie fantasy and American culture.

Hollywood's new democratic style appeared most simply in the form of local film openings across the nation. Small town premieres existed before the 1930s, but publicity pressbooks suggest an increasing scale and sophistication in efforts to disseminate the spirit of Hollywood Boulevard. Promoters of *Hell's Angels,* for example, utilized an aerial stunt show, military parades, and speeches by local officials to mark its "Hollywood-style" first night in Seattle. The 1936 pressbook for *Green Pastures* contained explicit instructions to local exhibitors on techniques for "Building the Opening," including radio broadcasts, streetside floodlights, and various "stunts." Under the heading "Photogs snare Crowds," the guide recommended, "How about having a few camera-snappers outside your theater, setting up their apparatus, blowing off flashlights. We suggest no plates in all but one of the cameras. Reason? It will make your opening look awful important and stunt won't cost much." Similar advice suggested that police be warned "to prevent too much jamming 'round theater. And by the way, if local photog takes picture of police holding back mobs, newspaper might think it exciting enough to publish." The language was all in the very folksy vernacular of the small town huckster, but the product, in its way, was big-time movie glamour.

By 1939 the clear message was that Hollywood "magic" knew no geographic bounds. The pressbook for *Juarez* pictured glittering Hollywood and New York openings, then told how local theaters, through proper devices, could follow suit. Exhibitors were directed, "See the picture of the throngs which tried to get into the theater, and you will see how this strategy successfully influences the masses." The opening night needed to be well publicized and packed with "action and excitement . . . flash bulbs

exploding. . . . Spotlights glaring on theater front . . . loudspeakers directing, announcing celebrities . . . radio microphones and announcers spiel-
ing off the activity . . . glitter and sparkle of women in gowns and jewels . . .
men in formal attire . . . all the razzle-dazzle necessary to start off your
engagement in big style."

Besides just good advice, the studios increasingly offered a more important commodity, the stars. For Busby Berkeley's 1933 extravaganza *Forty-
Second Street,* Warner Brothers used one of the first cross-country premiere
junkets. The "42nd Street Train," packed with stars and dancing girls,
stopped at cities across the nation until reaching its final destination:
Franklin Roosevelt's inaugural parade. Warner Brothers repeated the effort with its Gold Diggers series, movies which embodied the old qualities
of lavish, cosmopolitan frivolity, but which were promoted in the new democratic spirit of coast-to-coast tours with "personal appearances in America's key cities." These movie junkets, proclaimed *The New York Times,*
manifested an attempt "to bring the premieres to the people," thus signal-
ing a more egalitarian redistribution of Hollywood fantasy.

Small town "world premieres" at the end of the decade even more
clearly merged movie glamour with the heartland, New Deal values then
being celebrated by such filmmakers as John Ford and Frank Capra. A host
of movies embodying themes of Americana opened not on Hollywood
Boulevard, but in the towns and cities depicted on the screen. A reported
100,000 people lined Salt Lake City streets for the premiere of *Brigham
Young* (1940). For *Virginia City* (1940), a "16-car Southern Pacific Special
packed with the biggest names in show business" headed for Nevada. The
crowd allegedly doubled the state's normal population, and round-the-
clock showings at four theaters were utilized to accommodate everyone.
Also in 1940, trainloads of stars headed east for the world premiere of *Santa
Fe Trail.* The winner of a nationwide contest among schoolchildren received a free trip to join in the three days of festivities, after which a crowd
estimated at 10,000 bid farewell at the Santa Fe train station. Dodge City
made the premiere map by hosting the opening of the 1939 film bearing its
name. Fifty masked horsemen charged out of the American prairie to race
the celebrity train to the Dodge City depot, where nationwide radio broadcast the festivities.

Many of the middle America premieres attained a scale that even Sid
Grauman must have envied. For the Nebraska opening of *Boy's Town*
(1938), Omaha's mayor and council turned over the city to the actual Boy's
Town administrators on the day of the premiere. Participation in the festivities became a matter of civic pride. At the conclusion, Spencer Tracy
claimed the Omaha opening made "a Hollywood premiere look like a
dying hog." One year later, Omaha went even further. For weeks preceding
the opening of Paramount's *Union Pacific,* men grew beards, women wore
calico dresses and sunbonnets, while local merchants added false pioneer
fronts to their shops. Costumed actors departed Hollywood in a facsimile of
the first Union Pacific train, making stops in fifty-three cities along the way.
With schools and many businesses closed, an estimated 200,000 people
gathered at the Omaha depot, while a pioneer costume ball and banquet
highlighted the next three days of civic merriment. Cecil B. De Mille

remarked, "When I look at the crowds in Omaha . . . then Hollywood bows." But of course, the whole event—the false fronts, the costumes, the stars—was pure Hollywood. And everybody was in on the act.

Larger cities also shared in the events. One of the largest crowds in Detroit's history turned out for the 1939 opening of *Disputed Passage.* Twelve thousand Chicago women and 5,000 Chicago men entered beauty contests for the chance to sit with the stars at the Windy City's opening of *North West Mounted Police* (1940). And a Georgia state holiday honored the 1939 premiere of *Gone With the Wind* at an Atlanta theater draped in Confederate flags and covered over by a facade resembling one of the movie's fabled mansions. When the arriving celebrities got caught in the premiere crunch, Clark Gable, as MGM lore would have it, swept Margaret Mitchell into his arms, carrying her safely away from the threatening throng.

Yet probably no movie opening caught the spirit of the new patriotism so fully as South Bend, Indiana's 1940 premiere of *Knute Rockne—All American.* Trainloads of celebrities from movies, sports, and politics, joined 100,000 other visitors to the town. The governors of New York, Florida, Iowa, Tennessee, Louisiana, Georgia, and Massachusetts joined Indiana in proclaiming National Knute Rockne Week. High schools, civic organizations, and athletic teams partook of the festivities saluting Notre Dame's famed football coach. Highlighting a week of national radio broadcasts from South Bend, Kate Smith sang "God Bless America," and President Roosevelt's son recited a message from his father. The film's pressbook boasted, "Premiere activities for *Knute Rockne—All American* have loomed into a national celebration unequalled in the annals of motion picture history."

As for the actor playing the part of the legendary Notre Dame quarterback George Gipp, Warner Brothers predicted that "his stock will soar to starring level." That actor, Ronald Reagan, came in 1937 from the Midwest to Hollywood, seeking his own escape from Depression realities by way of movie fame and fortune. Previous employment as a radio announcer had helped him land one of his first talking roles in the 1938 film *Boy Meets Girl.* In it, Reagan played a radio commentator. He is broadcasting from the theater forecourt at a Hollywood movie premiere. While the camera pans the lights, grandstands, cameras, musicians, and even a small fight breaking out in the crowd, Reagan declares, "Your favorite stars, folks, in person, and the crowds! . . . Folks, I want to tell you this is the most thrilling premiere it's been my privilege to cover." The platitudes of "real-life" radio announcing sounded the call, while Reagan's vehicle to success, *Knute Rockne,* saluted the mixture of politics, sports, religion, and football so central to the new values for which Hollywood movie premieres were coming to stand.

As its new nationalist posture evolved, the premiere's older world of Hollywood carnivals seemed largely passé. In 1938 *Life* reported that film openings were "the most splendiferous social events in Hollywood," but its coverage suggested little more than "who's-with-whom" popularity pageants. At the 1938 opening of *Hurricane,* fans paid exorbitant prices to sit in grandstands where they put on leis and drank refreshments. And at the Chinese premiere of *Stagecoach* (1939), Americana prevailed, with nineteenth-century wagons rolling down Hollywood Boulevard. By the late 1930s, publicity brochures for the Chinese still boasted of its fabled premieres, but the theater's distinction by then derived more from the celebrity footprints in its forecourt cement.

Meanwhile, premiere energies away from Hollywood Boulevard crystallized in an increasingly militant form. At the Tacoma, Washington, opening of *Tugboat Annie Sails Again* (1940), thirty-five government planes, a sixty-piece Army band, a U.S. naval guard of honor, and blasts from the guns of offshore Coast Guard ships greeted the arrival of the stars. A premiere-day furlough for 40,000 local military personnel greatly augmented the crowd. Similarly, "a parade led by flag-carrying Boy Scouts and the Sons of the American Legion Drum and Bugle Corps" celebrated the 1941 "Hollywood-style" premiere of *Sergeant York* in Washington, D.C. The Undersecretary of War and several generals attended the festivities, while President Roosevelt met personally with Alvin York, real-life hero of the First World War. The Army, as part of its military preparedness and recruiting drives, volunteered to help theater owners stage local openings of the film.

Domesticated but not defused, Hollywood movie premieres thus firmly established their new political configuration on the eve of the war. The earlier glamorous crowds of the 1920s had excited powerful sentiments linked to deep-rooted needs for meaning, identification, and aspiration. It was their most volatile expressions, journalistically described in the language of "near riot," from which Nathaniel West so insightfully extrapolated in *The Day of the Locust*. "What a crowd, folks! What a crowd! . . . What excitement! Of all the premieres I've attended, this is the most . . . the most . . . stupendous, folks," screams West's premiere emcee, as the mob's increasing arousal brings Hollywood tumbling down. Written in 1939, the words echo those of Ronald Reagan from the previous year's *Boy Meets Girl*. But in fact, by decade's end, Hollywood has redirected premiere energies toward their new civic ends. They would seek release not in Hollywood Boulevard apocalypse, but in the more socially approved catharsis of patriotic militarism.

Befitting movie culture's potent mixture of reality and illusion, Hollywood's new real-life commitment to nationalist politics emerged most strikingly in a fanciful film of 1941. *World Premiere* is the comic tale of Germans and Americans fighting it out; the battlefield is a Hollywood movie premiere. The Americans intend to put on a gala Washington, D.C. opening for their film, *The Earth's on Fire*, which depicts the horrors of European facism. Nazi spies intend to substitute reels of German propaganda at the premiere showing. Most of the action occurs on the train heading from Hollywood to the nation's capital. "Premiere! Eselschwitz! I will show them premieres," rages the evil Nazi leader. When the German scheme to turn the opening—replete with stars and crowds—to their own advantage is finally foiled, they make one last desperate attempt to explode the theater itself. All appears lost until the bomb, at the climactic moment, falls to pieces, revealing the tag, "Made in Japan." The premiere is saved. It's on with the show. And Hollywood gave the nation a good belly laugh in 1941.

Hollywood would not long be laughing about Japanese explosives. A favorite truism had it that searchlights meant trouble in any part of the world except Hollywood, where they suggested only the fun of another gala movie premiere. The night of February 25, 1942, proved otherwise. According to news accounts, "powerful searchlights from countless stations stabbed the sky with brilliant probing fingers while anti-aircraft batteries dotted the heavens with beautiful, if sinister, orange bursts of shrapnel." The city was blacked out for five hours, and crowds gathered to watch the "explosions stabbing the darkness like tiny bursting stars." While the rhetoric and spectacle recalled Sid Grauman-style showmanship at its *Hell's Angels* best, and Secretary of War Stimson later announced the whole affair a terrible mistake, the explosions were real enough. Two months after Pearl Harbor, and two days after a reported Japanese shelling of a Santa Barbara oil field, high tensions combined with unidentified aircraft and wartime fears to bring home to Hollywood that real-life drama created once "the curtain of war lifted over a Nation."

Hollywood originally borrowed its bright lights from the First World War, and now they were to be relinquished to the Second. *The New York Times* reported, "Spotlighted openings are out for the duration, and photographer's flash bulbs may soon be rationed, so it is a safe bet that styles in premieres will soon revert to modesty." The vulnerability of Hollywood's lights became especially clear during the false attack. On the night of the panic, Vernon Farquhar, one-time president of the Hollywood Chamber of Commerce, remembered seeing "a bunch of people form into a mob when the blackout wasn't immediately effective everywhere. They went berserk, smashing lights. . . . They threw rocks . . . then they broke into businesses to dash lights." The Hollywood lighting and nightlife so cultivated in the early 1920s was thus one of the first casualties of war. Appropriately, Otto Oleson diversified his business. The outbreak of hostilities found the "King of Illumination" busily supplying lighting for War Bond rallies at the Hollywood Bowl.

Making do without klieg lights, movie premieres continued having, it was said, "their last fling." The August, 1942, opening of *Yankee Doodle Dandy* advertised "no pre-war searchlights calling attention to the theater, but . . . plenty of other bright lights—a condition that will not prevail after the Army's new dim out orders go into effect August 20." Staged as part of the Navy's "Build Ships" campaign, Hollywood celebrities bought up to $25,000 worth of War Bonds as the price of opening night admission. Sid Grauman, on hand for the affair, reminisced, "I hope, sincerely, that Wednesday night will not be the last of the premieres, that they will be resumed after the war. Premieres have given Hollywood color. They have given the fans a chance . . . to see the stars. And, since the advent of radio, such openings have been listened to by movie-goers throughout the country." Sam Goldwyn's *Pride of the Yankees* opened on Hollywood Boulevard the night before Hollywood went dark. "Thousands of fans stood outside the Pantages Theater, on Hollywood and Vine, and watched as stars and high-ranking Naval, Army and Marine officers entered." A new reality ushered forth a new kind of star crossing the symbolic theater threshold on opening night.

Despite the war, premieres did hang on, albeit in a subdued light. The marquee announced "Gala Premiere" for the 1943 opening of *This Is The Army,* and photographs show the traditional crowds gathering outside the theater well before sundown. But the affair was a fundraiser for the Army Emergency Relief, and in the film, war clearly takes center stage. Ronald Reagan again plays a master of ceremonies. Disorderly crowds, however, are nowhere in sight. Instead, Reagan oversees a production number in which choreographed soldiers put on the show. *This Is The Army,* like most other films which Warner Brothers "premiered" during the war— *Captains Of The Clouds* (1942), *Wings For The Eagle* (1942), *Destination Tokyo* (1943), *Hollywood Canteen* (1944)—formed part of the effort that merged Hollywood's older "dream factory" role into its newer function as the nation's most important mouthpiece for wartime propaganda. When publicist Russell Birdwell proposed an old-style gala opening as a press preview for a 1943 Howard Hughes film, Hughes aide Noah Dietrich was warned against "the old-fashioned, pre-war, Hollywood version of a super-duper opening . . . something which all the major film companies gave up for patriotic (real or pseudo) reasons even before Pearl Harbor. This kind of fanfare *at this time* is splitting Howard open for some unpleasant press criticism."

Yet certain remnants of the old-style Hollywood titillation persisted even without lavish premieres. Pinup girl Betty Grable reportedly earned $800,000 a year during the war, making her quite possibly the highest paid woman in American history up to that time. And while Hollywood gave million-dollar legs to the boys overseas, it offered the best set of blue eyes around to the girls at home. An RKO Inter-department memo concerning the promotion of Frank Sinatra's first speaking-role film, *Higher and Higher* (1943), advised that "the logical, and biggest thing you can do to cash in on this freak's current phenomenal popularity, and grab unlimited nationwide space for 'Higher and Higher' is to hire fifty extras to tear him to pieces at the Pasadena station." Fifty women should be "primed to literally rip the clothes off Sinatra when he steps off the train," and while the singer and his agents were to be told nothing, the memo recommended leaking to the press that "hundreds of women have phoned the studio and railroad offices regarding the time of Sinatra's arrival, and that there is certain to be fireworks at the depot." Whether such antics took place is unclear, but the 1944 "Columbus Day riots" greeting Sinatra's New York City singing engagements suggested that dimmed premiere lights did not short-circuit the most highly charged currents of show business glamour during the War.

"Razzle Dazzle: Movie Premieres are Back!" headlined *Look* in 1947. Indeed, war's end brought back the bright lights and former gaieties. Movies opened in subject matter locales, stars embarked on the old-style premiere junkets, and military uniforms gave way to good old Parisian fashions as favored premiere attire. In 1948 the film industry awarded a special Oscar to Sid Grauman, the "master showman who raised the standard of motion picture exhibition to a high art," and in 1949, the Hollywood Chamber of Commerce gave him a testimonial banquet. Nevertheless, times had changed. Americans at home experienced much of the war through the films and newsreels projected through the movie-house lens, and the country was ready for a break. Having more than doubled during the War, revenues and attendance peaked in 1946, after which the films, stars, and premieres never recaptured their former prominence.

Hollywood, stodgy grande dame of American mass culture by the 1950s, yielded considerably to the newer energies of television and rock 'n' roll.

Having so brilliantly envisioned Hollywood's apocalyptic rupture, Nathaniel West seemingly overlooked its more prosaic absorption into America's civic realm, a process well under way by the time of his death in 1940. Perhaps West had not so much overestimated the emotionally turbulent dynamism of movie culture, as he had underestimated the capacity and determination of America's institutions to harness that power for their own goals. Hollywood's raw, carnivalesque style of the 1920s had posed little threat to the nation's most important interests. Indeed, the exotic splendor, sensual titillation, and even frenzied seduction promoted by the premieres were consistent with the needs of a burgeoning commodity capitalism. Yet by the 1930s, a divergence threatened to develop between Hollywood fantasy and the nation's new political values. Where the "conservative" 1920s had thrived amidst novelty and excess, the "liberal" New Deal years stressed mostly traditionalist civic norms in the cultural sphere. "Hollywood politics" of the late 1930s are usually addressed in terms of left-wing scriptwriters, Popular Front sympathizers, and antifascist leagues. Be that as it may, "premiere politics" suggested that certain potentially subversive forces within the very fantasy–reality dynamics of movie culture itself had by the late 1930s been quite successfully tamed by the rising tide of an often conservative, platinum blond all-Americanism. The carefully staged New Deal premieres, like so many of the films themselves, spoke to this new political reality.

Yet Hollywood, even when most victimized, as during the Cold War inquisitions, should hardly be seen as a purely passive partner in this process of politicization. Civic culture was drawn to the movies because of their potent, captivating allure, and that allure depended upon movie culture's artful blend of the real and the imagined. If the nation's political institutions were able to adapt the transporting energies of modern show business to their own purposes, that process of incorporation necessarily transformed all parties. Just as Franklin Roosevelt quickly discovered the advantages of a radio and media persona, American politics in the postwar era increasingly became captive to the culture of manipulated symbols, images, and glamorous make believe. From the Camelot mystique of the Kennedy left to the *Rambo* and *Star Wars* dreaming of the Reagan right, we continue to live that fantastic reality. Hollywood movie premieres cannot, of course, claim sole credit for this ambiguous legacy. But with their brilliant capacity to confuse the illusory with the real, they played their part. Their bright lights between the Wars should help guard against any dimming of our memory of those early years.

PART FIVE

THE GREAT DEPRESSION, 1929-1938

When the stock market crashed in October 1929, nobody in America had the slightest idea just how bad things were going to get. President Herbert Hoover quickly reassured the public that the stock market meltdown was a temporary phenomenon, that if Americans just maintained a sense of optimism and confidence, the crisis would soon pass. But it did not pass. An economic malaise soon afflicted the whole country. Stock and bond prices, agricultural prices, real estate values, and foreign trade plummeted. Business and bank failures skyrocketed, as did the number of personal bankruptcies, foreclosures, and layoffs. In 1932 the unemployment rate reached 25 percent. One in every four people was out of work in an age when the safety net of unemployment compensation, food stamps, housing subsidies, and welfare did not exist. America was no longer the "land of plenty." Homeless, hungry people were everywhere. Whole towns sprouted in the garbage dumps and landfills of major cities as the poorest of the poor scratched out livings on the leftovers of others. When the election of 1932 rolled around, President Hoover and the Republicans did not stand a chance. Franklin D. Roosevelt was elected president of the United States, and he enjoyed huge Democratic majorities in the House and Senate.

President Roosevelt then launched the New Deal, a dramatic shift in the nature of public policy, using the federal government to provide jobs for those who could not find work on their own. In the process, Roosevelt became one of the most popular presidents in American history, at least to the working classes. But in spite of his willingness to take risks and use the power of the government in unprecedented ways, Roosevelt had a difficult time bringing the economy around. The depression was troublingly re-silient, succumbing only to the massive government spending increases of World War II.

The Great Depression had an enormous impact on American life and culture, shaping the way an entire generation viewed their lives and fu-tures. For a country worshiping the ideas of individual opportunity and economic progress, the Great Depression was profoundly disillusioning. Hoover's 1929 prediction that there would soon be "two chickens in every pot and a car in every garage" became a bad joke, repeated endlessly by down-and-out men and women whose only hope was keeping body and soul together. The most enduring images of the Great Depression were pictures of despair—grown men with stone faces selling apples on city streets; embarrassed men, hats in hands, standing at back doors begging for food or work; broken women sweeping dust bowl dirt out of their living rooms; uprooted families crossing the country for new beginnings; hoboes riding the rails; and auctions, everywhere auctions, where men and women lost everything they owned.

17. The Election of 1932

DAVID BURNER

Herbert Hoover was optimistic when he took the oath of office as president of the United States in March 1929. He predicted that a permanent end to poverty was just around the corner, that the nation's economic future was bright, that the time would soon come when there was a "car in every garage and a chicken in every pot."

Herbert Hoover was not much of a prophet. Six months after his optimistic inaugural address, the stock market crashed, plunging the United States into the Great Depression. Unemployment skyrocketed, reaching an unprecedented 25 percent by 1932. Herbert Hoover became the scapegoat. When 1932 rolled around, Herbert Hoover did not have a prayer for reelection. In the following essay, David Burner describes the events surrounding the election of 1932.

By 1932 many Americans believed their country to be crumbling fast. Brigadier General George Van Horn Moseley, deputy to Chief of Staff Douglas MacArthur, and a trusted confidant of Secretary of War Hurley and other prominent military figures, wanted something done.

Disturbed by what he perceived as Hoover's pacifist tendencies and inadequate leadership, General Moseley on May 24, 1932, wrote the journalist Herbert Corey—at least one other copy went out, to Charles Dawes —about how improvident and unready for emergencies Americans were. The numbers of "drifters, dope fiends, unfortunates and degenerates of all kinds" were growing. Without naming them, Moseley cited the testimony of a prominent senator who called for a dictatorship and a New York minister who suggested "military reinforcement" for civilian rule. Moseley recommended as a model the Spanish–American war experience in the Philippines. There the military had "ample authority" and "utter simplicity in government," free of a "multiplicity of laws, intricate procedures . . . weak . . . officials . . . [who] complicated the administration of justice." The military could simply ship undesirables "beyond the seas." He urged that a similar power be invested in government to

gather up the leading malefactors [including] important public officials when circumstances required and send them, let me suggest, to one of the sparsely inhabited islands of the Hawaiian group not suitable for growing sugar. On such an island, in a fine climate, they could stew in their own filth until their cases were finally disposed of with the return of normal conditions. We would not worry about the delays in the due process of law. . . . With carefully selected military governors installed in all our states and the District of Columbia, great economies could also be effected, for graft could be eliminated. . . . The return to normal conditions . . . might be on a competitive basis. . . .

Whether Moseley's letter came to Hoover's attention is not known, but similar calls for a "man on horseback" to set the nation right were familiar enough by the summer of 1932.*

*On March 7, 1932, "Bloody Monday," four demonstrators had been killed by police on the outskirts of Detroit—this "Ford Hunger March" set the tone for events later that year.

Even at the Republican Convention, held in Chicago from Flag Day, June 14, to the sixteenth, there was a lack of enthusiasm for Hoover's renomination. Progressive Republicans were hostile, the old guard unhappy. Colonel Robert McCormick's Chicago *Tribune*, repelled by Hoover's internationalist tendencies, declared it mandatory that the convention "look elsewhere" for a nominee. Dissident factions had talked of Coolidge and Senator Dwight Morrow of New Jersey, but Morrow had died late in 1931 and Coolidge had little strength. An incumbent President in control of patronage held the renomination for the asking. After a debate that lasted through much of the second night, the prohibition plank straddle won by 681 to 472 votes after 40 percent had voted for unrestricted repeal. Each day of the convention began with a clergyman speaking a prayer at the top of his lungs into a battery of microphones, photographers all the while perched above him on chairs snapping their bulbs. Floodlights for moving pictures threw the scene into an even brighter glare, and dozens of typewriters clicked away, recording the words.

The keynote speech, from Senator Lester Dickinson of Iowa, was addressed to a hall one-third empty; it became much emptier as his speech progressed because loudspeakers garbled "Hell-raising Dick's" words. Though an ardent dry, he omitted all mention of prohibition. Dickinson credited Hoover for speeding up public works projects but criticized the Democrats for recommending additional such ventures. Bertrand Snell, the permanent chairman, thanked God that Hoover had avoided "the deadly pit of the dole."

On the third day "that glorious Californian, Herbert Hoover," was placed in nomination by "Plain Joe" Scott of Los Angeles. Bands struck up "Over There" to recall Belgian relief, and the crowd demonstrated for more than twenty minutes. The display ended with Klieg lights, a blurred recording of Hoover's voice, slides of the President shown at both ends of the auditorium, and the thoughtless playing of "California, here I come, right back where I started from."

Dr. Joseph I. France, a former senator from Maryland, was offered as an alternative nominee; on the convention floor the microphone went dead and he was dragged off when he tried to withdraw in favor of Coolidge. A Hoover seconder, Roscoe Simmons of Chicago, added an unusual endorsement by Abraham Lincoln brought "fresh" from the Lincoln Memorial: "if you see him, speak to Hoover for me and say that his road is the one I traveled." Another seconder, Snell, compared Hoover to Washington, because both were engineers. After renominating Hoover by 1,126½ of 1,154 votes on the first and only ballot, the delegates grudgingly chose the bone-dry, seventy-one-year-old Vice-President Curtis as his running mate. Two less colorful candidates could scarcely be imagined. No picture of Hoover graced the convention hall.

The 1932 Hoover campaign staff was considerably different from that of 1928; Jeremiah Milbank, the Wall Street philanthropist, remained in his earlier position, that of Eastern campaign treasurer. Everett Sanders served as the fourth chairman of the national committee under Hoover. Silas Strawn of Chicago was campaign manager for the West and Felix Herbert of Rhode Island managed the East. Old friends George Akerson and Henry

J. Allen helped with publicity. The Chicago headquarters reported raising about $2.5 million, slightly more than the Democrats.

Behind the campaign stood a Republican organization with some years of troubles. David Hinshaw's *Washington,* an official Republican newsletter, had died in three strokes. For the first issue, it was disclosed, he had hired a Democratic printer, and then he dwelt at length on Hoover's "handicaps," notably an "inability to talk in the political vernacular." For the second, Hinshaw employed a non-union printer and Hoover ordered that the 5 tons of newsprint be destroyed. The third issue could not overcome the poor publicity generated by the first two. Succeeding the unfortunate Hubert Work as national chairman in 1929, Claudius Huston—once the head of a small business college—had collected large sums of money from sources he could not always recall, disbursing funds to people he could not remember. A Presbyterian and Mason, he had served as chairman of the Republican National Committee's Ways and Means Committee. When it became public knowledge that he had welched on an $80,000 poker debt and illegally used the funds of the lobby, the Tennessee River Improvement Association, to speculate in the stock market, Huston resigned. The next chairman, Senator Simeon Fess, allowed his assistant Robert Lucas to enter another man named George Norris in the Nebraska primary in an unscrupulous effort to unseat the progressive Senator Norris. Edward Sanders, Fess's successor in 1932, presided over a party in disarray.

Not long after the nomination an army of World War I veterans descended on the small Southern city of Washington. At first not much attention had been paid to reports of some three hundred unemployed veterans in Union Pacific freight cars rocking and swaying from Portland, Oregon, to Pocatello, Idaho. Some accompanied by their families, they all were headed for Washington seeking congressional approval for early payment of a soldier's bonus not scheduled for distribution until 1945. But this "Bonus Army" picked up fresh recruits at almost every city in the spring of 1932 and finally became national news when the B & O Railroad tried to stop it at the "Battle of East Saint Louis." Local railroad union leaders averted bloodshed by moving truckloads of men, women, and children across Illinois to the Indiana border. Then state governors hurried the band as swiftly as possible past Indiana, Pennsylvania, and Maryland until it reached the District of Columbia, there to meet other veterans from every state in the Union, a total of more than twenty thousand people.

General Moseley had prepared an order for Hoover to instruct federal troops to turn back the marchers before they entered the District. Secretary Hurley, according to Moseley, endorsed the plan, but "Mr. Hoover declined to execute it, calling it a 'temporary disease.'" Despite the entreaties of prominent Republicans, the President refused to follow the example of Grover Cleveland's administration, which thirty-eight years before had stopped the marchers of Coxey's army with federal injunctions. And once the veterans settled in abandoned buildings and on the largest site, Anacostia Flats in Maryland, Hoover quietly provided the District police commissioner, Pelham Glassford, with clothing, beds, tents, medical supplies, kitchen equipment, and army food free or at cost. Hoover wrote in early June that he expected no disturbance of the peace in Washington: "except for a few New York agitators these are perfectly peaceable people. . . ."

Like Hoover, Governor Franklin D. Roosevelt of New York disapproved early payment of the bonus, and offered his state's veterans both transportation home and guaranteed employment. Congressman LaGuardia and Senator Norris pointed out that many of the veterans were not poor people and deserved no special treatment. All of the President's cabinet opposed the bonus. Hoover had effectively centralized all veterans' activities in a new Veterans Administration under Frank T. Hines, and he had generously written or endorsed numerous pension and hospitalization bills for them. The President's disability bill for veterans was a model of generosity. By 1933 veterans' benefits accounted for one-fourth of the national budget. He had, however, made a dramatic trip to Detroit the previous October to give an eleven-minute speech to the American Legion Convention opposing early payment of the bonus and the Legion's idea of reinstituting a Council of National Defense with dictatorial powers. The Bonus Bill passed the House on June 15, 1932; but two days later the Senate soundly defeated it, 62 to 18. Next, Hoover initiated federal loans for transportation home to any veteran who applied. But some ten thousand stayed on, waiting for something to happen.

On July 9, some 250 Californians arrived, led by a navy veteran, Roy W. Robertson, who camped out with his men on the Capitol lawn. While in the service Robertson had broken his neck falling out of a hammock; he wore a leather brace supported by a tall steel column rising almost a foot above his shoulders, giving the eerie impression of a man with his head perpetually in a noose. For three days and four nights Robertson's men took turns slowly walking single file in a "Death March" vigil around the Capitol building. His head held high in the rigid brace, Robertson was a study in determination. While an angry mob of fellow veterans under Commander Walter W. Waters occupied the building's steps, Congress adjourned and its members escaped by subterranean passageways. Now the focus shifted to 1600 Pennsylvania Avenue. Hoover had earlier ordered guards not to arrest veterans or Communists picketing the White House, and he favored Glassford's policy of restraint. But after the siege of Congress the Secret Service urged the selective arrest of militant leaders, and Hoover went along when small groups of Communists attempted to draw the veterans into a bloody confrontation at the White House.

General Douglas MacArthur stood ready for trouble with a large regular army force under the command of Moseley. MacArthur personally commanded the most impressive display of military might that Washington had seen in many years. On July 28 the administration forced the eviction of veterans from a small downtown area of government buildings scheduled for demolition. A riot ensued between a gathering of as many as five thousand veterans and fewer than eight hundred police. One veteran was dead, another lay dying. The police commissioner, the District of Columbia commissioners informed Hoover, had concurred that army troops were necessary; Glassford later denied having made any such request.

MacArthur ordered his troops to assemble at the Ellipse behind the White House. Hoover specifically directed the general only to move the rioting veterans out of the business district and back to their camps. His staff aide, Major Dwight D. Eisenhower, was shocked when the Chief of Staff, resplendent in full military regalia, appeared personally to take command, although the President had ordered MacArthur to get his instructions from Glassford. Major George Patton was also on hand. Seeing "revolution in the air," MacArthur used cavalrymen with drawn sabers and infantry with tear gas, dispersing both veterans and spectators. After the downtown area was cleared, he stopped at the bridge leading to Anacostia for his men to have dinner. Ignoring the President, who issued contrary orders on at least two occasions, MacArthur and his troops then crossed over and the whole camp became ablaze with light. Setting fire to their own huts was a final symbol of the veterans' defiance. Eisenhower recalled "a pitiful scene, those ragged, discouraged people burning their own little things." Soldiers and District police fired the remaining, often unsanitary, empty huts. Fleeing the capital, the veterans became refugees from an apparently heartless government.

Hoover might have chosen to speak with representatives of the veterans, making an effort to reassure them of his concern. He had been notably restrained and tolerant about Communist demonstrations outside the White House in 1929 and 1931, and in January 1932 had provided army quarters for twelve thousand unemployed workers who came to protest. He met with their leader, Father Cox, at the White House. In 1928 he had even apologized that his *American Individualism,* written just after the war, was "a little out of date as it was written when we were somewhat more exercised over socialistic and communistic movements than we need to be today." Once the bonus marchers had been driven from town, he could have refrained from noisy propaganda about their iniquities. But he did not; and in the meantime the public had the memory of burning shacks within sight of the Capitol steps. The Bonus Army would become one of the most compelling stories of the coming presidential campaign.

The Bonus Army had posed a problem, not only for the government but for veterans in their crowded, unsanitary encampment, that any administration might eventually have responded to with some force. But why Hoover, who did upbraid MacArthur privately, nonetheless let him get away with insubordination we may only surmise. Part of the reason, perhaps, was a fear that firing the general might upset the country further. Personality, too, may have figured. MacArthur, as Moseley pointed out, "was a prima donna and insisted upon occupying the center of the stage; but he was the best performer, and that was the place for him." Hoover, not being one himself, could have had a certain grudging respect for a dramatic man of action. He was impressed that the army operations resulted in no casualties. Both men made much of Communist and criminal elements among the Bonus Army. MacArthur reported discovering machine guns and dynamite in the camps. These were, so it appeared, dangerous times: a plot to blow up Congress was discovered later in the month, and the President-elect narrowly escaped assassination during the interregnum. But Hoover's subsequent attitude toward the marchers appeared to be a part of a defensive, hard-tempered shift to the right as the presidential campaign progressed.

The Democrats and the liberal press portrayed Hoover's cruelty and ineptness in burning out the innocent veterans. *The Nation,* in an article entitled "Tear-Gas, Bayonets, and Votes," announced: "Hoover's campaign for reelection was launched Thursday, July 28, at Pennsylvania Avenue and 3rd Street, with 4 troops of cavalry, 4 companies of infantry, a mounted machine-gun squadron, six whippet tanks, 300 city policemen and a squad of Secret Service men and Treasury Agents." The customarily conservative American Legion denounced his actions. Much newsprint was devoted to the death of Bernie Myers, age eleven weeks, of tear gas. The infant had been diagnosed as having pneumonia by a District hospital; his parents, however, had refused to leave the child under medical care. A veteran's ear was supposedly severed by a cavalry saber, but the shorn man was never photographed or located. In the minds of most analysts, whatever doubt had remained about the outcome of the presidential election was now gone: Hoover was going to lose. The Bonus Army was his final failure, his symbolic end.

When Franklin Roosevelt heard about the rout of the Bonus Army, he turned to Felix Frankfurter and grinned: "Well, Felix, this will elect me." Roosevelt, named presidential candidate at the Chicago Democratic Convention a month before, had not won the nomination effortlessly. Some two hundred Eastern delegates who had favored Al smith lost in a fight with their old enemy from the 1924 convention, William Gibbs McAdoo. When the Californian delivered his state's votes and the nomination to FDR on the fourth ballot, someone remarked that McAdoo had buried the hatchet—in Al Smith's neck. Feelings ran so deep that Smith's advisor Belle Moskowitz suggested to a Hoover aide that the President should campaign first in the East. When Smith did speak for Roosevelt in Newark, he stuck to lambasting the "bigots" who had voted against him in 1928. Nor was Roosevelt—who in his Acceptance Address asked for a 25 percent cut in federal expenditures—widely regarded as a strong candidate. The choice of the alleged radical, John Nance Garner, as running mate also raised doubts about the strength of the ticket; Garner had opposed Roosevelt for the nomination.

But it gradually dawned on the public that this optimistic Roosevelt had survived the cruelest adversity in his own life—and might be able to overcome the nation's as well. His state had been in the forefront of those combating the Depression; in August 1931 its legislature passed his Temporary Emergency Relief Act. The New Yorker began his campaign before the convention closed: with his family he flew to Chicago, battling storms along the Great Lakes in a Ford Trimotor, to accept the nomination. Reflecting on the performance and the temper of the electorate, the Brooklyn boss James McCooey said that Roosevelt could go to Europe for the campaign and still win. Instead, to demonstrate his good health and vigor, FDR set out on a nationwide railway campaign trip and spoke sixty times, not including whistlestops where he jollied the crowds with local pleasantries. As Republican Senator Hiram Johnson of California remarked of his appearances there: "his very pleasing personality was quite attractive . . . enormous crowds . . . cordially gave him pretty general approval." Johnson complained of Hoover: "The money we so lavishly appropriated through the RFC . . . has not filtered through to those who most need it. I am afraid we began fertilizing the tree at the top and forgot the roots." Roosevelt's talks, vague in substance and dynamic in tone, went well in a Depression campaign; and he spoke effectively in numerous radio broadcasts.

The two candidates had some remarkable similarities. Both had been protégés of Woodrow Wilson. Both advocated rigid economy in government spending. Both were capitalists, Roosevelt probably being the wealthier of the two. Yet FDR had intangible virtues that, at least in retrospect, appear appropriate to a candidate in hard times: a confidence and ease and grace, the manners of inherited wealth, that could awaken trust and a sense of security within the electorate. Hoover, the self-made success and the technician, could not warm his audience. Ironically, though, he was capable of considerable personal warmth: Stimson remarked, after Hoover attended the funeral of William Castle's daughter, that "he is very considerate about these things and always goes out of his way to show human feeling and to make members of his administration feel that they belong to him." Roosevelt's presidential successes against the Depression would be in large part consistent with the character of his campaign: they were in essence political successes, a composing of diverse factions, in Congress and within the public, into a political community. If, of course, it had been Roosevelt who had presided over the beginnings of the Depression, and in consequence Hoover the victor in 1932, a historian could be pointing to Hoover's clipped competence as an asset, giving the electorate the promise of coldly sophisticated leadership. At a moment when the incumbent President was on his way out, any number of styles might have served his opponent; and FDR had a good one.

The Depression had converted the special virtues of Hoover in the 1928 campaign into liabilities four years later. Given the needs of the Depression, war relief no longer counted in the political scales—except as a source of embarrassment to Hoover. To rise from poverty was in good times a testimony to the working order of the system. In bad times, when people do not find themselves in control of their lives, they perhaps wanted a leader from a different and secure background—a Roosevelt who could relax and add grace. Roosevelt also appeared to be the national figure who could best unite rural and urban America against the threats of depression. Perhaps hard times, which mocked everything Hoover had worked for, awakened and validated in Roosevelt the right style for the right time. Like his cousin Theodore Roosevelt, he possessed a Burkean sense of a community's innate character—the sources of its energy, morale, equilibrium— that Hoover the progressive technocrat always had lacked. The astute politician, like a skillful clinician, senses the complex of elements needed to maintain the health of the organism. Hoover, as the historian Erick McKitrick has remarked, was prepared to let the most serious damage occur without quite realizing what the conservative's priorities were. He often faltered when he had to act in the medium of representative government.

In March 1931 Hoover vetoed the Muscle Shoals Bill and hoped that his strong words would be a good early opening to the campaign. He even believed the public would enthusiastically support his stand against the Bonus Army. In St. Paul just before the election, the press reported his comment: "Thank God we still have some officials in Washington that can hold out against a mob." Charles Michaelson, for three years the Democrats' director of campaign publicity, made the most of Hoover's gaffes and his policy of silence. To Michaelson, politics was a game played for power; to the naïve Hoover it was a solemn obligation for public service. John Nance Garner said: "It was Michaelson's job to whittle Hoover down to our size." Hoover's failures became much larger assets to the Democrats than all of Roosevelt's promises.

If Hoover's 1928 campaign speeches had seemed dull, his omnibus talks of 1932, crammed with statistics, were even duller and more platitudinous. The long, badly constructed sentences employed vocabulary on the order of *sisyphean, vacuous, supervened, attenuated, palpably.* Hoover delivered his talks in a flat, metallic voice. The speeches were unrelievedly conservative, a defense of the record, not a plan for reconstruction.

His acceptance speech delivered in Washington on his birthday, August 11, reads like a primer in economics. There was almost no applause at the end, wrote a British journalist, "due to the dispiriting influence of Mr. Hoover's personality, his unprepossessing exterior, his sour, puckered face of a bilious baby, his dreary, nasal monotone reading interminably, and for the most part inaudibly, from a typescript without a single inflection of a voice or gesture to relieve the tedium." In Des Moines on October 4 he addressed an audience of hand-picked Republicans on farm problems while two thousand demonstrators led by Milo Reno stood outside "to let the world know that there's folks in Iowa who's sour'n hell on Hoover." Not only did he fail to give the support he had been considering for the domestic allotment plan, but he repudiated the price-stabilizing provisions of the Agricultural Marketing Act. Years later the retired President told Charles Lindbergh the Des Moines speech had been a mistake; in politics one "learned not to say things just because they are true." The only personal portion of the talk—boiled down from a weighty seventy-one pages—came at the outset: Hoover's comment on the depression under way at the time of his Iowa birth and the Iowan's self-sufficiency then. But the present, he said somberly, "could be so much worse that these days now . . . would look like veritable prosperity." In Cleveland he bored an audience with a dreary account of the tariff. One *bon mot* on the tariff lightened the mass, the remark that Roosevelt's was "the dreadful position of the chameleon on the Scotch plaid." Hoover also took a swipe at the leaderless, irresponsible Democratic House for holding up passage of the national system of Home Loan Banks and thereby causing hundreds of thousands of unnecessary foreclosures. In Detroit an angry mob met Hoover at the railroad station. Numerous accounts state that the exhausted President shivered and trembled while delivering some of these talks.

Finally, in a vigorous speech at Indianapolis on October 28, Hoover took the offensive and sarcastically rebutted charges made by FDR. And he attacked an "atrocious slur": Roosevelt "implies that it is the function of the party in power to control the Supreme Court." On Halloween, in an overlong harangue at Madison Square Garden, he continued the attack, bravely repeating his promise of 1928 to banish poverty. If tariff protection were to be removed, he warned, paraphrasing William Jennings Bryan's "Cross of

Gold" speech: "the grass will grow in streets of a hundred cities, a thousand towns; the weeds will overrun the fields of millions of farms . . . their churches and schoolhouses will decay."* It was a contemptible appeal to fear. (The Democrats jovially responded in 1936 by driving an enormous harvester through the streets of Philadelphia.) Secretary of Agriculture Hyde unleashed a similar diatribe: "If Roosevelt is elected the homes and lives of one hundred million American people might be in jeopardy." According to Stimson, Hoover stimulated fears of what FDR might do because it was his only way to overcome feelings of hatred for himself.

Between June and October, as Hoover's candidacy faltered, considerable economic improvement was taking place. Stock prices increased by more than 50 percent; bank failures and applications for RFC loans declined. That August the Home Loan Bank System, with $125 million from the RFC, began to buy delinquent mortgages held by hard-pressed building and loan associations. But the requirement inserted by Speaker Garner in a funding bill, that all RFC loans be made public, may have been responsible for part of the drop in applications. In October repayments on previous RFC loans declined. And commercial lending by banks had not revived enough that industrial recovery could begin.

"Reemployment" schemes were advanced in 1932 by such varied business leaders as Julius Barnes, Bernard Baruch, and Owen Young. Hoover picked up parts of their programs when he employed the Banking and Industrial Committees of the twelve Federal Reserve banks to encourage the use of credit opportunities and so promote employment. "Enlightened self interest if not patriotism," said Walter Teagle, head of a Share-the-Work plan, required support of the scheme. Business periodicals backed the various reemployment plans. After the election, Hoover continued to press the program to make "purchasing power . . . confident and effective in speeding business recovery."

If there was one issue that could remotely compete with that of the Depression itself, it was the emotional and symbolic one of prohibition. The campaign blurred it. Attorney General Mitchell claimed that Hoover's administration had brought better federal enforcement, but observed that many states had abandoned or repealed their own "little Volstead Acts." The Republican platform's "dry, wet, damp" plank was the same, essentially, as that proposed by Al Smith in 1928 and by the Wickersham Report: a federal ban on the saloon, along with a reservation to each state of the right to regulate the sale of liquor within its borders. At the time of the plank's adoption Roosevelt was continuing to fudge the issue, and the Democratic Convention had not met. In his 1932 Acceptance Address Hoover admitted that prohibition had failed as the solution to the liquor problem. In 1932 the Republicans, like the Democrats in 1924 and 1928, were caught between the irreconcilable drys and the implacable wets. The Democrats called for outright repeal.

One measure of the President's troubles was that the state of Maine went Democratic by a close margin in its balloting of early September.

---

*Bryan had warned: "destroy our farms and the grass will grow in the streets of every city in the country."

Another was his loss of favor in the black community. Democrats reminded Negro voters of his "lily-white" delegates in 1928, his nomination of Judge Parker to the Supreme Court, and the army's segregation of black Gold Star mothers on their voyage to Europe to visit their sons' graves. FDR assured an integrated audience that his symbol of the forgotten man applied "absolutely and impartially" to all blacks as well as whites. For the first time the Republican party lost the support of most of the black press. Hoover would win a clear majority of the black voters; but 1932 forecast the loss to the Republican party of a once-faithful constituency.

On returning to California just before the election, Hoover's train was stopped near Beloit, Wisconsin, where a man had been found pulling up spikes. The President's car was pelted with rotten eggs in Elko, Nevada. The state's governor refused to appear publicly with Hoover; a senator did so and lost by five hundred votes. When Hoover reached Stanford he was described as a "walking corpse." One telegram to him suggested: "Vote for Roosevelt and make it unanimous." Hoover's candidacy was moving not even toward a decent and respectful repudiation but toward something ugly. As Elizabeth Stevenson, the popular historian, put it: his "reputation was murdered publicly, noisily, and painfully—as a thing once loved." The primitive impulse to personify misfortune was easy to understand, but there was a darker side to the hostility toward the President.

From 1930 to 1932, with the worsening of the Depression, a number of muckracking books had appeared, written by an assortment of critics ranging from honest radicals to dollar chasers, that purported to uncover wrongdoing in Hoover's business career: checks forged, workers exploited and chained to stakes in the sun, and other completely unsubstantiated charges. The books include *The Rise of Herbert Hoover* (1932) by Walter Liggett (the best of the lot), John Knox's *The Great Mistake* (1930), John Hamill's *The Strange Career of Mr. Hoover Under Two Flags* (1931; Hamill confessed under oath that this book was largely fabricated), James J. O'Brien's *Hoover's Millions and How He Made Them* (1932), and Clement Wood's *Herbert Hoover, an American Tragedy* (1932). Liggett—who was murdered while muckraking in Minneapolis during the 1930's—was writing in part from animosity developed out of his own work in Russian relief, which ran counter to Hoover's; O'Brien and Hamill worked together, financed perhaps by William Kenney, the New York Democrat; Samuel Roth, a convicted dealer in pornography, published Hamill's and Wood's books. Hamill's was sixth on Macy's non-fiction bestseller list. Some liberal journals like *The Nation* recommended books of this sort to their readers, and *The New Republic* said they must be answered. The scholar Harry Elmer Barnes was not untypical of certain liberal reviewers when he remarked that Hamill was "appalling if true and very likely true." At the height of the campaign Senator Norris's secretary repeatedly recommended that correspondents read Hamill and Knox: "Perhaps these books are in your local library." Democrats disagreed over whether to ignore such material. The Democratic Speakers' Handbook urged comment on opportune occasion about Hoover's "former partnerships which contracted cheap coolie labor in South African mines."

Hoover lost the election by 22,810,000 to 15,759,000 votes, receiving about 41 percent of the popular vote.* Roosevelt carried all but six states, winning 472 electoral votes to 59 for Hoover. But some of Roosevelt's states went for him by margins of less than 3 percent: Michigan, New Jersey, Wisconsin, Kansas, New Hampshire, Maine, Wyoming, and Delaware. In Congress 60 Democrats and 35 Republicans would sit in the Senate, 310 Democrats and 117 Republicans in the House.

Time labeled Hoover "President Reject." The event deserved a more dignified observation, for Hoover, a good but not guiltless man, had struggled against impossible odds. He blamed Wall Street for supporting the opposition "financially and otherwise. They opposed us because we were urging banking, public utility, and other reforms." He also blamed Congress for "the deliberate delay to recovery for purposes of the election." He should further have blamed his own inept campaign. At one point Stimson had to send researchers to New York so he could deliver a speech on Roosevelt's gubernatorial career. In 1932, as after World War I, incumbents in many countries were losing reelection. James Scullin, prime minister of Australia, served as the closest parallel. Taking office in October 1929 after a sweeping electoral victory, he along with his party was hurled from power twenty-six months later. At the December 1932 Gridiron Club dinner, Hoover managed to accept his defeat philosophically: "as nearly as I can learn, we did not have enough votes on our side." But for more than a generation Hoover and the Depression would serve as the Democrats' equivalent of the "bloody shirt" of Reconstruction. One of the first measures introduced in the December "lame duck" session of Congress was Congressman Lewis McFadden's to impeach Hoover for declaring the moratorium; eleven House members opposed tabling the motion. One ditty summed up the widespread feeling toward Hoover:

> O 'Erbert lived over the h'ocean
> O 'Erbert lived over the sea;
> O 'Oo will go down to the h'ocean,
> And drown 'Erbert 'Oover for me?

Just before and after the election, Nevada underwent a crisis that foreshadowed the events of Hoover's last months in office. Suffering from undiversified agricultural investments, the state banks had looked to the RFC for help. But the agency demanded very secure collateral for short-term loans. As a result, frequent and repeated requests were made to the RFC; upon refusal, the entire banking system shut down for some six weeks beginning October 31. Even after reopening—with the largest banking complex suspending operations—the state remained in desperate shape. The University of Nevada, for want of public funds lost in the crisis, was ready to close. It was probably the Nevada collapse as much as anything else that convinced Hoover of the need to use his option to extend the RFC's life beyond its one-year limit, and the RFC that its loans must be made

---

*Apropos of the election James Thurber wrote in *The New Yorker:* "Herbert Hoover is a great engineer and he should be released from burdens he doesn't understand in order to go back to his real work. Anybody who built the Great Wall of China, to name only one of his achievements, should not be President of this country."

more flexible. Only in Roosevelt's Hundred Days did authority come to loan to states directly.

In the succeeding months, as more and more banks across the nation closed while others stayed shakily open from day to day, they became the focus of a large economic failure. From twelve to fourteen million workers, nearly one-fourth of the labor force, had no jobs. Many farmers lost their lands or could not sell their produce at a tolerable profit. Hoover blamed the troubles on the proposed New Deal. In the long interregnum he sought FDR's cooperation toward balancing the budget, reorganizing the government, and changing the rules controlling banking and bankruptcy; more broadly he wanted to work with Roosevelt to achieve a public mood of confidence. Meanwhile the country floundered under a lame-duck Congress and a President who used his veto power repeatedly.

Another element complicated the situation: Hoover's own alarm at the New Deal's potential for radical mischief. He thought Roosevelt ill-qualified for the presidency and ill-informed about most pressing economic problems. New Dealers, he worried, might depreciate the dollar or experiment with deficit finance, controlled prices, or direct relief. Hoover was convinced that such measures would only aggravate depression, not cure it. So he set out during the interregnum to confine the scope of future New Deal reform by using the complexities of international finance, a field he thought he understood. Specifically, if the United States gave concessions for a promise to stay on the gold standard, the Democrats could not resort to monetary tricks without breaking treaties. A brazen, somewhat pig-headed effort—the people already had rejected his leadership— Hoover nonetheless pushed ahead. His was the patriotism of a higher order, he thought, for rescuing an unsuspecting country from an irresponsible man possessed of dangerous ideas.

From the time of his appointment to the World War Debt Commission, Hoover had been of all the members most willing to consider an easing of terms. After the election he thought of arguing for revision of debts as a method of reflating the economy, but Stimson and Mills dissuaded him. Hoover signaled a willingness to negotiate with Britain and France prior to the December payment, which allowed the work begun at Lausanne to proceed. On the issue of war debts he and the President-elect soon found themselves apart.

En route by train to Washington on the Sunday after the election, the President sent a telegram from Yuma, Arizona, to Hyde Park to inform FDR that Britain and most of America's other debtors had requested a review of war debts and a postponement of their December 15 payment. Hoover had earlier delayed these requests for fear of disturbing the presidential election. He asked FDR to a personal conference to discuss debts, disarmament, and the forthcoming World Economic Conference. The letter implied that the causes of the Depression were global, and Roosevelt correctly responded only in the most general terms to what looked like a more calculated political overture than Hoover wanted to realize.

At a meeting between the two men at the White House on November 22, Hoover tried to interest Roosevelt in the idea of jointly reconstituting the World War Debt Commission and softening the terms of payment. FDR did not reject the plan outright, and Hoover was led to think he approved.

Actually, compromising on the debts would have brought more risk than Roosevelt could afford of alienating Democratic congressional leaders. To the President, FDR's understanding of the problem appeared superficial. And he disliked Roosevelt's companion, Professor Raymond Moley of Columbia University, thinking him pompous and surmising that he had obtained his understanding of war debts from a recent *Saturday Evening Post* article. Hoover, however, was himself to blame for Moley's presence by having insisted that Secretary Mills be present. Hoover told Stimson they had educated "a very ignorant," and as he expressed it, "a well-meaning young man." Roosevelt did reveal himself at the meeting to be amenable to the principle of joint or mutual action: he asked the President in a moment of private conversation whether Hoover would support the domestic allotment plan for farming. Hoover said he would look at Roosevelt's version of the plan; but he was doubtful. According to John Nance Garner's biography, Garner, Senator Robinson, and Hoover favored some joint legislation to be enacted during the interregnum, but Roosevelt would not allow any.

A much more cordial meeting took place on January 9, 1933, between Roosevelt and Stimson, who would in 1940 join FDR's administration as Secretary of War. Roosevelt endorsed the Stimson Doctrine and Hoover's arms embargo message to Congress. Stimson in return agreed to express Roosevelt's views to foreign powers where possible. The Secretary of State obtained, he thought, Roosevelt's permission to negotiate an exchange of economic concessions: in return for canceling war debts, the United States would gain tariff concessions in Europe and Britain would return to the gold standard. Plans for just such a world economic conference were under way. Stimson remained in the background as advisor as the new administration came in, arranging another meeting between the departing President and his successor.

Roosevelt stopped in Washington on his way to Warm Springs, Georgia, on January 20, 1933. It was a dramatic session; even a last-minute wire from a diplomat overseas was rushed into the meeting. Frank Freidel, Roosevelt's biographer, has pointed out that the question of war debts was connected to that of the gold standard. At this January meeting, Hoover, committed to gold, raised the strategy of using the debts as a means of getting Britain to go back on the standard. He hoped that a United States commitment to gold would confine those New Deal proposals for a government-manipulated economy. But Roosevelt understandably wished to keep himself free on the gold issue. Yet he authorized the Hoover administration to open talks with major European powers about war debts and the coming World Economic Conference. No unified program came about. The question, Hoover had declared to Stimson, was whether the United States would take a courageous part in stabilizing the world economic situation. Roosevelt appeared to want only narrowly focused discussions on debts with the British, not the "best brains of both nations" going to work for "weeks and months." Nor was Roosevelt willing to write to the French asking for the December payment of their war debts, left unpaid perhaps because of his own inadvertent statements. The fault probably lay with the President, however, for throwing Roosevelt into the public spotlight. Informal, private conversations would have been a fairer, more effective way of testing Roosevelt's sincerity and finding their grounds of mutual concern and interest. The spectacle of misunderstanding between the two men, Walter Lippmann observed, was a bad example to the world.

Later in January the banking crisis quickened as major institutions throughout the country began to close. Near panic came in the final week of February, when banks lost over $73 million in deposits. The RFC could no longer cope with the cash demands, and state after state placed restrictions on withdrawals. Much of what FDR did subsequently—the bank holiday, the FDIC guarantee of $5000 of customer deposits, the Emergency Banking Act—was to implement plans Hoover and his advisors had articulated in this troubled period but lacked the political power to carry out.

Some of the worst trouble came in Michigan during early February. Henry Ford at first gave the RFC assurance that he would not withdraw $12.5 million of deposits from the Guardian Detroit Union banks. In an interview with Secretary of Commerce Roy Chapin and Arthur Ballantine, however, Ford said that if he had given the impression he would freeze his deposits, he "had not fully understood" and in any case "had changed his mind." When told of the consequences to small depositors, he replied: "Let them fail! Let everybody fail!" *He* would start over. Senator James Couzens would not use his personal fortune to save the Guardian banks and hastened collapse by demanding better security for RFC loans. The progressive Couzens wanted to help citizens directly and saw no reason to save unsound banks. Hoover was disgusted: "If 800,000 small depositors in my home town could be saved by lending 3 percent of my fortune, I certainly would do it." On February 13, however, Couzens offered to back half of such a loan, but Ford refused to do likewise. As a result, the governor closed all the state's banks for eight days on February 14; this was prelude to the national banking disaster three weeks later. Guardian bank stock dropped from $350 to zero: the banks themselves deserved no more, some of them having paid dividends while heavily in debt. Father Charles Coughlin, the radical radio priest of Royal Oak, Michigan, inveighed against "banksters"; this too invited withdrawal of funds. By now Hoover realized the inadequacy of the RFC policies, and recommended the issuance of clearinghouse scrip. He begged its new Democratic chairman, Atlee Pomerene, to take some form of action in behalf of Michigan. But Pomerene would not go beyond the letter of the law and the banks closed. The Michigan bank closings, which were largely extended until March 6, contributed to nationwide panic and the banking collapse.

After Roosevelt nearly fell victim to an assassin's bullet in Florida and the banking débâcle had taken place in February, Hoover once again sought a united policy. As pressure on the banks increased, he came to lay blame on Roosevelt for the heavy drain on federal gold reserves, which the President attributed to anticipation that FDR would take the country off gold. On February 18 Hoover wrote asking Roosevelt to make a public affirmation of orthodox fiscal and monetary principles and thereby quiet the fears that were leading to economic collapse. He proposed in effect a near-total abandonment of the New Deal. For days Roosevelt rested on Vincent Astor's yacht before he dignified Hoover's letter with a bland response. He also refused to risk his influence with Congress by supporting legislation to stop the dangerous bank runs. Hoover had a simple plan of closing the banks for a day and then placing the government behind the ones that were solvent. The President also asked Congress for greater RFC lending authority. Neither man stood ready to subordinate everything to the national interest. Hoover even asked Eugene Meyer of the Federal Reserve Board to resign at Roosevelt's accession to office.

The causes of the country's sudden crisis, Hoover wrote privately on February 22, were "simple enough. The public is filled with fear and apprehension over the policies of the new administration." And the public was unnerved by inflation, fear of an unbalanced budget, fear of projects that would overtax the government. The people "are acting in self-protection before March 4." But there was no reason to suppose that the withdrawals and the hoarding were on account of distrust of Roosevelt rather than simply distrust of the banks and the unfortunate constitutional situation. Hoover was personalizing large problems—a practice that had often dimmed his capacity for insight. Since economic conditions improved somewhat under the New Deal, he could only argue later that they would have improved more without it. Given the impotence of voluntarism in the face of huge economic forces, the demonstrated wrongheadedness of powerful individuals like Ford and Couzens, and the failure of Congress to endow the RFC with broader powers and of Hoover to provide it with leaders of greater vision, the policies of the Republican President and the Democratic Congress seemed now as bankrupt as the banks themselves.

To his credit, Hoover in these final days made every effort and several important compromises to try to obtain Roosevelt's cooperation. He finally chose a five-year, 50 to 75 percent guarantee on bank deposits, which Roosevelt and Senator Glass rejected, as the best answer to the crisis. Raymond Moley later called the principle "the greatest reform that came out of that whole period." Hoover also considered proclaiming a limited national banking holiday under authority of the Trading with the Enemy Act of 1917, even though his Attorney General doubted the constitutionality of such a step. But he came to prefer state holidays, and restrictions on gold exports or withdrawals, in the absence of firm, bipartisan planning about what should take place during a banking moratorium. Mills and Meyer favored the idea, and Meyer—whom Hoover later considered disloyal—conferred with FDR about it on March 2. Hoover asked Roosevelt to call a special session of Congress on March 5 for passage of the necessary emergency legislation or to promise to continue Hoover's own independent actions. But the incoming President, while he liked the notion of a holiday, refused to participate in any joint solution to the banking crisis. Hoover then asked state governors to announce bank holidays; Governor Pinchot had to be awakened from bed by a fire engine at 5:00 A.M. At least Hoover had tried. Now it was Roosevelt's turn to attempt to rise to greatness, and the bank closing announced his coming to power with dramatic force.

Saturday, March 4, was predominantly gray and bleak; the wind blew intermittent gusts of rain, although there was sometimes a ray of sunshine. The two men rode together to the inauguration, Hoover replying in monosyllables to FDR's clumsy attempts to make conversation. "My, Mr. President, what interesting steel structures," Roosevelt said on seeing some new buildings on the site of a skirmish with the Bonus Army veterans. Although Hoover scowled a bit during the famous Inaugural Address, he pressed forward to offer his congratulations when it was over.

Mills and other officials remained in Washington for a time to take essential roles in finishing the Emergency Banking Act of 1933. It had already been largely drafted on or before March 4. Mills told Hoover that if he and his associates had not stayed in Washington several days, the job "would not have been done. We have a country, you know . . . I am working for the country," he explained to the surly Hoover. Hoover agreed that the bank reorganization would create "some temporary inflation" and "give a fillip to the situation."

He left for New York by train, unprotected by the Secret Service. Since John Quincy Adams a hundred years before, no President had departed so caricatured as an enemy of the people. Indeed, he was another Adams in his dour public face, his heavily moral religion, his acquaintance with science, his interest in the physical plant of the United States, his familiarity with foreign countries, his long day spent at work in the White House, his embodiment of technology and education as components of disciplined character. He might have written Adams's famous report on weights and measures; his plans for developing waterways, building dams, and consolidating railroad and airlines systems recall Adams's internal improvements. And the forces that Adams had perceived as opposing him, personified in Andrew Jackson, were like the forces Hoover thought he saw in FDR: demagoguery, political patronage, opportunism.

18. The Indian New Deal

JAMES S. OLSON AND RAYMOND WILSON

The Great Depression of the 1930s aggravated already poor living conditions throughout the United States, but life was particularly difficult on Indian reservations. Reformers had long been calling for change in American Indian policy, and the Great Depression intensified those demands. When Franklin D. Roosevelt won the election of 1932, the reformers had a friend in the White House. Real change began when President Roosevelt appointed John Collier commissioner of Indian Affairs in 1933. A founder of the American Indian Defense Association, Collier had argued for years that Indian culture must be preserved if Native Americans were to survive. Despite protests from missionary groups, Collier set out to revive Native American culture by introducing bilingual education in the schools; ending requirements that children living at federal boarding schools attend Protestant church services; encouraging traditional dances, crafts, and drumming; and diverting federal funds used for suppressing peyotism to other purposes. Finally, he campaigned for the Indian Reorganization Act, which Congress passed in 1934. The years of John Collier's tenure as commissioner of Indian Affairs have been known as the "Indian New Deal" because of the dramatic changes he inaugurated in federal Indian policy. In the following essay, James S. Olson and Raymond Wilson describe the Indian New Deal.

John Collier became Commissioner of Indian Affairs on April 21, 1933, and he held the position for twelve years—longer than any other person. He became the most controversial and influential commissioner in United States history. His ideas invited debate and controversy, polarizing both the Native American communities and the European American community, with some of each group hailing him as a great reformer and others despising him as just another assimilationist, albeit a subtle one. Few people, however, questioned the profound influence he had on non-Native American opinion and on hundreds of thousands of Native Americans. Even now, nearly four decades after he left office, historians are still debating his career.

Born in Atlanta, Georgia, in 1884, Collier attended both Columbia University and the Collège de France in Paris, but he did not complete his studies at either place. In 1907 he found a job as civic secretary for the People's Institute in New York City, a job that shaped his ideas about ethnicity and social policy. The People's Institute worked to improve life for urban immigrants by promoting cooperative community action and preserving cultural traditions and communal lifestyles. Collier joined other social reformers at the Institute in the belief that cultural tradition tended to solidify and strengthen ethnic groups and that the vitality of such tradition in the process collectively enhanced political and social stability in American society as a whole. Ideally, cultural pluralism was a unifying force which represented ethnic differences and promoted a feeling of universal brotherhood. That belief strongly influenced his later service as Commissioner of Indian Affairs.

In September 1919 Collier moved to Los Angeles, where he accepted the directorship of public adult education in California. In his new post he stressed the importance of preserving community life in urban America and often cited the Bolshevik Revolution in Russia as a prime example of cooperative community action. State legislators in California frowned on Collier's "un-American" attitudes, and in 1920 he became a victim of the Red Scare and was forced to resign. Collier traveled to New Mexico to visit Mabel Dodge, an old friend from New York known for her support of the arts and the weekly salons she held in her Fifth Avenue apartment. Taos, New Mexico, where she had moved, had become a gathering place for hundreds of artists and writers. There Collier discovered his "Red Atlantis," the homeland of Pueblos still living together in a communal setting despite more than three centuries of attacks on their culture by generation after generation of Spanish, Mexican, and American settlers. For Collier, their cultural endurance demonstrated the vitality of communal relationships and ethnic pride.

Collier returned to California in 1921 and took a teaching post at San Francisco State College. But after a year of teaching psychology and sociology, he abandoned the academic life and joined the Indian Welfare Committee of the General Federation of Women's Clubs as a research agent. He quickly gained national recognition because of his efforts to block the passage of the Bursum Bill threatening the Spanish land grants to the Pueblos. In 1923 Collier became executive secretary of the newly formed American Indian Defense Association, an organization opposing the Bursum Bill, calling for termination of the Dawes Act, and encouraging preservation of Native American culture. In addition to organizing political lobbying efforts, in 1925 Collier began editing the magazine *American Indian Life,* a reform journal reflecting his basic values.

Throughout the 1920s Collier was in the vanguard of the reform movement, frequently publishing articles critical of the Bureau of Indian Affairs. He was also instrumental in convincing Secretary of the Interior Hubert Work to call upon the Brookings Institution to investigate reservation conditions, a proposal resulting in the Meriam Report in 1928. The Senate then decided to conduct its own investigation, and Collier served as a Senate investigator, an assignment which gave him an opportunity to visit a number of reservations and to observe the generally deplorable conditions. Among other things, he became convinced of the disastrous effects of the allotment and rapid assimilation policies.

When Franklin D. Roosevelt entered the White House in 1933, he selected Harold L. Ickes, a political liberal and former head of the American Indian Defense Association, as Secretary of the Interior. Ickes let it be known to the Senate and to Roosevelt that he wanted Collier to be his Commissioner of Indian Affairs. There was some opposition to Collier, especially from Senate Majority Leader Joseph T. Robinson of Arkansas, who wanted his brother-in-law, Edgar B. Meritt, a BIA employee for many years, as the new commissioner. With diplomatic skill, President Roosevelt informed Robinson that Collier was the choice, Robinson acquiesced, and Collier received Senate confirmation on April 21, 1933.

Collier enjoyed excellent rapport with Roosevelt and Ickes. Both men were willing to experiment with new and unconventional ideas, and because of their trust in Collier and the pressing duties imposed by the Great Depression they gave him virtually a free hand in making government policy. Collier immediately launched a new and, according to many people, revolutionary approach to Native American reform. Ever conscious of the importance of ethnic values and community solidarity, Collier attacked the concept of rapid assimilation of Native Americans into mainstream society. Instead of "getting the Indian out of the Indian," Collier sought to preserve tribal heritage and culture. Although many assimilationists cried that Collier was trying to "return Indians to the blanket," he was actually advocating more of an acculturated approach to solving the "Indian problem" based on his faith in cultural pluralism. The traditional goal was still the same: absorption of Native Americans into the dominant society, but at a slower and more equitable pace. Although some Native American critics would later call him an assimilationist, Collier was not committed to an inflexible timetable and believed that Native American culture, in the decades and even centuries before assimilation was complete, was absolutely necessary to Native American survival.

When he assumed office in April 1933, Collier had already developed a set of ideas about Native American affairs. He viewed the Bureau of Indian Affairs as an advisory rather than a supervisory agency and hoped to change the prevailing view among many full-bloods that the BIA was a manipulative, self-serving government bureaucracy. Collier was also adamant that the allotment program had been an economic and social disaster for Native Americans. Rather than breaking up tribes and distributing their land, Collier wanted to reconstitute the tribes politically, incorporate them economically, and restore their traditional land base. In one of Collier's earliest programs for self-determination, he wanted Native Americans to play a more active role in decisions affecting reservation life and to receive better training in the proper management of their land and natural resources. Regarding education, Collier believed that Native American children should attend community day schools or public schools on or near reservations instead of the distant boarding schools which separated them from their parents for long periods of time. Finally, Collier insisted that the federal government should no longer attempt to suppress Native American customs in the name of assimilation. The years of cultural imperialism had to come to an end. As a first step toward realizing his hopes, Collier convinced President Roosevelt to abolish by executive order the Board of Indian Commissioners, an agency created in 1869 to oversee the Board of Indian Affairs. Both Collier and Ickes considered the board an obstacle to reform, since its members and supporters remained intensely committed to the Dawes Act and to the eradication of tribal traditions. Roosevelt acted on Collier's request within days of his confirmation as commissioner.

With the influence of the presidency solidly behind him, Collier wasted no time in putting into motion a number of relief measures. On May 31, 1933, at Collier's request, Congress passed the Pueblo Relief Act granting additional payments to Native Americans and settlers who had been inadequately compensated by the Pueblo Lands Board in the 1920s. Collier also moved quickly to extend New Deal legislation to destitute Native Americans suffering from the effects of the Great Depression. Seasonal work for Native Americans in southern California and parts of Arizona, for example, had nearly disappeared. Many were also facing new difficulties in selling their products. The Navajos were receiving very low prices for their handicrafts, wool, lambs, and piñon nuts. Blistering summer heat and drought, as well as severe winter temperatures in 1932–33, increased the misery on the reservations. Although Native Americans were participating in the Civilian Conservation Corps established by Congress (in March 1933) to provide employment for young men in conservation work, Collier was instrumental in establishing the Indian Emergency Conservation Work program. Congress initially appropriated $5.9 million to the program, which funded the establishment of seventy-two camps on thirty-three reservations. Not only did the program permit Native Americans to work close to their families, but the conservation projects directly helped the reservation ecology. In New Mexico, Arizona, Oklahoma, Montana, South Dakota, and Washington, where reservation conservation programs were desperately needed, Native Americans constructed roads, storage dams, fences, and wells and put into effect proper fire control methods to protect their forests. Each worker received thirty dollars per month and many learned to operate machines and heavy equipment. Between 1933 and 1942 the more than eighty-five thousand Native Americans employed in the Indian Emergency Conservation Work program built a total of 1,742 dams and reservoirs, 12,230 miles of fences, 91 lookout towers, and 9,737 miles of truck trails. They conducted pest control projects on 1,315,870 acres of land and removed poisonous weeds from 263,129 acres of reservation farm and grazing land. Collier also established a magazine, *Indians at Work,* which promoted the "Indian CCC" and later served as a vehicle to garner support for Collier's other legislation.

Collier also managed to channel funds from other government agencies to benefit Native Americans. Secretary of Agriculture Henry A. Wallace used his influence to help Native Americans purchase purebred cattle from non-Native Americans through an eight-hundred-thousand-dollar allocation from the Agricultural Adjustment Administration. Between 1933 and 1939 Native American cattle herds increased from 167,373 to 267,551 head. Collier convinced Harry Hopkins, director of the Federal Emergency Relief Administration, to supply relief money to the reservations not included in the original legislation of May 1933. From the Department of War, poverty-stricken Native Americans received army surplus clothing, including 35,000 pairs of pants, 33,000 shirts, 40,000 coats, and 24,000 pairs of shoes. Under the Civil Works Administration, thousands of Native Americans were employed during the winter of 1934—such employment in addition to that made possible through the IECW program. The CWA also employed fifteen Native American artists and twenty-five craftsmen to paint pictures and make jewelry, rugs, and pottery. The Bureau of Indian Affairs then displayed the finished products in its offices.

The Public Works Administration, the Works Progress Administration, the National Youth Administration, and the Resettlement Administration provided more relief in the form of jobs and improved reservation conditions. The PWA, for example, employed Native Americans in building or improving reservation hospitals, schools, and sewage systems. The WPA hired over ten thousand Native Americans a year to index and file records for the Bureau of Indian Affairs, while the NYA provided six dollars monthly to each Native American student enrolled in day school for clothing, supplies, and lunches. The Resettlement Administration assisted

Native Americans in North and South Dakota by constructing needed water wells. The agency also purchased nearly one million acres of grazing land for the Pueblos and Navajos. Finally, the Resettlement Administration encouraged Native Americans to help themselves and allocated money to instruct them in developing root cellars, canning centers, and low-cost housing.

To further assist Native Americans, Collier convinced Secretary Ickes to cancel their debts to the federal government. Ickes had authority to do so through an act of Congress passed on July 1, 1932. In 1933 the Roosevelt administration canceled debts worth more than $3 million; by 1936, debts exceeding $12 million for the construction of roads, bridges, irrigation projects, and the purchase of tribal herds had been eliminated. Because of the debt cancellation and the appropriation of more than $100 million in relief programs, Native Americans were able to survive the worst years of the Great Depression. Indeed, many Native Americans enjoyed a higher standard of living during the 1930s than they had in the 1920s, in large measure due to Collier's efforts to make available to them a healthy share of such depression relief.

In the field of education Collier followed the recommendations of the Meriam Report. Will Carson Ryan, Jr., remained as director of Native American education until 1936, when Willard W. Beatty, an educator from Illinois, succeeded him. Collier, Ryan, and Beatty continued to close boarding schools in favor of day schools. Using $3.6 million in PWA Funds, Collier ordered the construction of one hundred day schools. Consistent with Collier's philosophy, the day schools served as community activity centers where both children and adults could learn domestic skills and health care and participate in preserving tribal culture. Beatty also worked to improve the quality of teachers hired, and he expanded curricula by inaugurating summer school classes in anthropology, home economics, arts and crafts, rural sociology, health, and tribal languages. He also supported bilingual education as one of the best ways to increase literacy among Native Americans.

In addition to relief measures and educational reform, Collier tried to improve health conditions. Securing $1.7 million from the Public Works Administration in 1933, he ordered the construction of eleven reservation hospitals and the substantial improvement of ten others. He also saw to the employment of more part-time doctors, nurses, and dentists. More comprehensive treatment programs for trachoma and tuberculosis were soon made available. Between 1939 and 1943 the incidence of trachoma dropped from 20.2 percent to 7.2 percent. And throughout the 1930s and early 1940s, Collier recognized the inadequacy of government health programs on the reservations and demanded increased appropriations for the Indian Medical Service.

Many New Dealers felt that Collier had achieved some remarkable results in 1933 and early 1934. But he was not without his critics. Many Native Americans and non-Native Americans complained that either too much money was spent on programs that were not needed or that too little money went to critically necessary programs. Others complained of government-sponsored blunders, such as the time when inexperienced work parties of Klamaths in Oregon mistakenly destroyed timber on their reservation. Problems still plagued Native American education. Appropriations were inadequate to provide needed teachers, classrooms, and lunch programs. Navajo students at day schools in 1937 received only thirteen cents per day for lunches, a figure well below the minimum recommended in the Meriam Report. Day schools among the Navajos were largely unsuccessful because the lack of reservation roads and the Navajos' nomadic ways meant low attendance. Additionally, many Navajos preferred boarding schools simply because their children had received better meals there. Flora Warren Seymour, a staunch opponent of Collier and formerly a member of the Board of Indian Commissioners, tried to ruin him politically when it became clear that the Navajos preferred boarding schools. Christian missionaries greatly resented Collier's decision to extend religious freedom to Native Americans by restricting religious instruction in day and boarding schools. He also angered them by ending compulsory religious services and providing voluntary instruction in native religions. Some Christian Native Americans also protested Collier's orders. At the Pine Ridge Reservation in South Dakota, 962 people signed a petition addressed to Eleanor Roosevelt expressing the fear that their children would no longer receive Christian instruction in BIA schools. Collier had to remind all these critics that he was not anti-Christian but was merely concerned that native religions receive equal time. Religious freedom, he argued, was not limited to instruction in the tenets of Christianity. To soothe any misgivings President Roosevelt had about the criticisms, Secretary Ickes wrote to him that he had been

a real White Father to the Indians and they appreciated it deeply. . . . Your administration will go down in history as the most humane and far seeing with respect to the Indians that this country ever had.*

Despite the gains of 1933, Collier still felt that the overall approach had been piecemeal and that a more carefully planned and comprehensive approach to Native American affairs still had to be developed. The relief measures passed in 1933 had been absolutely necessary, as had the changes in education policy in reservation schools. Preservation of Native American culture, new support for Native American education, and the end of the allotment program were all keys to Collier's philosophy; and in 1934 and 1935 the federal government took major steps toward implementing his ideas in these regards.

In 1934 Secretary Ickes named a committee to study means of protecting and marketing Native American arts and crafts, and the next year Congress authorized the Department of the Interior to create an Indian Arts and Crafts Board, operating on an initial budget of $45,000. The five-member board was to improve the quality and widen the distribution of tribal arts and crafts and, through the use of government trademarks on products, to guarantee to purchasers that the items were Native American-made. The board created craft guilds on reservations to operate as "training centers" for Native American artists and craftsmen and as direct

*Quoted in Kenneth R. Philp, *John Collier's Crusade for Indian Reform, 1920–1954* (Tucson: University of Arizona Press, 1977), 126.

marketing outlets, bypassing middlemen who siphoned off profits. It sponsored art classes in BIA schools, helping to inspire young artists and to preserve native traditions. The board also conducted weaving, silverwork, leatherwork, and beadwork projects. Collier took great pride in the board's work. He was delighted with the superb products exhibited by the Navajo Arts and Crafts Guild at the 1939 World's Fair in San Francisco.

The New Deal launched a new approach to Native American education on April 16, 1934, when Congress passed the Johnson–O'Malley Act, which authorized the Secretary of the Interior to negotiate contracts with any state or territory for monetary relief in the areas of Native American education, medical aid, agricultural assistance, and social welfare. Although Collier had high hopes that the Johnson–O'Malley Act would improve conditions and provide better services to Native Americans, especially in the field of education, there were several problems inherent in the law. The act was passed on the assumption that state administrators and federal officials could work together. Collier believed that better programs could be developed by combining federal and state resources. But the Bureau of Indian Affairs was deeply concerned that the states would be more interested in the money they received from the act than in providing special programs and classes for Native American students. State administrators, on the other hand, guarded their authority jealously and resented any federal interference with their schools.

The idea of Native Americans attending public schools was hardly new. Since the end of the nineteenth century, Native American students had attended public schools through federal contracts with individual school districts, and by 1928 more of them were in public schools than in BIA schools. Before the Johnson–O'Malley Act, however, the funding method was cumbersome and inefficient, with the BIA Education Division responsible for contracting with hundreds of individual school districts instead of working directly with officials of the state departments of education. Will Carson Ryan, Jr., director of the BIA Education Division, complained that the method was "administratively absurd" and violated "every right principle of Federal–State relationship in education."* With the passage of the Johnson–O'Malley Act, the BIA was able to contract on a federal–state basis.

The Education Division of the BIA stressed the importance of handling each state's situation individually because of the complex differences in local tribal groups. Both Arizona and Oklahoma, for example, had large Native American communities, but only a small number of Native American children in Arizona went to public schools, while more than three-fourths of them in Oklahoma attended public schools. Federal funding for these educational programs had to be different because of the number of Native American students involved and because the sources from which the states drew their revenue varied greatly.

Between 1934 and 1941, California, Washington, Minnesota, and Arizona negotiated contracts with the Bureau of Indian Affairs. Except in Minnesota, the harmonious working relationship Collier had so desper-

---

*Quoted in Margaret Connell Szasz, *Education and the American Indian: The Road to Self-Determination since 1928* (Albuquerque: University of New Mexico Press, 1977), 90.

ately wanted never materialized. California was the first state to receive federal funding under the new act. Mary Steward, the BIA Superintendent of Indian Education for California and a well-known educator, immediately encountered difficulties with state education officials who did not want the federal government to "dictate" educational policy to them. She finally resigned in disgust in 1941, and the next year her position was eliminated. State officials then played a much more active role in allocating Johnson–O'Malley funds. Similar problems erupted in Washington between Homer L. Morrison, the BIA superintendent, and the state Superintendent of Public Instruction. Although there were few problems in Arizona, primarily because most Native American children were in BIA schools, it was only in Minnesota that the state department of education worked hard to cooperate with the BIA.

The competitive problem in education, of course, did not always involve state education leaders. The effectiveness of the Johnson–O'Malley Act was also limited by BIA fears as well as by local attitudes. A number of BIA officials regarded federal schools as better fit to accommodate the needs of Native American children. They felt that most public school administrators were too inexperienced to develop adequate programs for Native Americans. Public school instruction was seriously flawed in several areas. A primary problem was the anti-Native American prejudice so common to teachers and administrators. Some teachers were openly prejudiced, while others were subtly cruel. Public schools also lacked courses in tribal culture, and a capability for bilingual instruction was commonly inadequate or nonexistent. It was no wonder that Native American students did not do well in public schools. Too often their physical needs—food, clothing, shoes, and transportation—were not met, while their emotional needs—ethnic pride and a sense of belonging—were ignored completely. Yet public schools continued to draw Johnson–O'Malley money while failing to provide adequate programs for Native American children. Instead, in most instances they channeled the money into their general operating expenses and made little effort to meet specifically the needs of Native American students. Collier's hopes for drastic educational reform were dashed on the rocks of federal–state rivalry and racism.

The third and most profound piece of New Deal legislation directly affecting Native Americans was the Indian Reorganization Act of 1934. A denunciation of the allotment policy, this act was an open admission that the Dawes Act, after forty-seven years of operation, was a devastating blunder. Collier had always been an outspoken critic of land allotment, and in August 1933 he had ordered federal agents on reservations nationwide to stop selling trust land and to cease submitting certificates of competency, fee patents, or removal restrictions on Native American land to the BIA except in cases of grave distress. Early in 1934 Collier joined with William Zimmerman, Assistant Commissioner of Indian Affairs, and Nathan Margold, Felix Cohen, and Charles Fahy, members of the Interior Department legal staff, to draw up the piece of legislation which later became the Indian Reorganization Act. The forty-eight-page bill was sent to Senator Burton K. Wheeler of Montana and Representative Edgar Howard of Nebraska, chairmen of the Senate and House Committees on Indian Affairs, and they introduced it to Congress in mid-February.

The Wheeler–Howard Bill was divided into four titles involving self-government, education, land, and a special court for Native American affairs. Title I allowed Native Americans residing on reservations to establish local self-governments and tribal corporations to develop reservation resources. The Secretary of the Interior would issue a charter of home rule and right of incorporation to a tribe after one-fourth of its adults petitioned for such a charter and after three-fifths of them ratified the charter in a tribal election. Collier hoped that these newly formed local governments would operate like municipalities, each having a voice in congressional bills affecting them and ultimately assuming most of the functions of the Bureau of Indian Affairs. Title II permitted the federal government to train Native Americans in forest management, public health, law enforcement, and record keeping and provided scholarship money for gifted students. Money was also allocated for courses in tribal culture in BIA boarding schools. Title III ended the Dawes Act and provided for the consolidation of allotted and heirship lands into productive units for chartered community use. Individuals affected by the consolidations would receive either compensation or interest of equal worth in tribal lands. Those holding fee patent titles could participate on a voluntary basis. The Secretary of the Interior was also authorized to buy property for Native Americans through a congressional appropriation of $2 million annually. Title IV established a special federal court, the Court of Indian Affairs, for the chartered communities. The court would have jurisdiction over reservation crimes and cases where at least one of the parties was a Native American.

In order to garner support for the bill, Collier had ten meetings with Native Americans in South Dakota, Oregon, Arizona, New Mexico, California, Oklahoma, and Wisconsin in March and April 1934. He spent most of his time at the meetings dealing one at a time with the numerous particular and often unique apprehensions and problems presented by representatives of the many tribes involved. Several Sioux delegates, for example, wanted all land exchanges under Title III to be voluntary instead of compulsory, and Collier agreed to amend the bill. Papago delegates doubted whether self-government would work among their independent farming and ranching communities; they opposed the bill. The Pimas and San Carlos Apaches feared loss of their mineral rights or tribal herds. And the Navajos tended to link the Wheeler–Howard Bill to Collier's unpopular program of stock reduction of Navajo sheep and goats, instituted to prevent overgrazing and long-term environmental damage to the reservation. Many mixed-bloods simply wanted to retain their individual allotments; they had no desire to return to communal living under tribal direction. Nevertheless, Collier later informed Congress that polls taken at the ten meetings revealed that fifty-four tribes representing 141,881 individuals approved the bill, while only twelve tribes totaling 15,106 opposed the measure.

The bill was stiffly opposed by several groups, mostly for traditional reasons. The Indian Rights Association believed that the bill perpetuated the segregation of Native Americans, isolating them forever from the mainstream of social life in the United States. Many congressmen seriously questioned the idea of communal ownership of property and feared that the creation of "independent" tribal-chartered communities would severely threaten the process of assimilation, which they felt was the only realistic way of dealing with the "Indian problem." Collier responded to them by citing the Mormon success with cooperative land allotment, agricultural, and economic programs during the early decades in the Great Basin, arguing that Native Americans too could benefit from similar programs. Some people accused Collier of attempting to restore pagan ideas and of being an advocate of communism. Joseph Bruner, a full-blood Creek and later president of the American Indian Federation, denounced Collier and considered him a communist and an atheist. Many western congressmen, reflecting the demands of economic interest groups, feared the permanent loss of reservation resources to outside development. In Arizona, for example, where certain Papago lands had been temporarily withdrawn for mineral exploitation by non-Native American mining interests, Senator Henry F. Ashurst believed that the Wheeler–Howard Bill would permanently deny non-Native American entry to these lands. He vociferously opposed the bill. Eventually, Collier agreed to thirty amendments to the Wheeler–Howard Bill, most of them based on congressional criticisms of the original draft of the bill and the proposals made at the ten regional conferences. Included in those proposed changes were the individual's consent to the transfer of allotted land to community ownership, the protection of individual mineral rights to allotted lands, and the retention of the right to partition farm lands among heirs as long as the procedure remained economically sound. Many in Congress, however, remained opposed, most of them along traditional lines: liberal reformers feared the end of assimilation; those with an eye to increased land holdings feared the permanent inaccessibility of those Native American-controlled resources that remained.

Frustrated and angry at the opposition to his proposals, Collier finally turned to President Roosevelt for assistance. The President had previously expressed his support for the bill, and both Secretary Ickes and Secretary of Agriculture Henry Wallace began soliciting Roosevelt's open support for the measure. Roosevelt insisted that Democratic congressmen join in support of the Wheeler–Howard Bill, and in June 1934 Congress passed the bill but only after reducing its benefits and protections. The appropriation for helping organize tribal governments was reduced from $500,000 annually to $250,000; benefits were denied to all Native American groups not formally recognized by the BIA as a tribe or band; provisions to consolidate allotted lands were weakened; tribes were prevented from simply taking over heirship lands; and the provision for a special Court of Indian Affairs was eliminated. Despite Collier's hopes, Congress had very little interest in restoring Native Americans to a position of political, economic, and cultural independence.

In its final version, the Indian Reorganization Act repealed the allotment laws, restored certain surplus reservation lands to tribal ownership, and permitted voluntary exchanges of allotments for interests in tribal corporations. Congress agreed to appropriate $2 million annually to the Secretary of the Interior for the acquisition of additional lands for tribes. Congress also authorized the expenditure of $250,000 a year for the organization of tribal governments and tribal corporations, which could then borrow money from a $10 million revolving credit fund—later increased to $12 million—to finance economic development of reservation resources. The law also created a $250,000 annual scholarship fund for Native American students and gave Native Americans preferential treatment in securing civil service positions in the Bureau of Indian Affairs.

The Indian Reorganization Act required tribes to accept or reject the act through referenda. Similarly, the provision establishing tribal self-governments was decided through referenda. When a majority of the adult members of a tribe voted to approve the Indian Reorganization Act, they could then write a constitution which had to be approved by another majority vote of the tribe and by the Secretary of the Interior. At first, in order to expedite implementation of the Indian Reorganization Act and avoid delays that would inevitably arise because of tribal factionalism, the Interior Department arbitrarily counted all eligible adult voters who failed to vote as favoring the measure. As could be expected, the results were extremely biased in favor of acceptance. At least seventeen tribes who voted to reject the act were considered as being in favor of it because a high number of qualified adult voters did not cast ballots. California Mission Native Americans at the Santa Ysabel Reservation, for example, overwhelmingly voted to reject the Indian Reorganization Act by a vote of forty-three to nine; but since sixty-two eligible members did not vote, the Secretary of the Interior declared the tribe in favor of the new law. Thousands of Native Americans denounced the election method, claiming that it favored mixed-bloods, who were more likely to vote, over full-bloods, many of whom were isolated in distant parts of the reservations and were less likely to vote. The last thing Collier wanted was to appear dictatorial, so in 1935 he convinced Congress to pass legislation defining "majority" as half plus one of those Native Americans actually participating in the election.

Tribes accepting the Indian Reorganization Act could then, by majority vote, elect a tribal council which possessed all powers already vested in the tribe by "existing law." The tribal council had a right to hire legal counsel, to prevent the sale or lease of tribal lands without its consent, to enter into negotiations with federal or state agencies for public services, and to review federal appropriations affecting the tribe before such measures were submitted to either Congress or to the Bureau of Indian Affairs. In the 1960s and 1970s Native American activists built on this idea of tribal self-determination. When one-third of the adult tribal members petitioned the Secretary of the Interior for a tribal charter of incorporation, and a simple majority of tribal voters ratified the charter, tribes could then form corporations to develop reservation resources and business enterprises.

To assist Collier in his efforts to organize tribal self-government and restore tribal life, the federal government sought help from recognized anthropologists. Dr. Duncan Strong, an employee of the Bureau of American Ethnology, and several university anthropology professors agreed to serve as consultants. The Bureau of Indian Affairs established the Applied Anthropology Unit in 1935 under the direction of Dr. H. Scudder Mekeel, a former Harvard anthropology professor. Mekeel's staff conducted reservation fieldwork in an effort to prepare tribes to adopt the Indian Reorganization Act and to write constitutions. But over the years, internal conflicts over policy decisions between BIA administrators and anthropologists, including Collier and Mekeel, weakened the effectiveness of the division, and in 1937 Congress cut appropriations and disbanded the unit. Collier continued, however, to consult anthropologists and other social scientists. Their expertise was especially useful in instructing employees and teachers in the BIA Education Division on Native American culture.

To further assist tribes in drawing up constitutions, Nathan Margold, Felix Cohen, and other members of the Interior Department's legal staff prepared a model constitution to follow. The model helped some tribes, but its abundance of "legalese" made it difficult to comprehend, and it was too general to take into account the particular needs and expectations of individual tribes.

In 1936 the Bureau of Indian Affairs established an Indian Organization Division to aid tribes in administrative details after they had prepared their constitutions. Division field representatives—most of them Native American employees of the BIA—provided political, economic, and social assistance to tribal councils. For example, they examined how well the tribal councils operated, helped settle some problems the tribal councils faced, and assisted them in their efforts to develop economic and social programs.

As Collier and others in the Bureau of Indian Affairs tried to implement the Indian Reorganization Act, critics attacked it on the grounds that the law segregated Native Americans from European American society, prevented "efficient" development of reservation resources, ignored tribal prerogatives and customs, or supported anti-Christian and communistic principles. Such criticism was effective to the extent that congressional appropriations to the Indian Reorganization Act programs were cut beginning in 1935.

Still, Collier had other successes. For example, he convinced Congress to pass legislation in 1936 providing self-government and financial assistance to Native Americans in Alaska and Oklahoma. Native Americans in Alaska, due to an oversight in the law, had not been permitted to establish constitutions or tribal corporations or to draw from the revolving credit fund under the Indian Reorganization Act. To remedy this situation, Congress passed the Alaska Reorganization Act in 1936, extending these privileges to Alaskan natives and authorizing the creation of reservations on land occupied by Native Americans. With Native American approval, the Secretary of the Interior established six reservations in Alaska in 1944. Since Alaskan Native Americans were more village than tribal oriented, villages were allowed to establish corporations and constitutions. Forty-nine villages with a total native population of 10,899 drew up constitutions and charters of incorporation. An Alaska Native Industries Cooperative Association was created to borrow money from the revolving credit fund for the promotion of Native American business ventures.

Oklahoma congressmen objected so bitterly to the Indian Reorganization Act—on the grounds that it would retard assimilation—that the tribes there were excluded from many of the act's provisions. But Collier was not satisfied, and in the fall of 1934 he went with Senator Elmer Thomas, who had been opposed to the act initially, and visited many tribes, soliciting their opinions, especially about the right to establish tribal governments and tribal corporations. He met with very mixed feelings. Some of the delegates from the Five Civilized Tribes, for example, favored the establishment of self-government and charters of incorporation, while others, wishing to be left alone on their individual allotments, rejected all or most programs of a communal nature. Delegates representing the Kiowas and Potawatomis also voiced disapproval and supported the older allotment policies. Shawnee, Sac and Fox, and Iowa delegates tended to approve of the creation of tribal corporations, and the Pawnees and Comanches were bitterly divided.

Convinced that Native Americans in Oklahoma could benefit from the extension of certain provisions of the Indian Reorganization Act to them, Senator Thomas and Representative Will Rogers introduced a bill drafted by Collier. The Thomas–Rogers Bill proposed to place Native Americans in Oklahoma under federal guardianship; but in order to satisfy non-Native] American assimilationists, mixed-bloods, and assimilated Native Americans, the bill allowed Native Americans of less than one-half Native American ancestry to be "relieved of all restrictions" on their property. The Secretary of the Interior would make the final decision in lifting such restrictions, based on recommendations from a special competency commission. Other provisions involved better protection of heirship lands, tribal self-government, tribal incorporation charters, communal ownership of land, acquisition of additional property (which would be tax exempt), reservation expansion, and increased educational and health care.

The bill encountered stiff opposition from Native Americans and non-Native Americans at congressional hearings. Joseph Bruner, the Creek president of the American Indian Federation, again argued that such a bill would retard assimilation. Legislators and businessmen in Oklahoma echoed similar sentiments and complained about the loss of state taxes on withdrawn tribal lands and mineral deposits. Others feared that the competency commission would function like previous commissions and indiscriminately give fee patent titles to "incompetent" Native Americans who would then lose their lands to European Americans or mixed-bloods. As had been the case in many previous pieces of Native American reform legislation, the Thomas–Rogers Bill was controversial for both Native Americans and non-Native Americans.

Collier revised the Thomas–Rogers Bill to meet many of the criticisms, and Congress passed it as the Oklahoma Indian Welfare Act in June 1936. The law permitted the state of Oklahoma to levy a "gross production tax" on oil and gas leases on reservation land and deleted all provisions regarding the degree of Native American blood required to remove restrictions on Native American land. The act made no mention of improving educational and health services but did provide for communal ownership of property and the creation of tribal constitutions and corporations. The Oklahoma Indian Welfare Act also permitted ten or more Native Americans to establish local cooperatives and secure money from a special $2 million credit fund.

For a variety of reasons, only a minority of Native Americans ever really came under the umbrella of the Indian Reorganization Act and the Oklahoma Indian Welfare Act. Because the Indian Reorganization Act denied eligibility to all groups not officially recognized as tribes or bands by the Bureau of Indian Affairs, more than 50,000 Native Americans were excluded at the outset. The 103,000 Native Americans in Oklahoma were similarly excluded from the IRA. With the vote counted, approximately 181 tribes numbering 129,750 people accepted the Indian Reorganization Act, while 77 tribes with a total population of 86,365 rejected it. Less than 40 percent of all Native Americans were eligible for IRA benefits from the beginning.

Moreover, not all tribes approving the Indian Reorganization Act or the Oklahoma Indian Welfare Act adopted constitutions or incorporated. Ninety-three tribes or bands ultimately adopted constitutions under the IRA, and only seventy-three had charters of incorporation. Despite Collier's hard work on the Oklahoma Indian Welfare Act, most Oklahoma Native Americans did not avail themselves of the law, preferring instead to keep their own land allotments. Indeed, between 1936 and 1945 only eighteen Oklahoma tribes or bands numbering 13,241 people wrote tribal constitutions, and only thirteen of them, numbering 5,741 people, set up charters of incorporation. Among the Five Civilized Tribes, for example, only the Cherokee Keetoowah band and the three Creek towns adopted constitutions and corporate charters. By 1945 tribes representing only a small percent of Native Americans had opted for the provisions of the Indian Reorganization Act and the Oklahoma Welfare Act. Most individuals continue to live on allotted lands in Oklahoma. Only one reservation remains, and that for mineral rights only. (Only 12 percent of its residents were Native Americans in 1980.)

Despite his understanding of and respect for Native American culture, Collier had underestimated its diversity, as well as the intensity of Native American factionalism. His ideas had come from his experience with the isolated, high-context cultures of the Navajos and Pueblos—the "Red Atlantis" of the Southwest. But relatively few Native Americans lived in such highly integrated, monolithic cultures. The idea that Native Americans functioned as unified tribes was an inherent flaw of the Indian Reorganization Act, since many Native Americans were more band (even family) oriented than tribal oriented. Thus, the formal tribal governments on the level envisioned by the architects of the Indian Reorganization Act never really existed among many tribes, even before the time of European or European American contact. The Indian Reorganization Act imposed rigid political and economic systems which were often alien to Native American peoples. Voting by majority rule posed problems for a people who had a long tradition of reaching decisions by consensus or persuasion. To them, majority rule was arbitrary, rigid, and inconsiderate of the feelings of the minority; and the result, even when the tribe approved the Indian Reorganization Act, was considerable disaffection among many members of the tribe. Rivalries and factionalism on the reservations militated against the Indian Reorganization Act as well. Native American factionalism, not always clear-cut or well defined, was as common in the 1930s as it had been throughout American history. Simply stated, it usually pitted full-bloods against mixed-bloods and traditionalists against progressives.

The Crows of Montana, for example, rejected the Indian Reorganization Act even though their native superintendent, Robert Yellowtail, urged support. Full- and mixed-bloods united to defeat the measure, believing that acceptance would inevitably result in the loss of their lands. Full-blood

Northern Cheyennes in Montana supported the Indian Reorganization Act because they viewed it as a means of gaining control of the tribal business committee which mixed-bloods, a numerical minority, had controlled for years. At the Rosebud Reservation in South Dakota, the full-blood Sioux, who generally still retained their land allotments, opposed the act, charging that it would favor the mixed-bloods who had disposed of their allotments. In the referendum voting, both the Northern Cheyennes and the Rosebud Sioux accepted the Indian Reorganization Act; but the full-blood Northern Cheyennes gained control of tribal enterprises while the mixed-blood Sioux gained more control over tribal decisions and property.

In the Southwest, the Papagos voted to accept the Indian Reorganization Act; but they had no tradition of tribal unity. Their language had no word equivalents for "representative" and "budget" and only one word to describe a superintendent or commissioner, a president, or a king. The Hopis were also village-oriented people and had little knowledge of centralized tribal government. Their constitution established a tribal government respecting the authority of individual villages in certain matters, but inter-village rivalries undermined its effectiveness. Although most of the New Mexico Pueblos accepted the act, it was only a token gesture. Very few of the Pueblo communities wrote constitutions because most Pueblo leaders held tenaciously to their traditional forms of authority and feared that those powers would be threatened if they wrote constitutions establishing self-governments based on majority rule.

Another major disappointment to Collier was the rejection of the Indian Reorganization Act by the Navajos, the largest tribe in the United States. They turned down the act by a close vote of 8,197 to 7,679 in June 1935, largely because they related it to the unpopular government programs to reduce their stock herds. The BIA had recommended the reduction of Navajo livestock because reservation land was being damaged by overgrazing. But the number of animals a Navajo owned was a status symbol among tribesmen, and, although the stock reductions could be seen to be a long-range benefit, Navajos still resented the decreases. Collier visited the Navajos in 1933 and convinced their tribal council, which had been created by the Interior Department in 1922 to represent the tribe in oil leasing of reservation land, to accept the stock reductions. Securing a grant of $200,000 from the Federal Emergency Relief Administration, the Bureau of Indian Affairs purchased 100,000 head of sheep; but the reductions were done on an across-the-board scale rather than a graduated one, which favored the large herd owners at the expense of the smaller owners.

In March 1934 Collier again visited the Navajos and explained the proposed Indian Reorganization Act to them. He also requested a second stock reduction. Although the Navajo Council finally agreed to a reduction of 150,000 goats and 50,000 sheep, the BIA again implemented the program too rapidly, and the Navajos used the livestock reduction programs in their campaign against the Indian Reorganization Act. Jacob C. Morgan, a Navajo graduate of Hampton Institute and a staunch assimilationist, led the faction opposing the Indian Reorganization Act. Chee Dodge, a recognized tribal leader of long standing and an avid traditionalist, was Morgan's archrival and threw his support behind Collier and the Indian Reorganization Act.

Morgan argued that acceptance of the Indian Reorganization Act would segregate the Navajos from the dominant society and "return them to the blanket." He condemned the closing of boarding schools (he had had a successful experience as a boarding school student) and the increased enrollment of Navajo children in day schools. In his campaign of opposition Morgan effectively converted hostility to the livestock reductions into resentment for both the Bureau of Indian Affairs and the Indian Reorganization Act.

Most traders and missionaries among the Navajos similarly disapproved of the new law. The traders worried about their own economic survival, fearing that the Navajos, under the Indian Reorganization Act programs, would banish them and establish cooperatives. The Protestant missionaries also harbored fears of expulsion and viewed the new tribal independence and tribal governments as a threat to Christian assimilation.

Dodge, on the other hand, believed that acceptance of the Indian Reorganization Act would create genuine self-government for the Navajos. But Dodge was not nearly as effective a campaigner as Morgan, who especially influenced the eastern and northern Navajos. Their votes proved decisive in defeating the Indian Reorganization Act in June 1935. Collier was deeply disappointed over the rejection; he tried repeatedly to persuade the Navajos to hold another election on the act—to no avail. Throughout the 1930s and early 1940s the Navajos, outside the provisions of the act, argued with Collier and the BIA over such issues as land management, livestock regulation, and the power of the Navajo Tribal Council.

Other tribes, however, took advantage of the Indian Reorganization Act by forming tribal corporations and borrowing money from the revolving credit fund. The Manchester Band of the Pomos in California, for example, established a dairy and farming business, and the Chippewas at the Lac du Flambeau Reservation in Wisconsin built a number of tourist cabins to generate income. Native Americans on the Swinomish Reservation in Washington started an oyster fishing project, and in Montana the Northern Cheyennes and Rocky Boy Band of Chippewa Crees received loans to increase and feed their cattle herds. In the Southwest, the Chiricahua and Mescalero Apaches (on the Mescalero Apache Reservation) secured loans of more than $240,000 for the improvement of reservation housing and agricultural and livestock production, while the Jicarilla Apaches used a loan from the revolving credit fund to establish a tribal store, the first of its kind operated exclusively by Native Americans. Tribal corporations also gave loans to individual Native Americans so that they could improve their own economic situations. These loans were repaid promptly; by 1945 less than 1 percent of the loans from the revolving credit fund were in default. Still, only 8 percent of adult Native American males in the United States ever participated in the revolving credit fund program.

Further problems magnified Collier's unpopularity. The creation of the Technical Cooperation–Bureau of Indian Affairs project in December 1935, a joint venture by the Department of Agriculture and the Interior Department to survey reservation resources and recommend means of economic development, caused many Native Americans to fear reductions of their lands and livestock. At Zuñi Pueblo, tribal members complained that Collier had placed them under the jurisdiction of the United Pueblo

Agency and had appointed a woman—medical doctor Sophie Aberle—as general superintendent without their consent. At Taos Pueblo, where Collier had first encountered his "Red Atlantis" in the 1920s, disputes over the use of peyote brought more controversy and bitterness. The peyotists were a minority there, but problems between the two factions had existed for years. In February 1936 the antipeyotist majority stopped a peyote ceremony, and the peyotists protested vehemently. Collier went to Taos Pueblo in June and managed to arrange a compromise that allowed the peyotists to practice their religion on a restricted basis, but the agreement soon degenerated into more bitterness and contention. More serious for Collier, the antipeyotists among the Pueblos resented his interference, as did Mabel Dodge, his old friend. She had long viewed peyote as a dangerous drug and believed that Collier's unilateral decisions regarding the Zuñis were deplorable. At an All Pueblo Council meeting in April 1936, Collier defended his actions, while Dodge and the antipeyotists criticized him. Their arguments were carried nationally in the media, and in August the United States Senate held hearings in Santa Fe. Although Collier's decision on peyote stood, along with his willingness to let the Native American Church function on the reservations, his popularity suffered a serious setback.

As the 1930s drew to a close, the "Indian New Deal" had become the object of intense criticism. Even Burton K. Wheeler, one of the sponsors of the original Indian Reorganization Act, began expressing misgivings about the program. He had never really supported Collier's views on communal societies and the values of ethnic pluralism, and he had become critical of BIA controls over Native Americans. By the late 1930s he also came to believe that the tribal corporations were becoming too powerful and that the Bureau of Indian Affairs was discriminating against the tribes which had rejected the Indian Reorganization Act. Wheeler's disaffection from Collier grew more intense in 1937 when Collier wrote an editorial in *Indians at Work* supporting Roosevelt's attempt to pack the United States Supreme Court. To Collier's great dismay, Wheeler introduced a bill in the Senate in 1937 to repeal the Indian Reorganization Act. Collier fought the repeal, arguing that Native Americans were not being segregated from European Americans, that tribal corporations were only exercising powers specifically granted to them in previous laws and in the provisions of the Indian Reorganization Act, and that those Native Americans rejecting the New Deal program were not being mistreated or ignored. The repeal was defeated, but it was a continuing sign of congressional resentment over the "Indian New Deal."

The American Indian Federation also remained a major critic of the "Indian New Deal." Leaders of that organization even solicited aid from the Nazis, who had declared that Native Americans were members of the Aryan race and a suppressed minority in the United States. (The German-American Bund carried on a propaganda campaign, condemning Collier's "communistic" reforms and the presence of Jewish employees in the Department of the Interior.) Federation spokesmen were allowed to express their views at Senate Indian Affairs Committee meetings, and in 1939 they managed to submit a bill exempting certain tribes from the Indian Reorganization Act. However, the House revised the legislation to allow tribes who had already accepted the law to vote again on provisions they might have already approved but now found objectionable. Collier fought the bill and it died in committee, but the "Indian New Deal" barely survived the assault.

World War II eventually accomplished, however, what the critics of the 1930s had failed to do. Because of the tremendous growth of federal agencies and the shortage of office space during the war, in December 1941 the Bureau of Indian Affairs was transferred to Chicago, far from the seat of power. It became almost impossible for the BIA to work with other government departments in cooperative programs to assist Native Americans. John Collier no longer had the ear of President Roosevelt, who was too absorbed with military, diplomatic, and economic concerns to worry about Native American affairs. More than eight hundred employees of the Bureau of Indian Affairs left the agency during the war, either going to work for other federal agencies or joining the armed services. Congressional appropriations to the bureau dwindled, and deterioration of roads, housing, and medical care on the reservations ensued.

Even more significant were the ideological pressures created by total war. The Japanese attack on Pearl Harbor inspired nearly four years of patriotic fervor, anti-Axis propaganda, and obsessive concern for national unity; in the process Collier's emphasis on ethnicity and community independence seemed counterproductive at best and dangerous at worst. Between 1941 and 1945 the need for unity and consensus was overwhelming, and most Americans were simply unwilling to accept Native Americans as a permanently separate set of subcultures in the United States. Karl Mundt, a prominent congressman from South Dakota, called for a complete investigation of Native American affairs in 1943 and suggested abolition of the BIA and the end of federal control over Native Americans.

In 1944 Senator Thomas issued a scathing attack on Collier and the "Indian New Deal," and Senator Wheeler concurred. The Senate Subcommittee on Indian Affairs suggested a return to the old allotment policies. That same year Senator Harlan Bushfield of South Dakota sounded a similar theme in demanding repeal of the Indian Reorganization Act. Additionally, the National Council of Churches once again proposed a return to the traditional policies of individualism, private property, and assimilation in Native American communities. Disgusted with the criticism and the pressure, John Collier resigned on January 10, 1945.

Achievements of the Indian Reorganization Act were limited—far short of expectations. The Department of the Interior spent more than $5 million purchasing four hundred thousand new acres of land, and several pieces of congressional legislation added another nine hundred thousand acres. The Interior Department returned more than a million acres that had not been homesteaded as well as a million acres of public-domain grazing land. With their own funds Native Americans managed to purchase four hundred thousand new acres, so that in all they recovered nearly 4 million acres of land they had lost under the Dawes Act. That was not much, especially in view of what they had lost since 1887, but at least the Indian Reorganization Act had stopped the allotment program before it had done any more damage. Also, the tribal structures of some tribes had been repaired and the federal government had given at least lip service to the principle of self-determination for Native Americans.

Still, overwhelming problems remained for the more than five hundred thousand Native Americans living in the United States in 1945. They had lost over 90 million acres of land since 1887, and much of what they had recovered since 1934 was of little value—land that European American settlers had not wanted. Economic dependence on the federal government remained a fact of life. Poverty, disease, and unemployment continued to be far higher than among other Americans.

As had occurred so often in the past, European American attitudes and Native American factionalism had stalled reform movements, and the "Indian New Deal" had been no exception. Although it had many shortcomings, it was an unprecedented effort to protect Native American heritage and provide political and economic assistance. Collier failed, however, to appreciate the complexity of Native American tribalism. He expected all Native Americans to accept political and economic institutions created along European American rules of individual aggrandizement and majority rule. The "Indian New Deal" had been a noble, albeit flawed, attempt to reverse the trends of the past. A viable but mutually accommodating policy had yet to be formulated.

19. John Dillinger: Public Enemy

MARK SUFRIN

It is not often that murderers and bank robbers become popular national heroes; the times must be particularly unique to produce such an extraordinary development in popular culture. The 1930s were such a time in the United States.

After the stock market crash in 1929, the economy slipped deeper and deeper into the Great Depression. Farm prices collapsed, unemployment rose to a staggering 25 percent, and banks closed by the thousands. Since federal deposit insurance did not exist, millions of Americans lost all of their savings. Those banks that did survive were forced to foreclose on the farms, tractors, automobiles, houses, and businesses of Americans who could not pay their bills. Bankers became the fall guys in a society embittered by economic decline.

When criminals like John Dillinger, Bonnie and Clyde, Baby Face Nelson, Ma Barker, and Pretty Boy Floyd started robbing those banks, they struck a responsive chord in the heartstrings of America. Bank robbers became larger-than-life folk heroes, celebrities who gave the bankers a dose of their own medicine. The fact that the bank robbers were little more than murderous thugs did not seem to faze the public. In the following article, Mark Sufrin describes the life of John Dillinger, whom FBI director J. Edgar Hoover dubbed "Public Enemy Number One," and how his escapades infatuated the American public in the 1930s.

In the Great Depression of the early 1930's an obscure group of criminal psychopaths quickly became notorious. They were native-born Americans from isolated dirt farms and dusty small towns, some descended from the James brothers, the Youngers, and Daltons, and briefly were figures in the national folklore.

In those terrible years hungry, jobless people, frightened of and helpless against forces they didn't understand, made heroes of men who took what they wanted at gunpoint. These hayseed buccaneers evoked nostalgia for a vanished past that probably never existed—angry wild boys out of the hills forced into a life of crime, Robin Hood avengers fighting the predatory railroads and banks . . . the swan song of an American breed, the last rugged individualists who took all the risks themselves. They were nothing more than depraved killers and thieves, but American myths die hard. More than thirty years after their rampage, a farmer near Palmyra, Missouri, spoke this eulogy for the outlaws:

"Why, Johnny Dillinger and all them fellows, they came from this part of the country. They was real Americans—not like them city gangsters, a lot of greasy foreigners. These boys was the stock that made this country. Hell! If they stole from the banks—well, it was hard times then and the banks took our farms and money. They didn't do no worse than what the James boys did."

Of all these lurid desperadoes, one man, John Dillinger, came to evoke the era, and stirred mass emotion and worship to a degree rarely seen in this country. He lived a myth first created by Matt Leach, Director of the Indiana State Police, a man Dillinger constantly outwitted and humiliated, then exaggerated by the press until Dillinger himself became possessed by the legend. His career was brief and violent, and his death, supreme melodrama that loosed an awesome madness in the public.

He was a paradox: a creature of driving will, a self-pitying, warped man who murdered with morbid calm, then wept, not for his victims, but something sentimental suddenly remembered about his sisters whom he loved. He thought kidnappers were "dirty skunks," he seldom smoked, cursed or drank (he refused to buy his girl Evelyn Frechette booze because she was half-Sioux). He bored his gang with lectures on loyalty, but when she was arrested he did nothing to help though only a few feet away in a car and armed with a tommy gun. When John Hamilton, his top gun, was badly wounded, Dillinger refused to take him to a doctor, waited until he died a lingering, painful death from gangrene, then buried him in a gravel pit and poured lye over his face to prevent identification. "Sorry old pal," he said, "I know you'd do the same for me."

Dillinger was a tomcat with the women—and a loser all the way. His first love probably helped trigger his vicious, dismal life, and the last woman he met fingered him to the FBI, and a violent end. He was tough and courageous, with a sharp intelligence, and he gripped the public's imagination through virtues Americans understand: Dillinger was, simply, the most energetic, successful, and efficient thief of that genre, and his flair for the dramatic and brazen made it look easy.

John Herbert Dillinger was born on June 22, 1903 in the Oak Hill section of Indianapolis, a middle-class residential neighborhood. His father, a hard working grocer, raised him in a bewildering atmosphere of disciplinary extremes, harsh and repressive on some occasions but generous and permissive on others.

Young John's mother died when he was 3, and although his father remarried six years later, Dillinger apparently resented his stepmother, seeing his father giving her the affection that he craved.

In adolescence, the flaws in his bewildering personality became evident. Maddeningly restless, convinced that his teachers abused him for no reason, he was frequently in trouble. Finally, he quit school and got a job in a machine shop in Indianapolis. Although intelligent and a good worker, he soon became bored and often stayed out all night. His father, worried that the temptations of the city were corrupting his teen-aged son, and wanting, himself, to retire from the grocery business, decided on a move to the country. He sold his property in Indianapolis and moved his family to a farm near Mooresville, Indiana. But young John reacted no better to life on the farm than he had to that in the city and soon began to run wild again.

A break with his father and trouble with the law (auto theft) led him to try something new. He enlisted in the Navy but, hating the discipline, he soon got into trouble and finally deserted his ship, the *Utah*, when it docked at Boston.

Returning to Mooresville, he married a local flapper, 16-year-old Beryl Hovius in 1924.

She had the itch, wanted to get out of "this jerk town" and head for the big city. Her dazzling dream of bright lights and excitement was Indianapolis. Dillinger, a confused bridegroom, pleaded that he was a farmer and wanted to stay put, but Beryl kept nagging. He tried to find work in the city but had no luck. When Beryl pouted and took to sleeping alone on the couch, Dillinger, wild to please her, hooked up with the town pool shark, a skinny, jug-eared hustler named Ed Singleton, in the search for easy money.

Their first caper was a farce. They tried to rob a Mooresville grocer and were caught red-handed. Singleton pleaded not guilty, stood trial, and got two years. Dillinger, on his father's advice to remember the moral teachings learned in church, confessed. The senile, vindictive judge sentenced him to ten to twenty years.

Stunned by the injustice, Dillinger became a tortured, bitter man in prison. A man who served time with him saw what was happening:

"You get to recognize a killer in prison. There's a lot come in that way or it makes them. First we thought he was just a hardheaded hick who got a lousy break. Then you'd see him in a fight, and it was like he didn't care whether he got killed or the other guy, just so someone got it. We learned to keep out of his way. Even inside, cons joke and are friendly. But year by year, Dillinger just got quieter and madder. I used to sweat every time he looked at me. He always had this expression on his face, his mouth twisted on the left side, like he was under pressure every minute. Some guys try to look tough, then they forget and it's gone. But he had that look all the time. I tell you, I knew as soon as they let this guy out, someone was gonna walk away from his hat."

The first year of his infamy and the last year of his life began on May 22, 1933, when he was released from the Michigan City, Indiana penitentiary after serving nine years. On the way back to Mooresville, he seemed inconspicuous—5 feet 9, 170 pounds, wavy reddish-brown hair, a stolid face with a mole between the eyes and a slightly receding, dimpled chin—another farmer or small town clerk in a cheap suit, denim shirt, and high black shoes. But Dillinger's sour-lined mouth, the dead cast of his strange lynx eyes, his big hands locked tightly together, all revealed an almost unbearable tension.

He found trouble at home. His stepmother was dead. Beryl, who had divorced him five years before, had remarried and moved to Denver. His father had only a week to raise money on the mortgage or lose the farm to a bank. Everything fed Dillinger's self-pity and the hate he had nurtured in prison. That same night he left for Chicago, reassuring his father he would get him the money.

He teamed up with an ex-con named Homer Van Meter and others, knocked off several small banks and other firms in the area, and paid off the mortgage. Dillinger began to dream of a gang that could strike fast and hard throughout the Midwest and grab a fortune. He figured he needed four more men to work with himself and Van Meter, four specialists. The men he wanted were still in the Michigan City pen: fat and genial Charlie Makley, John "Three-fingered Jack" or "Red" Hamilton, handsome Russell "Boobie" Clark, and burly Harry Pierpont. None had gone beyond the 8th grade, all had had gonorrhea, and they were vicious—but they were professionals. Dillinger had a contact in the factory that supplied thread to the prison shirt shop, and knew that Pierpont always opened the crates. He smuggled in arms and money ($1,000 in small bills) and sent word via the grapevine: *Watch for a crate splashed with black paint.*

While they waited, he and Van Meter robbed the State Bank in Indianapolis of $37,000. Both had been identified by witnesses to the first three holdups, and Matt Leach linked them to the latest job. Van Meter escaped, but a stool pigeon turned in Dillinger. On September 6, 1933, he was captured without a struggle in an apartment in Dayton, Ohio, then removed to the county jail at Lima.

On September 26 Dillinger's four recruits escaped, killing a guard and taking two guards as hostages. On October 12 the fugitives, wearing snappy new suits and snap brim hats, arrived at the Lima jail, posing as deputies from Michigan City who had come to take Dillinger back. When Sheriff Jesse Sarber asked for their credentials, Pierpont reached inside his jacket, drew a gun and fired, fatally wounding the lawman. The sheriff's wife and a deputy ran in; Makley and Clark killed the man, locked the woman in a cell, and then freed Dillinger.

The gang began to scourge the Midwest, hitting banks, and raiding police stations when they needed weapons and bulletproof vests (first casing them as writers for a detective magazine eager to publicize the local lawmen). Dillinger decided their next heist would be the National Savings and Trust Company in Greencastle, Indiana. The others argued that it was too risky, that there were too many people always around the courthouse across the street. Dillinger said they would take the bank, and no one would know it was being robbed.

One day a raffish-looking film crew drove up to the red brick building. Makley, his cap turned backwards, was the "cameraman"; Hamilton, the "director," wore puttees and an open-necked shirt and carried a megaphone; Van Meter, the "assistant director," ran around shouting directions as Clark, the "assistant cameraman," measured distances between the camera and bank entrance. Dillinger and Pierpont, wearing bright yellow makeup and primping before mirrors, were the "actors."

Hamilton explained to the watching crowd that they had come from Hollywood to film a bank robbery in an authentic setting. They went through a couple of rehearsals, but Hamilton was dissatisfied:

"That's lousy. I want to make this look more realistic. I'm going in there and show you how to make a bank holdup look like the real thing. And I want those people inside to yell like they really been robbed. This time when you escape, do it different—get away in the car."

Two minutes later, Hamilton with Dillinger and Pierpont ran from the bank followed by shouting people. *"It looks real as hell,"* said a man in the crowd. The three bandits jumped into the car and started up the street as Clark, Makley, and Van Meter leaped onto the running board, and they kept going straight out of town. The take was $87,389.14.

After a side trip to virgin territory—Farrel, Pennsylvania where a stickup netted $26,000—Dillinger decided to make his headquarters in Chicago. The city had definite advantages: it was big, had a crooked police department, a lot of women, and was a central point from which he could raid. He took up light housekeeping with the 27-year-old Evelyn Frechette, a singer in a cheap North Clark Street Club.

Dillinger got a straight one-fourth cut from all proceeds. There was never any argument about the split until "Baby Face" Nelson—the only bandit without a single redeeming trait—joined the gang. Dillinger let him divide the take. He wasn't scared of Nelson, merely prudent. The homicidal runt was jealous of Dillinger.

In December 1933 Dillinger and Makley, out for a walk, saw a notice posted on the Unity Trust and Savings. The bank was closed, it said, but the room containing the safe-deposit boxes was open for business. Posing as salesmen of burglar alarms, they were surprised when the lone attendant, an elderly man, said the building didn't have sufficient wiring, hence there was really no need for such a device. Back on the street, Makley wanted to hit the bank right then. But Dillinger, always a cool tactician when it came to money, had another plan. For this job he conceived something new in lookouts—a phony Santa Claus. "Fat" Makley was the obvious choice: ruddy-cheeked, with a deep "Ho-Ho-Ho" laugh, and two automatics tucked under his red shirt. On the afternoon of December 13 Pierpont, Hamilton, and Dillinger emerged from the bank, the leader carrying a suitcase stuffed with $220,000 in cash and negotiable bonds. He bid the "Santa" out front a Merry Christmas, dropped a few coins in the iron pot, and merged with the crowd of shoppers.

The newspapers emitted an outraged blast and even the live-and-let-live Chicago police, prodded by Matt Leach who was certain it was Dillinger's work, threw every man it could muster into the search. One night Dillinger and Hamilton were at a newstand. A detective spotted the latter's missing finger, swung his gaze toward Dillinger and started to draw. Dillinger was quicker and killed him. Chicago became too hot and the gang took a brief Florida vacation.

Back in Chicago they held up the Beverly Gardens night club and a roadhouse, then Dillinger had to shoot his way out of a police trap while visiting a dentist. His picture was on the front pages every day, on magazine covers, flashed on movie screens in newsreels, his description given every hour on the radio. But he hit five banks in eight days. Racine, Wisconsin; Montpelier, Indiana; Bluffton, Ohio; Decatur, Illinois; Sioux Falls, South Dakota. He killed two bank tellers and two policemen.

After that orgy Dillinger split the gang. Pierpont, Makley, and Clark were sent to Tucson, Arizona, with orders to stay low. Dillinger, Hamilton, and Van Meter hit an East Chicago, Indiana bank for $43,280, and killed a cop in the getaway. Dillinger fled to Tucson and joined the others in the Congress Hotel. The building caught fire and one of the firemen recognized the bandits from pictures in a detective magazine. They were taken prisoner without a shot being fired and put under guard by forty picked men. Pierpont, Makley, and Clark were taken back to Lima, Ohio to be tried for the murder of Sheriff Jesse Sarber. Dillinger, shackled hand and foot and guarded by a hundred police armed with submachine guns, was returned to Chicago. Three states were fighting to get him, but Bob Estill, an ambitious county prosecutor in Indiana, won the legal wrangle and the outlaw was delivered to the Crown Point, Indiana jail that had been converted into a stronghold.

"Not even Harry Houdini could crack this place," said one courthouse wag.

Smirking, Dillinger posed for photographs with his arm around Estill, and the woman sheriff, Mrs. Lillian Holley, alongside. He was a model prisoner, but on March 3, 1934, nine days before his trial for murder, he broke out using a "gun"—fashioned, he said, from a piece of wood and black shoe polish. With a murderer named Herbert Youngblood, he stole the sheriff's car, grabbed a deputy as hostage, and headed for Illinois.

The legend was growing: a derring-do escape, a country boy using good old Yankee ingenuity by whittling a weapon. The true story came out later but people refused to believe it. It was too disillusioning. Dillinger's lawyer had bribed a prominent Indiana judge, who smuggled in a real gun. To save face, the authorities planted the story of the phony. Dillinger, a supreme egotist and his own best press agent, never did anything to dispel the legend.

But when he escaped from Crown Point, he made his first bad tactical mistake. By transporting a stolen car across a state line, he had committed a Federal offense; this brought the FBI into the hunt. The fear he inspired was at a peak. Every cop in the Midwest carried his picture and it was pasted behind every bank teller's cage. Jittery bank employees pressed the alarm button at the first hint of anything suspicious; in one day Chicago cops responded to eight false alarms in different banks. Dillinger became the popular phantom of everyone's imagination. In a single week he was reported in Omaha, Council Bluffs, Savannah, New York, San Diego, Mexico City. As one newspaper editorial facetiously put it: "Dillinger—wherever he is—seems to have kept out of London, Paris, Berlin, Rome, Moscow, Vienna, and Paducah, Kentucky." Newspapers and police were bombarded with tips from cranks and practical jokers.

Newsreel shots of Dillinger were greeted with applause, cheers, and whistles. Newspapers played up the color, dubbing him "The New Jesse James." President Roosevelt said that he was "shocked by the public adulation of a vicious criminal . . . it permits police to be corrupted or intimidated, and romanticizes men who are nothing but insane murderers." A London editorial asked, "What is happening to America?" German newspapers shrieked: "No voice in America should be raised against Hitler as long as Dillinger is loose." Then they advised Americans to follow the Nazis' "deep sense of responsibility" and sterilize all gangsters. Will Rogers, commenting about a Dillinger holdup when more innocents than bandits were shot by trigger-happy cops, remarked:

"Well, they had Dillinger surrounded and was all ready to shoot him when he came out, but another bunch of folks came out ahead of him, so they shot them instead. Dillinger is going to accidentally get with some innocent bystanders sometime—then he'll get shot up like a sieve."

On April 8, 1934, lonesome for his family, he risked his life to return home for a Sunday dinner. Back in Chicago the next day, Evelyn Frechette was picked up by police while Dillinger, unrecognized, sat in a car a few feet away with a loaded tommy gun. He made no move to help her but afterward sent money to her for a lawyer through a go-between, a third of the sum disappearing en route. He wrote his father:

"I got here all right and found I don't have many friends. Would liked to have stayed longer at home. I enjoyed seeing you and the girls so much. I have been over a lot of this country, but home always looks best to me. . . ."

Late in April, holed up in a northern Wisconsin lodge called Little Bohemia, the gang was trapped by forty-eight agents and twelve local lawmen under Melvin Purvis, head of the FBI's Chicago field office. But they shot their way out. The only casualties were three more innocents, shot by mistake by the lawmen, and two agents killed by Nelson. Hunted, a big price on his head, obsessed with getting a stake big enough to escape to Mexico, Dillinger continued to hit banks.

Ten strong anticrime bills were pushed through Congress to give the FBI teeth in its fight against Dillinger. Every Midwestern city had a special Dillinger squad and sharpshooters to pick him off on sight. The Indiana National Guard wanted to use tanks, planes, and poison gas to run him to earth, and the American Legion offered to arm 50,000 of its members to act as vigilantes to assist in his capture.

There was too much pressure, and the decline began. Dillinger had a plastic operation performed on him by a drug-addicted doctor and almost died from an overdose of ether. It was a failure, his face mutilated but little altered, the fingerprints still detectable. He trusted no one and paid to stay alive. He bought protection from crooked cops, criminals, and paid stoolpigeons more than they could get from the law for turning him in. Most of what he stole went for living expenses and "grease" (he paid as much as $200 for a filthy room). Hamilton was dead. Clark, Makley, and Pierpont were sentenced to death in Ohio. Pierpont ("I'm what you would call an abnormal mental case, but once I was normal") was killed attempting escape, and the others were executed.

Dillinger tried one more bank job to get his stake. It had to be a good haul: he needed $10,000 just to buy his way out of the country, and at least $30,000 for living expenses. Van Meter cased the Merchants' National Bank in South Bend, Indiana and figured there was at least $200,000 in the till. They hit the bank on June 30, 1934—and it was a disaster. The city was a nest of heroes . . . it was Northfield, Minnesota, all over again, when townfolk butchered the James–Younger gang in 1877.

First, one man thought he recognized the bandits (all were dressed in straw hats and overalls) and tried to steal their car keys when they entered the bank. A jeweler named Harry Berg ran from his shop and opened fire on Nelson, standing outside. Saved by his bulletproof vest, Baby Face spun and fired wildly down the street. A teenager jumped him, but Nelson flung him into a plate glass window and fired from ten feet. The slug pierced the kid's palm and shattered the window. Nelson was about to kill him but was driven off by Berg's fire. A man leaving a sporting goods store with a new shotgun kneeled and loaded and hit Van Meter. An elderly judge using an heirloom cavalry pistol wounded Dillinger and Tommy Carrol, then Berg gunned down Eddie Green. The bandits' bullet-riddled Hudson slewed around a corner and swung south, pursued by a police car. They made their escape, but each man's share came to only $4,800.

After the fiasco at the Little Bohemia Lodge, FBI Director J. Edgar Hoover had sent Special Agent Samuel Cowley to Chicago to head a special Dillinger squad.

Back in Chicago in July, Dillinger—calling himself "Jack Lawrence"—picked up blonde Polly Hamilton in a diner. She took him home to the apartment she shared with Anna Sage, her former boss in a Gary, Indiana brothel. Fighting deportation to her native Rumania for her record of prostitution, Anna felt certain "Lawrence" was the wanted killer. She figured she could make a deal with the government and contacted an East Chicago cop who took her to see Purvis. She offered to turn in Dillinger in return for her freedom. The FBI man said he could only make a favorable recommendation for her to the immigration service if she would help capture the outlaw. Anna agreed, said that she would talk Dillinger into taking her and Polly to a movie the next day, July 22—either the Mabro or the Biograph, but probably the latter because it had a Clark Gable film and he was Dillinger's favorite actor. She said she would wear a bright red dress for identification.

Both theaters were inspected and agents staked out. Early in the evening of July 22, 1934, Purvis waited nervously for Anna Sage's call, afraid Dillinger might have fled. The phone rang and he heard the woman's urgent, whispered voice:

"We're leaving in about five minutes . . . the Biograph."

While Cowley and one squad of agents waited at the FBI offices in the Bankers' Building for the final word of Dillinger's appearance, Purvis drove to the Biograph Theater.

At 8 P.M., seated in a parked car, Purvis saw three people approach the theater: a buxom, dark-haired woman in a red dress, a thin blonde, and a stocky man in gray pants and a white shirt. Dillinger looked relaxed, the familiar smirk on his tight mouth. Six agents followed him into the theater. Purvis settled back to wait until the show ended, but never took his eyes off the theater entrance. Meanwhile Purvis' companion, Agent Ralph Brown, telephoned the news of Dillinger's arrival at the Biograph to Cowley who soon arrived at the theater with his men.

Munching sunflower seeds, Dillinger watched the film, *Manhattan Melodrama,* blinking back tears at the end as Gable walked to the electric chair with these words, *"Die the way you lived . . . that's the way to take it."* The house lights went up and the audience started out of the theater. The six FBI agents fell in behind Dillinger and the two women as they walked out into the stifling summer night. Purvis saw them emerge and suddenly thought of the veiled but definite order from Homer Cummings, the United States Attorney General:

"Take Dillinger under circumstances that will make a trial unnecessary."

Purvis and Cowley were taking no chances that Dillinger would slip through their hands this time. In case the outlaw escaped the squad to his rear, pairs of agents were staked out all along the street to stop him. As the hunted outlaw neared Purvis, their eyes met for an instant. Possibly Dillinger saw nothing more than a casual glance. But Purvis was scanning his face quickly. He thought Dillinger looked different, something about the nose, the entire face. For an anxious moment, he thought Anna Sage was mistaken. Then Purvis saw the menacing lynx eyes and realized that Dillinger had had his face lifted. He had his man.

Purvis lit a cigar: the signal that he had made positive identification. The six agents began to close in. Two more agents walked toward Dillinger from the front, cutting off escape. The two women began to drop back slowly. Suddenly sensing danger, Dillinger broke for an alley, reaching for the .45 Colt pistol in his right hand pocket, trying to jerk it free. He took only a few lunging strides when the first slug tore into the back of his neck and spun out under his right eye. Several more bullets struck him and he was dead before he hit the ground. He lay face down in the alley, his feet extending into the glare of the electric signs. Blood spurted from his fatal wounds onto the white pants of the first agent to reach him.

The neighborhood suddenly exploded with excited, morbid crowds. Hysterical women surged forward in a frenzy, screeching in almost sexual ecstasy, scratching and fighting the agents and police in their attempt to reach the body. One fat-breasted woman with stringy red hair broke through the cordon and dipped her handkerchief in the blood, clutched it to her sweaty dress and waddled off down the street, her face fixed in tense passion. A man offered the FBI agent $50 for the bloodstained pants. The crowd was sobbing, babbling, laughing wildly.

Dillinger had $7.87 in his pocket—from an estimated $200,000 share of the holdups. If he had any money stashed away, he never told anyone the hiding place.

A month later, still recuperating from his shotgun wounds, Van Meter was gunned down in St. Paul, also betrayed by a woman. Baby Face Nelson succeeded Dillinger as Public Enemy Number One. On November 27, 1934, he and his wife were caught in a Wisconsin roadblock. Nelson killed two FBI men, Cowley and Hollis, who had been at the theater when Dillinger was killed. Nelson escaped, but was mortally wounded. The next morning, stripped nude to prevent immediate identification, his body was found in a ditch thirty miles away.

After an inquest, Dillinger's body went on display at the Chicago morgue and thousands passed by in a line a mile long. The majority were women.

"I wouldn't have wanted to see him," said one, "only it's a moral lesson. I think I'll go through once more, but he looks just like any other dead man."

The mob followed the corpse to the mortuary. Barkers passed through the crowd, shouting, "Here you are, an original guaranteed swatch of Dillinger's blood on a handkerchief."

Dillinger's brain was removed for examination—and somehow "mislaid."

At a funeral home in Mooresville, crowds broke the place apart and stole or trampled every flower.

One Communist commentator said Dillinger was "a product of capitalism."

A Virginia newspaper branded the FBI agents as "cowards" for not giving Dillinger a chance to shoot.

There were rumors that it wasn't Dillinger at all. He had fooled the law again.

Purvis resigned from the FBI to accept a lucrative offer from Post Toasties Cereal—organizing Junior G-Men. He committed suicide in 1960.

It was an incredible circus, but Dillinger was finally buried (the grave reinforced with iron and concrete to keep out ghouls) in the same cemetery with other noted Hoosiers: President Benjamin Harrison, a Vice President, two governors, three senators, and poet James Whitcomb Riley.

A week after his son's death, Dillinger's father, an old stooped farmer, left on a vaudeville tour of the country with his daughter and son-in-law. The billing style was Old Time Carnival:

Hear From Their Own Lips Incidents in the Life of the Late John Dillinger, Jr.—and of His Visit to the Kindly Old Father's Home April 8, When the Entire Nation Was Searching for Him!

Tourists still come to gawk at the site of the Biograph Theater, now torn down, and the alley where he died. And the legend persists. A few years ago, with the renewal of interest in the 1930's because of the enormous success of the film, *Bonnie and Clyde,* a reporter visited Mooresville to talk to the townfolk about Dillinger.

"I saw Johnny not long ago in a motel up in Michigan," said one man.

"Johnny drove through town only a few days ago," another insisted. "He smiled at me and winked. . . ."

20. The Night of the Martians

EDWARD OXFORD

Historians are fond of saying that it was World War II, not the New Deal, that really brought an end to the Great Depression. Although Americans worried about "bread and butter" issues throughout the 1930s, the winds of war were blowing over Europe late in the decade, and there were unsettling fears in the United States that the world was about to enter another global conflict. In 1938, Adolf Hitler and the German army occupied Austria in what became known as the Anschluss, *and later in the year the Nazis invaded the Sudetenland in Czechoslovakia, all in the name of reuniting the German-speaking people of Europe. Benito Mussolini's Italian army had stormed through Ethiopia in 1936. In East Asia, Japan attacked Manchuria in 1931 and China in 1937. Great Britain, France, Belgium, The Netherlands, Poland, and the Soviet Union braced themselves for war.*

Americans felt a bit safer. The Atlantic and Pacific Oceans provided some insulation, but since they had not proven enough of a barrier to keep us out of World War I, there was no real sense of optimism. Newspapers were full of talk about invasion and war. American nerves were already frayed in 1938 when Orson Welles decided to produce a radio dramatization of H. G. Wells's The War of the Worlds. *The ensuing panic and controversy became legend in the annals of American broadcasting. In the following essay, Edward Oxford describes the night America was invaded by Martians.*

A little after eight P.M. on Halloween eve 1938, thirteen-year-old Dick Stives, his sister, and two brothers huddled around their family's radio. They were in the dining room of their grandfather's farmhouse near the hamlet of Grovers Mill, four miles east of Princeton, New Jersey. Their mother and father had dropped them off there and gone to the movies.

Dick worked the radio dial, hunting for the station that carried the *Chase and Sanborn Hour,* his—and the nation's—favorite Sunday evening program. As he scanned the airwaves, Dick tuned in the local affiliate of the Columbia Broadcasting System (CBS). A commanding voice—that of Orson Welles—riveted his attention.

". . . across an immense ethereal gulf, minds that are to our minds as ours are to the beasts of the jungle, intellects vast, cool, and unsympathetic, regarded this earth with envious eyes and slowly and surely drew their plans against us. . . ."

Dick Stives turned the dial no further. Instead, during the next hour he and millions of other listeners sat glued by their radios, convinced by an alarming series of "news bulletins" that monster aliens from Mars were invading America. Dick's village of Grovers Mill—the supposed landing site for these invaders—became the focal point of a panic wave that rapidly swept across the nation.

The program—the *Mercury Theatre on the Air* adaptation of H. G. Wells's *The War of the Worlds*—would later be remembered as the most extraordinary radio show ever broadcast. And Orson Welles, its brilliant young producer, director, and star, would be catapulted to nationwide fame overnight.

As the wonder boy of the performing arts, Orson Welles had by age twenty-three already appeared on the cover of *Time* magazine; built a considerable reputation as a radio actor; set the stage-world on its ear with a *Julius Caesar* set in Fascist Italy, an all-black *Macbeth,* and a production of Marc Blitzstein's opera *The Cradle Will Rock;* and founded—with his partner-in-drama John Houseman—the revolutionary and often controversial Mercury Theatre.*

In midsummer 1938, the Columbia Broadcasting System, impressed by Welles's meteoric success, offered him and his repertory company a grand stage, radio—"the Broadway of the entire United States"—on which to deliver a sixty-minute dramatization each week.

Broadcast from the twenty-second floor of the CBS building in midtown Manhattan, the *Mercury Theatre on the Air* had no commercial sponsor. The show was subsidized by the CBS network, and its bare-bones budget provided no money for expensive, original plays. "We offered the audience classic works from the public domain—*Julius Caesar, Oliver Twist, The Heart of Darkness, Jane Eyre,* and such," recalls John Houseman. "Orson and I would select the book. Sometimes it was my task to fashion the original into a workable radio script."

For the last program of October, the seventeenth in their series, Welles and Houseman wanted to "throw in something of a scientific nature." They settled on an adaptation of *The War of the Worlds,* a science-fiction novel written in 1898 by British author H. G. Wells. Houseman assigned the script to a recent addition to the company, writer Howard Koch [see "Words on a Yellow Pad"].

For the fall season CBS had moved the *Mercury Theatre on the Air* from Monday evening to the Sunday-night eight-to-nine-o'clock slot, an "unsold" time period. During this hour much of America tuned in to the competing NBC Red network for the *Chase and Sanborn Hour,* which featured ventriloquist Edgar Bergen and his wooden-headed "dummy" Charlie McCarthy. The Crossley ratings of listenership gave Charlie McCarthy a "thirty-five" (roughly 35 percent of radio listeners at that hour tuned in), while the *Mercury* usually scored about "three."

During the week before the October 30 broadcast, Welles nonchalantly put in his own typically frantic week while Houseman, Koch, and the cast struggled to ready the show. Welles spent much of his time not in the CBS studios at 485 Madison Avenue, but on the stage of the Mercury Theatre on West 41st Street, rehearsing his repertory company for the opening of a new play. He hurried back to CBS at odd hours to try out some of his lines, listen to run-throughs by the radio show's cast, and render his inimitable revisions.

Welles and his company spent much of Sunday amid a litter of sandwiches and coffee cups in Studio One, adding final touches to their version of *The War of the Worlds* and conducting a dress rehearsal with full music and sound effects.

---

*Up to this time Welles was probably best known to radio audiences as "Lamont Cranston," alias "The Shadow," on the popular Sunday afternoon mystery program of the same name. But he also appeared frequently on many other shows, including *The March of Time,* and was said to be earning $1,000 a week from his radio commitments alone.

WORDS ON A YELLOW PAD

"When John Houseman handed me a copy of the H. G. Wells novel, *The War of the Worlds,* I felt it wouldn't work," says Howard Koch, who wrote the radio script of that novel. "It was too far afield, being set in England, and twenty years in the past. I asked that some other story be chosen. John relayed my request to Orson. But Orson insisted on *The War of the Worlds.*"

Koch was used to working six days a week, morning to night, dramatizing novels or short stories chosen by Orson Welles and John Houseman for the *Mercury Theatre on the Air* broadcasts. They paid Koch about $75 for each sixty-page script he wrote.

About all Koch could use from the Wells novel was the invasion concept; the rest of the script he invented, shifting the scene of the drama from England to the United States. Koch also conceived the idea of interrupting the narrative with sudden "bulletins" to set the action in a seemingly here-and-now time frame.

On the Monday before the broadcast—the one day of the week that he had off—Koch drove from his Manhattan apartment to his parents' home in Kingston, New York. The writer had not yet thought of a landing site for the Martian invaders, so, on his way back, he stopped at a gas station in New Jersey and picked up a road map.

"I just closed my eyes," he said. "Jabbed the point of my pencil straight down onto the map, then looked at the name of the place it had hit. Grovers Mill. A crossroads near Princeton, New Jersey. It had a good sound. That's where I decided the first Martian machine would land.

"I wrote *The War of the Worlds* script in pencil on a lined, yellow pad," he recalls. "A typist deciphered my scrawl. Each day John Houseman would shuttle back and forth between my apartment and the studio to pick up my ten or fifteen new pages and bring back changes that Orson and he had made on my prior batch."

Koch worked right up until the show's Sunday noon deadline. That night he listened to the program and then, exhausted, fell asleep.

Next morning, as he walked along 72nd Street toward his barber shop, Koch heard people talking about "invasion" and "war." He thought Hitler had unleashed his forces on Europe. At the shop, Koch's barber held up a newspaper and said, "Haven't you heard?" Center-page was a picture of Welles, arms outstretched in innocence, and underneath was the opening scene of Koch's play.

"That was an odd moment in my life but all ended well," says Koch. "Life went on. The show got a prestigious sponsor. I received a raise to $150 a week. Orson Welles and the Mercury Theatre players moved into the national limelight—and on to Hollywood."

And there Koch, in time, would win acclaim for writing the scripts for such films as *The Letter, Sergeant York, In This Our Life,* and *Letter From an Unknown Woman.* He would also share an Oscar for the screenplay of the unforgettable *Casablanca.*

Today, still lean and vigorous at eighty-five years of age, the self-effacing playwright lives in a stream-side home in Woodstock, New York. "I hold the rights to the radio script of *The War of the Worlds,*" he says. "But at this point, the story belongs to the people. It has become a part of the American memory."

Just before 8 P.M., Eastern Standard Time, Welles, conductor-like, stood poised on his platform in the middle of the studio. He had at his command not only his loyal band of actors, but also a small symphony orchestra. Wearing a headset, the multifaceted genius was prepared to read his own lines, cue the other actors, signal for sound effects, summon the orchestra, and also keep in touch with the control room.

At the stroke of eight o'clock, he gave the cue for the start of the *Mercury* theme—the Tchaikovsky Piano Concerto No. 1 in B-Flat Minor.

For the next unforgettable hour, Dick Stives at Grovers Mill, along with several million other Americans, sat transfixed as the airwaves brought word of weird and almost incomprehensible events that seemed to unfold with terrifying reality even as they listened.

It was not as though listeners hadn't been warned. Most simply didn't pay close attention to the program's opening signature (or tuned in a few seconds late and missed it altogether): "The Columbia Broadcasting System and its affiliated stations present Orson Welles and the Mercury Theatre on the Air in *The War of the Worlds* by H. G. Wells. . . ."

Many in the radio audience failed to associate what they heard with prior newspaper listings of the drama. And, by the time a single station break came late in the hour with reminders that listeners were hearing a fictional story, many others were too agitated to comprehend that they had been deceived.

Skillfully choreographed by Welles and Houseman, the program—a play simulating a montage of real-life dance band "remotes" and news bulletins—began with deliberate calm. Millions of listeners, conditioned by recent news reports of worldwide political turmoil—and by their inherent trust in the medium of radio—believed what they heard.

Just two minutes into the show, audience perception between fantasy and reality began to blur when, following Welles' dramatic opening monologue, the microphone shifted to a "network announcer" reading an apparently routine report from the "Government Weather Bureau."

Programming then shifted to "Ramon Raquello and his orchestra" in the "Meridian Room" at the "Hotel Park Plaza" in downtown New York City.

During rehearsals for the show, Welles had insisted—over the objections of his associates—on increasing the broadcast time devoted to the fictional orchestra's soothing renditions of "La Cumparsita" and "the ever popular 'Stardust.'" As he had anticipated, the resulting "band remote" had a disarming air of reality—and provided emotional contrast to the intensity of later news bulletins.*

Just when Welles had calculated that listeners might start tuning out the music in search of something more lively, an announcer broke in with a bulletin from the "Intercontinental Radio News": "Professor Farrell of the Mount Jennings Observatory" near Chicago had reported observing "several explosions of incandescent gas occurring at regular intervals on the planet Mars. . . . The spectroscope indicates the gas to be hydrogen and moving toward the earth with tremendous velocity."

---

*The format was a familiar one to radio listeners. "Big band remotes"—network broadcasts featuring America's best-known dance bands as they played at one-night stands in ballrooms from coast to coast—were a staple of broadcasting during the 1930s.

The dance music resumed, only to be interrupted repeatedly during the next several minutes by other bulletins. The tempo of events—and listeners' interest—began to intensify.

From a "remote pickup" at the "Princeton Observatory," reporter "Carl Phillips" interviewed famous astronomer "Richard Pierson" (played by Welles). As the clockwork mechanism of his telescope ticked in the background, Professor Pierson described Mars as a red disk swimming in a blue sea. He said he could not explain the gas eruptions on that planet. But skeptical of anything that could not be explained by logic, the astronomer counted the chances against living intelligence on Mars as being "a thousand to one."

Then Phillips read a wire that had just been handed to Pierson: a seismograph at the "Natural History Museum" in New York had registered a "shock of almost earthquake intensity occurring within a radius of twenty miles of Princeton." Pierson played down any possible connection with the disturbances on Mars: "This is probably a meteorite of unusual size and its arrival at this particular time is merely a coincidence."

Again the program returned to music, followed by yet another bulletin: an astronomer in Canada had observed three explosions on Mars, confirming "earlier reports from American observatories."

"Now, nearer home," continued the announcer, "comes a special announcement from Trenton, New Jersey. It is reported that at 8:50 P.M. a huge, flaming object, believed to be a meteorite, fell on a farm in the neighborhood of Grovers Mill, New Jersey, twenty-two miles from Trenton. The flash in the sky was visible within a radius of several hundred miles and the noise of impact was heard as far north as Elizabeth."

Listeners leaned closer to their sets. In Grovers Mill, Dick Stives stared at the radio and gulped.

Again the broadcast returned to dance music—this time to "Bobby Millette and his orchestra" at the "Hotel Martinet" in Brooklyn. And again the music was interrupted by a news flash. Having just arrived at the scene of "impact" on the "Wilmuth farm" near Grovers Mill, reporter Carl Phillips, accompanied by Professor Pierson, beheld police, state troopers, and onlookers crowding around what appeared to be a huge metallic cylinder, partially buried in the earth.

About this time, some twelve minutes into the broadcast, many listeners to the *Chase and Sanborn Hour*, momentarily bored by a guest musical spot, turned their dials. A lot of them stopped in sudden shock as they came upon the CBS wavelength. The events being described seemed real to listeners—quite as real to them as reports, not many months before, that Adolf Hitler's troops had marched into Austria.

"I wish I could convey the atmosphere . . . the background of this . . . fantastic scene," reported Phillips. "Hundreds of cars are parked in a field back of us. . . . Their headlights throw an enormous spot on the pit where the object is half-buried. Some of the more daring souls are venturing near the edge. Their silhouettes stand out against the metal sheen. . . ."

Professor Pierson described the object as "definitely extraterrestrial . . . not found on this earth. . . . This thing is smooth and, as you can see, of cylindrical shape." Then Phillips suddenly interrupted him:

"Just a minute! Something's happening! Ladies and gentlemen, this is

terrific! This end of the thing is beginning to flake off! The top is beginning to rotate like a screw! The thing must be hollow! [shouts of alarm]
Ladies and gentlemen, this is the most terrifying thing I have ever witnessed. . . . Wait a minute! Someone's crawling out of the hollow top.
Someone or . . . something. I can see peering out of that black hole two
luminous disks—are they eyes? Good heavens, something's wriggling out
of the shadow like a gray snake. . . . I can see the thing's body. It's large as a
bear and it glistens like wet leather. But that face. It . . . it's indescribable. I
can hardly force myself to keep looking at it. The eyes are black and gleam
like a serpent. The mouth is V-shaped with saliva dripping from its rimless
lips that seem to quiver and pulsate. . . ."

Thirty state troopers, according to the reporter, now formed a cordon
around the pit where the object rested. Three policemen carrying a white
handkerchief of truce walked toward the cylinder. Phillips continued:

"Wait a minute . . . something's happening. [high-pitched, intermittent whine of machinery] A humped shape is rising out of the pit. I can
make out a small beam of light against a mirror. . . . What's that? There's a
jet of flame springing from the mirror, and it leaps right at the advancing
men! It strikes them head on! Good Lord, they're turning into flame!
[screams and shrieks] Now the whole field by the woods has caught fire!
[sound effects intensify] The gas tanks, tanks of automobiles . . . it's
spreading everywhere! It's coming this way now! About twenty yards to my
right [abrupt silence]."*

Now terror was afoot. A series of voices—fictional "announcers," "militia commanders," "network vice presidents," and "radio operators"—took
up the narrative. At least forty people, according to the radio bulletins, lay
dead at Grovers Mill, "their bodies burned and distorted beyond all possible recognition." And in a Trenton hospital, "the charred body of Carl
Phillips" had been identified.

A current of fear flowed outward across the nation. Real-life police
switchboards, first in New Jersey, then, steadily, throughout the whole
Northeast, began to light up: "What's happening?" "Who's attacking America?" "When will they be here?" "What can we do?" "Who are they—these
Martians?"

By now, according to the broadcast, "eight battalions of infantry" had
surrounded the cylinder, determined to destroy it. A "Captain Lansing" of
the "Signal Corps"—calm and confident at first, but with obviously increasing alarm—described what happened next:

"Well, we ought to see some action soon. One of the companies is
deploying on the left flank. A quick thrust and it'll all be over. Wait a
minute, I see something on top of the cylinder. No, it's nothing but a
shadow. . . . Seven thousand armed men closing in on an old metal tube.
Tub, rather. Wait, that wasn't a shadow. It's something moving . . . solid
metal. Kind of a shield-like affair rising up out of the cylinder! It's going
higher and higher! Why, it's . . . it's standing on legs! Actually rearing up

*Phillips's narrative bore a perhaps-not-coincidental resemblance to a famous eyewitness
report by Chicago radio newsman Herb Morrison, who on May 6, 1937, had described the
explosion and destruction of the German dirigible *Hindenburg* as it was about to moor at
Lakehurst, New Jersey.

on a sort of metal framework! Now it's reaching above the trees and searchlights are on it! Hold on [abrupt silence]."

In a matter of moments, a studio "announcer" gave America the incredible news:

". . . Those strange beings who landed in the Jersey farmlands tonight are the vanguard of an invading army from the planet Mars. The battle which took place tonight at Grovers Mill has ended in one of the most startling defeats ever suffered by an army in modern times; seven thousand men armed with rifles and machine guns pitted against a single fighting machine of the invaders from Mars. One hundred and twenty known survivors. The rest strewn over the battle area from Grovers Mill to Plainsboro crushed and trampled to death under the metal feet of the monster, or burned to cinders by its heat ray. . . ."

Grovers Mill's couple of hundred real-life residents hardly knew what to make of it all. Young Dick Stives was stunned. He and his sister and brothers pulled down the shades in the farmhouse. Their grandfather shoved chairs against the doors.

Teen-aged Lolly Dey, who heard about the "invasion" while attending a church meeting, consoled herself by saying: "I am in the Lord's House." Another resident seeing what he thought to be a Martian war machine among the trees (actually a water tower on a neighbor's property), peppered it with shotgun blasts. One man packed his family into the car, bound for parts unknown. He backed right through his garage door. "We're never gonna be needing that again anyway," he muttered to his wife.

"The monster is now in control of the middle section of New Jersey," proclaimed the voice on the radio. "Communication lines are down from Pennsylvania to the Atlantic Ocean. Railroad tracks are torn and service from New York to Philadelphia discontinued. . . . Highways to the north, south, and west are clogged with frantic human traffic. Police and army reserves are unable to control the mad flight. . . ."

Life was soon to imitate art. A wave of terror, unprecedented in its scope and rapidity, swept across New Jersey. A New Brunswick man, bound for open country, had driven ten miles when he remembered that his dog was tied up in the backyard of his home. Daring the Martians, he drove back to retrieve the dog.

A West Orange bar owner pushed customers out into the street, locked his tavern door, and rushed home to rescue his wife and children.

Twenty families began to move their belongings out of a Newark apartment house, their faces covered by wet towels to repel Martian rays. Doctors and nurses volunteered to come to hospitals to help handle the "war casualties."

At Princeton University, the chairman of the geology department packed his field equipment and headed into the night to look for whatever it was that was out there. The governor of Pennsylvania offered to send troops to help New Jersey. A Jersey City man called a bus dispatcher to warn him of the fast-spreading "disaster." He cut their conversation short with: "The world is coming to an end and I have a lot to do!"

Meanwhile, on the radio, the "Secretary of the Interior," speaking in a voice much like that of President Franklin D. Roosevelt, announced that he had faith in the ability of the American military to vanquish the Martians.* He solemnly intoned:

". . . placing our trust in God we must continue the performance of our duties each and every one of us, so that we may confront this destructive adversary with a nation united, courageous, and consecrated to the preservation of human supremacy on this earth."

A Trenton store owner ran out screaming, "The world is ending! The world is ending!" Another man dashed into a motion-picture theater in Orange, crying out that "the state is being invaded! This place is going to be blown up!" The audience hurriedly ran out to the street.

A woman in a Newark tenement just sat and cried. "I thought it was all up with us," she said. A man driving westward called out to a patrolman: "All creation's busted loose! I'm getting out!"

More grim reports issued from the radio. Scouting planes, according to the broadcast, had sighted three Martian machines marching through New Jersey. They were uprooting power lines, bridges, and railroad tracks, with the apparent objectives of crushing resistance and paralyzing communications. In swamps twenty miles south of Morristown, coon hunters had stumbled upon a second Martian cylinder.

In the Watchung mountains, the "22nd Field Artillery" set down a barrage against six tripod monsters—to no avail. The machines soon let loose a heavy black poisonous gas, annihilating the artillerymen. Then eight army bombers from "Langham Field, Virginia," attacked the tripod machines, only to be downed by heat rays.

Thousands of telephone calls cascaded into radio stations, newspaper offices, power companies, fire houses, and military posts throughout the country. People wanted to know what to do . . . where to go . . . whether they were safer in the cellar or the attic.

Word spread in Atlanta that a "planet" had struck New Jersey. In Philadelphia, all the guests in one hotel checked out. Students at a college in North Carolina lined up at telephones to call their parents for the last time. When a caller reached the CBS switchboard, the puzzled operator, asked about the end of the world, said: "I'm sorry, we don't have that information."

Radio listeners soon heard an "announcer," said to be atop the "Broadcasting Building" in Manhattan, describe a doomed New York City:

"The bells you hear are ringing to warn the people to evacuate the city as the Martians approach. Estimated in last two hours three million people have moved out along the roads to the north. . . . No more defenses. Our army wiped out . . . artillery, air force, everything wiped out. . . . We'll stay here to the end."

Something like madness took hold among the radio listeners in New York City. People stood on Manhattan street corners hoping for a glimpse

*Network censors, concerned that the drama might sound too factual, had earlier requested more than thirty changes in the script. Thus, although he still sounded like Franklin Roosevelt, the "President" became the "Secretary of the Interior." The "U.S. Weather Bureau" was changed to the "Government Weather Bureau," the "National Guard" became the "State Militia," etc.

of the "battle." Thirty men and women showed up at a Harlem police station wanting to be evacuated. A woman had her husband paged at a Broadway theater and told him of the Martian landings; word spread quickly and a throng of playgoers rushed for the exits.

The radio voice continued: "Enemy now in sight above the Palisades! Five great machines. First one is crossing the river . . . wading the Hudson like a man wading through a brook. . . . Martian cylinders are falling all over the country. One outside Buffalo, one in Chicago, St. Louis. . . . Now the first machine reaches the shore! He stands watching, looking over the city. His steel, cowlish head is even with the skyscrapers. He waits for the others. They rise like a line of new towers on the city's west side. . . ."

A Bronx man dashed into the street and saw people running in all directions. One New Yorker claimed he heard the "swish" of Martian flying vehicles. Another told of machine-gun fire. Atop a midtown Manhattan building a man with binoculars "saw" the firing of weapons. In Brooklyn, a man called the police station: "We can hear the firing all the way here, and I want a gas mask. I'm a taxpayer."

An NBC executive was upset because *his* network wasn't carrying the ultimate news event. One man sped at eighty-miles-an-hour to reach a priest before the "death rays" overtook him; his car flipped over twice, but he lived.

The program played out the drama of doom right to its end.

From atop his fictional building, the "broadcaster" continued his "eye-witness" report: "Now they're lifting their metal hands. This is the end now. Smoke comes out. . . . People in the streets see it now. They're running towards the East River . . . thousands of them, dropping in like rats. . . . It's reached Times Square. . . . People trying to run away from it, but it's no use. They . . . they're falling like flies. . . ."

Meanwhile, in real life, Boston families gathered on rooftops and thought they could see a glow in the sky as New York burned. A horrified Pittsburgh husband found his wife with a bottle of poison, screaming: "I'd rather die this way than that!"

People called the electric company in Providence, Rhode Island, to turn off the city lights to make it a less visible target. A motorist rode through the streets of Baltimore, Paul Revere-fashion, blowing his horn and warning of the Martian invasion.

The staff of a Memphis newspaper readied an extra edition on rumored landings in Chicago and St. Louis. In Minneapolis, a woman ran into a church yelling: "This is the end of the world! I heard it on the radio!"

Back on the broadcast, the forlorn announcer carried on: "Now the smoke's crossing Sixth Avenue . . . Fifth Avenue . . . [coughing] a hundred yards away . . . it's fifty feet . . . [thud of falling body, then only sound of ships' whistles]."

In Salt Lake City, people started to pack before heading into the Rocky Mountains. One man, in Reno for a divorce, started to drive east, hoping to aid his estranged wife. A man and woman who'd run out of gas in northern California just sat and held hands, expecting any minute to see the Martian war machines appear over the tops of trees. Electric power failed in a village in Washington; families started to flee.

In Hollywood, John Barrymore downed a drink, went to his kennels and released his Great Danes. "Fend for yourselves!" he cried.

Then, from the radio, came the mournful call of a "radio operator": "2X2L calling CQ . . . New York. Isn't there anyone on the air? Isn't there anyone?"

Forty minutes into the broadcast, Welles gave his distraught audience a breather—a pause for station and program identification.

In the control room, CBS staffer Richard Goggin was startled as telephones there began to ring. That would only happen in an emergency. "Tension was becoming enormous in Studio One," he later recalled. "They had a tiger by the tail and couldn't let go."

For those brave enough to stay tuned, Welles was able to match the program's stunning first portion with an equally remarkable concluding sequence. In what amounted to a twenty-minute soliloquy, he, in the role of Professor Pierson, chronicled the events that followed the Martians' destruction of New York City. Welles's spellbinding voice—magnetic, doom-filled, stirring—held listeners mesmerized.*

In the script, a stoic Pierson, still alive in the rubble, made his solitary way toward the ruins of New York, hiding from the invaders as he went.

Along the way he met a "stranger," a former artilleryman. This survivor feared the Martians would cage and enslave any humans still alive. The stranger was determined to outwit and outlast the Martians and, in time, to turn the heat-rays back on the invaders and even—if need be—upon other humans. And so, one day, new leaders would rule a new world.

Pierson, unwilling to join the stranger's cause, continued his lonely journey. Entering Manhattan through the now-empty Holland Tunnel, he found a lifeless city:

"I wandered up through the Thirties and Forties . . . stood alone on Times Square. I caught sight of a lean dog running down Seventh Avenue with a piece of dark brown meat in his jaws, and a pack of starving mongrels at his heels. . . . I walked up Broadway . . . past silent shop windows, displaying their mute wares to empty sidewalks. . . ."

There seemed to be little hope left for the human race. Then Pierson "caught sight of the hood of a Martian machine, standing somewhere in Central park, gleaming in the late afternoon sun":

"I rushed recklessly across Columbus Circle and into the park. I climbed a small hill above the pond at Sixtieth Street, and from there I could see standing in a silent row along the mall, nineteen of those great metal Titans, their cowls empty, their steel arms hanging listlessly by their sides. I looked in vain for the monsters that inhabit those machines. Suddenly my eyes were attracted to the immense flock of black birds that hovered directly below me . . . and there before my eyes, stark and silent, lay the Martians, with the hungry birds pecking and tearing brown shreds of flesh from their dead bodies."

The mighty Martians had fallen: ". . . it was found that they were killed

*Welles's closing narrative, fictionally dramatic in style and compressing months of events into twenty minutes, contrasted sharply with the realism of the first portion of the program. Nevertheless, many listeners apparently remained convinced that Martians had landed.

by the putrefactive and disease bacteria against which their systems were unprepared. . . . slain, after all man's defenses had failed, by the humblest thing that God in His wisdom put upon this earth."

In a sprightly epilogue, Welles then explained away the whole unsettling broadcast as the Mercury Theatre's "way of 'dressing up in a sheet and saying Boo!' . . . We annihilated the world before your very ears, and utterly destroyed the CBS. You will be relieved, I hope, to learn that we didn't mean it, and that both institutions are still open for business."

He tried cheerily to dispel the darkness: "So goodbye everybody, and remember . . . the terrible lesson you learned tonight. . . . And if your doorbell rings and nobody's there, that was no Martian . . . it's Hallowe'en."

The joke was on the listeners. More than one hundred and fifty stations affiliated with CBS had carried the broadcast. About twelve million people had heard the program. Newspapers estimated that at least a million listeners, perhaps many more, had thought the invasion real.

Back in Grovers Mill, disenchantment began to take hold. Twenty-year-old Sam Goldman and three pals had been playing cards when they heard that the Martians were on the move down by the mill. They had thrown down their cards and jumped into a car, ready to face the invaders. "We got there and looked around," Sam said, "and nothing was going on."

A squad of New Jersey state troopers equipped with riot guns had deployed near the crossroads. They found little more than the dilapidated old mill itself.

Nearby, in their grandfather's farmhouse, Dick Stives, his sister, and brothers talked excitedly about the "men from Mars." Then their mother and father came home from the movies and told the children about the "make believe" on radio that everyone was talking about. Dick, more confused than ever, went upstairs to go to sleep, still half-sure that what he heard was "really real."

For the players who had inadvertently just made radio history, the next hours turned into a nightmare. As soon as Welles left the twenty-second-floor studio, he was called to a telephone. He picked it up, to hear the irate mayor of Flint, Michigan, roar that his city was in chaos because of the program and that he, the mayor, would soon be on his way to New York to punch one Orson Welles in the nose.

"By nine o'clock several high-ranking CBS executives had arrived or were in full flight toward 485 Madison. We were in trouble," recalled Larry Harding, a CBS production supervisor for the Mercury Theatre show.

Policemen hurried into the CBS building. Welles, Houseman, and the cast were held under informal house arrest. Staffers hastily stashed scripts, memoranda, and the sixteen-inch acetate disks upon which the show had been recorded.

Welles was taken to a room on the seventeenth floor, where reporters battered him with questions about whether he knew of the deaths and suicides his broadcast had caused (none have ever been documented), whether he knew ahead of time how devastating an effect his show would have (he said he didn't), and whether he had planned it all as a publicity stunt (he said he hadn't).

Finally, at about one o'clock Monday morning, Welles and the cast were "released," free to go out into the streets of New York where not a

Martian was stirring. Welles walked a half-dozen blocks to the Mercury Theatre, where, even at that hour, members of the stage company were still rehearsing their new play.

Welles went up on stage, where news photographers were lurking. They caught him with his eyes raised, his arms outstretched. The next day his photograph appeared in newspapers throughout the country, over a caption that blurted: "I Didn't Know What I Was Doing!", or words to that effect.

The next morning headlines in major city newspapers reported the hoax: "Radio Listeners in Panic, Taking War Drama as Fact" (*New York Times*); "U.S. Terrorized By Radio's 'Men From Mars'" (*San Francisco Chronicle*); "Radio Drama Causes Panic" (*Philadelphia Inquirer*); "Listeners Weep and Pray, Prepare for End of World" (*New Orleans Times-Picayune*).

Many of the listeners who had been deluded laughed good-naturedly at one another—and at themselves. Some professed not to have been taken in by what one woman called "that Buck Rogers stuff." But others turned their wrath on Welles, on the network, and on the medium that had turned their Sunday evening into a time of unsolicited terror.

CBS apologized to the public, but also pointed out that during the program no fewer than four announcements had been made stating that it was a dramatic presentation, not a news broadcast.

A subdued Welles, believing his career was ruined, dutifully followed suit. "I don't think we will try anything like this again," he stated.

For two or three days, the press would not let Welles, nor radio, off the front page. Media rivalry played its part; newspaper publishers seemed anxious to portray radio—and Welles—as villains. The clipping bureau that served CBS delivered condemnatory editorials by the pound.

While newsmen "tsk-tsked," government officials fumed. Senator Clyde Herring of Iowa, reflecting the anger of many citizens, stated his support for legislation to curb such "Halloween bogymen." The Federal Communications Commission (FCC), flooded with complaint letters, tried to find a philosophical stance somewhere between imposing severe censorship and permitting unbridled expression.

Novelist H. G. Wells cabled his disregards from London. Although he had given CBS permission to air his novel, he complained that "it was not explained to me that this dramatization would be made with a liberty that amounts to a complete reworking of *The War of the Worlds*."

But some columnists and editorialists began to perceive significant merit in the program. Essayist Heywood Broun interpreted the broadcast as a cautionary tale: "Jitters have come home to roost. The peace of Munich hangs heavy over our heads like a thundercloud." *Variety*, under a headline stating "Radio Does U.S. A Favor," described the program as a warning to Americans of the danger of unpreparedness.

In a column that turned the tide of public opinion in favor of Welles and company, Dorothy Thompson called the broadcast "the news story of the century—an event which made a greater contribution to an understanding of Hitlerism, Mussolinism, Stalinism, anti-Semitism, and all the other terrorism of our time than all the words about them that have been written by reasonable men."

Welles, to his relief, soon learned that he would not be consigned to durance vile. "Bill Paley, the head of CBS, brought Orson and me up on the carpet and gave us a reprimand," Houseman later recalled. "But there was ambivalence to it. The working stiffs thought we were heroes. The executives thought of us as some sort of anarchists. But reason—and revenues—prevailed. A few days after the broadcast, when it was announced that Campbell's Soup had become a sponsor, the boys at the top began to think of us as heroes, or at least as employable persons, as well."

Some critics continued to decry the credulity of the American people. They spoke of the compelling power of the human voice emanating from the upper air. Radio, ominously, seemed able to reduce an entire country to the size of one room; it exerted unexpected power over susceptible millions.

For a book-length study titled *The Invasion from Mars,* Princeton University psychology professor Hadley Cantril interviews scores of persons who had listened to the program. Speaking with them shortly after "that night," he received responses ranging from insecure to phobic to fatalistic.

"The coming of the Martians did not present a situation where the individual could preserve one value if he sacrifices another," Professor Cantril concluded from his research. "In this situation the individual stood to lose all his values at once. Nothing could be done to save any of them. Panic was inevitable."

Did Welles intend the panic? Had he hoped, by means of his magnificent dramatic powers, to gain all those headlines?

Houseman dismisses such conjecture as "rubbish." He declares: "Orson and I had no clear pre-sense of the mood of the audience. *The War of the Worlds* wasn't selected as a parable of invasion and war in the 1930s, but just as an interesting story unto itself. Only after the fact did we perceive how ready and resonant the world was for the tale. Our intent was theatre, not terror."

Welles and his players could not know that they had portrayed the shape of things to come. The program was, in a way, quite prophetic. Barely two weeks later, German foreign minister Joachim von Ribbentrop chillingly commented: "I would not be surprised if in the United States eyewitness reports are under consideration in which the 'Giants from Mars' marched up in brown shirts waving swastika flags."

Sooner than the peoples of the world could guess, a true nightmare—that of World War II—would be upon them.

Welles, of course, went on to memorable successes in motion pictures and theater. And his *War of the Worlds* broadcast became the most famous radio program of all time.

These days, the crossroads village of Grovers Mill is much the way it was that spectral night half a century ago. There are, however, signs of strangers nearby—new homes sprouting up among what had been potato fields. And futuristic shapes—sleek, glass-walled, high-technology industrial buildings—stand amid the trees.

But the old mill itself is still at the intersection of Millstone and Cranbury roads—a dot east of Princeton on the highway map. The weatherworn wooden structure, with a few of its millstones scattered about, stands lonely vigil.

Here fate tossed its random lightning-bolt. Here the "Martians" made their landing on what is now a municipal park. Nearby, ducks glide on a big, placid pond.

The former Wilson farm (the script spoke of the "Wilmuth" farm, but sightseers made do with the Wilson place) has long since been cut into smaller properties. Here Martian-hunters once tramped across the cornfields looking for traces of the invaders.

Wayfarers from all parts of the world still occasionally wander the roads and fields of Grovers Mill. They know they will see no Martians, find no burn-marks on the earth left by war machines from outer space, nor come upon charred ruins wrought by the alien's devastation. Still, drawn by curiosity, they come and look and wonder.

Not all Grovers Mill residents find such doings fascinating. The proprietor of a nearby gas station, for example, remembers the night of the "invasion," but didn't think much of it then and thinks as little of it now. "It doesn't make sense," he says with disdain. "Never has. Never will."

But for Dick Stives, now sixty-three, the "panic broadcast" still holds disquieting memories. Not long ago he walked around the "Martian landing ground."

"When I was a kid," he recalled, "I would crawl down near the wheel of the old mill, just by the pond there, and shuck my clothes and go in swimming. It was just a pond on a farm. But now, looking at it, I have to wonder why people still come so far to find a place where something that was supposed to happen didn't happen.

"I still remember," he said, "how I felt that night, up there in the bedroom in my granddad's place, in the dark, trying to sleep, thinking about what we had heard on the radio. The nighttime would make me think about how almost anything, just about anytime, could happen anywhere—even in Grovers Mill. Things in the shadows. Things I didn't understand."

PART SIX

GENDER AND SEXUALITY IN MODERN AMERICA

When scholars finally write the history of the United States in the twentieth century, they will no doubt identify gender roles as those that underwent the greatest change and precipitated the most intense debates in American society. In 1900, most women labored on farms within family economic units and enjoyed few civil rights and no other economic opportunities, unless they were desperately poor and willing to work as domestics in the homes of well-to-do women or in industrial sweatshops. The cult of domesticity was overpowering, insisting that women find fulfillment only within the home as wives and mothers. Those women who sought a life outside that domestic framework, especially when economic circumstance did not require it, found most occupations closed or, at best, severely restricted. Only teaching and nursing, both of which fit into the domesticity stereotype, were socially acceptable.

World War I and especially World War II were crucial to the birth of economic liberation for women. Both conflicts resulted in large-scale conscription of young men into the military, creating labor shortages in the booming industrial economy. Suddenly, jobs formerly closed to women were open, as were the recruiting, training, and decent pay that went with them. To be sure, when the war ended, most women lost those jobs to returning veterans, but the American workplace, and the cult of domesticity, would never be the same. Women's expectations—their consciousness—had been raised as never before, and those expectations fueled the women's movement of the twentieth century.

In the nineteenth and early twentieth centuries, the women's movement had revolved around the campaign to achieve the right to vote. It began with the Woman's Rights Convention in Seneca Falls, New York, in 1848 and culminated with the ratification of the Nineteenth Amendment to the Constitution in 1920. But the right to vote did not mean full civil rights. In the 1920s, women could not run for public office or serve on juries in many states; surrendered citizenship if they married foreigners; enjoyed few property rights; and rarely got custody of children in divorce cases. With the franchise secure, the crusade for women's rights broadened to include a larger social as well as political agenda. The National Woman's Party proposed an Equal Rights Amendment to eliminate all discriminatory legislation against women. A variety of interest groups—such as the National Consumers' League, General Federation of Women's Clubs, and National Women's Trade Union League—campaigned for federal maternal and infant protection legislation, federal aid to education, and an end to child labor. Activists like Margaret Sanger and Mary Ware Dennett crusaded against the Comstock Law, which prohibited the distribution of birth control devices and contraceptive information in the U.S. mail.

By the end of World War II, most women found themselves living in cities with new economic opportunities. Although the cult of domesticity still tried to keep them within a social and cultural cage, and forced many of them out of the World War II workplace, industrialization and urbanization had created a different economic reality. For the first time in American history, women could see economic opportunities outside the home—the ability to survive, and sometimes prosper, without a husband. The women's movement was still in its infancy in 1945, at least compared to what it would become in the 1970s, 1980s, and 1990s, but the foundation for the future was well in place.

21. The Case for Birth Control

MARGARET H. SANGER

The newspaper headlines and evening news broadcasts in 1993 and 1994 carried dozens of stories about Jack Kevorkian—"Dr. Death"—the physician who assisted terminally ill people commit suicide. In most states, physician-assisted suicides were against the law—misdemeanors or felonies—as well as contrary to the Hippocratic oath American physicians take when they are licensed. But for Kevorkian, the right to choose the timing of one's death was beyond statute law. He was a crusader, refusing to obey what he considered to be immoral laws, and he was jailed many times for his beliefs.

Whether or not Jack Kevorkian becomes known to history as a great civil rights crusader remains to be seen, but his implacability is reminiscent of an earlier crusader—Margaret Sanger—who at the time was considered equally radical. In 1914, Sanger founded the American Birth Control League, the forerunner of Planned Parenthood of America, to overthrow the Comstock Law, which prohibited the dissemination of birth control devices and birth control information through the U.S. post office. Sanger also campaigned for state and federal public health programs that included family planning education. More than once she was jailed for her activities, but Margaret Sanger would not be quieted. In the annals of the women's movement today, she is considered a hero. The following essay, written in 1917, provides an early look into Sanger's ideas.

For centuries woman has gone forth with man to till the fields, to feed and clothe the nations. She has sacrificed her life to populate the earth. She has overdone her labors. She now steps forth and demands that women shall cease producing in ignorance. To do this she must have knowledge to control birth. This is the first immediate step she must take toward the goal of her freedom.

Those who are opposed to this are simply those who do not know. Any one who like myself has worked among the people and found on one hand an ever-increasing population with its ever-increasing misery, poverty and ignorance, and on the other hand a stationary or decreasing population with its increasing wealth and higher standards of living, greater freedom, joy and happiness, cannot doubt that birth control is the livest issue of the day and one on which depends the future welfare of the race.

Before I attempt to refute the arguments against birth control, I should like to tell you something of the conditions I met with as a trained nurse and of the experience that convinced me of its necessity and led me to jeopardize my liberty in order to place this information in the hands of the women who need it.

My first clear impression of life was that large families and poverty went hand in hand. I was born and brought up in a glass factory town in the western part of New York State. I was one of eleven children—so I had some personal experience of the struggles and hardships a large family endures.

When I was seventeen years old my mother died from overwork and the strain of too frequent child bearing. I was left to care for the younger children and share the burdens of all. When I was old enough I entered a hospital to take up the profession of nursing.

In the hospital I found that seventy-five per cent of the diseases of men and women are the result of ignorance of their sex functions. I found that every department of life was open to investigation and discussion except that shaded valley of sex. The explorer, scientist, inventor, may go forth in their various fields for investigation and return to lay the fruits of their discoveries at the feet of society. But woe to him who dares explore that forbidden realm of sex. No matter how pure the motive, no matter what miseries he sought to remove, slanders, persecutions and jail await him who dares bear the light of knowledge into that cave of darkness.

So great was the ignorance of the women and girls I met concerning their own bodies that I decided to specialize in woman's diseases and took up gynecological and obstetrical nursing.

A few years of this work brought me to a shocking discovery—that knowledge of the methods of controlling birth was accessible to the women of wealth while the working women were deliberately kept in ignorance of this knowledge!

I found that the women of the working class were as anxious to obtain this knowledge as their sisters of wealth, but that they were told that there are laws on the statute books against importing it to them. And the medical profession was most religious in obeying these laws when the patient was a poor woman.

I found that the women of the working class had emphatic views on the crime of bringing children into the world to die of hunger. They would rather risk their lives through abortion than give birth to little ones they could not feed and care for.

For the laws against imparting this knowledge force these women into the hands of the filthiest midwives and the quack abortionists—unless they bear unwanted children—with the consequence that the deaths from abortions are almost wholly among the working-class women.

No other country in the world has so large a number of abortions nor so large a number of deaths of women resulting therefrom as the United States of America. Our law makers close their virtuous eyes. A most conservative estimate is that there are 250,000 abortions performed in this country every year.

How often have I stood at the bedside of a women in childbirth and seen the tears flow in gladness and heard the sigh of "Thank God" when told that her child was born dead! What can man know of the fear and dread of unwanted pregnancy? What can man know of the agony of carrying beneath one's heart a little life which tells the mother every instant that it cannot survive? Even were it born alive the chances are it would perish within a year.

Do you know that three hundred thousand babies under one year of age die in the United States every year from poverty and neglect, while six hundred thousand parents remain in ignorance of how to prevent three hundred thousand more babies from coming into the world the next year to die of poverty and neglect?

I found from records concerning women of the underworld that eighty-five per cent of them come from parents averaging nine living children. And that fifty per cent of these are mentally defective.

We know, too, that among mentally defective parents the birth-rate is four times as great as that of the normal parent. Is this not cause for alarm? Is it not time for our physicians, social workers and scientists to face this array of facts and stop quibbling about woman's morality? I say this because it is these same people who raise objection to birth control on the ground that it *may* cause women to be immoral.

Solicitude for woman's morals has ever been the cloak Authority has worn in its age-long conspiracy to keep woman in bondage.

When I was in Spain a year ago, I found that the Spanish woman was far behind her European sisters in readiness or even desire for modern freedom. Upon investigation as to the cause of this I found that there are over five thousand villages and towns in Spain with no means of travel, transportation and communication save donkeys over bridle paths. I was told that all attempts to build roads and railroads in Spain had been met with the strongest opposition of the Clergy and the Government on the ground that roads and railroads would make communication easier and bring the women of the country into the cities *where they would meet their downfall.*

Do we who have roads and railroads think our women are less moral than the Spanish women? Certainly not. But we in this country are, after all, just emerging from the fight for a higher education of women which met with the same objection only a few years ago.

We know now that education has not done all the dreadful things to women that its opponents predicted were certain to result. And so shall we find that knowledge to control birth, which has been in the hands of the women of wealth for the past twenty-five years, will not tend to lower woman's standard of morality.

Statistics show us that the birth-rate of any given quarter is in ratio with and to its wealth. And further figures prove that in large cities the rich districts yield a birth-rate of a third of that of the poor districts. In Paris for every 1,000 women between the ages of 15 and 50 the poor districts yield 116 births and the rich districts 34 births. In Berlin conditions are approximately the same. For every 1,000 women between the ages of 15 and 50 the poor districts yield 157 births while the rich yield 47. This applies also to all large cities the world over.

It can be inferred from these figures that the women of wealth use means to control birth which is condemned when taught to the poor. But the menace to our civilization, the problem of the day, is not the stationary birth-rate among the upper classes so much as the tremendous increase among the poor and diseased population of this country. . . .

Is woman's health not to be considered? Is she to remain a producing machine? Is she to have time to think, to study, to care for herself? Man cannot travel to his goal alone. And until woman has knowledge to control birth she cannot get the time to think and develop. Until she has the time to think, neither the suffrage question nor the social question nor the labor question will interest her, and she will remain the drudge that she is and her husband the slave that he is just as long as they continue to supply the market with cheap labor.

Let me ask you: Has the State any more right to ravish a woman against her will by keeping her in ignorance than a man has through brute force? Has the State a better right to decide when she shall bear offspring?

Picture a woman with five or six little ones living on the average working man's wage of ten dollars a week. The mother is broken in health and spirit, a worn out shadow of the woman she once was. Where is the man or woman who would reproach me for trying to put into this woman's hands knowledge that will save her from giving birth to any more babies doomed to certain poverty and misery and perhaps to disease and death.

Am I to be classed as immoral because I advocate small families for the working class while Mr. Roosevelt can go up and down the length of the land shouting and urging these women to have large families and is neither arrested nor molested but considered by all society as highly moral?

But I ask you which is the more moral—to urge this class of women to have only those children she desires and can care for, or to delude her into breeding thoughtlessly. Which is America's definition of morality?

You will agree with me that a woman should be free.

Yet no adult woman who is ignorant of the means to prevent conception can call herself free.

No woman can call herself free who cannot choose the time to be a mother or not as she sees fit. This should be woman's first demand.

Our present laws force woman into one of two ways: Celibacy, with its nervous results, or abortion. All modern physicians testify that both these conditions are harmful; that celibacy is the cause of many nervous complaints, while abortion is a disgrace to a civilized community. Physicians claim that early marriage with knowledge to control birth would do away with both. For this would enable two young people to live and work together until such time as they could care for a family. I found that young people desire early marriage, and would marry early were it not for the dread of a large family to support. Why will not society countenance and advance this idea? Because it is still afraid of the untried and the unknown.

I saw that fortunes were being spent in establishing baby nurseries, where new babies are brought and cared for while the mothers toil in sweatshops during the day. I saw that society with its well-intentioned palliatives was in this respect like the quack, who cures a cancer by burning off the top while the deadly disease continues to spread underneath. I never felt this more strongly than I did three years ago, after the death of the patient in my last nursing case.

This patient was the wife of a struggling working man—the mother of three children—who was suffering from the results of a self-attempted abortion. I found her in a very serious condition, and for three weeks both the attending physician and myself labored night and day to bring her out of the Valley of the Shadow of Death. We finally succeeded in restoring her to her family.

I remember well the day I was leaving. The physician, too, was making his last call. As the doctor put out his hand to say "Good-bye," I saw the patient had something to say to him, but was shy and timid about saying it. I started to leave the room, but she called me back and said:

"Please don't go. How can both of you leave me without telling me what I can do to avoid another illness such as I have just passed through?"

I was interested to hear what the answer of the physician would be, and I went back and sat down beside her in expectation of hearing a sympathetic reply. To my amazement, he answered her with a joking sneer. We came away.

Three months later, I was aroused from my sleep one midnight. A telephone call from the husband of the same woman requested me to come immediately as she was dangerously ill. I arrived to find her beyond relief. Another conception had forced her into the hands of a cheap abortionist, and she died at four o'clock the same morning, leaving behind her three small children and frantic husband.

I returned home as the sun was coming over the roofs of the Human Bee-Hive, and I realized how futile my efforts and my work had been. I, too, like the philanthropists and social workers, had been dealing with the symptoms rather than the disease. I threw my nursing bag into the corner and announced to my family that I would never take another case until I had made it possible for working women in America to have knowledge of birth control.

I found, to my utter surprise, that there was very little scientific information on the question available in America. Although nearly every country in Europe had this knowledge, we were the only civilized people in the world whose postal laws forbade it.

The tyranny of the censorship of the post office is the greatest menace to liberty in the United States to-day. The post office was never intended to be a moral or ethical institution. It was intended to be mechanically efficient; certainly not to pass upon the opinions in the matter it conveys. If we concede this power to this institution, which is only a public service, we might just as well give to the street car companies and railroads the right to refuse to carry passengers whose ideas they do not like.

I will not take up the story of the publication of "The Woman Rebel." You know how I began to publish it, how it was confiscated and suppressed by the post office authorities, how I was indicted and arrested for bringing it out, and how the case was postponed time and time again and finally dismissed by Judge Clayton in the Federal Court.

These, and many more obstacles and difficulties were put in the path of this philosophy and this work to suppress it if possible and discredit it in any case.

My work has been to arouse interest in the subject of birth control in America, and in this, I feel that I have been successful. The work now before us is to crystallize and to organize this interest into action, not only for the repeal of the laws but for the establishment of free clinics in every large center of population in the country where scientific, individual information may be given every adult person who comes to ask it.

In Holland there are fifty-two clinics with nurses in charge, and the medical profession has practically handed the work over to nurses. In these clinics, which are mainly in the industrial and agricultural districts, any woman who is married or old enough to be married, can come for information and be instructed in the care and hygiene of her body.

These clinics have been established for thirty years in Holland, and the result has been that the general death-rate of Holland has fallen to the lowest of any country in Europe. Also, the infant mortality of Amsterdam and The Hague is found to be the lowest of any city in the world. Holland proves that the practice of birth control leads to race improvement; her increase of population has accelerated as the death-rate has fallen.

In England, France, Scandinavia, and Germany, information regarding birth control is also freely disseminated, but the establishment of clinics in these countries is not so well organized as it is in Holland, with the consequence that the upper and middle classes, as in this country, have ready access to this knowledge, while the poor continue to multiply because of their lack of it. This leads, especially in France, to a high infant mortality, which, rather than a low birth-rate, is the real cause of her decreasing population.

We in America should learn a lesson from this, and I would urge immediate group action to form clinics at once. We have in this country a splendid foundation in our hospital system and settlement work. The American trained nurse is the best equipped and most capable in the world, which enables us, if we begin work at once, to accomplish as much in ten years' time as the European countries have done in thirty years.

The clinic I established in the Brownsville district of Brooklyn accomplished at least this: it showed the need and usefulness of such an agency.

The free clinic is the solution for our problem. It will enable women to help themselves, and will have much to do with disposing of this soul-crushing charity which is at best a mere temporary relief.

Woman must be protected from incessant childbearing before she can actively participate in the social life. She must triumph over Nature's and Man's laws which have kept her in bondage. Just as man has triumphed over Nature by the use of electricity, shipbuilding, bridges, etc., so much woman triumph over the laws which have made her a childbearing machine.

22. Illegal Operations: Women, Doctors, and Abortion, 1886–1939

ANGUS McLAREN

Not since the pre–Civil War debate over slavery and its abolition has the United States witnessed a social issue as controversial as abortion. At one extreme are passionate right-to-life advocates who oppose abortion for any reason. Whether a woman is pregnant because of rape or incest, or whether the pregnancy threatens her life, is irrelevant to purists, who view the fetal right to life as inviolate. At the other extreme are those who claim that the Fourth and Fifth Amendments to the Constitution give a woman "reproductive rights"—absolute control over her own body and the right to terminate a pregnancy anytime before birth. In between these two positions are 90 percent of Americans who believe that abortion, at least under some limited circumstances, is legitimate.

The Supreme Court's 1973 decision in Roe v. Wade *tried to find a middle ground, authorizing abortions up through the second trimester of pregnancy but prohibiting them thereafter unless the mother's life was seriously threatened by a full-term pregnancy. The decision satisfied many Americans but certainly not all. Of all the social issues currently being debated on the American political landscape, abortion is the most likely to continue indefinitely. In the following essay, Angus McLaren describes illegal abortions occurring in the United States during the late nineteenth century and the first four decades of the twentieth century.*

On 9 July 1919 Sarah Robins, mother of three small children, died in Vancouver General Hospital, her septic poisoning the aftermath of a bungled abortion. In the dying declaration which the doctors extorted from her, Robins left an agonizing portrayal of the last days of her life.

My trouble started with going to a doctor in Vancouver, Dr. Thomas Vernon, Lonsdale Avenue, North Vancouver . . . I was told of him by a Mrs. Peters, Denman St., West End, Vancouver. I saw him last Friday week. I told him I was six weeks overdue in menstruation. I asked him if he could do anything for me and if there was any risk. He asked me who my husband was, and said he charged $100 and there was no great risk as he did eight and ten a day. I went home and my husband implored me not to go. I went the next day Saturday with $75 and told him that was all I could afford. He told me he would not do it. I cried to him and eventually he did. I was ill on Saturday night and the Sunday and the Monday I phoned him. He said he did not remember me. When I asked him what to do for the pain in the abdomen, he said "Better get used to it," said "Take a hot soap-suds douche" which I did. Continued sick as ever. I went to see him on Wednesday. He felt my pulse and said I would get along alright. On Thursday at 4 o'clock in the morning my husband phoned him and demanded him out at once. My husband met the six o'clock boat. He came and curetted me and douched me without anaesthetic.

A few days later Sarah Robins was dead.

Women seeking to control their fertility have had recourse, as far back as it is possible to trace, to abortion. Such a "back-up method" of fertility control was essential given that until the 1930s coitus interruptus was the main means of contraception. Demographic historians and historians of the family have gone so far as to speak of an abortion "epidemic" occurring in the western world at the turn of the century, when the rate of induced miscarriages rose to account for perhaps one-sixth of all pregnancies.

Because such risky strategies were labelled "crimes" it is difficult to analyze the obviously important question of why so many women adopted them. The decisive role played by the medical profession in both North America and Britain in the increased restriction of the law on abortion does not have to be pursued here. It suffices to say that the criminalization of abortion in the nineteenth-century meant that neither those who sought to induce their miscarriages nor their accomplices wanted their activities made public. Court reports are accordingly especially valuable for researchers attempting to trace the history of such practices, spotlighting as they do the fact that abortions were not carried out in isolation; they were social acts the investigations of which reveal the particular nature of the relationships of women like Sarah Robins with their male partners, their friends, their doctors, and ultimately the judiciary.

The main purpose of this paper is to use legal sources to explore the decision to abort in the last decades of the nineteenth and the early decades of the twentieth century, an era in which the state and the professions took an unprecedented interest in the fertility control decisions of ordinary women and men. As the pressures to limit fertility increased and recourse to abortion rose, the criminal nature of the act necessarily tainted the relationships of women, men, doctors, and magistrates. The fate of women burdened with unwanted pregnancies, whose well-being was most placed at risk by the law, is the chief concern of what follows. A subsidiary preoccupation of this paper is to investigate the law-induced biases inherent in the sources which the historian of abortion necessarily employs—the court records.

The study exploits the strikingly graphic and intimate information generated by inquests and trials concerning one hundred British Columbian women who, between 1886 and 1939, attempted to induce a miscarriage. The woman who merely sought as well the woman who succeeded in inducing her own abortion, those who assisted such women, and anyone who directly procured an abortion were all, according to Canada's Revised Statutes of 1892, guilty of an indictable offense. But the same statutes held that doctors were not liable for inducing a miscarriage which in their opinion was necessary to protect the life of the mother. The same sorts of laws were in force in the United States and Great Britain.

To whom could women turn, in whom could they confide, when a crisis like the need to terminate a pregnancy occurred? How did their female friends, their male partners, their doctors, and finally the courts respond? The great value of the legal documentation is that it contains rare accounts of women and men forced to talk of interactions that would normally have been cloaked in silence, hidden from history. But before plunging into an investigation of such sources some provisos are in order. The first pertains to the women whose stories we are told. Abortions usually

only came to the attention of the authorities when something went tragically wrong; in three quarters of our cases the woman had died. Since
courts tended to hear only about unsuccessful attempts at abortion the
women whose fates they discussed were usually the most unfortunate, desperate and unlucky. But such women represented only a small fraction of
those who sought to terminate a pregnancy; the many more successful
attempts at induction of miscarriage necessarily escaped public scrutiny.
Moreover it has to be kept in mind that the courts often consciously played
up the dangers of abortion with the obvious intention of policing female
sexuality. Repeated reports of deaths due to illegal operations served as a
chilling reminder to all women—both married and unmarried—of the
fate of those who sought to free themselves from an unwanted or unexpected pregnancy.

The second point to be made about the law-induced bias of the
sources is that while they exaggerated the unfortunate fate of women who
aborted they minimized the role of the men involved. The only single men
who emerge from the records are those few who, failing to abscond, became entangled in the law. The courts generally refused, for reasons which
will be explored, to hold husbands responsible for their wives' abortions.

The third point to be kept in mind is that doctors' involvement in
abortion was also likely to escape full judicial scrutiny. For an illegal operation even to be brought to light usually required medical testimony. When
a case threatened the reputations of their hospital or their colleagues many
doctors' natural response was to look the other way. Quacks and the occasional maverick physician, who failed to enjoy collegial support, ran the
greatest risk of being reported.

One final proviso. Although witnesses swore to tell the truth, the
"truth" was only recognized by the court when expressed in a language that
it found acceptable. The legal records were written by and for lawyers; all
those involved knew or were soon instructed on what they had to say. Only
by constantly reading between the lines can one tease out something of the
"actual" experiences of the actors from the ritualized assertions recorded
in the transcripts.

Turning at last to our sources, the first question to be asked is why did
women seek recourse to abortion? Abortion was, of course, not the first line
of defense against unwanted pregnancies, but evidence came out in court
that at the turn of the century reliable contraceptive protection was for
many simply not available. Condoms were expensive and unreliable. Peter
Adams who courted Kitty Morris in 1895, knowing she was afraid of becoming pregnant, promised to obtain contraceptives. "I told her I would buy a
French protector, I then went to the Doctor and bought one and I showed
it to her . . . she examined it and said too thin may break and I want none
of that." Some women douched with "Zycol" which was, a doctor explained,
similar to "Lysol." "It is a disinfectant and women use it as a means of the
prevention of conception." And if all else failed celibacy could be tried.
When in 1901 Sarah MacDonald and her husband decided they could not
afford to have any more children they simply abstained from intercourse.
The fact was that prior to World War Two most Canadian couples hoping to
contracept employed the age old method of coitus interruptus. In the

absence of reliable means of contraception "accidents" inevitably occurred and couples intent on limiting fertility then had to contemplate recourse to abortion.

Why would women be so determined to avoid childbearing as to risk the dangers of abortion? Some contemporary commentators accused them of acting irrationally. "Well it is surprising," retorted one doctor, "the number of times it is done by people who have absolutely no reason in the world for doing it, other than the fact that they don't want to have another child." Such middle-class male commentators failed to realize what a burden pregnancy could pose. When it came to listing motives for recourse to abortion economic need was, for the married, always paramount. Mary Barnett stated in her dying declaration, "My husband and I want to get it done because we were so hard up and we were out of work." "We agreed we did not want any children," declared Henry Diederichs, "because we could not afford it." Rosaria Silletta had three children and did not want any more. Diana Baker had six under the age of twelve. Alice Nixon had lost two children, but still had six living. Some women could not envisage bearing another child; a few had been warned by doctors that it would be dangerous. In 1886 Annie Emberly told a friend "that she thought she was pregnant and that she was going to take medicine if she could get it by any means . . . that she would never have another child as it would kill her." The public tended to imagine that most women seeking abortion were single victims of seduction and abandonment, but the "typical" case which emerges from the early twentieth-century inquest and court records is that of the married woman in her mid-twenties. Many were already mothers. They turned to abortion, not to postpone having children, but to limit their number.

For the single or separated abortion was at first glance apparently not so much linked to family planning as motivated by the desire to protect one's reputation. Real desperation was evident in the 1896 case of Sarah Rosenzweig, a divorced mother who, believing herself pregnant, first sought an abortion and then drowned herself. Jennie Quinlan, who died in 1919 as a result of trying to abort with a catheter, was presumably seeking to hide her pregnancy from her overseas husband. Edith Niemi, a single Finnish maid, did not want her employer to know of her condition. Nellie Rae died in 1926 of a miscarriage induced "to relieve herself of a pregnancy produced by a man who had raped her."

The age and marital status of the women seeking abortion have been regarded by researchers as important because from such facts one can infer motive. The presupposition is that a young, single woman would have been motivated by a desire to protect her reputation; a married woman by the need to limit family size. But a close examination of the court files reveals that the motivations of the married and the single could not always be clearly separated. In 1920 Agnes Michaels became pregnant and sought to abort while her husband was away. In 1923 Annie Mulvaney, who was separated from her spouse, sought to terminate her pregnancy. Hazel Snowden, whose husband was an inmate of the New Westminster asylum, took similar action. An unexpected pregnancy could, in short, pose as great a threat to such married women's reputations and well-being as it did to the unmarried's.

Who provided women with abortions? Women often refused to implicate third parties and despite incriminating evidence insisted that they had induced their own miscarriages. In some cases while admitting the assistance of others, women attempted to protect those who tried to help, feeling that they were not to blame. Margaret Roberts, though dying, refused to give the name of her abortionist because she did not want to be responsible for sending to jail a woman who had three children. But doctors and police were for their part often intent on tracking down accomplices. Keeping in mind that the involvement of others was difficult to trace the one hundred cases reveal the following: self-induction was claimed in twenty-seven, the aid of an abortionist or supplier of drugs was admitted in fifty-one, and no clear determination was made in sixteen.

Attempts at self-inducement were no doubt common. A nurse was told in 1913 by Nellie Andrews that she had precipitated her own abortion. "She said she'd used a catheter that day and I told her she couldn't do it and do it properly. Then she said I have done it before about a year ago and it brought on an abortion." The use of instruments was by all accounts the leading method of abortion. The woman would squat and with the help of a mirror insert in the cervix a catheter, speculum, sound, pencil, bougie, needle, crochet or button hook. The second most important method was consumption of pills or drugs containing such irritants and emmenagogues as quinine, aloes, or ergot; the third, douching by syringe or enema bag with lysol, carbolic acid, turpentine or simple soap and water; and the fourth dilation of the cervix by inserting slippery elm or packing the vagina with cotton batten. In 1930 one Canadian researcher found that out of a sample of seventy-one self-inductions forty-seven were by vaginal insertion, twenty by drugs, and four by vaginal douches. Many of the women had previously aborted successfully. A witness testified that Marjorie Coffin, who died in 1935 after employing a hot water douche and slippery elm, said "this is the sixteenth time and someone told me I would do it once too often." All methods practiced outside a hospital setting were dangerous. Infection—either peritonitus or septicemia—accompanied by the tell-tale chills and fever was the primary cause of death. Hemorrhaging due to rupture of the uterus and drug toxicity also took their toll. Vascular accidents—occurring when air or soapy water, which having been pumped into the uterus, penetrated and obstructed an artery—became more common after World War Two.

Coroners consistently used abortion death inquests as occasions to call for tighter restrictions on the sale of patent medicines that could be used to induce miscarriage. But women could always try common household supplies such as castor oil, Beecham's Pills, and epsom salts which they had at hand before turning to such compounds as "Dr. Hunt's Female Pills," "French Female Pills" and "Nadruco Female Regulating Pills." Dr. F. C. Curtis said of abortifacients: "Anyone can get them, they are patent medicine. . . . It is said in the advertisement that they are used for regulating monthly flow but really and truly they . . . are intended to bring about abortion." At the same trial a druggist described the policing of ergot and savin: "They both come under Schedule A of the B.C. [British Columbia] Pharmacy Act and must be signed for by the parties purchasing them . . . Under the Act we are entitled to sell them on signature but very few drug stores will sell them even on a signature." Nevertheless a herbalist shop in downtown Vancouver was a well known outlet for such products.

If self-induction failed outside help would be sought. Eighteen year old Josephine Stearns had learnt of abortion, so her mother reported, from school mates. Single women usually appeared to be especially reliant on their male partner's assistance, often not being able to tell friends or family of their predicament. Married women, who enjoyed more extensive networks of support, first turned to relatives and neighborhood female friends. Alice Peters recalled at the 1919 inquest into the death of her neighbor Sarah Robins a conversation they had had two years previous about limiting family size.

. . . she said "We are not so wise as you." I said "Wise, I don't know I am sure—I have four. I don't know what you call wise," and she said if I did anything and I said nothing whatever. And she said "I am sure you do" . . . she told me before the child was born she had been to Seattle to have an operation performed but they wanted far too much, $250. I said to her, "Why I understand that they did these operations right here in Vancouver."

Annie Woodward in 1910 finding herself several weeks late went to buy ergot pills, "Mrs. Sunner's Remedies," and a package of womb tonic from a shop on Vancouver's Keefer Street. Annie Mason, the clerk, referred Woodward to a Mrs. Matthews who in turn put her in contact with a Richard Beveridge. Beveridge offered to perform an abortion for twenty-five dollars. In 1915 Concuilla Kappel reported her attempts at aborting to a Mrs. Reed,

who told her to take pennyroyal. It did no good and she was scared her people would find out that she was married. Mrs. Reed told her of a doctor in Vancouver who did that sort of thing and gave her a letter written in German.

In this fashion Kappel met "Dr." Joseph Kanstrup, a massage parlour operator.

Women had abortionists recommended to them by others who had availed of their services. Sisters and sisters-in-law helped out. Female friends and neighbors knew what was going on and kept tabs on those in distress. In 1920 Harriet Brown testified that she was aware of the five occasions on which Dr. Bamberg had visited Agnes Michaels. When such cases came to court women were in general far more candid than men— more so even than husbands—in admitting to knowing of their neighbors' attempts to terminate pregnancies.

For those who could go further afield the Vancouver newspapers contained advertisements for abortion services in Washington state.

Dr. David Andrews. Women's Disorders Specialty. 25 Years Experience. Suite 400 Pantages Building, Seattle.

Dr. J. Dunn. Women's Disease Specialist. European Hospital Experience. 317 Walter Building, Seattle.

Sound View Hospital. Specialist in Women's Diseases.

Women went across the border to American towns like Sumas and Blaine and many references were made at trials to operations sought in Seattle. In

1911 Augusta Benn, after reading an advertisement for the services offered in Seattle, went to be operated on by Dr. Catherine Harriman. In 1917 Mary Dawes was sent by her father to the same city for the same purpose. Nineteen year old Frances Pike died in 1918 as a result of a Seattle operation; her mother testified she thought her daughter was visiting friends. Nurse Fromm was implicated in the February 1920 deaths of two British Columbia women who were operated on in her 20th Avenue South Seattle clinic on the same day.

Who were the abortionists? Sixty individuals were cited in fifty-one cases; often an accomplice—usually a single woman's male partner—was indicted along with the practitioner. Forty-seven of the sixty could be called abortionists; the other thirteen were accused of supplying medicines, being accessories, or aiding and abetting. Of twenty-eight women named nine were identified as doctors, nurses or midwives. Clara Kaufman, a Victoria masseuse reportedly assisted over a hundred women for fees of fifty to a hundred dollars each. "You don't have to go to Seattle to get rid of your trouble," she was quoted as saying at her 1917 trial, "I am a woman's friend." In Vancouver nurse Clara Jesson, despite three trials, enjoyed a reputation as a skilled practitioner, advertising her services for "private maternity cases" at her home which had four upstairs bedrooms. In the 1930s Mrs. Esther Morris established a similar operation, the "Home Private Hospital." Hazel Dalton advertised in the papers as "Specialist in female remedies." Edith Pierce provided abortions in downtown Vancouver at "Adam and Pierce's Electrical Steam Treatments."

Women received most of their support from other women; recourse to abortion was commonly regarded as very much a woman's means of birth limitation. But where did men figure in all of this? In the case of the married couple living together the decision to terminate a pregnancy was often obviously a joint undertaking. In 1914 a woman dying in the Vancouver General Hospital explained, "My husband and I want to get it done because we were so hard up and we were out of work." Another stated, "Well, we [meaning her husband and herself] put some slippery elm up the womb." In some instances the abortion was more the husband's idea than the wife's. Phyllis Villeneuve said she went to an abortionist because she believed that her spouse did not want the baby; at the subsequent inquest he was portrayed by witnesses as a wife beater.

When an abortion case resulting in death ended up in the courts the husband, while admitting knowledge of his wife's attempts to abort, commonly claimed that he opposed recourse to the final deadly operation. Nellie Andrews's separated husband testified: "I knew of her using an instrument known as a catheter . . . I was not in favor of it. . . . She always had one. Whenever she became pregnant she always had all kinds of things to prevent her going her time." Likewise in 1898 one man testified at his wife's inquest:

Up to this time I did not know that she had been taking any medicine to bring on a miscarriage. I knew that she had used natural means to bring on a miscarriage. She put her feet in hot water. I mean by what I said that she had a little flow but that it did not come as she thought it ought to. She asked me to go to the store to get her something to bring on her periods more freely, or to produce a better flow.

He said he brought back whiskey, but she had already procured a pill from the druggist.

She said she had taken it to induce the menstrual flow . . . she had been passing an instrument into her womb so she told me. . . . She had several miscarriages before and in one case she had used a lead pencil and I had attended her and she got better.

Similarly Arnott Woods testified that he accompanied his wife to a pharmacist's to obtain drugs, but opposed the idea of an instrumental abortion. "I would not hear of an operation, and I left them. . . . When I returned . . . my wife was suffering from an attempted abortion." Robert Blatchford stated that he knew his wife was taking "dope" and douching herself, but that he forbad her to go to Seattle where she had the operation from which she ultimately died.

Some husbands were no doubt kept completely in the dark. Annie Emberly told her friend Mary Jane Drew "that she had been using a syringe on herself; and that I was not to tell Dr. Walker or her husband when they came." When Orlan Gaynor was told of his wife's abortion he replied "that it was possible my wife might have done something to herself." Of course, it was in the man's interest to feign ignorance of his wife's actions. Few husbands probably needed legal counsel to realize that not to do so could possibly lead to their being charged as an accomplice. On occasion such duplicity was publicly revealed. Henry Andrews's testimony that he opposed his wife's abortion was directly contradicted by a female witness who declared that Nellie Andrews "told me that the husband insisted that she have it done and that the husband wanted her to go to Seattle." Mark Baker said of his wife, "She never discussed very much about those affairs or I don't think we would have had so many children" whereas she stated that he had actively assisted in her aborting.

But even when the husband was obviously involved, the authorities would rarely charge him as an accomplice. Bertrand Barnett was initially prosecuted in 1914 for involvement in his wife's abortion death, but the case seems to have been dropped. The general feeling was that to jail a man who had already lost his wife would be a cruel and unnecessarily harsh course of action.

When an abortion involved a married woman the courts tended to downplay her husband's participation; when abortion involved a single woman the police frequently assumed that her male partner had been actively involved. Such a man, it was felt, clearly had much to lose if the woman's pregnancy was not terminated. This presupposition was apparently borne out in 1895 when the court heard that Locksley Lyons, having impregnated his fifteen year old sister-in-law, Kate Burns, provided her with medicine. Kate testified that it consisted of "black pills and a dark brown medicine . . . there was no name on it but he said he got it from Dr. Sloan living at Ladner. He gave me the pills two at a time; he gave me the medicine night and morning and two pills a day; he gave me three doses of pills." Though the medicine did not work Lyons was charged with both intent to procure a miscarriage and seduction.

An equally active bachelor was David McHenry who in 1904 sought the assistance in Vancouver of Dr. Alexander Stewart Murrow, who reported him as saying,

there was a girl who had missed her menses. The girl lived over on Vancouver Island and he wanted to get some medicine to bring her menses on because he said as you know I am engaged to Miss Bolen and I don't want to have any trouble occur before the wedding.

Murrow refused but a Vancouver Island doctor proved more accommodating. Often these careless lovers were charged. The court declared a married Agassiz chiropractor, who in 1929 provided his eighteen year old nurse with pills, not guilty of abortion; this was hardly surprising since he had in fact failed to abort her. But he was found guilty of her seduction and sentenced to a year in prison.

When a single woman died as a result of an abortion the courts were likely to prosecute the man, assuming he had taken the initiative in suggesting the operation. In July 1934, noticing that her daughter Veronica had missed her period Anna Kuzyk asked the local coroner if Carl Schwam, her daughter's boyfriend, had to marry her. Dr. Truax said there was no legal compulsion, but the Kuzyks could talk to Schwam. They apparently forced him into an engagement, but on 11 September Mrs. Kuzyk reported her daughter missing. The police located Veronica Kuzyk in the nearby town of Greenwood a week later in a state of ill health that required her hospitalization. She was released on 25 September but returned to hospital on 28 September. In a dying statement Veronica Kuzyk declared that Carl had given her lots of pills and, those failing, took her to Grietje Sandstrom, a Greenwood midwife. In return for twenty dollars Sandstrom "mixed up some soap and something in a small bottle and put [it] in a glass pump which she put inside me." Six such attempts failing Sandstrom then "used a button hook."

Schwam initially denied complicity and later only admitted that he had advised Kuzyk on whom to contact and provided money for the operation. He was charged with conspiracy, tried, convicted and sentenced to five years in prison; Sandstrom was sentenced to a mere twenty-three months. Going a step further, in a 1931 case the police cited the female abortionist as an accessory, but charged the dead woman's fiancé with her abortion.

Single men, when named as accomplices, frequently sought to save themselves by casting all the blame on the woman. Such was the case when William Underwood was charged in 1911 with having supplied his fiancée Angelica Stagg with drugs and a syringe with the intent to procure a miscarriage. Underwood's lawyer, by portraying Stagg as an immoral "half-breed" from Lillooet who had wanted the abortion, succeeded in getting Underwood off. But such tactics did not always work. In 1915 Walter Irwin, a separated thirty-four year old construction worker, failed to shift the blame onto eighteen year old Gladys Bolton. The court responded that ". . . a woman may be immoral and yet very truthful. . . . This is not a question of morals."

But, of course, as far as the man was concerned the courts made it clear that it was a question of morals. Husbands were rarely charged as accessories, not because they were less likely than single men to bully their partners into abortion or to support a freely made decision, but because the courts tacitly recognized that as married men they had a "right" to be so involved. Bachelors did not have such rights, indeed they were regarded as usurping the parents' right of surveillance of their unmarried daughters. Single men in short were prosecuted as much for their sexual activities as for their involvement in the abortion that made such "immorality" public knowledge. Such prosecutions, in allowing the justice system to present itself as chivalrously punishing unscrupulous males, gave it a rare opportunity of providing those members of the public that might doubt the fairness of the abortion law with badly needed evidence that it was not aimed simply at women.

Of the thirty-five men cited in abortion cases fifteen were physicians. Doctors could provide safe abortions, but by law only for medical reasons. The special nature of abortion in medical practice was spelled out by a physician testifying at a 1920 inquest.

A. Occasionally we sanction the doing of an operation to save the mother's life.
Q. But just to get rid of the child . . . is not a legal operation?
A. It is not sanctioned by the medical profession and is an illegal operation . . . And the medical Council does not sanction it.

A woman seeking an abortion or assistance in recovering from one could accordingly not expect to receive from her doctor ordinary medical care.

Abortion was one of the rare medical procedures which, save for exceptional cases, was a crime. Doctors on occasion complained about this encroachment by the law on medicine. What they tended to forget was that in Canada as elsewhere physicians, in order to eliminate the competition of midwives and irregular practitioners, had been in the nineteenth century the most vocal proponents of the criminalization of abortion. One consequence was that a doctor who did not report an abortion death risked being implicated in it. Some physicians saw themselves obliged to assume the role of police informers. If a woman were dying in hospital as the result of a bungled abortion a statement was taken if only to protect the doctor and the hospital staff. No doubt many doctors wanted to help track down dangerous abortionists, but some medical personnel showed themselves more interested in protecting themselves than in caring for their patient. In 1922 Dr. Alexander Stewart Murrow cruelly threatened the dying Jennie Young that he would not treat her for septic poisoning if she did not tell him who had performed her operation. Similar pressure was presumably applied to Winnifred Lewis because her inquest jury was told that her statement was not made voluntarily. When Sarah Robins was dying at Vancouver General Hospital in 1919 the examining physician went so far as to stimulate her with drugs to acquire a declaration that would protect the hospital staff. Such dying declarations had special force in court, having the status of sworn testimony. Accordingly Dr. Boak testified that he was "satisfied" that Mary Dalziel knew she was dying when she made hers at Victoria's Jubilee Hospital in 1917.

When a woman entered a hospital showing signs of abortion, but her life was not in danger the examining physician had to decide whether or not to make a report. Marian Noel, who had endured an operation on a kitchen table carried out by a midwife with "some sort of long thing made to prick the womb" and then went to hospital, ended up having to testify in court because the attending physician alerted police. The same thing occurred when nineteen year old Isabella Arcand was hospitalized in October 1921. In 1938 twenty-three year old stenographer Ann Tandberg passed out after her third visit to nurse Hazel Dalton and was taken to Vancouver General Hospital where her abortion was completed and reported. Such reports were far from random. The likelihood was that hospital staff would see and report poor women rather than private patients and the single rather than the married.

The extent of reportage also depended on the zeal of the attending physician. The point that many doctors had little appetite for pursuing such enquiries was made in a 1921 inquest.

Q. Doctor Fuller, it is not really customary to report these cases when they get better?
A. I don't know. As a matter of fact I guess not many are reported but I thank the Lord I have so few of them I don't know from my experience. I think if a doctor could find any information that would do any good, most of them would be willing and glad to give information, but what is the good of going to a whole lot of expense when you cannot do anything.

In the privacy of their offices doctors obviously provided some patients with abortions, but naturally enough never admitted in court to carrying out illegal operations. In 1886 Dr. William McNaughton reported that Annie Emberly, who had been cautioned she would never live through another confinement and found herself pregnant, told him that although she wanted an abortion she did not wish to see him in the penitentiary. Presumably she hoped he would courageously offer his services; McNaughton did not. In 1904 Dr. Ernest McLean likewise testified that he had been asked by Jennie Gammon to help her out of her difficulty, but he had refused. Some women felt there was no one else to whom they could turn. After her doctor rejected her request "to do something" Annie Fields ended her life with cyanide of potassium.

As regards their private patients' discussions of abortion doctors reported that some were too reticent, refusing to say what had befallen them. Other patients were too candid; doctors claimed to be shocked to find that such women insisted on their assistance. Explaining why he provided a patient with ergo-apiol pills one physician whined, "When a patient comes to us like that you have got to do something for her or they get angry with you." The doctors' worse fear was to be "taken advantage of" by their patients. Such apparently was the case in 1922 when Annie Mulvaney visited Dr. Albert Ross and gave him her maiden name, purposely failing to reveal that she was married and separated. When he asked why she did not resolve the problem of her pregnancy by marrying she replied that if her parents knew of her condition they would turn her out of the house. Ross, in return for fifty dollars, accordingly operated on Mulvaney; a few weeks later he found himself charged with performing an abortion and Annie Mulvaney testifying against him.

Courts were repeatedly told that doctors, to protect themselves from being suspected of providing abortions, were duty bound to notify colleagues of any suspicious cases. "Practically every medical man when he gets a case of this kind immediately calls a consultant. He does that for his own protection." Before a legal therapeutic abortion could be carried out,

a consultation of two or more medical men, and in the case of the hospital the heads of the hospital are notified . . . that the patient has been notified . . . and that the doctor's opinion is corroborated by that of another doctor who is in good standing and so forth.

In 1915 an inquest jury found Dr. Samuel Bamberg negligent in not calling in other doctors in consultation in an abortion case and he was finally charged with the woman's death. In 1920 Bamberg was again charged with murder, but again found not guilty. A Vernon doctor tried to have it both ways. Gerald Wilson privately treated a young woman who had been taking abortifacient pills; only when it became clear a week later that she was not going to survive—possibly due to his incompetence—did he call in a colleague for assistance.

The courts frequently expressed the concern that some doctors concealed evidence of inducement of miscarriage. More than one inquest jury recommended that physicians be forced to make public anything they knew of abortion. Suspecting a medical cover-up in 1919 the Vancouver coroner warned,

It is a very serious matter, you know, this abortion business—criminal abortion— anybody that advises it or tries to cover it up in any way is guilty, and medical men may run themselves into trouble, because if they grant a certificate in a case that should be reported to the coroner it is an offense, and a criminal offense.

The cruel irony was that the doctor whom the coroner suspected colleagues were protecting—Dr. Thomas Vernon—was himself the coroner of the neighboring municipality of North Vancouver. Vernon was implicated in Sarah Robins' abortion death in 1919 and Margaret Graham's in 1926, but in neither case were charges ever filed.

Abortion raised the complex issue of who should discipline doctors— the courts or the medical profession. In 1904 Dr. Robert Temple was initially charged with the murder of Hetta Bowes. "I took some pills today that Dr. Temple gave me," she had told a female friend, "and they nearly killed me." Temple was ultimately tried and found not guilty of the lesser charge of manslaughter, but nevertheless struck off the medical register for unprofessional conduct. He carried on a long campaign for reinstatement and was finally successful. By the 1930s a qualified doctor, so an inquest jury was told, was rarely prosecuted or censured for involvement in abortion: ". . . there is nothing to it . . . because this goes on every day unfortunately."

Before leaving the discussion of what went on in hospital wards and doctors' offices it has to be noted that many women who had illegal abortions, but did not end up in court, were nevertheless "punished." Those doctors who saw themselves first as moral guardians and second as caregivers subjected such women to humiliating interrogations, threatened to withhold from them medical treatment, and extorted dying declarations which both publicized the most intimate details of their private lives and incriminated their friends and neighbors. Given that one doctor might discreetly offer desperately needed services whereas another might call the police, women in distress necessarily approached medical professionals with caution.

What treatment could women expect to receive from the courts? An abortion was most likely heard of, as we have seen, when it resulted in a woman's death. Such a calamity could not be ignored; the police and judiciary had to act. But if the medical fraternity did not like abortion cases, the crown also viewed them with distaste. Evidence was difficult to obtain; the key witnesses were usually party to the crime. Consequently few abortion cases ever made it to court. In only thirty-four of our hundred abortions cases were charges filed. And in the even fewer number in which prosecutions were successfully pursued the sentence levied for procuring abortion was usually no more than a two year prison term. In a handful of cases stiffer sentences were given. In 1910 Richard Beveridge was tried and convicted of manslaughter and sentenced to ten years in prison. In 1914 Enid Shelbourne, a mother of an eight year old, was sentenced to seven years for the manslaughter death of Mary Barnett.

If a death had not occurred the likelihood was that an abortion attempt would only come to the police's attention because an overzealous attending physician had noticed and reported the suspicious causes of a woman's hospitalization. These sorts of cases were inevitably messy. Judges did not like them. Juries often refused to convict no matter how overwhelming the evidence. On occasion the courtroom drama, instead of properly impressing the public by a demonstration of the power and prudence of the law, brought it into disrepute. The 1902 case of Rex versus Bella Howe climaxed in what the local press called a "sensational finish." Bella Howe had been charged in Nelson with attempting to induce her own miscarriage. The attending physician testified that Howe, having been hospitalized, admitted to attempting to abort by inserting a rigid catheter. The medical witness regarded it as pertinent that Howe was a prostitute. "She is pretty tight," he coldly commented, "evidently she has not been in her occupation very long." Such a charge of self-inducement was rare inasmuch as the woman—despite what the law said—was usually regarded by the public as a victim driven by desperation. On this occasion the charge was presumably only laid because the crown thought it could make an example of a woman of the streets who had no family support. But the jury was more sympathetic and followed tradition in refusing to convict a woman of her own abortion. Mr. Justice Martin, outraged that the jurymen should blatantly ignore the testimony of the doctors, the police and the accused herself, ordered the jury to be locked up overnight to reconsider their verdict; they returned the next morning with the same verdict of "not guilty." The judge was helpless, but before discharging the jury subjected its members to a "whigging," declaring that they had "signally failed to appreciate the responsibilities of [their] office." Of course, it was the crown that had failed to appreciate its duty—that of levelling charges that it was confident that the community would sustain.

Perhaps the most surprising discovery made in the legal records is that the courts offered the opportunity for one or two vengeful women to report their own abortions in order to implicate their male partners. Although the abortion law clearly victimized women, in such cases women sought to turn a bad law to their own advantage. A case in point was revealed in the press' accounts of Sarah McPhee's extra-marital affair with Dr. Peter Van Kampen which began in Armstrong in 1901. They apparently did not employ effective contraceptives because, according to Sarah McPhee, Van Kampen aborted her in September 1901, November 1902, and February 1903. In late 1903, pregnant again, McPhee left British Columbia for California where in 1907 she instituted divorce proceedings against her husband. But when the single Van Kampen subsequently refused to marry her she in revenge successfully pressed charges against him for her earlier abortions. A similar scenario was played out in 1914 when Phila Marsden, "mistress" of Dr. Charles Maclean, charged him with aborting her against her will. The defense countered that because of the doctor's refusal to marry her she was out to get him. The crown, after the jury had failed on two occasions to come to a decision, eventually stayed the proceedings. Phila Marsden had nevertheless won a victory of sorts. Not only had she dragged Maclean's name through the mud for months in a trial which set a record as the longest in the province's history; she was sympathetically portrayed in press accounts headlined: "Would Forgive Man She Claims Wronged Her. Pathetic Story is Told by Main Witness in Retrial of Local Medico."

What was printed in the columns of the local newspapers represented for some the potentially most damaging punishment. Doctors were naturally frightened at the prospect of the tarnishing of their reputation that the appearance of their names in the news could cause. Women dreaded having their most intimate acts made a subject of public discussion. But more importantly press reports, in dwelling on gruesome deaths, both made an example of the "guilty" woman who had died at the hands of an abortionist and warned off all the others who might contemplate a similar gamble. Headlines such as "Her Horrible Death," "Young Life Cut Off Very Suddenly," "Illegal Operation Results in Death of Woman and a Charge of Murder" carried the moral that the woman who tried to interfere with nature inevitably paid a terrible price. Such lurid stories made good copy. It could be argued that newspaper editors were not necessarily trying to play up the dangers of abortion, that they were only alerted to and reported on the most tragic cases, but to do so would require crediting journalists with an unlikely ignorance of what was actually taking place in their communities.

The historian is supposed to differ from the journalist in being candid about the shortcomings of his or her sources. In drawing to a conclusion our analysis of abortion we have to recall our opening proviso that inquest and court records tell only part of the story. Because our sources draw primarily from disastrous attempts at abortion we have only had brief glimpses of women—facing the crisis of an unwanted pregnancy—supported by their male partners and their female friends and neighbors. Nevertheless the dogged determination and courage of individual women, often abandoned by those closest to them, is undeniable. Much of what we have reviewed makes for unpleasant reading: married mothers of children dying of septic poisoning, husbands pretending not to know what was going on, young men bullying young women into dangerous operations, doctors refusing to help, and incompetence abortionists demanding money. But we should not forget that almost everyone was victimized by an inequitable and unenforceable law.

What did the law accomplish? Though there was scant evidence that its avowed purpose of protecting fetal life was served, the law did have its uses. Some regular physicians found that it could be employed to shore up their profession's monopolization of the provision of medical services. The abortionists who were convicted were usually not doctors, but midwives, masseuses, and herbalists. When a maverick physician like Dr. John Garden was found guilty of abortion in 1895 it was chiefly because he did not have the support of the medical profession; he himself declared that he was a victim of a conspiracy of doctors. The law similarly extended the reach of the judiciary. The courts, abetted by the press, brandished the accounts of horrific abortion deaths as a warning to all women and so sought to police the morality of both sexes. Abortion trials, which contain potentially disturbing evidence of class and gender inequities, were "turned to account" in defense of the social and sexual status quo.

At best coroners and jurors simply ignored the law. At worse, as was made chillingly clear in 1936, such a statute could blight more than one life. In that year Helen McDonald died as a result of a botched operation, her fiancé—who considered himself responsible—committed suicide, and Edith Pierce, the abortionist, having endured a trial and two appeals, took her own life.

Given the limitations of the sources used here the claim could never be made that the entire impact of the criminalization of abortion has been surveyed. But this analysis—of the negotiations of husbands and wives, of single men and single women, of doctors and patients, of police and the public—does reveal the ways in which the law poisoned relationships which were often already inherently difficult. It is not necessary to argue that people are innately good, to recognize that such laws made many worse than they had to be.

23. "I Want a Girl, Just Like the Girl That Married Harry James": American Women and the Problem of Political Obligation in World War II

ROBERT B. WESTBROOK

It was, without question, the most enduring popular culture image in the United States, evident wherever American soldiers were training and fighting, during World War II. Betty Grable, the blonde actress who danced with Fred Astaire in a dozen films and married big band leader Harry James, is dressed in high heels and a one-piece, low-backed bathing suit, smiling coquettishly over her right shoulder at the camera, her hands resting casually on her hips. The "pin-up" photograph was taped to windows, foot lockers, tank turrets, bomber panels, and diaries around the world, a fitting image of "American womanhood," what the boys were fighting for in Europe, North Africa, the Pacific, Asia, and the Philippines. The United States government approved of the pin-up, as well as those of such other actresses as Rita Hayworth and Jane Russell, to encourage the troops to crush the Axis powers and whatever threat they posed to American women.

During the war, American women felt obligated to live up to the pin-up image, to be the pure, white, beautiful person Betty Grable embodied. Soldiers played the role of protectors, and American women became the protected. Soon after the end of World War II, a powerful feminist critique of stylized body images emerged in the United States. Such women as Betty Friedan, Kate Millett, Gloria Steinem, and Susan Brownmiller labored, with crusading zeal, to liberate women from the rigid physical standards the culture imposed on them. The "pin-up girls" of World War II pre-dated those criticisms, but the obligations they imposed on men and women helped fuel the subsequent feminist movement. In the following essay, Robert B. Westbrook discusses the "pin-up girls" of World War II.

As the 1988 presidential campaign wound down to its conclusion, a reporter from the *New York Times* made a valiant effort to elicit the candidates' opinions on "the subject of culture." Perhaps unduly worried about Southern votes, George Bush went on at length about his fondness for country music and *Bassmaster* magazine. He also revealed that, when he was a young navy pilot in the Second World War, he had named four of his planes "Barbara" after his girlfriend, but he denied that he had gone in for pin-ups of Betty Grable or Rita Hayworth. "I didn't pin 'em up because I was, like, engaged to Barbara Bush. . . . those pin-ups were all over our ship, but I'd like to plead innocent myself." Bush did, however, confess that he "glanced" at the pin-ups of his shipmates, and when he glanced, he said, he liked Doris Day best.

What follows suggests that Bush need not have been so sheepish on the subject of pin-ups. The sailors who pinned up Rita Hayworth were engaged in a common activity with those, like the President, who named their planes after their fiancées. Though Barbara Bush may not have been "just like the girl that married Harry James," she and Betty Grable were part of the same story.

Before I tell that story, I would like to explain my interest in pin-ups, for the source of that interest is not what one might expect. I started thinking about pin-ups in the context of a study on the way in which political obligation was conceived in America during World War II. This study is an effort to see whether the conclusion of a number of political philosophers that liberal theory lacks a coherent conception of political obligation (a conclusion I find persuasive) is reflected empirically in the political culture of a liberal polity like that of the United States. My aim is to identify the philosophy of obligation at work in American practices and institutions and to highlight its distinctive features by means of a case study of a moment when Americans had reason to be more explicit than usual about such matters.

My working hypothesis (consistent with the expectations derived from political theory) is that, with some exceptions, Americans during World War II were not called upon to conceive of their obligation to participate in the war effort as a *political* obligation to work, fight, or die for their country. By and large, the representatives of the state and other American propagandists relied on two different moral arguments, neither of which constituted a claim of political obligation. First, they appealed to putatively universal moral values—such as those enumerated in the Atlantic Charter or Franklin Roosevelt's "Four Freedoms" speech—values such as "freedom," "equality," and "democracy" transcending obligations to the United States as a particular political community. Second, and more interestingly, they implored Americans as individuals and as families to join the war effort in order to protect the state that protected them, an appeal, philosophers have argued, characteristic of liberal states and one that, at bottom, is an appeal to go to war to defend *private* interests and discharge *private* obligations. Over the course of the war, this latter sort of prescription became increasingly prominent, and the more elusive evidence of the felt obligations of Americans suggests that it was this sort of appeal that was most compelling for them and coincided most often with their own notions of "what we are fighting for."

One important body of evidence supporting this hypothesis is what might be termed the cultural construction of women as objects of obligation. This process is one I want to analyze here, examining principally the fabrication by communication elites of women as prescribed icons of male obligation. I also will suggest the ways in which women functioned as such for soldiers and the manner in which women themselves participated in their mobilization as a private interest for which men would fight. My focus will be on the pin-up, one of the most prominent documents in the material culture of World War II and, in particular, on the image of the most popular of the movie stars who found their way onto the walls of barracks from the Aleutians to North Africa: Betty Grable (hence my title).

LIBERAL OBLIGATIONS

Before I turn to pin-ups, more should be said about the theoretical concerns that lie behind this effort to offer something other than the obvious reading of these documents—an attempt to see them as part of the wartime discourse on obligation without gainsaying their place in the story of the exploitation of women and their bodies in American mass culture. Wartime pin-ups can tell us much about liberal political theory, as well as much about sexual politics. Or, to be more precise, they can tell us something about the ways in which the American state attempted to draw on the moral obligations prescribed by prevailing gender roles to solve the problem of obligation posed by liberal ideology.

Arguing from a variety of perspectives, a number of philosophers have offered a powerful critique of the efforts of the giants of the liberal philosophical tradition from Thomas Hobbes to John Rawls to provide an adequate basis for political obligation and have concluded, as Carole Pateman puts it, that "political obligation in the liberal democratic state constitutes an insoluble problem; insoluble because political obligation cannot be given expression within the context of liberal democratic institutions." This critique of the liberal theory of political obligation has advanced on at least two fronts. On the one hand, philosophers such as John Simmons have used the tools of analytic philosophy to demonstrate that the traditional foundations of the liberal theory of political obligation—the notion of "tacit consent" and the claim that citizens are obligated to a liberal state because of the benefits they receive from it—cannot provide an adequate account of or justification for political obligation. On the other hand, communitarian critics of liberalism such as Michael Walzer have slighted these difficulties in favor of raising doubts about whether liberal theorists can be said to have ever advanced an account of *public* obligation, that is, obligation to a political community. It is this latter critique that is most pertinent to discussing the construction of women as icons of obligation.

In an essay entitled "The Obligation to Die for the State," Walzer addresses the problem of obligation in the context of war and asks whether the obligation citizens have to the state can be made the motive for risking their lives. The answer to this question, he suggests, depends in critical respects on the nature of the state, and, in the case of the liberal state, the answer is no. The reason, he argues, is that the end of the liberal state—as conceived in the social contract tradition of Hobbes, Locke, and their successors—is the security of the lives of the individuals who form it. Consequently, "a man who dies for the state defeats his only purpose in forming the state: death is the contradiction of politics. A man who risks his life for the state accepts the insecurity which it was the only end of his political obedience to avoid: war is the failure of politics. Hence there can be no political obligation either to die or to fight."

When a war begins, political authorities in a liberal society invite their subjects, as Hobbes put it, to "protect their protection"—an admission on their part of a failure to hold up their end of the bargain on which the state rests. Peculiar in any case as a call to men and women to risk their lives for their instrument, the invitation is doubly peculiar as one to defend an instrument that has failed its function. As Walzer says, when individuals "protect their protection they are doing nothing more than defending themselves, and so they cannot protect their protection after their protection ceases to protect them. At that point, it ceases to be their protection. The state has no value over and above the value of the lives of the concrete individuals whose safety it provides. No man has a common life to defend, but only an individual life."

Walzer goes on to link more closely this problem that liberalism has with the "ultimate obligation" to its individualism and largely negative conception of liberty—which make for a conception of the citizen as an individual whom the state protects from interference by other individuals or by the state itself. This liberal view suggests "an indefinite number of distinct and singular relations between the individual citizens and the authorities as a body—a pattern that might best be symbolized by a series of vertical lines. There are no horizontal connections among citizens as citizens." The state is conceived "as an instrument which serves individual men (or families) but not or not necessarily as an instrument wielded by these men themselves" as constituents of a political community. Walzer concludes that any theory like liberalism which "begins with the absolute independence of freely willing individuals and goes on to treat politics and the state as instrumental to the achievement of individual purposes would seem by its very nature incapable of describing ultimate obligation."

It is very important to add, as Walzer does, that this difficulty in liberal theory does not mean that the citizens of a liberal state will not go to war and fight and die on behalf of ethical, if not political, obligations. As he says:

Moved by love, sympathy, or friendship, men in liberal society can and obviously do incur ultimate obligations. They may even find themselves in situations where they are or think they are obliged to defend the state which defends in turn the property and enjoyment of their friends and families. But if they then actually risk their lives or die, they do so because they have incurred private obligations which have nothing to do with politics. The state may shape the environment within which these obligations are freely incurred, and it may provide the occasions and the means for their fulfillment. But this is only to say that, when states make war and men fight, the reasons of the two often are and ought to be profoundly different.

This argument leads one to expect that liberal states, bereft of a compelling argument for political obligation, will attempt to exploit private obligations in order to convince its citizens to serve its defense. Indeed, it was precisely these sorts of private obligations—to families, to children, to parents, to buddies, and generally, to an "American Way of Life" defined as a rich (and richly commodified) private experience—that formed a crucial element in the campaign to mobilize Americans for World War II. Yet few private obligations were more apparent in pronouncements about "why we fight" than those binding men and women.

PIN-UPS AS MORAL ARGUMENTS

Three years before American entry into the war, a team of copywriters drew up a recruiting advertisement to show what wartime enlistment propaganda might look like. Though the most apparent feature of this ad is its racism—its call to white Americans to prevent "yellow feet" from ever reaching American soil—it is also a document that anticipates the privatization of obligation in World War II propaganda. Men are urged here to enlist in order to discharge a private (the "'other fellow' won't stop them") obligation to the women they, as individuals, protect ("*your* sister, *your* wife, *your* sweetheart"). This sort of appeal distinguishes this ad from other instances of the prominent genre of Allied "rape propaganda" of which it is a part. Often in such propaganda women are portrayed simply as the booty of war, and the appeal is to men to protect their property in women's bodies from enemy male competitors. In the "*Your* Sister" ad, however, a more complex bond of obligation is said to tie American men to the women of their society. The copy suggests that the rights American men claim to "their" women's bodies are linked to a set of corresponding obligations; the threat of the "yellow hand of lust" is here less that of the expropriation of the bounty of their own lust than the rupturing of a moral relationship between themselves and the women in their lives. It also indicates that this relationship extends to their sisters and to other women to whom they have no proprietary sexual claim. When American soldiers said, as they often did, that it was American women that they were "fighting for," they sometimes, to be sure, were identifying women as the spoils of war, but more often "for" meant "for whom" or "on behalf of." They were articulating the moral obligations of the "protector" to the "protected," a relationship ethically problematic in its own right but nonetheless different from that of a man to a woman viewed simply as sexual property.

A similar argument is implicit in one of the ubiquitous visual components of the cultural landscape of the war: the pin-up. Unlike the "naughty postcard" that American troops brought back from France in World War I, the pin-up circulated above ground in World War II, and the Hollywood pin-up did so with official sanction. Despite the concerns of religious groups and some officials about the immorality of pin-ups, the United States government and the film industry cooperated closely during the war in the production and distribution of millions of photographs of Hollywood's leading ladies and rising starlets, and these pictures decorated the walls of barracks, the bulkheads of ships, and the fuselages of planes on all fronts. I suspect that many historians whose fathers fought in the war might find evidence in family archives of the avidity with which soldiers collected pin-ups.

Obviously, pin-ups functioned as surrogate objects of sexual desire for soldiers far from home, and I do not mean to discount this. Soldiers viewed them as such, and some complained that the pin-ups in semi-official publications like *Yank* were too tame. "I know you want to keep it clean," wrote one private to *Yank*, "but after all the boys are interested in sex, and *Esquire* and a few other magazines give us sex and still get by the mail, so why can't *Yank*?" They reacted bitterly to charges that pin-ups were immoral and to the threat of censorship. "Maybe if some of those 'panty waists' had to be stuck out some place where there are no white women and few native women for a year and a half, as we were," wrote some GIs in Alaska, "they would appreciate even a picture of our gals back home."

American military officials linked the aggressiveness of the effective soldier with healthy, heterosexual desire and worried about sustaining such desire and thwarting homosexuality. Thus, it is plausible, as John D'Emilio and Estelle Freedman have said, that pin-ups were intended by the government to "encourage heterosexual fantasy in the sex-segregated military." Concerned also about epidemics of venereal disease, the government sought to provide activities in which sexual desire could be sublimated and even endorsed a measure of "autoeroticism," provided it did not become "habit-forming."

However, pin-ups were more than masturbatory aids. They also functioned as icons of the private interests and obligations for which soldiers were fighting. Several pieces of evidence suggest this point. First of all, many pin-ups were, as the complaints of some soldiers indicate, relatively demure. As Paul Fussell has said, they were hardly "triggers of lust," which is, in part, attributable to censorship; the War Department and Hollywood were only willing to go so far. Yet to attribute the limited erotic charge of pin-ups to censorship alone fails to explain why some of the most popular pin-ups were not those that flirted with the limits imposed by the censors. Above all, it fails to account for the appeal of far-and-away the most sought-after pin-up—that of Betty Grable—for which, at one point, there were twenty thousand requests per week and which, by war's end, had been put in the hands of five million servicemen. This pin-up was modest compared with others like that of runner-up Rita Hayworth, suggesting that Grable and many of the other most popular pin-up models were viewed not only as objects of sexual fantasy but also as representative women, standing in for wives and sweethearts on the homefront. "If I had a wife I would make sure her picture was up," one sailor remarked, "but Irene Manning will do until that big day." Reporting on behalf of the Hollywood Victory Committee, Alan Ladd observed in 1943 that those who had entertained the troops had learned that the boys preferred women who reminded them of their mothers and sisters. In search of "girls they can prize," servicemen were not interested in "flash." They preferred movies "whose components—street scenes, normal people on the streets, women who look like mothers, wives, sweethearts—bring them near home."

Betty Grable's appeal, in particular, was less as an erotic "sex goddess" than as a symbol of the kind of woman for whom American men—especially American working-class men—were fighting. She was the sort of girl a man could prize. Her image, carefully cultivated by the star-making machinery of Twentieth Century Fox, was "straight-arrow, chintz-table-cloth." Darryl Zanuck, the head of the studio, correctly guessed that Grable would appeal to soldiers, and he featured her in a series of Technicolor musicals that highlighted her "pastel charms." In her movies, Grable repeatedly portrayed a young woman tempted by "flash" but, in the end, claimed for gentility. In *Pin-Up Girl* (1944), for example, she played Laurie Jones, a local pin-up girl popular with the soldiers at the USO Club in Missoula, Montana, who is possessed of a vivid imagination and a weakness for the white lie. After moving to Washington to take up a job as a government stenographer, Laurie attempts to win the heart of Guadalcanal hero Tommy Dooley by pretending that she is glamorous showgirl "Laura Lorraine" only to discover that what Tommy really wants and needs is a girl like the real Laurie Jones: "sincere, honest, with both feet on the ground." In the film's finale, she reveals that Laurie Jones and Laura Lorraine are one and the same woman and accepts herself as she is: a level-headed small-town girl who happens to know her way around an elaborate production number.

This reading of Grable's appeal is not to deny a sexual dimension to her popularity. It is rather to situate her sexuality within a configuration of attributes that established her as a principal icon of obligation. Grable's sexiness was, as condescending middlebrow critics often sneered, "of the common sort"—and this was a key to her success. The consensus of opinion, including Grable herself, was that, as *Time* put it, "she can lay no claims to sultry beauty or mysterious glamor. . . . Her peach-cheeked, pearl blonde good looks add up to mere candy-box-top prettiness." If we place Grable's image within the context of the discourse of obligation as well as that of soft-core pornography, we can explain how it flourished despite bucking what André Bazin perceived as a drift of the gaze of American men during the war from the leg to the breast. By these lights, Grable's standing as the premier pin-up girl is inexplicable given that her legs were said to be her most striking attribute. Of course, Bazin might have been wrong, and Grable's popularity, compared to Rita Hayworth and Jane Russell, merely might indicate that "leg-men" still outnumbered "breast-men" during the war. Yet this conclusion, I think, is too simple. Even Grable's legs were celebrated less for their exceptional beauty than for their approximation to the "average." As *Life* reported, Grable's legs—"her private trademark"—were celebrated not as extraordinary but as "the Great American Average Legs: straight, perfectly rounded and shaped, but withal judged by the same standards as millions of others."

Finally, one must not forget that the war in the Pacific was a race war, and Grable's obvious "whiteness" gave her an advantage over competitors such as Hayworth (née Margarita Cansino) in the eyes of white soldiers waging a brutal struggle against a racial enemy in a setting in which, as they often complained, white women—especially women as white as Grable—were in short supply. As *Time* reported, soldiers preferred Grable to other pin-ups "in direct ratio to their remoteness from civilization." Here again, in a nation still firmly in the grip of white supremacy, Betty Grable provided the superior image of American womanhood.

Packaged as the serviceman's favorite, Grable quickly caught on as such. No one received more fan mail from soldiers, and by the end of the war she was the most popular star in Hollywood, earning the largest salary of any woman in America. Summing up the attitude they held toward her, one veteran told Grable:

There we were out in those damn dirty trenches. Machine guns firing. Bombs dropping all around us. We would be exhausted, frightened, confused and sometimes hopeless about our situation. When suddenly someone would pull your picture out of his wallet. Or we'd see a decal of you on a plane and then we'd *know* what we were fighting for.

In October 1943 *Modern Screen* reported that a soldier had died clutching Grable's photograph. If, as Richard Schickel scoffed, she was "democratic womanhood's lowest common denominator," it was precisely for this reason that she came to stand for those worth dying for. "In her time," as Jane Gaines has said, Grable was "model girlfriend, wife, and finally mother."

Indeed, her popularity *increased* after she married bandleader Harry James in 1943 and had a child later that year. She fared as well, if not better, as "pin-up mamma" as she had as pin-up girl.

Perhaps the most striking evidence of the way pin-ups functioned as wartime discourse about obligation is the way soldiers plastered the image of Grable and others to the machines of war, where they competed with and upstaged the insignias of the state. As John Costello observes, "by 1945 there was hardly a tank or a plane in the U.S. military that was not adorned with its own painted icon of femininity as a good-luck talisman that also showed the enemy what it was that red-blooded Americans 'were fighting for.'" This practice was not just a matter of naming planes after girls (or of comparing girls to planes) but of removing the obfuscating veil of arguments for a soldier's obligation to die for the liberal state in order to reveal (nakedly) the private obligations upon which such states ultimately relied.

In suggesting that there was more to pin-ups than sexual exploitation and that pin-ups advanced a tacit moral argument, I do not mean to endorse the substance of that argument, for it is a troubling one. As Judith Hicks Stiehm has observed in an acute discussion of the disquieting features of the asymmetrical relationship between "protectors" and "protected," at the heart of this argument is the assignment of women to the role of the protected simply by virtue of their gender. Moreover, this argument has some disturbing effects on male protectors.

Men, who have a monopoly on the use of violent power, find their identity bound up with the effectiveness of the protection they provide to their dependents. Hence, they may tend to "overprotect" them, and, even more disturbing, "there is a tendency for the protector to become a predator" who turns on his dependents, especially when things go badly.

When there is no real work or duty required of a protector the role is satisfying, it makes one proud. As role demands increase, and/or as the chances of fulfilling the role decrease, the practice of the role becomes less and less attractive. The protected become a nuisance, a burden, and finally a shame, for an unprotected protectee is the clearest possible evidence of a protector's failure. . . . As one gains ascendancy one gains dependents, as one gains dependents their requirements for protection increase. . . . Thus the most wholly dependent protectees may be just the ones most likely to trigger a nihilistic impulse in their protector.

The dynamic that Stiehm describes may help explain the misogynistic, often violently misogynistic, character of much of the literature produced by soldiers, which such critics as Susan Gubar have analyzed. Though pin-ups are not the best documents through which to explore this dynamic, there is a hint of it in the use of a Grable pin-up to instruct troops in map reading. This device was said to be an aid to concentration, but it is difficult not to view it also as a "targeting" of Grable's anatomy, in which case Grable's image proved eminently adaptable to an expression of the darker side of the pressing obligations connecting men and women during the war.

RECIPROCITY

Though male soldiers were the principal collectors of pin-ups, the pin-up girl also addressed herself to American women, suggesting that, if men were obliged to fight for their pin-up girls, women were in turn obliged to fashion themselves into pin-up girls worth fighting for. Pin-ups, that is, argued for a reciprocity of obligation. Amidst a call to women to do their part by taking up (for the duration) the jobs that men had left behind, there was a simultaneous appeal to them to discharge an obligation to be the sort of women their men would be proud to protect.

Here too Betty Grable was an important figure. She was admired by women as well as men. Her rise to box-office champion during the war was due as much to the women who flocked to her movies as to the soldiers who pinned her up overseas. "Girls can see me in a picture," she said, "and feel I could be one of them." During the war, she was offered to women—especially working-class women—as a model of female virtue on the home-front. "Men are so right about everything, especially Betty Grable," declared *Photoplay*. "Girls who want to be brides should aim to be like Betty." Young working-class women avidly followed Grable's career in the fan magazines where her domestic life, as they portrayed it, was held up as an example to readers. As Gaines says, "even though Grable was making a six-figure yearly salary, in the fan magazines she was still the little family budget-keeper, living within her million-dollar means and outfitting the ranch house with bargains from the Sears catalogue." Above all, it was Grable's self-effacing modesty that recommended her to women. Advising her readers on how to please men, she said: "Remember to follow their lead, from dancing to conversation. Talk about *them*. The most popular girls at the Hollywood Canteen, for instance, are the really good listeners; the ones who hang onto a man's words as if he were the Oracle of War and the only person in the room." Betty Grable, *Photoplay* observed, "is as modest as the girl who married Dad."

It is important, of course, to try to figure out the extent to which the obligation of American women to be pin-ups men would die for was felt as well as prescribed, but it is much more difficult to find evidence on this score. Here I can only say that what evidence I have been able to gather thus far suggests that it was an obligation that many women took to heart. American soldiers marched into battle with pin-ups of not only Betty Grable but also of their own wives and girlfriends. Grable both explicitly and by example urged women who thought they looked good in a bathing suit to send a snapshot to servicemen, and many heeded her advice. Like Rita Weinberg of the Bronx, thousands of American women provided soldiers like Bernie Kessel with photographs to tuck in their helmets and pin to their weapons, and in these photographs women often expertly constructed their images through the conventions of the pin-up: the one-piece bathing suit or sweater, high heels, the over-the-shoulder look, the "pleasing convexities" of the bent knee, and the bright, coy "come on" smile. Even my mother, I must say, proved adept at this, carefully tailoring her photographic image to conventions established by Lana Turner and others. Moreover, though homemade cheesecake circulated as widely as the Hollywood variety on the battlefront, soldiers often opted for apple-pie. As the American Expeditionary Force gathered in Northern Ireland in 1942 for the invasion of North Africa, they held a contest for the "Sweetheart of the AEF," and the winner was Janet ("Angel") Barry of Belmar,

New Jersey—a pin-up at which even George Bush might, in good conscience, have sneaked a peak.

LIVING THEORY

Occasionally, citizens recognize that political theory is something more than the labor of those specialists called political theorists and come to realize that, in their everyday experience as citizens they are *living* theory. One of those occasions on which they become aware of this is when their nation goes to war. Reflecting then on the problems of political obligation, they ask themselves why they are obliged not only to obey the laws of their state but why they (or their loved ones) are obliged to risk their lives to defend that state. The representatives of the state supply them with answers to these questions that best serve their purposes, and citizens often accept these answers, which accord with their own sense of where their obligations lie, a sense developed within the confines of a particular political culture.

Because of the thinness of public life in a liberal political culture like that of the United States, modern American statesmen and their allies have found it difficult to call upon their fellow citizens *as citizens* to defend their nation in time of war. Though given to justify wars on behalf of principles transcending the values of any particular political community, they also have relied heavily on appeals to private (which is not to say selfish) obligations in order to legitimate the sacrifices of war, including the moral commitments believed to exist between men and women. These arguments are sometimes explicit; often they are not. As living theory, they can be found in some unexpected places, even in pin-ups.

Given the centrality of the mutual obligations, both prescribed and felt, between men and women to American mobilization in World War II, it is not surprising that pin-ups were sanctioned by the state. Nor is it surprising that the photograph that has come to signify the end of American participation in the war is one portraying the consummation of the bargain between protector and protected. . . . In Times Square in August 1945, *Life* photographer Alfred Eisenstadt captured a protector exacting his reward from a woman he grabbed on the street, a representative of the protected who happened to be close at hand. Apparently this sailor shared the conviction of fellow soldiers in New Guinea who, earlier in the war, had remarked that "we are not only fighting for the Four Freedoms, we are fighting also for the priceless privilege of making love to American women." Having helped win that fight, the sailor and other soldiers returned home to reap the rewards they believed were their due. If I am right about the character of American discourse concerning obligation during World War II, it is fitting to mark the end of the "Good War" with a representative kiss, manifesting in its mix of joy and violence the ambiguities of the moral contract binding protective men and protected women in a liberal state.

24. We Also Served

DORIS BRINKER TANNER

During the Persian Gulf War, military women piloted a number of combat aircraft, and several women were among the casualties of the war. In January 1994, Secretary of Defense Les Aspin announced that by the end of the year most combat positions in the United States military would be open to women. Feminist critics had for years charged that military women did not enjoy the same promotion opportunities as men because they were denied combat positions, which traditionally have been very important in career advancement. Aspin's announcement was an attempt to correct much of that injustice.

During World War II, because of severe shortages of pilots, women were trained as WASPs—Women Airforce Service Pilots—ferrying combat aircraft from the factories where they were produced to the operational airfields where they fought the war. Their service shattered more than a few myths about the capabilities of women pilots. In spite of their service, however, Congress refused to grant the WASPs full military status, and as soon as the labor shortages ended in 1945, they were displaced by male pilots. In the following essay, Doris Tanner describes the Women Airforce Service Pilots program during World War II.

Plunged into World War II on December 7, 1941, the United States soon experienced a desperate labor shortage, necessitating that women participate in many activities previously reserved for men. Government agencies launched a nationwide media blitz through newspapers and radio, urging women to work outside the home and thus help bring the war to an early, victorious end. Women responded in overwhelming numbers.

No field of endeavor during that time was more tradition-shattering than women's roles in the military services—and none of these was more revolutionary than women flying aircraft for the Army Air Forces. The World War II achievements of the Women Airforce Service Pilots (WASP) have received slight attention from military historians, but their record nevertheless stands as an important and interesting milestone in history. Except for nurses, very few women had previously served in military units, and none in the dangerous, demanding jobs of military aviation. Later, following disbanding of the WASP, it would be 1977 before women would again graduate from Air Force pilot training. This subsequent accomplishment came about in large part due to the performance of the courageous group of women who earned silver wings during the war years of 1942 to 1944.

The idea of enlisting women pilots for domestic military flying duties, thus releasing men for combat-related operations overseas, was primarily the brain child of aviatrix Jacqueline Cochran. Less well-known than her friend Amelia Earhart, Cochran had a remarkable flying career. In 1935 the twenty-five-year-old flyer became the first woman entrant in the famous Bendix Transcontinental Air Race, and three years later she took first place over experienced male competitors. In 1940 Cochran broke speed records for both men and women, and over a twenty-five-year period she would set some two hundred other flying records. Her many awards would include the Harmon International Trophy for the world's outstanding woman flyer (fifteen times), the Distinguished Flying Cross (three times), and the Air Force Distinguished Service Medal (for which she was the first woman to be so honored).

Cochran also made aviation history on July 1, 1941, when she became the first woman to ferry a Lockheed Hudson bomber across the Atlantic for delivery to the besieged British. This exploit brought her headlines in the *New York Times* and a luncheon invitation from the White House that resulted in a long conversation with President Franklin D. Roosevelt.

Roosevelt was so impressed with Cochran's ideas about women's potential for military flying duties that he arranged for her to talk with his assistant secretary of war for air, Robert Lovett. This meeting led in turn to conferences with the officer in charge of the Ferry Command, Colonel Robert Olds, and the commanding general of the Army Air Forces, Henry "Hap" Arnold.

General Arnold assigned to Cochran the monumental task of compiling data on the number of women pilots qualified for military flying jobs, and to formulate a plan for utilizing their skills. Her comprehensive proposal was presented to him in August 1941.

But even an innovative, advanced thinker like General Arnold—one of the first American military leaders to visualize the potential of air power—was skeptical about putting a "slip of a young girl" into the cockpit of one of his planes. Although he knew the duties that both British and Russian women pilots were already performing, Arnold decided that the United States was not yet in need of such extreme measures. However, as preparation for a possible emergency, he suggested that Cochran return to England to gain firsthand knowledge and experience with a group of English women pilots serving in the Royal Air Force Air Transport Auxiliary. Commanded by Pauline Gower, they were dubbed "ATA girls," and as ferry pilots were making a significant contribution toward retaining aerial superiority above the British Isles.

The Japanese attack on Pearl Harbor in December 1941 led Cochran to question entering service with England, since the security of her own country was now in jeopardy. But General Arnold assured her that the experience would be a vital preliminary step toward the formation of any such group in the United States—and that while no such organization was yet planned, he would recall her if and when such a move was made.

Consequently, in the spring of 1942 Cochran was commissioned a flight captain with the ATA. Twenty-two other experienced American pilots joined her in the venture; these women serving with the Royal Air Force constituted the first organized group of American women pilots in the war.

During the bleak summer of 1942 General Arnold informed Jacqueline Cochran that the time had come for her to return home, where her expertise was now needed to plan, organize, and direct a program to train women pilots for service with the Army Air Forces. As quickly as possible, she completed her responsibilities to the Royal Air Force, and returned to New York on September 10, 1942. To her amazement, that same day's edition of the *New York Times* contained an article announcing the formation of an organization of women pilots under the Army Air Forces Transport Command, with Nancy Harkness Love as director.

Twenty-seven-year-old Nancy Love, a skilled pilot and wife of Colonel Robert Love, deputy chief of the Air Transport Command, had urged the employment of women ferry pilots by the command for many months. An announcement at a conference of the air staff that a women's program had been approved prompted General Harold L. George, commander of the Ferry Command, to authorize immediate action; the need for pilots to fly new planes from factories to military fields was critical. Air Transport Command orders authorizing the employment of women flyers were issued on September 5, 1942. Eighty-three experienced women pilots received application; twenty-three were immediately accepted, and four more joined later.

When informed of this swift action by a subordinate, General Arnold summoned his officers of the Ferry Command and explained that a much larger and more comprehensive program than hiring a few women civilians to ferry planes for the Air Transport Command was planned. Nevertheless, these unusual circumstances resulted in the initial coexistence of *two* fledgling organizations of women pilots.

The organization responsible for recruitment and training of women pilots was designated the 319th Army Air Force Flying Detachment and was based in Houston, Texas. Jacqueline Cochran was named director and Leni Leoti Clark Deaton chief administrative officer.

At the same time, Nancy Love headed the Air Transport Command Squadron, comprised of women pilots with at least five hundred hours of flying experience. It was designated the Women's Auxiliary Ferry Service, or WAFS, and was based at New Castle Army Air Base in Delaware.

The two units operated separately until June 1943, when Arnold ordered their consolidation into one organization, known thereafter as Women Airforce Service Pilots, or WASP. Cochran became director of all WASP activities, while Love was made staff director of all WASPs assigned to the Air Transport Command. Love and the women already employed continued their ferrying duties, but all others, even veteran pilots returning from ATA service in England, were now required to complete a rigorous military training program.

News of the opportunity for women to fly for the Army Air Forces spread like wildfire across America. More than 25,000 young women flooded Cochran's office with applications; of these 1,830 were accepted.

Requirements stipulated that successful applicants must be American citizens between twenty-one (later reduced to eighteen and one-half) and thirty-five years of age, stand at least sixty (later raised to sixty-four) inches tall, and pass the high standards of the Form Sixty-Four physical examination by a flight surgeon. The key requirement was that applicants have at least two hundred (subsequently reduced to thirty-five) hours of logged, certified flying time. Cochran or her representative personally interviewed each applicant before acceptance and assignment to a class.

The first class of twenty-eight recruits assembled on November 16, 1942, at the Howard Hughes Municipal Airport in Houston, Texas. Aviation Enterprises Limited, a civilian contract school under the Gulf Coast

Air Force Training Center of the Training Command, was awarded the contract to train the women in the Army method of flying.

Legislation giving the women pilots complete military status was awaiting action in Congress; in the meantime the students were accepted as federal employees on temporary Civil Service status. As such they did not qualify for flight pay or other standard military benefits, nor did the organization yet have an official uniform.

The training program included over four hundred hours of ground school, with instruction in aircraft design and theory of flight, engines and propellers, mathematics, physics, navigation, instruments and instrument flying, weather, code, calisthenics, and close-order drill. The most important part of the course, however, was the 210 hours of flight instruction. Twenty-seven weeks were scheduled to complete the program.

To compensate for delays caused by fog and other bad weather, the women often flew six and seven days a week. But they had come to Texas to fly and to serve their country during the crisis of war, and they willingly and cheerfully endured the grueling schedule. Their training compared in every way to that of male cadets, except that formation and aerobatic instruction were not included officially; such skills were needed for combat duty, and law forbade women in combat.

Chief Administrative Officer Leni Leoti Deaton was responsible for much of the initial success of the unique and "avante garde" project, finding solutions for the unprecedented problems arising from trying to make civilian volunteers fit into a military organization. Cochran and Deaton followed military procedures and Army regulations wherever possible, but the quasi-military, quasi-civilian structure hampered operations severely. Adding to their difficulties were the challenges of obtaining adequate transportation, food, living quarters, and medical services in a region already flooded with war workers and military personnel.

The second class of trainees arrived in December 1942, and another new group each month thereafter. By the time several classes had entered training, flying conditions at Houston were becoming increasingly overcrowded and dangerous. Plans to increase the number of students to 750, then to 1,000 for 1944, made it obligatory to find more adequate facilities.

When a male cadet program was scheduled for phasing out at Avenger Field in Sweetwater, Texas, Deaton was asked her opinion of moving the women's program there—being cautioned at the same time that the move would temporarily involve side-by-side training with male cadets, and that any resulting problems would be hers. Deaton's enthusiastic "My grandfather pioneered coeducation, let's go," made it possible to turn the 319th into a much better organized, equipped, and disciplined unit: the 318th Army Air Force Flying Training Detachment. Until the last male cadets at Sweetwater were graduated, this was the first, though brief, coeducational flight training program in American military aviation history.

Conditions at Sweetwater, located two hundred miles due west of Dallas–Fort Worth, were a great improvement over those at Houston, but the training remained extremely difficult and exhausting. The ninety-five women of Class 44-W-4 who reported to Avenger Field on November 1, 1943 (the author was a member of this group), were typical WASP trainees.

The students had come from all parts of the United States and from many backgrounds, and included former teachers, nurses, secretaries, factory workers, waitresses, students, housewives, debutantes, actresses, and the wife of famous Broadway playwright Damon Runyon.

Following check-in and the filling out of myriad government forms, we were assigned alphabetically to typical one-story Army barracks, six women to a bay. We soon found that the total lack of privacy necessitated a frank and open attitude and willingness for cooperation. Surplus Army mechanics' olive drab overalls, size forty-four and up, dubbed "zoot suits," replaced our civilian clothes, while cosmetics and fancy hair styles quickly became relics of the past. Biting winds from the west Texas plains drilled sand into our clothes, skin, teeth, ears, eyes, and hair.

Our typical day began before the chilly dawn with the trumpet blast of reveille, followed by a hasty dressing in three or four layers of clothing, and falling in for roll call and breakfast formation. We then policed our quarters and fell in again for ground school or flight line. For one week Flight I attended ground school each morning while Flight II (my group) flew; then the schedule was reversed. Saturday morning was the occasion for a stringent inspection of our quarters by male officers.

The seventy-hour primary phase of flying began in a 175-horsepower Fairchild PT-19 primary trainer, a silver, streamlined, open-cockpit, low-wing monoplane. It was the fastest and heaviest plane most of the trainees had ever flown, as most of their prior experience was in 65-horsepower Piper Cubs. Soon after 44-W-4 started flying, the PT-19 was replaced by the Stearman PT-17, a sturdy, stable, 225-horsepower, bi-wing trainer.

Following approximately six to eight hours of "dual" instruction on takeoffs, climbs, turns, stalls and spins, and landings, the civilian instructor climbed out of the plane and the student flew her first solo flight. The first woman to solo was hailed as the class "hot" pilot and dunked in the cold water of a fountain called the wishing well; the honor for 44-W-4 went to Dorothy Britt from Oklahoma.

Subsequent solo flights involved long hours of intense practice to perfect loops, chandelles, pylon eights, spins, and all of the elementary maneuvers necessary to prove one's proficiency on an Army "check" ride. Total concentration was imperative to master the exact precision demanded for an "S" or satisfactory grade. It was easy, especially on a hazy or windy day, to concentrate so completely on maneuvers that check points or markers back to the home base were lost.

Faye Wolfe of Grand Rapids, Michigan, for example, had been practicing spins for an hour when she realized that her "point" had disappeared. She flew in each direction looking for a familiar landmark without success. Just as panic began to set in, another Stearman with a woman pilot came reassuringly into view. Saved, Faye happily followed it, but when her guide continued on a steady westward course, Faye realized that it was not headed for Avenger Field at all. With sunset approaching, she now had no alternative but to follow. The two planes finally landed at an Army field forty miles from Avenger, where Faye learned that her guide was not another student but a graduate WASP ferrying a new Stearman to California!

Martha McKenzie from McKenzie, Tennessee, was even less fortunate than Faye. Following one last practice spin late one afternoon, she realized she was lost. As the sun plummeted lower and lower, her engine sputtered out on its last drops of fuel. Selecting a field clear of obstacles, she managed to bring the Stearman down unharmed, then climbed out and began walking toward the lights of a nearby farmhouse. Suddenly McKenzie grew aware of some approaching presence behind her, then heard the sound of pounding hooves. She turned to face an approaching herd of Herefords aroused by the roar of the plane's engine. A burst of adrenalin enabled her to run faster than ever before, and she outdistanced them all, including the bull, to the fence. McKenzie beat on the front door of the house until it was opened by an incredulous old deaf farmer who kept repeating, "Well, I'll be darned, it's a girl," as he drove her down the road to the nearest telephone.

No less alarming than getting lost was encountering one of the numerous natives of west Texas—rattlesnakes. During a solo flight Shirley Tannehill looked out on her right wing to see—slowly inching its way up the aileron and onto the leading edge—the biggest, meanest-looking snake she had ever seen. Fortunately the slipstream caught the rattler and it sailed off into space, much to the shaken pilot's relief. The size and validity of Tannehill's snake story went unchallenged by her barracks bay mates as she awoke screaming from nightmares on several nights. Thereafter, trainees examined their cockpits very carefully before taking off, and especially before climbing in for the first flight of the day.

Occasionally a primary student became a member of the Caterpillar Club. The women of Class 44-W-4 were always careful to fasten their seat belts after hearing of the experience of a Class 44-W-1 trainee who, accompanied by her instructor, was practicing spins. After holding the plane in a right wing spin for the customary three revolutions, she recovered with the standard technique of pushing hard opposite rudder and popping the control stick forward as far as it would go, which resulted in a steep dive. The student, whose belt had inadvertently become unfastened, was stupified to find herself sailing out into space while the plane and startled instructor cruised on past her. Automatically she pulled the D-ring ripcord, her parachute opened, and she landed frightened but unharmed.

Flying dominated every waking moment as well as some sleeping moments for the students, as some mumbled acronyms for cockpit procedures, such as CIGFTPR [controls, instruments, gas, flaps, trim, prop, radio] throughout the night. Flying was their single-minded consuming passion, and they were determined to master the skills that led to graduation and silver wings.

Despite that great determination, students usually experienced various degrees of debilitating stress prior to the periodic check rides. Called "checkitis," it was accompanied with loss of appetite and sleep, which caused even more anxiety and tension.

A flustered pilot was a dangerous pilot, and instructors often deliberately tried to rattle a student suspected of instability. All the maneuvers taught during the primary phase had to be executed precisely, from regular takeoffs and landings to emergency or forced landings. Unexpectedly the testing pilot would pull the throttle back to kill the engine; the trainee then had to quickly point to the field selected for such an emergency, and "dead-stick" the plane to a low-level simulated landing. It was essential to think quickly, calmly, and carefully under such pressure, and there was no tolerance for emotional reaction or hysteria.

The results of each test ride determined whether the student passed and moved on to the next phase of training or failed and was sent home. The elimination rate for females for flying deficiencies during training was comparable to that of male cadets. It varied from time to time, but averaged 30.7 percent over the duration of the program.

For the women who washed out, the sting of failure often left deep scars despite the knowledge that elimination was preferable to an accident or fatality. No alternative training as bombardiers or navigators—options for men failing pilot training—was available for the women.

Following successful completion of the Primary phase of flying, Class 44-W-4 ordinarily would have gone into the Basic phase, which included instrument flying. However, the Army was searching for a way to eliminate the waste of time and money when cadets passed through Primary and Basic only to wash out during the final or Advanced phase. Class 44-W-4 served as guinea pigs to test the feasibility of skipping directly from Primary to Advanced. The policy proved completely successful and was thereafter instituted for the training of all cadets, male and female.

But the abrupt change to the North American AT-6 advanced trainer gave the women of 44-W-4 some anxious moments. The "Texan" had a 650-horsepower Pratt & Whitney engine and a retractable landing gear, which made it a "hot" plane to fly in comparison with the slower, sturdy Stearman. When grounded because of snow and ice, the students would spend their time in the AT-6 cockpit just to get used to its more complex instrument panel.

As familiarity with the AT-6 increased, however, it became a great favorite with the women. It epitomized the joy and pride we found in flying—explanations as to why always sounded vague, poetic and mystical, corny, or jingoistic. But to walk out on the ramp in front of the hangars to see the neat rows of handsome, powerful planes shining in the sun always produced a thrill and sense of pride.

Self-confidence grew as our skills increased. The satisfaction or achievement brought a profound sense of self-sufficiency and a deeply personal possession of one's own soul, which produced an even deeper sense of worth and feeling of dignity and integrity.

Then suddenly AT-6 training was finished and instrument training began. A renewed sense of humility quickly returned with the realization of how much more we still had to learn.

Instrument training was part of the curriculum for every military aviator, and for this the fixed-gear, 450-horsepower, closed-canopy BT-13 was used. Dubbed the "Vultee Vibrator," it shuddered violently in a spin and recovered level flight slowly.

Contact flying "by the seat of your pants" was impossible when the weather turned stormy and a thick overcast cut off all visual contact with the world. The "feel" of the plane, developed so carefully over so many hours of practice, now became a liability. Flying under the hood with reference only to the instrument panel required total concentration, patience, endurance, and determination, but it was an essential skill in case of an emergency or the necessity of flying at night.

After mastery of the essentials of instrument flying with an instructor, we flew together on "buddy rides." One acted as a lookout for other aircraft while the other pulled the blackout curtain around her canopy and practiced flying straight and level, then climbing and turning with reference only to the instruments, and finally working into even more difficult navigation using radio beams.

The "buddy rides" led us to develop greater trust and respect for one-another's flying ability, for we were literally putting our lives in each other's hands. No instructor was there to bail you out of trouble—only another student such as yourself. Each fervently hoped the other was capable. It took only a few rides to discover that she was.

Exacting as such flying was, flying at night challenged us even more. What had been so familiar in the daylight grew eerie and unreal when the plane shot up into the black void of night. Disorientation resulted at first, as it seemed almost impossible to get one's bearings when stars above, stars to the right, stars to the left, and a confusion of lights on the ground all merged together. But initial twinges of panic passed as proficiency increased, and soon night flying, too, was "duck soup."

A favorite pastime for us was to stand out on the flight line and watch the red and green wing lights as the planes circled overhead. The steady drone of the engines became sweet, familiar music. But one night that steady drone sputtered and stopped abruptly. An engine had quit on take-off. The nose dropped into a glide but held a straight course dead ahead. Then a brilliant flash lit the sky as the ship plowed through high tension wires and plunged the entire field into darkness.

Fear engulfed the entire base—fear for the woman in the plane, fear for those waiting on taxi strips to take off, fear for those circling overhead. Within seconds the control tower operator announced in a matter-of-fact voice what had happened and calmly called each lane down by number. All came in with beautiful, smooth landings in clock-like precision, each clearing the runway quickly for the next incoming plane. No pilots anywhere, at any time, could have handled the emergency more efficiently.

Two hours later rescuers located the trainee still safely buckled in her cockpit, flashing her lights in the SOS Morse distress signal. She had cut the engine switch to avoid fire, and when she felt the gear drag through brush and strike ground, she pulled back on the stick and pancaked the plane into the ground. She escaped with no more than bruises and scratches, and was in the air again the next morning. Daylight revealed that the plane had stopped only a few feet short of a ravine.

Not everyone was so fortunate, for night flying had already claimed its first victim. Apparently an engine caught fire in flight and the plane crashed. The bodies of Jane Champlin and her instructor, Henry Awbrey, were found in the charred wreckage. Such tragic accidents increased our determination to succeed at any cost and justify the faith Cochran and Arnold had placed in us. The cost was high. During World War II eleven WASPs were killed in training, and twenty-seven more died during performance of active duty.

By the spring of 1944, Class 44-W-4 entered the final phase of its training—cross-country navigation. We studied maps and charts, and learned to plot wind drift and courses with precision. Small groups went

276 PART SIX GENDER AND SEXUALITY IN MODERN AMERICA

out on short flights in primary trainers; then we flew AT-6s for longer distances east to Shreveport, Meridian, and Atlanta, or west to Tucson, Yuma, and Santa Fe.

For many this was their first sight of the rugged western mountains and magnificent stretches of desert valleys. The peacefulness of the seemingly endless land, and the dazzling, unforgettable beauty of blazing orange, pink, and gold sunsets made indelible impressions. Here many found a new appreciation of the beauty of nature and a sense of the presence of God. We women pilots viewed America from a perspective then shared by few other groups—and we deeply, sincerely loved our country.

By the time of these cross-country flights, the May 23 graduation seemed assured. New Santiago-blue uniforms were issued and altered, and group photographs taken for the class yearbook. Of the original ninety-five entrants, fifty-three could now visualize the approaching touch of silver wings.

A fifteen-miles-per-hour southeasterly wind, with ceilings and visibility unlimited under sunny Texas skies, were the weather conditions on April 16 as members of the class headed back to Sweetwater from cross-country flights to a variety of destinations. We were in high spirits, with the anticipation of visits from families and friends on graduation day, and excited over our prospective active-duty status, assignments, and new flying duties ahead. Almost six months had passed since November 1, 1943, but it seemed a lifetime ago. Few families realized the rapid maturity their "girls" had achieved, or could relate to these changes in them.

Twenty-five-year-old Mary Howson's family was no exception, but they appreciated their only daughter's sense of accomplishment even though they may not have fully understood it. With two sons already in military service, the Howsons were making plans for the long trip from Philadelphia to Texas to see Mary receive her wings.

Howson's April 16 cross-country hop to San Antonio and back would bring her total flying time to 165 hours, with nearly 50 of these in the AT-6. Approaching Avenger Field early in the afternoon, she descended to the eight-hundred-foot traffic pattern altitude and turned west onto the forty-five-degree leg for entry onto the downwind leg.

At the same moment Elizabeth Erickson of Class 44-W-6, with ten hours in the AT-6, was on her first solo flight out of traffic. She started her re-entry onto the forty-five-degree leg from an easterly direction. Suddenly the peacefulness of the Texas sky was shattered by a deafening explosion as the two planes roared head-on into each other. Mary attempted to jump, unfastening her seat belt and pulling her ripcord pin. The canopy and shroud lines burst from the case, but there was insufficient altitude left for the chute to open. Her body was found about thirty feet from the scattered fragments of wreckage. Elizabeth Erickson was pinned in her aircraft and died instantly.

The tragic circumstances of the two fatalities cast a pall over both classes, but depression was especially acute for the seniors. Mary Howson's body was accompanied to her birthplace of Wayne, Pennsylvania, by one of her classmates, Mickie Carmichael of Tyler, Texas. The military escort and government-issue pine box provided for deceased male fliers were not available. Her classmates provided Mary's coffin, and all of the trainees, army officers, and other personnel at Avenger Field contributed to the casket blanket of purple irises with WASP spelled out in yellow daisies. No military services or flag were authorized, despite the WASP director's condolence telegram to the Howsons that "Mary had lost her life in the service of her country."

Not even death could cancel the absolute necessity of keeping up the daily schedule. Class 44-W-4's flight leader reminded them that flying would go on the following day.

Graduation day soon came, and families and friends arrived. VIPs occupied the reviewing stand on the flight line. Class 44-W-4 was the first group of WASPs to be honored with an all-trainee wing review parade. Each class composed and sang a special song in tribute to the departing graduates; one favorite parodied "Yankee Doodle Dandy":

> *We are Yankee Doodle pilots,*
> *Yankee Doodle do or die;*
> *Real live nieces of our Uncle Sam,*
> *Born with a yearning to fly.*
> *Keep in step to all our classes,*
> *March to flight line with our pals;*
> *Yankee Doodle came to Texas*
> *Just to fly the PTs,*
> *We are those Yankee Doodle gals.*

Singing had been an important feature of their daily life, for they were usually an exuberant, energetic, and happy group. Their lyrics combined bawdy with bravado. They sang to keep cadence while marching from barracks to mess hall or flight line, or while riding the "cattle" trucks to auxiliary fields. Singing bolstered their spirits when they were discouraged, tired, or just plain scared, and it helped develop the great camaraderie among them.

Of that camaraderie one wrote:

"All of us realized what a terrific spot we were on and drew closer together as a result. I've seen everything now, for I have seen the miracle of women working together in cooperation and friendliness; for we knew that on our efforts hung the fate, at least in any military form of endeavor, of not us alone but of the untold future of women pilots. . . ."

The climax of each graduation was the moment the trainee had her official silver wings pinned to her stunning Santiago-blue uniform. The WASPs were the first to wear Air Force blues, and their uniform, selected by the Chief of Staff General George C. Marshall, was considered by many to be the most attractive of all the World War II uniforms.

One of the most impressive WASP graduation ceremonies was held on March 11, 1944, when General Hap Arnold delivered the principal address to an assemblage that included seven generals as well as Jacqueline Cochran and Nancy Love.

By that date, 441 trainees had graduated and were performing a variety of essential jobs in active service, many of which were nevertheless considered monotonous by most male pilots.

One of the most tedious of such duties was towing target sleeves for ground antiaircraft gunnery practice and for B-17 gun crews, on missions sometimes lasting up to five hours in duration. Not every such flight was boring, however: on one occasion bullets came so close to the tow plane cockpit that the unflappable WASP pilot informed the gunners over her radio that she was pulling the target sleeve, not pushing it!

Other WASPs "slow-timed" new engines and test-hopped planes newly repaired by maintenance crews or modified at repair depots. They transported administrative officers from base to base; acted as copilots for male officers logging their required flight time; transported nurses and medical personnel; served as flight instructors; and flew Chinese cadets on cross-country training flights. One WASP spent her free Sunday mornings flying a Catholic priest to remote Army bases in Arizona so that mass could be held.

One of the chief flying duties for WASPs remained ferrying aircraft. The experiences of Ann Hamilton, assigned to the Air Transport Command, were typical:

"The modification center was located at Evansville [Indiana]. Each day for three weeks I flew a P-47 to Oakland, California, returning at night on a military C-47 shuttle where I got my sleep. The C-47 had bucket seats, but I preferred to sit on the floor. I had a way of sitting with my knees to my chest, curled up. I'd get inside my parachute bag and have someone zip from both sides. There was no heat in the cabin."

In all, the WASPs delivered more than twelve thousand aircraft, logging over sixty million miles in every type of plane (over seventy) the Air Force had in operation. They took their duties seriously and performed them in an unobtrusive, matter-of-fact, common sense manner with as little fanfare as possible. Their World War II service and records contributed significantly to establishing knowledge and respect for women's capabilities and potential.

At the WASP graduation exercises on March 11, 1944, General Arnold concluded his laudatory speech by stating that, if necessary, everything needed short of actual combat could be done by women pilots. He paid the organization further tribute by presenting a bronze plaque dedicated to the "Best Women Pilots in the World."

Despite these accolades, just seven months later each WASP received a letter containing stunning and disappointing news from her general:

HEADQUARTERS OF THE ARMY AIR FORCES
WASHINGTON, D.C.

1 October 1944

To Each Member of the WASP:

I am very proud of you young women and the outstanding job you have done as members of the Air Forces Team. When we needed you, you came through and have served most commendably under very difficult circumstances.

The WASP became part of the Air Forces because we had to explore the nation's total manpower resources and in order to release male pilots for other duties. Their very successful record of accomplishment has proved that in any future total effort the nation can count on thousands of its young women to fly any of its aircraft. You have freed male pilots for other work, but now the war situation has changed and the time has come when your volunteered services are no longer needed. The situation is that, if you continue in service, you will be replacing instead of releasing our young men. I know that the WASP wouldn't want that.

So, I have directed that the WASP program be inactivated and all WASP be released on 20 December 1944. I want you to know that I appreciate your war service and that the AAF will miss you. I also know that you will join us in being thankful that our combat losses have proved to be much lower than anticipated, even though it means inactivation of the WASP.

I am sorry that it is impossible to send a personal letter to each of you. My sincerest thanks and Happy Landings always.

H. H. ARNOLD
General, U.S. Army
Commanding General, Army Air Forces

Arnold's final graduation address sounded an ironic valedictory. More than one hundred WASPs on active duty returned to Sweetwater on December 7, 1944, and listened in total dismay:

"I want to stress how valuable I believe this whole WASP program has been for the country. If another national emergency arises—let us hope it does not, but let us this time face the possibility—if it does, we will not again look upon a women's flying organization as an experiment. We will know that they can handle our fastest fighters, our heaviest bombers; we will know that they are capable of ferrying, target towing, flying training, test flying, and the countless other activities which you have proved you can do.

"This is valuable knowledge for the air age into which we are now entering. But please understand that I do not look upon the WASP and the job they have done in this war as a project or experiment. A pioneering venture, yes, solely an experiment, no. The WASP are an accomplishment.

"We are winning this war—we still have a long way to go—but we are winning it. Every WASP who has contributed to the training and operation of the Air Forces has filled a vital and necessary place in the jigsaw pattern of victory. Some of you are discouraged sometimes, all of us are, but be assured you have filled a necessary place in the overall picture of the Air Force.

"The WASP have completed their mission. Their job has been successful. But as is usual in war, the cost has been heavy. Thirty-seven WASP have died while helping their country move toward the moment of final victory. The Air Forces will long remember their service and their final sacrifice.

"So this last graduation day, I salute you and all WASP. We of the Army Air Forces are proud of you; we will never forget our debt to you."

Despite the continuing national emergency, services of the WASP had been terminated abruptly through the action of the United States Congress. Their dismissal at the height of mobilization appeared dangerously shortsighted, and in terms of the time, effort, and money invested in the program, such action seemed incredibly irresponsible. The failure of Congress to militarize the women pilots who had proven so valuable in helping to build the greatest air power in the world can be explained only by a review of the complexities of the situation.

Requests from the military forces for legislation during the war were seldom denied. Support for militarization of the women's service detachments was relatively strong in 1942 and 1943, when their assistance was clearly essential for national security.

House of Representatives Bill 4219, the long-awaited legislation designed to grant the WASPs full military status (and with it, for the first time, insurance coverage, hospitalization, burial benefits, and veteran status) was introduced on February 17, 1944. Unfortunately for the WASPs, new factors were by this time influencing Congressional decisions.

By 1944, the Air Forces' massive flight training program was reaching its peak. Plans for the coming invasion of Europe now necessitated the shifting of priorities to ground troops. As a consequence, there was a cutback in Air Forces training programs that affected two groups of males: (1) nine hundred civilian flight instructors and five thousand civilian trainees in the Civil Aeronautics Administration's War Training Service Program; and (2) eight thousand civilian flight instructors employed by the Air Forces in their contract schools for cadets.

These men were dismissed when the Air Forces shut down various flight schools—thus removing them from the draft-deferred status many held as reservists. The Air Forces accepted as many of these men as possible, but many were unable to meet the demanding physical and mental requirements for military pilots.

Threatened with induction into the infantry, these pilots exerted intense lobbying pressure on their Congressmen to defeat Bill 4219 and instead pass legislation favorable to their employment. The resulting controversy was heightened by political and emotional overtones.

It was inconceivable to General Arnold that well-trained, qualified women pilots not be utilized. On March 22, 1944, he testified to the House Committee on Military Affairs that "we should use every means we can to put women in where they can replace men. This bill [House Bill 4219] will help to do that but will also make for more effective employment of the present WASPs that we have in our service."

Discussion in the Commission on Military Affairs centered around the protests of the released men who demanded the positions occupied by the WASPs. Statistics showed that one-third of the men had been assimilated into the Air Forces. General Arnold adamantly refused to reduce standards in order to accommodate others who could not pass qualifying tests. Military pilots held a highly respected position, and he wanted no erosion of that hard-won recognition.

In executive session with the House Military Affairs Committee, Arnold again expressed his preference for the services of the more highly qualified, trained, and better motivated WASPs over the male civilian pilots. He was disgusted with the men's demands for preferential treatment in spite of the new needs of the country and the necessity to coordinate overall manpower requirements for the projected invasion of Normandy. He questioned the integrity and capability of a man who had held a "safe" noncombat job for so long and then insisted on dodging more hazardous duty.

The Military Affairs Committee agreed with the general, releasing a two-page report that recommended passage of the bill to commission the WASP. But lobbying efforts of the men grew stronger, even bitter.

The chairman of the Civil Service Committee, Robert J. Ramspeck of Georgia, instituted an investigation of the WASP (technically Civil Service employees), ostensibly to find out how public funds were being spent on a program about which he knew little. The majority report of Ramspeck's investigation concluded that the WASP was "wasted money and wasted effort."

Most damaging of all was the committee's accusation that the authority of Congress had been bypassed, and that Congress had never authorized the WASP program. The War Department responded that its authority for such action was based on the 1943 military budget section that provided for such "salaries and wages of civilian employees as were deemed necessary."

Ramspeck disagreed that such salaries were necessary; twelve committee members sided with him. General Arnold's arguments for the WASP failed to change the committee's recommendation that the training program be discontinued, although a minority opinion stated that the War Department, not Congress, should decide what was necessary. The committee also recommended that the male pilots be utilized immediately.

Again the War Department assured Congress that the men had received every consideration, that the two issues should be viewed separately, and that the WASPs should not be victimized by pitting them against the men.

The press, earlier supportive of women pilots, now turned antagonistic. Although the *New York Times, New York Herald Tribune,* and *Boston Globe* favored militarization of the WASP, writers in other papers throughout the country supported the male pilots against the women. The media, which had aroused women to answer their government's call to war work outside their homes, now swung public opinion against those who had done so.

Editorial writers for the *Washington Post, Washington Star, Washington Daily News, Washington Times-Herald,* and *Time* magazine led the opposition to continuation of the WASP program. Several such articles, heavily weighted with emotional and social bias, were read and recorded in the Congressional Record. Representative James Morrison of Louisiana quoted a statement by a *Washington Daily News* writer that "it [WASP] smells like a racket of some kind." Representative Compton I. White of California read a May 29, 1944, *Time* editorial that stated that:

"The need to recruit teen-aged schoolgirls, stenographers, clerks, beauticians, housewives, and factory workers to pilot the military planes of this government is as startling as it is invalid . . . the present program should be immediately and sharply curtailed. . . ."

An unusually vicious article entitled "Those Charming People," by Austine Cassini, appeared in the June 14, 1944, edition of the *Washington Times-Herald:*

"In the last week the shapely pilot [Jacqueline Cochran] has seen her coveted commission come closer and closer . . . One of the highest placed generals, it seems, gazed into her eyes, and since then has taken her *cause celebre* very much 'to heart' . . . She's such an attractive composition of windblown bob, smiling eyes, and outdoor skin, nobody blames him. It's whispered he's battling like a knight of olde, or olde knight, for the faire Cochran."

Such insinuations could not escape notice by Arnold's family. Public opinion was altered; morale plummeted among the women pilots. One WASP resigned, basing her action on the August 6, 1944, *Washington Post* column of Drew Pearson:

"Magnetic Miss Cochran has even persuaded the Air Force's smiling commander to make several secret trips to Capitol Hill to lobby for continuation of her pets, the WASPs. After Congress refused to let WASPs into the Army, Arnold and Cochran adopted backdoor strategy . . . The WASPs, like the WACs, claim they were recruited to release men for active service. Now they say the WASPs are just 'replacing men, period.'"

Far from being pictured as heroines, the WASPs were now regarded as participants in a frivolous program that had wasted millions of dollars of tax money.

The competent, proven performance of the women was never the issue. Congressional debate on Bill 4219 lasted forty-two hours and culminated on Wednesday, June 21, 1944, shortly after the D-Day invasion of Europe. A roll call vote was taken, with 188 yeas, 169 nays, and 73 not voting. By nineteen votes the WASP militarization bill advocated by the Administration, the Secretary of War, the House of Representatives Military Affairs Committee, and the General of the Army Air Forces was defeated.

The message from the legislative branch of government was clear: women must not occupy positions in the military if men were available for them. The bold experiment was ended, for it could not continue without Congressional approval and appropriation. The WASP became the first of the women's services to be disbanded, and the battle to give women equal opportunity in military cockpits was lost. The backlash of official government action against the WASPs deeply hurt and bewildered them, but they clung to the knowledge that their service record had been outstanding.

On June 23, 1972, 315 former WASPs met for a thirtieth-anniversary reunion at their old training base in Sweetwater, Texas. Time had grayed their hair and wrinkled once-suntanned complexions, but none noticed or cared as they relived long-ago hours spent in the air and at the old hangar. Following an air show, the unveiling of a marker by Jacqueline Cochran, and a banquet and speeches, they gathered around their motel pool to look at old picture albums and reminisce. Conversations generated a spontaneous desire to somehow return to December 20, 1944, and correct the injustice dealt them by a strange set of circumstances.

By the next reunion in 1974, a Militarization Committee under the guidance of Colonel Bruce Arnold, U.S. Air Force (retired), the son of deceased General Hap Arnold, had been formed. Several more years of concerted political action by WASP members, under the leadership of Senator Barry Goldwater,, plus help from all of the female members of Congress, produced Congressional bills and hearings.

On September 20, 1977, a select Congressional subcommittee on veteran affairs in the House of Representatives heard testimony on Bill 3277, designed to provide long-overdue recognition to the Women Airforce Service Pilots and deem their World War II service to have been active duty in the armed forces for the purposes of laws administered by the Veterans Administration.

During the hearings, committee member Margaret Heckler questioned witness Bruce Arnold why he had devoted so many hours to the cause of the WASP. Colonel Arnold replied:

"This was one of my father's desires . . . he would have been right here doing this too, if he were alive, and . . . I am carrying on some of his unfinished work. My father worked on the principle of 'get it done now and work out the details later.' "

It was indeed later, but despite forceful opposition, efforts were rewarded as Congress finally decided to recognize the WASP, providing the Secretary of Defense determined that the service had been *de facto* active military duty.

On May 21, 1979, the Assistant Secretary of the Air Force, Antonio Chayes, presented the first authentic WASP discharge, stating that "the efforts and sacrifices of a talented and courageous group of women have been accorded [retroactive] status as military veterans . . . and inspire the forty-seven thousand Airforce women who now follow in their footsteps." The unknown, gutsy women of the World War II Army Air Forces at last occupied their rightful place as the first female military pilots in American history.

PART SEVEN

WORLD WAR II,
1939-1945

On Sunday morning, December 7, 1941, Japanese fighters, bombers, and torpedo planes carried out a surprise attack on the American fleet at Pearl Harbor, Hawaii. Four days later, Adolf Hitler honored the Axis alliance with Japan and declared war on the United States. Once again, a little more than two decades after the end of World War I, the United States found itself in a global conflict, but this one really was global in scope, with military fronts in Europe, North Africa, Asia, and the islands of the Pacific. President Franklin D. Roosevelt marshaled the country's resources, placed the economy on a war footing, and unleashed a level of military and economic power that dumbfounded friends and foes. Protected from the conflict by the space of two oceans, the American economy produced an enormous volume of goods during the war—275,000 military aircraft, 75,000 tanks, 650,000 pieces of artillery, 55 million tons of merchant shipping, and more than 1.5 million tons of synthetic rubber. The United States was the "Arsenal of Democracy."

The war also accelerated a number of demographic trends already at work in American life. Factory jobs were abundant in major cities throughout the country, and the pace of urbanization increased as rural Americans moved downtown looking for wartime wages. The migration of African Americans to northern cities and Mexican workers to the commercial farms and factories of the Southwest, both of which had stalled during the Great Depression, picked up again in 1940. During the course of the war, more than ten million men and women entered the military and found themselves stationed, training, and fighting far from home. The war helped break down some of the regional and ethnic clusters in the United States and promoted ethnic and religious assimilation. With so many men in military units, and the economy so desperate for workers, large numbers of women entered the labor force for the first time. Although many of them were displaced after the war when the soldiers returned, the experience of earning good money and controlling the purse strings had an empowering effect on millions of women and contributed directly to the growth of the women's movement in postwar America.

The social, economic, and demographic changes proved to be stressful when Americans found themselves living and working with people from different backgrounds. African-American workers experienced systematic discrimination in defense factories, and only their own protests, led by people like A. Philip Randolph, head of the Brotherhood of Sleeping Car Porters, forced the federal government to address the problem. Race riots erupted in a number of cities during World War II, the worst of them in Detroit, Michigan, in 1943, when dozens of black people were slaughtered by marauding groups of whites. In Los Angeles, the so-called "Zoot-Suit" riots broke out when Anglo-American sailors on liberty attacked groups of Mexican-American youths in the downtown area. More than 100,000 Japanese Americans living on the Pacific Coast ended up spending World War II in concentration camps. For all the economic prosperity of the early 1940s, few Americans remembered them as "the best of times."

But they did remember the era as a heady, if difficult, time. Germany surrendered in May 1945 and Japan followed suit three months later. The American military machine was the most powerful in the world, and American values of egalitarianism and democracy had been projected on a worldwide scale. In September 1945, when World War II formally ended, the United States was unrivaled in its global status. No other nation could doubt the country's military might or economic capacity, and Americans had no doubt about their own collective virtue. The age of the "American century" in world history was under way.

25. America's Nazis

SUSAN CANEDY CLARK

During the Great Depression, the United States suffered economically as never before. The stock market crashed, banks failed by the thousands, land values plummeted, business and home foreclosures skyrocketed, and unemployment rose to 25 percent. Only one out of four people looking for work could find it. Hunger, homelessness, and misery were commonplace. So were proposals to make life better. Communists confidently predicted the end of capitalism was near, that workers were about to rise up and seize the means of production themselves. Norman Thomas and the Socialist Party of America called for a government takeover of the major corporations and construction of a social welfare safety net to prevent widespread poverty. Demagogues like Huey Long and Father Charles Coughlin spread conspiracy theories about the reasons for the country's plight. One of the fascist groups to appear in the United States late in the 1930s was the German-American Bund, a pro-Hitler, pro-Nazi organization. Adolf Hitler had used economic misery and anti-Semitism to take control of Germany in the 1920s and early 1930s, and the fanatical members of the German-American Bund hoped to do the same in the United States. Susan Clark describes these "American Nazis" in the following essay.

"My fellow countrymen! We German-Americans are unequivocally committed to the defense of the flag, Constitution, and sovereignty of our United States. We stand before you—loyal and law-abiding . . . resolved to restore America to the true Americans . . . Free America!"

So began the opening address by the national secretary of the German-American Bund at a massive rally held in New York City's Madison Square Garden on February 20, 1939. The Garden was filled to capacity, with attendance estimated at over twenty thousand. A two-block perimeter had been cordoned off around the building in anticipation of a counter-demonstration, and more than two thousand New York policemen were on hand.

Inside, the hall was resplendent with American flags, and a huge poster of George Washington hung behind the podium. On the platform hung the flags of the United States, Italy, and Nazi Germany.

The aisles were lined with uniformed men—the Bund's equivalent of Hitler's storm troopers—and armbands abounded. In turn, officers of the Bund arose to glorify American purism and to condemn the racial amalgamation that had occurred since George Washington's time; anti-Semitism and the perils of racial mongrelization were the major themes. All of the speeches were given in English to a crowd that rocked the great hall with sharply punctuated cheers of "Free America!"

The last speaker was forty-two-year-old Fritz Kuhn, national leader of the Bund. During Kuhn's speech, in which he heartily denounced Jews and praised the Ku Klux Klan, the crowd suddenly rose to its feet and roared in anger. A young man, Isadore Greenbaum, had broken through the ring of uniformed guards and rushed at Kuhn. Knocked down by a dozen troopers, Greenbaum was badly beaten.

Once order was restored and the rally had concluded, the Bundists left the hall to find the New York police protecting them from an angry mob of approximately one hundred thousand people. America was growing concerned about its Nazis.

With uniforms and trappings patterned after those of the Third Reich, the German-American Bund advocated a version of National Socialism as a solution to the Great Depression: America had to be cleansed of its undesirable elements, the Bundist doctrine proclaimed—notably of Jews and Communists. At its strongest between 1936 and 1939, the Bund boasted of having a membership of twenty thousand, with sympathizers three to five times that number. Bund units supposedly existed in forty-seven states, with activities ranging from paramilitary forces and youth groups to publishing houses and business corporations.

The German-American Bund was an outgrowth of the Association of the Friends of New Germany, formed in 1933 when Nazi sympathizers took over control of the United German societies of New York and Detroit. Although characterized as an extension of Hitler's National Socialist German Workers' Party (NSDAP), the Bund was first and foremost an extension of its leader, Fritz Kuhn. Assuming leadership of the movement in March 1936, Kuhn fashioned it as a mirror-image of Hitler's, outfitting his followers in swastikas and jackboots and mimicking Hitler's speeches in his own heavily accented English. Slowly he shifted the driving force behind the movement from Hitler to himself, building a powerful fascist cult of his own.

Like Hitler, Kuhn was described by the media as everything from a social misfit and illiterate thug to a man endowed with considerable force and intelligence. Born in Munich in 1896, Kuhn was in fact fairly well educated and had served as an officer in the German Army during World War I. After emigrating to the United States, he had for a time worked in the auto industry in Detroit. Surviving former Bundists paint a picture of a man capable of inspiring great admiration and trust. In the eyes of most Americans, however, Kuhn epitomized all that was evil and dangerous about Nazi Socialism.

Upon taking leadership of the Bund, Kuhn dropped the title of president, preferring instead the name of *Bundesfuehrer.* He proudly announced to audiences in Madison Square Garden, the Yorkville (New York) Casino, and the German-American Bund home in Union City, New Jersey, that National Socialist Germany pointed the way to America's future. Dressed in the uniform of the Third Reich, he offered himself as an American Hitler. Glorying in Germanism, Kuhn made liberal use of his personal magnetism and penchant for the sensational as he transformed the Bund into an aggressive arm of American fascism.

The Bund was directed almost exclusively by German nationals, recently naturalized as United States citizens, and it commanded its greatest following in cities with large German immigrant populations. The true size of the organization is difficult to establish, for most membership lists and related documents were destroyed at Kuhn's command in the face of impending congressional investigations. Given the public's rising fear of fascism, fueled by the Bund's extreme visibility, its size and scope of operation was often exaggerated, and the membership figures expanded or contracted in relation to the emotional climate.

Kuhn officially placed the Bund membership at 8,299, though the U.S. Department of Justice reduced that number to 6,617 (of which an estimated 4,529 were concentrated in the metropolitan New York area). But when forced to testify before a congressional committee in 1939, Kuhn boasted of a membership of twenty thousand, stating that the Bund was organized in every state but Louisiana, with one hundred local units. On the other hand, the Federal Bureau of Investigation presented statistics to show the Bund so small that it constituted "no threat," and the Bund's principles of organization were "not destructive to the government of the United States." Membership figures, real or invented, only served to confuse and anger an America preparing to wage war on all things German.

The organic structure of the Bund was highly regimented, with administrative units flowing downward from the national level to the individual member. This chain of command led from the national office in New York City to "areas" (major national segments), "regions" (groups of states), "circuits" (individual states), "districts" (groups of counties), "precincts" (villages, towns, or cities), "squares" (subdivisions of towns), "blocks" (subdivisions of squares), and finally "house groups" (subdivisions of blocks).

Below the national level, the Bund was divided into three areas—the Eastern, Midwestern, and Western. Each of the subdivisions operated on its own leadership principle: a *fuehrer* was responsible for his own area and reported directly to the next higher leader. Each level had precisely defined tasks and responsibilities. The national office prided itself on the claim that all members could be informed of events within a twenty-four-hour period. Kuhn thus controlled a tightly-knit organization of dedicated followers by a preset means of daily contact.

Power concentrated upward in accordance with the leadership principle. Each level held annual elections by secret ballot, and each branch sent delegates to an annual convention to fulfill the same purpose on the national level. But more often than not these elections functioned as mere votes of confidence. In reality, all officers within the administrative units were appointed by the respective *fuehrer* of the level above.

The most visible aspect of the German-American Bund was its Uniformed Service or *Ordnungs-Dienst* (OD). Viewed by the press as Kuhn's storm troopers, and by the Bund membership as its protective shield, the OD functioned alongside and within the Bund. This paramilitary group was organized on all local levels that had the membership to support it. The OD was open to every male member eighteen years of age or older with proof of Aryan origin.

Membership figures for the OD are practically nonexistent. A 1939 report by the Congressional Committee to Investigate Un-American Activities and Propaganda estimated that the Bund could muster a uniformed force of five thousand troops. Speaking at the 1939 Bund Convention, Kuhn declared, "I calculate that approximately ten percent of membership should belong to the OD. That is approximately the proportion of the SA [Sturmabteilung, predecessor to the German SS] to the membership of the NSDAP." Parallels between the two martial forces would not go unnoticed by an increasingly paranoid public.

In response, the Bund declared that the OD was not a military or even a paramilitary body. It was, the leaders maintained, simply a group whose major function was to keep order during meetings and rallies—its members being likened to theater ushers. Training consisted of marching, singing, and calisthenics and was described as being no more than one aspect of personal discipline.

OD men carried no firearms, which were prohibited by organizational guidelines. This, however, did not prevent them from exercising brute force when necessary. In fact, had it not been for their protection, Fritz Kuhn and other members of the Bund leadership might well have been killed during the many attempts on their lives. And with its high visibility, SA look-alike uniforms, and proudly displayed martial capabilities, the OD did in fact present itself as a parallel to Hitler's storm troopers.

All ceremonial occasions called for the employment of the Bund salute, identical to the outstretched arm, open-palmed salute of the Third Reich. Here, however, the salute was described as being "a friendly greeting with an open hand that carries no weapon." The official spoken salutation of the Bund, in place of "Heil Hitler!", was "Free America!" Only for the "Star-Spangled Banner" and "America" was a military salute required.

Equally important in Bund doctrine was the formation of youth camps. Kuhn's youth group was a carbon copy of Hitler's *Jugend,* or Youth Movement. During the summer months, the children were sent to one of twenty-four recreational camps owned by the Bund. Organized by age and gender, they participated in a variety of activities that included nationalistically oriented singing, dancing, arts, crafts, sports, and military drill.

While the total number of children who participated in the movement is not clear, during the summer of 1937 nearly two hundred children were registered at Camp Hindenburg, near Grafton, Wisconsin, and twice that number were enrolled at Camp Nordland, near Andover, New Jersey. Activities in the youth camps were highly regimented, and much time was devoted to the study of *Mein Kampf* and National Socialism in general. A typical day at Camp Nordland began with reveille at 6 A.M., followed by swimming and exercising. After breakfast the boys practiced marching while the girls attended lectures on National Socialism. Afternoon activities included public speaking, music, gymnastics, and a variety of sports.

Adults, too, had access to the grounds of the recreational camps. Former Bundists still nostalgically recall watching athletic demonstrations by the children, and participating in celebrations and rallies, dances, dining, and camping.

The camps were set up to provide the members with facilities and organized events common with their cultural heritage. Their pursuit of the Wagnerian dream, however, was visibly stamped with the harshness of German National Socialism. Columns of goosestepping, uniformed children and OD men marched against a backdrop of dirndled women serving beer.

The Bund was, in fact, nothing short of being a sister movement of Hitler's National Socialist German Workers' Party. Not only the structure of the organization but also its aggressive and vociferous stance paralleled that of the Third Reich. This did not go unnoticed in a sensitive United

States straining to remain neutral in the face of a fast-approaching world conflict.

Curiously, Fritz Kuhn was gratified by the image, for he was most anxious to become Hitler's official representative in America. Kuhn felt sure that recognition from Hitler would be forthcoming, and to solicit the Fuehrer's support, he and fifty members of the Bund traveled to the Reich in June 1936.

During his visit, Kuhn wallowed in the magnetism of the New Germany. The highlight of the trip was an unexpected audience with *Der Fuehrer* himself. Kuhn presented Hitler with more than two thousand dollars collected for the German winter relief program and a leather-bound pictorial history of the Bund from 1924.

Unimpressed and distracted, Hitler simply advised Kuhn to "go over there and continue the fight." In reality, Hitler's audience with Kuhn seems to be only one of a long procession of meetings with foreign visitors. Germany was, after all, on display that Olympic summer, and Hitler played every part the host.

Kuhn left Germany with no more assurance of support or responsibility than he had arrived with. He received promises of propaganda material but nothing more: his long-sought-after recognition as the American *fuehrer* would have to be self-manufactured.

And so it was. Kuhn had been to Germany, he had participated in Party activities, and he had met with Hitler. Few though they were, these facts were enough to form a powerful base from which to operate. Kuhn's trip was given widespread coverage in the Bund's publications and picked up by others as well. The American public was treated to every detail of the visit, from Kuhn's reception in Berlin and his meeting with Hitler to the march of a contingent of OD men down the Unter der Linden Strasse. Something of a furor was created as Americans became convinced that Hitler sanctioned and supported the Bund as an outpost of German National Socialism.

By cleverly publicizing his link to Hitler, Kuhn infused new life and direction into the Bund. Upon returning to America he issued Bund Command Number One, in which he announced his determination to bring the organization into national prominence. "Today I know better than ever before the direction in which our Bund must go," he said. "I know that it is not only important to continue our work, I understand that the German-American Bund is called to assume the political leadership of the German element in the United States."

To facilitate this program, Kuhn moved to consolidate a number of ancillary organizations under his control. These included the German-American Business League, the AV Development Corporation, the AV Publishing Company, the Prospective Citizens League, the German-American Settlement League, and the German-American Bund Auxiliary. Ownership and consolidation of these organizations opened avenues for expansion and financial security. Individually they put out propaganda, published newspapers, bought and maintained properties, and monitored trade among the neighborhood grocers.

Within a short period of time, Bundists found that it was possible to live virtually one's entire existence within the group's framework. The

Bund gave members the camaraderie they yearned for, and their common cultural heritage provided ties during an era of economic depression and social change. Social projects were encouraged, and the Women's Auxiliary regularly put together bundles of food, clothing, and household necessities for distribution to the needy within the group. Marriages, births, and deaths were handled within the movement, adding to the sense of community. Indeed, a large portion of the German-American community joined the Bund, not to implant National Socialism on American soil, but rather to preserve their cultural heritage in what was becoming a highly intolerant society.

Moving up from the grassroots level, however, the character of the Bund changed dramatically. While the general membership clung to the organization largely for the order and stability it gave to their lives, the leadership was rabidly National Socialist. Parroting Hitler's proposals "for the betterment of mankind," it intended to clean up America as Hitler had cleaned up Germany. Reworking the basic tenets of National Socialism to fit the American way of life, Kuhn envisioned a major political party to be built around the Bund.

Kuhn appealed to members on the grounds that Germans were superior to other peoples by virtue of their genetic and cultural heritage, and that racial comrades were linked by a community of blood. Blood and race were the determinants of German superiority, not environment or location. This racial elitism, as explained in the *Yearbook,* was the hallmark of the German-American Bund: "Present day Germany considers that every person of German ancestry and German blood who adheres to German language and culture is a German racial comrade. Germany does not ask you to neglect your duties as an American, but Germany says, only he who is a good German can become a good American."

Growing public concern over a possible fifth column naturally intensified with the Bund's continuous outpourings. Driven by the fear of an increasingly dangerous foreign influence and potential infiltration, America unleashed her investigatory bodies to muzzle the Bund, as well as all other organizations that moved too far from center. Citizens and civic organizations, as well as state legislative and judicial bodies, launched investigations to probe the Bund's structure and motives.

This led to national action, and in January 1937 Representative Samuel Dickstein introduced a resolution in Congress to investigate the Bund's activities. Following suit, the Federal Bureau of Investigation began a cursory examination of the German-American recreation camps. This activity emboldened individuals and groups dedicated to ferret out subversion. Although the U.S. Attorney General announced to a press conference on January 5, 1938, that its investigation had found no evidence the Bund had broken any federal law, the public lashed out.

In May 1938, Congress authorized the formation of the House Committee to Investigate Un-American Activities, to be chaired by zealous Martin Dies of Texas. Heartily backed by public opinion, the Dies Committee (as it came to be known) vigorously embarked on a search for subversion, acts of sabotage, and individuals connected to foreign governments.

The Bund was the first organization to come under the Dies Committee's scrutiny. During the opening sessions in the summer of 1938, Bundists, sympathizers, and myriad cooperative citizens were called before what Kuhn termed the "Un-American Committee for the Persecution of German-Blooded Americans." While the Bund was far from lily-white, the committee's questioning often worked against its own best interests by being leading, prejudiced, and biased. Staff members manipulated testimony to confirm the suspicious activity the committee was dedicated to find.

Despite the Dies Committee's efforts, however, its investigation was not what finally brought the German-American Bund to its knees. It was, rather, the Special Tax Emergency Investigation, authorized by Mayor Fiorello H. LaGuardia of New York City, that broke the organization. An inquiry was launched to investigate the Bund's financial activities and to ascertain whether the Bund had paid New York City taxes on the sale of National Socialist paraphernalia. The investigation revealed a substantial amount of missing funds, and in May 1939, three months before Kuhn was to appear before the Dies Committee, he was indicted on charges of theft of the Bund's funds. Kuhn's passport was immediately confiscated, and he was later arrested near Allentown, Pennsylvania.

Despite the indictment by the New York grand jury, Kuhn was re-elected president of the Bund at a secret convention in July 1939. He maintained the position until the day he went to prison in December 1939, but it was a hollow leadership by that time. Increasing harassment of the organization and its members by numerous organizations, along with the impending war, had caused a significant exodus from the Bund, especially among the old guard. Their departure precipitated a breakdown in the chain of command. Some left the movement outright, frustrated in their efforts to build a National Socialist Party in the United States, while others merely withdrew their financial support.

Despite Kuhn's claims of support from Germany, none was forthcoming, nor was there a call from Hitler inviting his disciples home. The Bund was not strong enough to withstand the scrutiny and subsequent intolerance levied by the frightened American public, and it started to disintegrate. The final blow came with Kuhn's conviction and imprisonment.

On December 6, 1939, the day after Kuhn went to prison, the Bund's executive committee met and deposed him. Gerhard Wilhelm Kunze, former national publicity director and vice-leader, was named as Kuhn's successor. But under constant pressure of investigation, financially crippled, and drained of its membership, the Bund had little left to sustain it. The movement survived until 1942 but only as a shell of its former self. Mention of the group in the newspapers virtually halted, and although the Dies Committee continued its investigations, its attention shifted to the Communist Party and other left-wing organizations.

The spotlight faded for Kuhn as well. After serving three-and-a-half years in prison, Kuhn was paroled in July 1943 and shipped to an internment camp for enemy aliens in Crystal City, Texas. He spent over two years in various camps, awaiting the deportation that finally came after V-J Day in September 1945. He returned to Germany, only to be apprehended by the United States's occupation forces and jailed as a war criminal. Kuhn died in obscurity in 1951, nearly ten years after the breakup of his organization.

At the conclusion of its investigations, the House Un-American Activities Committee reported that the Bund had received its "inspiration, program, and direction from the National Socialist government of Germany," and therefore must be classified as an agent of a foreign government. The committee did not note, however, that it had discovered any concrete administrative or financial links between the Bund and the National Socialist German Workers' Party. Such collusion was never proven. (And certainly the Bund had proven to be more of a hindrance and an embarrassment than a help to the German government at a time when it was seeking to soothe anti-Nazi concerns in the United States.)

Ironically, it was Kuhn's own actions and words that constituted the Dies Committee's best evidence. Kuhn had bragged of his influence over German consular officials and boasted of ties to Hitler, when, in fact, neither claim could be substantiated. The publicity generated by such fabrications only amplified the dangerous and subversive image the Bund had fashioned for itself and proved counterproductive to Kuhn's goals of an expanded membership and German support. In effect, the Bund fell victim to its own propaganda, antagonizing an America that was marshalling its strength against the growing Nazi menace overseas.

26. The Making of a Madman: The Childhood and Rantings of Adolf Hitler

JAMES S. OLSON

INTRODUCTION

An adorable little boy looks at us from a distance of about a hundred years. Just a year old, he must have been entranced by either the camera or the photographer, because his wide, round blue eyes stare ahead intently. Adolf Hitler was a beautiful baby. What factors led this child to grow into a man who would murder 6 million Jews?

During his life Hitler acquired an extraordinary hatred of Jews. One incident especially illustrates the malignancy of his passion. Late in 1944, with Russian troops bearing down on Germany from the east and British and American soldiers coming from the west, Hitler knew that the war was lost. There would be no thousand-year reich. But he nurtured a warped vision of his own historical legacy. Hitler honestly believed that future generations would revere him for resolving the "Jewish question." At the time, one Jewish community still survived in Europe—the 750,000 Jews of Hungary. To guarantee his place in history and complete his life's work, Hitler diverted badly needed troops, fuel, supplies, and railroad cars from the military front, debilitating his own army in the process, to make sure that Hungary's Jews were delivered to Auschwitz and exterminated before the surrender. For the Führer, Jews were the source of all evil in the world; genocide was the historical solution. How could the feelings of that little Austrian become so convoluted?

As a child, Adolf Hitler could have avoided developing negative feelings about Jews only with the greatest difficulty. Anti-Semitism was an integral part of the cultural world into which he was born. To most Austrians, Judaism seemed an alien religion in a Christian society. German Catholics, along with European Catholics in general, literally believed that Jews—all Jews—were responsible for the crucifixion of Jesus Christ; the Roman Catholic Church had maintained that position for centuries. Protestantism's founder, Martin Luther, accused Jews of carrying "vermin and diseases" and warned Christians to keep their distance from Jews. Germans also believed that Jews were inordinately rich and successful, usually in banking and commerce, and that they conspired to get more than their fair share of Europe's financial resources.

But Hitler's rabid anti-Semitism had deeper roots. Mass murderers don't just act on external impulses. Buried deep in their psyches are primal fears and forgotten symbols that find expression in violence. Hitler was no exception. When he ordered Jews into the railroad cars for the gas chambers of Auschwitz, Bergen-Belsen, Treblinka, and the other concentration camps, Adolf Hitler was not fulfilling any historical imperative, nor even pandering to the anti-Semitic expectations of the German people. Instead, he was responding to the psychotic demands of his own insecurities, to demented voices speaking from the depth of his own soul.

The deepest of those voices came from his own ancestry. Throughout his life, Hitler was plagued with rumors about his own family. His father, Alois Schicklgruber, was illegitimate. When he was born in 1837, Alois's mother, Marie Schicklgruber, was working as a maid in Graz, Austria, for a prominent Jewish family. Rumor had it that the teenaged son had fathered the child, making Alois half-Jewish. Although the rumors were never confirmed, they were nevertheless persistent and followed Alois all his life. In 1842 Marie Schicklgruber married Johann Hitler, but she died five years later and Johann soon abandoned Alois. Alois then spent three years with a step-uncle before leaving home for good in 1850. He grew into a gruff, insensitive, abusive adult plagued by being an orphan and by the possibility that he was half-Jewish.

The illegitimacy of Adolf Hitler's father left the son potentially one-quarter Jewish. German and Austrian anti-Semitism was more than a social artifact for Hitler; Austrian culture and his own genealogy had become tangled. The specifics of the Reich Citizenship Law of 1934 were no coincidence. Germans had to come up with a definition of just what constituted a Jew, because so many intermarriages occurred in the nineteenth and twentieth centuries between German Christians and German Jews. The decision was simple: People with more than one-quarter Jewish ancestry were defined as Jews; those with one-quarter Jewish ancestry or less were not Jews. Even if the rumors about his background were ever confirmed, Hitler was safe with this law's tenets.

When Alois Schicklgruber was 48 years old, he married Klara Polzl, his 25-year-old niece from Spital. Alois was a notorious philanderer, and his first wife divorced him when she learned of his affair with their maid, Fannie Matzelberger. He married Fannie two years later, but when she developed a severe case of tuberculosis, Alois invited his niece Klara to move in and help care for his wife and two small children. Klara performed more than simply household duties. When Fannie died in 1884, Klara was already pregnant with Alois' child. Local gossip had it that Alois purchased the coffin before Fannie died. He married Klara in January 1885, four months before Gustav was born. A daughter Ida was born in 1886, and Otto in 1887. The infant Otto died two weeks later, and diphtheria killed Gustav and Ida early in 1888. Klara was devastated and went into a deep depression.

Her fourth child, Adolf, was born on April 20, 1889. Typical of women who have lost earlier children, Klara lavished her new baby with love and protection, nursing him into his fifth year. This was an unusually long time for nineteenth-century Austria. Women regularly nursed their babies for about two years, simply because the process of nursing often postponed the return of ovulation and new pregnancy. But at the same time that Klara was showering Adolf with attention, Alois was administering abuse masked as discipline. He beat Adolf and his other siblings unmercifully, sometimes into unconsciousness, and daily meted out vicious attacks on the family dog. Adolf despised his father. When the old man died in 1903, the 14-year-old Adolf secretly celebrated. Tension left the house with Alois' body.

By that time Hitler was already infatuated with all things German: the lower-Bavarian dialect spoken in southeastern Germany, the legends of Teutonic mythology, and Wagnerian operas. The contrast with the political views of his deceased father could not have been more striking. Alois, an ardent Austrian patriot, supported the Hapsburg regime, proud to wear his army uniform on ceremonial occasions even as an old man. Alois looked with disdain and suspicion on German growth and unification in the nineteenth century. The young Adolf expressed his hatred for his father in his own pan-German patriotism and his decision to join the German—not the Austrian—army in 1914. When Hitler conquered Austria in the *Anschluss* of 1938 and rode through the streets of Vienna in a convertible draped with the German flag, he no doubt took pleasure in achieving exactly what his father had feared and loathed.

In contrast to his feelings about his father, Hitler adored his mother. Her death in 1907 was particularly difficult for him. In January she began complaining of chest pains. Dr. Edward Bloch, a Jewish physician, examined her at home and discovered an advanced breast cancer. She underwent a double mastectomy three days later. Although Klara recovered from the surgery, the tumors had already spread to the pleural tissues of the chest.

In October she again sought the help of Dr. Bloch. He warned Hitler that his mother was gravely ill, probably terminal, and that her only chance was a controversial, experimental chemotherapy treatment that was both painful and expensive. It involved reopening the mastectomy scars and applying massive doses of iodoform, an iodine-based medicine, with gauze to the open wounds. The chemical burned its way into the tissues, with Klara screaming and writhing through the treatment and then whimpering afterward for hours. The iodoform paralyzed her throat so that she could barely swallow.

Bloch performed the treatment for forty-six consecutive days, sometimes twice a day, in November and early December. Adolf was beside himself, watching his mother go through the ordeal. It was to no avail. She died on December 21, 1907. Hitler was inconsolable.

Two days later Hitler visited with Dr. Bloch, expressed sincere gratitude to him for his diligent care of Klara, and paid him in full—359 Kronen, a considerable sum of money. Years later Hitler saw to it that Bloch got exit visas from Austria, exempted him from the confiscatory Jewish tax laws, and let him emigrate to New York before the Holocaust was underway. It was a curious irony: While Hitler was engineering the liquidation of 6 million Jews, he made sure that one escaped. Consciously he was thankful for Bloch's treatment of his mother. But subconsciously, Hitler remembered he had daily watched Bloch deliver terrible, and in the end unnecessary, pain to his mother. In Hitler's warped inner vision, Klara had died at the hands of a Jew.

After his mother's death, Hitler spent several years in Vienna. He fancied himself an artist, painted landscape scenes for tourists to support himself, and desperately wanted to study at the Academy of Fine Arts. But each time he sought admission, a faculty committee rejected his portfolio as didactic and uninspired, not worthy of further training. Terribly disappointed, Hitler could not accept his work as mediocre. He eventually concluded that it was the Jewish faculty members who had turned him away and shattered his dreams. He spent several years in abject poverty, surviving in hostels and welfare hotels and living off soup-kitchen food.

Still, Hitler was not openly espousing a paranoid's anti-Semitic theories or expressing anti-Semitic feelings. He had several Jewish acquaintances and sent Christmas cards to Dr. Bloch regularly. Buried deep in his psyche, however, were images of his father's Semitic origins, his mother's excruciating death, and his own rejection from the university. World War I brought those buried images to the surface and transformed Adolf Hitler into a passionate, hungry fanatic—a megalomaniac.

When World I erupted Hitler lived in Munich, Germany. Rather than join the Austrian army and fight for his father's beloved Hapsburgs, Hitler enlisted in the Germany army to fight for his "own country." He proved to be a good soldier, courageous and well-disciplined, if a bit too enthusiastic for many of his comrades. In 1918 an Allied offensive left Hitler unconscious when he got caught in a cloud of mustard gas. The coma lasted for several months. When he recovered, Hitler seemed a changed man, possessed of a different personality. Anti-Semitism suddenly became an obsession, something to be discussed long after his associates bored of his rantings. Hitler's constant theme was the same: Jews were responsible for all of Germany's problems.

When Germany signed the armistice in November 1918, Hitler blamed Jewish radicals for undermining the German will to resist. After the war, as Germany endured political humiliation from the Allies and went into a severe economic tailspin marked by hyperinflation and high unemployment, Hitler became even more convinced that Jewish radicals and Jewish financiers were to blame. Jewish communists had imposed the peace on Germany, Jewish bankers were exploiting the German economy, and British and American Jews were conspiring to keep Germany prostrate. Before Germany would ever be great again, Hitler argued, something had to be done about "the Jewish question." Beginning in the 1920s, campaigning for political recognition, Adolf Hitler had his own answer to the Jewish question. Hitler conceived of "the final solution." More than twenty years later, "the final solution" became the Holocaust—the near annihilation of European Jewry. The following documents are speeches Adolf Hitler delivered. His blatant hatred of Jewish people was already fully developed.

The Aryan regards work as the basis for the maintenance of the national community as such; the Jew regards work as a means of exploiting other peoples. The Jew never works as a productive creator without the great prospect of becoming the master. He works unproductively, using and profiting from the work of others. We therefore understand the iron words once pronounced by Mommsen: The Jew is the ferment of the decomposition of peoples. This means that the Jew destroys and has to destroy, because he is completely lacking in any concept of work for the common good. It does not matter whether the individual Jew is "decent" or not. He has certain traits which nature has given him and he can never rid himself of these traits. The Jew is harmful to us. Whether he harms us consciously or unconsciously is not the question. We must consciously protect the welfare of our people . . .

We were finally the ones who pointed out to the people on a large scale the peril which crept into our midst, a peril which millions of people did not realize, but which will nevertheless lead us all to ruin—the Jewish peril. Today people again say that we are "agitators." In this respect I should like to make reference to someone greater than myself. Count Lerchenfeld declared in the last session of the *Landtag,* that his feeling "as man and as Christian" keeps him from being an anti-Semite. I say: My feeling as a Christian points me to my Lord and Savior as a fighter. It points me to the man who, once lonely and with only a few followers, recognized these Jews for what they were, and called men to fight them, and who, so help me, was greatest not as a sufferer but as a fighter. With boundless love, as a Christian and as a man, I read the passage which relates how the Lord finally gathered His strength and made use of the whip in order to drive the usurers, the vipers, and cheats from the temple. Today, 2000 years later, I recognize with deep emotion Christ's tremendous fight for this world against the Jewish poison. I recognize it most profoundly by the fact that He had to shed His blood on the cross for this fight. As a Christian it is not my duty to permit myself to be cheated but it is my duty to be a champion of truth and of right.

As man it is my duty to see to it that humanity will not suffer the same catastrophic collapse as did an old civilization about 2000 years ago, a civilization which was also driven to destruction by the Jewish people. . . . (Munich, April 12, 1922)

If you wish to live, you must fight against the annihilator of our people, for the fate of the middle class is the fate of the German people. Our fighters must come from the ranks of the middle class. Necessity teaches us to pray, but it also teaches us to fight. God gave man prayer, but He refuses to grant the fulfillment of prayer if man does not fight for it. All the disinherited from every side should come together in the ranks of the National Socialists. They all should know that there is one place where faith in the future has not been lost. We need those as fighters who have been uprooted. We need them for rebuilding the future Germany, a Germany founded not on a Jewish basis but on a Germanic basis. . . . This Germany must, moreover, establish the basis of an Aryan *Weltanschauung.*[1] In this regard we must not ask whether it is possible to attain this goal, but whether it is necessary. If it is impossible, then we shall try our best and perish in the attempt; but if it is necessary and proper, then we must believe that it is possible. We need this faith. A thousand years [of German history] look to us, and the future demands sacrifices from us. If we fail, our people will sink into the grave. Whether our people will survive or whether it is doomed to destruction—this is the fateful question. That is why the truth must be told, the truth about the unprecedented world-fraud of the Jews. (Munich, September 29, 1922)

There were times when there was no danger of a Jewish bastardization of the people. A Goethe still had the natural instinct to say: Marriage between a Jew and a Gentile seems to me something against nature; it is impossible and cannot be. For generations, therefore, no laws concerning this question were necessary. Racial instinct protected the people; the odor of that race deterred Gentiles from marrying Jews. At present, in these days of perfume, where any dandy can assume the

[1]World view.

same odor as anyone else, the feeling for these finer distinctions between peoples is being lost. The Jew counts on that. The eye also becomes accustomed to differences between peoples. In this respect, knowledge must come to our aid. What generations once did instinctively, we must by necessity do consciously, lest we perish. And with that we come to the basic principle of our *Weltanschauung.* Instinct is the sound *Weltanschauung* of the primitive man reared in nature. As long as his instinct remains sound, his *Weltanschauung* is sound. Instinct keeps him from the wrong ways of thinking. (Munich, November 29, 1929)

Because I believe in the idea of race I fight in all matters pertaining to public life against the Judaization of our people, against the poisoning of our people with foreign blood. A National Socialist will never tolerate that a foreigner—and that means the Jew—should have a position in public life. He will never tolerate that a foreigner hold a government position. A National Socialist will not even ask, Is he capable? No, my *Weltanschauung* tells me that I must keep our national organism free from foreign blood.

As a National Socialist I will deal with all questions of education in the community as well as in the state from the point of view of the preservation of my blood, that is, the preservation of my people. The people comes first, the state is secondary. The people is the most important consideration; everything else must be made subservient to it alone. An educational system is as it should be if it gives my *Volksgenossen* the power of resistance in all fields, if it makes them recognize the fundamental principles of their own lives. A National Socialist will never tolerate that a non-German should be the educator of a German, that a Jew should be the teacher of our people. If the People's Party (*Volkspartei*) tells us that we have no legal basis, we answer that it is our state. In our state only a German can be a citizen, and only the citizen can hold public office. You say to us that we have no means of enforcing this. And we answer: All measures which are necessary for the preservation of a people in its substance are justified. (Munich, November 29, 1929)

I do not even want to speak of the Jews. They are simply our old enemies, their plans have suffered shipwreck through us, and they rightly hate us, just as we hate them. We realize that this war can only end either in the wiping out of the Germanic nations, or by the disappearance of Jewry from Europe. On September 3rd, I spoke in the Reichstag—and I dislike premature prophecies—and I said that this war would not end the way the Jews imagine, that is, in the extinction of the European Aryan nations, but that the result of this war would be the destruction of Jewry. For the first time, it will not be the others who will bleed to death, but for the first time the genuine ancient Jewish law, "an eye for an eye, a tooth for a tooth," is being applied. The more this struggle spreads, the more anti-Semitism will spread—and world Jewry may rely on this. It will find nourishment in every prison camp, it will find nourishment in every family which is being enlightened as to why it is being called upon to make such sacrifices, and the hour will come when the worst enemy of the world, of all time, will have finished his part for at least one thousand years to come. (Berlin, January 30, 1942)

27. Even Hell Wouldn't Have It

JOHN F. WUKOVITS

It was just one square mile of coral atoll, the tiniest of islands, located six thousand miles west of Los Angeles, out in the middle of the Pacific Ocean. Few Americans had the foggiest notion where Betio or the Tarawa Atoll or the Gilbert Islands were located, but during three days in November 1943, the islands made their way into the front pages of newspapers all over the United States. During those seventy-two hours, 3,301 of America's best young men—soldiers in U.S. Marine Corps rifle platoons— died there under withering Japanese fire.

Tarawa was part of the Gilbert Island chain, the first stepping stone in the American march across the Pacific toward Japan during World War II. The Japanese troops fought valiantly, even fanatically, refusing to surrender under any circumstances, fighting to the death, every last one of them. America had not seen so much blood shed over so little territory since the horrific battles of the Civil War. But the battle was necessary. With the Gilbert Islands secured, Admiral Chester Nimitz led American forces on to the Marshall Islands in February 1944, the Marianas Islands in July 1944, Iwo Jima in February 1945, and Okinawa, just off the coast of Japan, in April 1945. In the following essay, John F. Wukovits discusses the bloodletting on Tarawa.

Something was seriously wrong, realized war correspondent Robert Sherrod. By now he should be scurrying around the little Pacific island gathering material on this amphibious operation for his editors at *Time* magazine. Yet here he was, still standing in neck-deep water several hundred yards from shore, dodging enemy gunfire.

He was not alone, but that made the situation even more perilous. Those Marines around him should have been ashore, too. Wherever he turned he could see men struggling to get to the beach. Many, he saw, were not making it.

The situation ashore was not going smoothly, either. Most Marines there were pinned down behind a four-foot-high sea wall. Burning amphtracs and smashed tanks littered the beach and water, and everywhere the tiny island shook as it absorbed still one more blow from huge naval guns offshore.

Sherrod knew that he could not remain in the water, for it would be only a matter of time before a Japanese bullet or shell hit him. His only choice was to join those Marines who were already wading the bloody gauntlet toward shore. Thinking that "I was scared as I had never been scared before," Robert Sherrod took his first wet step into the hell that was the battle of Tarawa.

It was the morning of November 20, 1943, and Sherrod was struggling toward Betio, an island on Tarawa Atoll in the Central Pacific. Located in the Gilbert Islands group, some twenty-five hundred miles southwest of Hawaii and near the equator, Tarawa is a triangular-shaped atoll of about twenty-five islands. The islands are coral, built up on extinct volcanoes, and are covered with sand and dotted with palms. One renowned nineteenth-century visitor to the region, Robert Louis Stevenson, described the Gilberts as "a treasure trove of South Sea island beauty."

Surrounding Tarawa is its most imposing physical feature—a jagged coral reef that presents a formidable menace to those wishing to cross it. Marines would be taught a bloody lesson for underestimating this reef.

Betio is the largest of Tarawa's islands, yet it is only two miles in length and at no spot wider than one-half mile. Why was this scraggly bit of coral, less than half the size of New York's Central Park, so important? It was vital because the U.S. Navy wanted its four-thousand-foot airstrip. In Japanese hands, planes stationed at Betio threatened the lines of communication between Australia and the United States. But, in American possession, this threat would be eliminated, and the airfield could be used as a base in the advance toward Japan.

American war planners also had another reason. Admiral Chester W. Nimitz, commander of the Pacific Fleet, wanted to attack Japanese bases in the larger and more strategic Marshall Islands. Attacking the Marshalls would require unleashing a large amphibious operation, with still-unproven troops, against a heavily fortified enemy—a risky endeavor that had never before been attempted. He and Admiral Raymond Spruance, the sea commander for the planned Marshalls assault, believed that Betio would be a useful preliminary target that, in addition to its airstrip, would provide the Marines with valuable experience in amphibious operations. Mistakes made at Betio could be corrected for the later, more difficult landings in the Marshalls.

For the assault on Tarawa, Admiral Nimitz assembled what was up to that time the most powerful naval force in U.S. history, covering eight square miles of ocean. The force was placed under the command of Admiral Spruance, hero of the recent battle of Midway. Spruance was a quiet, modest man who worked at a stand-up desk to keep meetings with visitors brief. To help plan the landing, Spruance chose two men who were every bit as loud and brash as he was unassuming: Marine General Holland "Howling Mad" Smith, known for his quick temper, and Admiral Richard Kelly Turner.

Their plan was to attack Betio from its lagoon side. Betio runs generally west to east, with the ocean to the south and the lagoon to the north, all of it surrounded by a coral reef approximately seven hundred yards out. The Marines would land on three connecting north beaches on both sides of a long pier that extended out over the coral reef. Once on shore, the Marines would punch straight ahead, capture the airfield in the center of the island, and split the Japanese defense in two by reaching the ocean shore. This would pin most of the remaining defenders on the eastern, narrow end of the island, where they could be mopped up the next day.

The plan was simple, but it included a major gamble—that there would be enough water over the reef to allow the landing craft to cross. Betio has very unpredictable tides in November, and Admiral Turner received conflicting reports from hydrographers and from former British and Australian residents of the atoll. Some believed that there would be barely sufficient water for the larger landing craft to cross, and others warned that there would be even less.

If Turner sent in the landing craft and there was not enough water, only the Marines in the first three waves, using about one hundred small, agile tracked vehicles called amphtracs, could get over the reef. These men would be stranded on the beach while waiting for their reinforcements (in deeper-draft Higgins boats) to wade in the final seven hundred yards. After weighing the available intelligence, Admiral Turner decided that the two-to-one odds for favorable tides on November 20 made that day the best the Marines were likely to have.

Rear Admiral Keiji Shibasaki, the Japanese commander on Tarawa, left little to luck. He planned to make any invader pay dearly in any attempt to take the island. His contingent of 4,836 men, many of whom were members of the crack Special Naval Landing Forces, worked feverishly to change Betio into a formidable bastion bristling with armaments.

Enemy landing craft would first be met by underwater obstacles, including concrete pyramids and mines, that would channel them into the path of pointblank fire. The barriers on the ocean side of the island had already been completed, and now Shibasaki's men were readying the lagoon side.

If any invader was fortunate enough to make it through this initial onslaught and reach the beach, he would be halted by a three- to five-foot-high coconut-log sea wall. Troops could crouch behind this for protection—practically the only protection they would find on the island—but Shibasaki ensured that the safety would be only temporary. As one Marine described it, "An American helmet reared above this sea wall would be as clear and helpless as a fly walking down a windowpane. And, if the Americans crouched beneath it, Betio's mortars would dye the sands with their blood. The mortars had the beaches registered—and they were behind a formidable array of machine guns and light artillery interlocked to sweep the lip of the sea wall."

The "array of guns" consisted of some two hundred heavy weapons varying in power from machine guns to eight-inch cannon. They were strategically placed throughout the island, and since no point on Betio was more than three hundred yards from a beach, most of the weaponry could be targeted on an invading force. The guns were entrenched in hexagon-shaped pillboxes of double-tiered coconut logs hooked together with railroad spikes. Sand had been poured between the tiers for reinforcement, and on top, half-inch steel roofs were covered with three feet of sand.

Between the pillboxes were even stronger blockhouses with five-foot-thick concrete walls. This formidable system was connected by a network of trenches, and was devised so that each position would be safe from any but a direct hit by the largest bombs. In this manner Shibasaki was forcing any Americans who made it to shore and over the sea wall to take each separate spot in the most brutal of ways—hand-to-hand combat.

The efficient Admiral Shibasaki had installed what one historian has called "the most complete defensive system . . . that could have [been] devised . . . Corregidor was an open town by comparison." In fact, Shibasaki was so confident in his preparations that he boasted, "A million men cannot take Tarawa in a hundred years."

The American planners hoped to take it in two days.

The American forces approaching Betio in November 1943 temporarily basked in another, more peaceful world. The Marines who were en route to the island were battle-hardened Guadalcanal veterans of the Second Marine Division, which was judged to be the best unit ever sent on an amphibious operation. They sailed amidst a tropical beauty that bathed the entire enterprise in a luxurious glow, creating the illusion that they were almost on a pleasure cruise. Correspondent Sherrod marveled at "the brilliant sunlight, the far-reaching, incredibly blue Pacific, the soft breezes at evening and the Southern Cross in the sky." Some Marines began to optimistically wonder if the Japanese had pulled out of Betio as they had recently done at Kiska in the Aleutians.

Optimism prevailed even among some of the operations leaders. Rear Admiral Howard Kingman, in charge of the naval fire support group, boasted to Marine officers, "We will not neutralize; we will not destroy; we will obliterate the defenses on Betio!" Rear Admiral Harry W. Hill, Southern Force commander, confidently predicted that "we're going to steamroller that place until hell wouldn't have it!"

Neither officers nor troops anticipated the reception that Admiral Shibasaki had prepared for them. As the force neared its position off Tarawa on the still night of November 19, 1943, these officers and men silently prepared themselves for what many hoped would be an easy victory.

Not everyone on board the ships was as confident. General Julian Smith, commander of the Marines landing at Betio, reminded fellow officers that "when the Marines land and meet the enemy at bayonet point, the only armor a Marine will have is his khaki shirt."

Invasion day began with reveille sounding through the ships shortly after midnight. A hearty breakfast of steak, eggs, French fries, and coffee was served to those who could think of food while staring into the face of death.

After breakfast, the men readied themselves for battle. The equatorial heat was stifling in the still darkness, drenching the Marines in sweat and soaking through the fresh uniforms they had put on one hour before to minimize infection if wounded. Some men joked to relieve the tension, asking each other how many "Japs" they would get. Officers reassured their men that there was "no necessity for anyone to get killed, although possibly someone might get slightly wounded." Correspondent Robert Sherrod took out two fresh notebooks because "if I were killed I did not want the Japs to learn anything about us from the notes I had made during the convoy trip."

At 2:50 A.M. Betio was sighted by the approaching armada, and within an hour, men for the first three waves silently began climbing down cargo nets into landing craft. The battle was about to begin.

Across the calm waters, on the beaches of Betio, Japanese troops wrapped protective cloths called *semin bari* around their waists. Each stitch in the cloth had been sewn by a different friend wishing the soldier good luck, and would, according to tradition, bring divine protection. The cloth also served as a reminder of each soldier's duty according to the simple code, "Honor is heavier than the mountains, and death lighter than a feather."

Two tough forces, the Marine Second Division and the Japanese Special Naval Landing Forces, had been maneuvered opposite each other.

Perspiring in the humid tropical night, they waited in silence for the fight to begin.

The first shots were fired shortly after 5:00 A.M., just as dawn was casting its initial faint light. At 5:10 the battleship *Maryland* catapulted her spotter plane into the air. The Japanese, mistaking this for the start of the battle, began firing at the American force. Fifteen U.S. ships immediately unleashed a thundering reply, lighting up the night with deadly brilliance. "First you would see a big flash at sea," said one observer, "then a graceful slow-moving arc of twin balls with bright flashes where they hit. Then would come a rumble like distant thunder."

After a brief cessation for a U.S. air strike, the ships resumed firing, and during the next two-and-one-half hours poured two thousand tons of explosives onto Betio, ranging from five-inch diameter shells weighing fifty pounds to sixteen-inch projectiles weighing over a ton. Ten tons of shells were fired at each acre on the islet in the most intense preinvasion bombardment in naval history. Admiral Spruance's chief of staff, Captain C. J. Moore, later recalled that "fires were burning everywhere. The coconut trees were blasted and burned, and it seemed that no living soul could be on the island . . . it looked like the whole affair would be a walkover."

Some Japanese troops were in fact killed in the bombardment, and most of the above-ground installations were destroyed. Most importantly, Shibasaki's communications network was knocked out, isolating him from his troops and making efficient coordination of the island's defense practically impossible. But the bombardment had done little damage to the well-constructed Japanese bunkers and deeply burrowed troops. Most Japanese defenders emerged from this shelling untouched.

Consequently, the American amphtracs that began carrying the first three waves of Marines on their fifteen-minute journey to shore would not, as many prayed, approach silent bunkers filled with dead Japanese. The Marines would instead be welcomed by alert defenders with fire in their eyes—eyes that already were peering over gunsights aimed directly at khaki shirts.

At 8:55 A.M. the bombardment ended. In the sudden silence, as the amphtracs inched toward shore, Admiral Shibasaki switched his defenders to the lagoon side of the island. Every Japanese gun on Betio was now pointing at the approaching Marines.

The first three waves were commanded by Colonel David M. Shoup, a bull-necked writer of poetry who was described as "the bravest, nerviest, best soldiering Marine." His men would land in three connecting sections on either side of the five-hundred-foot pier extending to the reef from the island's midsection.

Shoup's first task was to clear out the pier to eliminate crossfire. He sent in First Lieutenant William D. Hawkins's elite scout-sniper platoon five minutes ahead of the first wave for this purpose. Known as "Hawk" to his men, Lieutenant Hawkins was a dedicated Marine who believed he would not survive the war, even telling a friend when he joined the Marines, "Mac, I'll see you someday, but not on this earth."

Following Hawkins's platoon came Shoup's three waves of ninety-three amphtracs carrying nearly two thousand Marines, each wave separated by three hundred yards of blue-green water. Shoup quickly discovered that the American command had lost its battle with the tide—barely three feet of water covered the reef. His amphtracs could churn across the shallow water, but the following waves of deeper-draft Higgins boats carrying men and heavier equipment would not be able to penetrate to the beachhead. Their cargo would have to be shuttled from reef to shore by amphtracs, and the men would have to wade much of the way. If the Japanese resistance was strong, many Marines would die.

Those who hoped the bombardment had neutralized Betio quickly found otherwise. Plodding ahead at the speed of four knots, the first amphtracs came under fire from Japanese artillery while still three thousand yards from shore. At two thousand yards, Japanese machine guns joined in, agitating the water with thousands of bullets. By the time the amphtracs were crawling over the reef eight hundred yards from shore, every gun and mortar on Betio was pumping away at the shocked Marines, turning the normally placid lagoon into a watery inferno.

The approach turned into what one historian called a "nightmarish turtle race," with the slow-moving amphtracs providing easy targets for the Japanese. "The bullets were pouring at us like a sheet of rain," said Private N. M. Baird, who landed in the first wave. "The enemy fire was awful damn intense and gettin' worse. They were knockin' boats out left and right. A tractor'd get hit, stop, and burst into flames, with men jumping out like torches."

Machine gunners on each amphtrac fired back, but it was an almost futile gesture since each gunner was exposed from the waist up while his enemy was hidden. Three hundred twenty-three of the five hundred amphtrac crew members were killed or wounded while trying to land the Marines in the midst of ever-growing carnage.

The enemy fire was so accurate that shells hit some landing craft just as their ramps came down, leaving some in pools of blood, completely destroying others. Battalion commander Lieutenant Colonel Herbert Amey led his men off an amphtrac by shouting, "Come on men. We're going to take the beach. Those bastards can't stop us now!" Before he could take another step, a Japanese machine gun ripped open his chest and head, killing him instantly. One amphtrac coxswain became so confused and petrified by the unfolding horror that he stopped his amphtrac and yelled to the twenty Marines inside to get out. "This is as far as I go!" he screamed, then watched in terror as the twenty Marines jumped off the ramp into fifteen feet of water, drowning under the weight of their equipment.

Slowly, a handful of men began reaching the sea wall. Small groups of Marines hugged the relative safety of the four-foot log barricade, confused and leaderless. In a few places, small dents were punched into the Japanese defenses. Major Mike "Iron Mike" Ryan scratched out a tenuous foothold with his two companies on the west beach, but was immediately pinned down by blistering fire. Within two hours he had lost half his men. On the east side, two amphtracs churned their way one hundred yards inland before being stopped at the airfield.

Colonel Shoup managed to reach shore by edging in along the pier until an amphtrac picked him up. On shore, the wounded officer set up his command post within six feet of a large Japanese bunker and began to

assess the desperate situation. He tried to get a message through for reinforcements, but all of his radios had been ruined by seawater. Ninety long
minutes would pass before he would find a workable radio set and could
send out a plea for more troops. In the meantime, he would have to
depend on the Marines in the following waves. But, when Shoup turned his
gaze from the shore to the reef, he saw that these men were experiencing a
hell even more intense than what he had just come through.

"Oh, God, I'm scared," muttered one debarking Marine when he saw
what stretched before him. Since the boats in the later waves were too large
to get over the nearly exposed reef, their occupants had to wade the
remaining seven hundred yards to shore, every step heading directly into
the carnage being carved out by deadly Japanese gunfire. Already there
were thousands of dead fish and hundreds of dead and dying Marines
floating on the lagoon waters, yet there was no alternative but to continue
on. They had to wade straight into the inferno, or they would die on the
reef. Doing what they had to do, Marines began taking their first steps
toward the beach.

The men in Robert Sherrod's boat jumped into neck-deep water and,
"no sooner had we hit the water than the Jap machine guns really opened
up on us. There must have been five or six of those machine guns concentrating their fire on us . . . which meant several hundred bullets per
man . . . bullets were hitting six inches to the left or six inches to the right.
I could have sworn that I could have reached out and touched a hundred
bullets."

Marines began falling into the water, their mangled bodies staining the
lagoon. "The water was red with blood," recalled a Marine. "All around me
men were screaming and moaning. I never prayed so hard in all my life."

One Marine described his walk "like being completely suspended, like
being under a strong anesthetic; not asleep, not even a nightmare, just
having everything stop except pain and fear and death. Everyone was
afraid . . . Our voices sounded like the voices of complete strangers, voices
we had never heard before."

Yet, they waded on.

A naval airplane observer, Lieutenant Commander Robert McPher-
son, circled above the madness, feeling outrage over his inability to help
the men struggling and dying in the water. He watched men work toward
the beach, and felt tears fill his eyes as so many disappeared under a hail of
bullets or explosions: "The water never seemed clear of tiny men, their
rifles held over their heads, slowly wading beachwards. I wanted to cry."

Somehow, men began to reach the beach in spite of the tremendous
barrage thrown at them by the Japanese. Although they were still subject to
heavy fire, and Japanese mortars were lobbing shells onto the beaches
with frightening accuracy, those Marines who came through the gauntlet
clutched the sea wall as a man would grasp a long-lost friend. Carl Jonas, a
Marine, struggled ashore by using a rifle as a cane to push his exhausted
body forward, and when he finally collapsed on the beach, "it seemed like
the sweetest earth this side of paradise, and I wanted to lie there forever
without moving a muscle."

The Marines on shore found little safety either. Most were confined to
the sea wall and a mere twenty feet of beach, from which they could easily

be dislodged by a Japanese counterattack. Mortars were zeroing in on their positions, and snipers were picking off any heads that peered over the wall.

In a few places some progress was made to expand the tenuous toehold, but Shoup could do no real damage without more men and armor. Around 10:30 A.M. he finally contacted Admiral Hill with a desperate message for reinforcements. Hill was able to release some reserve troops, but they, too, were stopped at the reef by the low tide and had to wade in, reaching the beach tired and decimated. Shoup would have to hold the beachhead until the tide was high enough for heavier artillery and equipment to come in over the reef.

Throughout the long afternoon, troops continued to filter into the beachhead, until by nightfall there were five thousand exhausted Marines ashore. In this first day of fighting, fifteen hundred Marines had become casualties. Medics tried to help the wounded, but since so many medical personnel had been hit coming in, unattended casualties piled up. And their supplies were desperately short, forcing at least one medic to dash back into the water to salvage medical supplies from dead bodies. Another had to operate without anesthetic because he had depleted his supply.

As darkness settled over the island, numbed, tired Marines lay still with their thoughts and awaited the seemingly inevitable Japanese counterattack against their thin beachhead. It had certainly not been the kind of day any of the survivors had expected. "I was quite certain that this was my last night on earth," wrote Robert Sherrod.

The expected counterattack never came. Because the preinvasion bombardment had severed his communications, Admiral Shibasaki found it impossible to coordinate an assault that could have swept the Marines off the island and possibly ended the battle. The Japanese commander could do little but wait for dawn.

On the morning of November 21, Marines wading ashore found the situation as serious as it had been the previous day. The men already on shore knew they had to get off the beach, where they were still receiving intense fire, and move inland. The only way was to expose themselves to direct Japanese fire by jumping over the sea wall, and advance yard by yard over land infested with snipers and machine guns. Japanese pillboxes were arranged so that Marines attacking one emplacement would be under fire from two others. The defenders were solidly dug in. "They are the damnedest diggers in the world," said one sergeant of the Japanese. "It's like pulling a tick out of a rug to get one out of his hole." Progress would be slow, and measured in yards and in blood.

Yet, in the beating heat of the tropical sun, at scattered points across the beachhead, men began to rise above their fears and leap over the wall to engage the enemy. Brutal losses were commonplace: some units suffered more casualties in twenty-four hours at Betio than they had in six months at Guadalcanal.

Again in the forefront was Lieutenant William Hawkins, who amazed other Marines with his disdain for personal safety. Attacking nest after nest of machine-gunners, he rested only when returning for more ammunition. "He is a madman . . . I never saw such a man in my life," said one Marine.

Hawkins refused medical treatment after being shot twice through the shoulders, but finally his premonition was fulfilled and he was cut down by an explosive shell. He died shortly after dawn the following day. Hawkins would later be awarded one of four Congressional Medal of Honor citations given for Tarawa. (The Tarawa airstrip was also named Hawkins Field in his memory.) Colonel Shoup, who would also receive a Medal of Honor, praised Hawkins for spurring his men to victory. "It's not often that you can credit a first lieutenant with winning a battle," he said, "but Hawkins came as near to it as any man could. He was truly an inspiration."

Other Marines were motivated into action by Staff Sergeant William Bordelon, who took out three pillboxes by approaching their flanks and heaving demolition charges in through their narrow gun slits. Wounded in his third attempt, but refusing medical aid, he heard cries of help coming from the water and dashed in to drag out two wounded men. Then he grabbed another demolition charge and attacked his fourth pillbox, where "the Japanese gunners saw him coming and shot him dead." Bordelon, too, received the Congressional Medal of Honor.

Not all Marines would receive the acclaim given these men, but what they did was almost as courageous. Ordinary men were doing extraordinary deeds, in most cases by simply conquering their own fears and doing what had to be done. Colonel Shoup's proudest memory of this battle was of the teen-age corporal he saw shaking in fear on the beach. When Shoup asked him where the rest of his squad was, the corporal replied that he was the only survivor. Shoup ordered him to form another squad. In a terror-creaked voice, the corporal said he did not know how, so Shoup told him to go up and down the beach telling one straggler, then another, to "Follow me." The young man walked off down the beach and Shoup returned to pressing matters. An hour or so later, Colonel Shoup heard his name being called and turned around to view the young Marine now standing proudly at the head of a squad.

Not all were heroes on the island. One officer started inland with one hundred Marines, but by the time he reached his objective, all but three had fallen back. Another officer complained to Shoup that none of his men would follow him to attack a machine gun nest.

But enough Marines did conquer every soldier's worst enemy—fear—and in doing so began swinging the battle in the Americans' favor. The beachhead slowly began to expand. Then around noon, the other enemy that had almost defeated the Marines—nature—began to cooperate with a rising tide. Soon there was enough water over the reef for the larger boats to bring in badly needed food, water, ammunition, artillery, and men.

Freshly reinforced, one unit of Marines advanced across the middle of Betio and cut the Japanese defenses in two, while a second unit began mopping up the southwest sector. Although fighting was still brisk, Colonel Shoup felt confident enough by late afternoon to notify Admiral Smith: "Casualties many; percentage dead not known; combat efficiency: we are winning."

As the Marines dug in for the night of November 21–22, far more confident now than they had been twenty-four hours earlier, Admiral Shibasaki radioed a message to Japanese headquarters. He had claimed that he could hold this island "for a hundred years," but now he admitted defeat and signaled, "Our weapons have been destroyed and from now on everyone is attempting a final charge . . . May Japan exist for ten thousand years!" The Japanese knew they could no longer win this battle, but they would continue to make the Marines suffer for their victory.

The following morning, while destroyers lobbed shells onto the tail end of Betio, Marines began the arduous job of mopping up the remaining Japanese strongholds. Using TNT, hand grenades, and flame throwers, they assaulted any pillbox that the tanks were unable to knock out, or called up bulldozers to smother the enemy with dirt.

One stronghold eliminated that morning was Admiral Shibasaki's huge bombproof headquarters. Around 9:30 A.M., Lieutenant Alexander Bonnyman led a small group onto the top of the blockhouse. Japanese defenders poured out to shove off the threatening Marines, but found their way blocked by Bonnyman, who fired round after round at them. Although outnumbered, he roused his men by rushing at the enemy while yelling, "Follow me!" His men held the top, but Lieutenant Bonnyman fell, dying of numerous wounds. Bonnyman would receive the fourth Medal of Honor.

Bulldozers sealed up the blockhouse entrances with sand, trapping two hundred defenders inside. Marines then poured gasoline down the air vents and dropped in hand grenades. In a matter of minutes Admiral Shibasaki's fortification, which he had claimed was untouchable, became a coffin for him and his men.

The elimination of the headquarters symbolically finished the Japanese. Japanese defenders, realizing the end was near, began committing suicide by thrusting bayonets into their stomachs, holding grenades to their heads, or placing rifles against their throats and pulling the triggers.

In one final spasm of fury on the night of November 22, four hundred surviving defenders threw themselves against the Marines in a banzai attack, screaming "Marines, you die!" and "Japanese drink Marines' blood!" Furious hand-to-hand fighting ensued, with the Japanese nearly breaking through the lines. But the attack was repulsed, and the next morning Marines counted 325 slain Japanese around their foxholes.

Finally, at noon on November 23, a Hellcat fighter piloted by Ensign W. W. Kelly became the first American plane to land on Betio's battle-scarred airstrip, and the Marines could proudly boast that they had accomplished their main goal. Some fighting would continue on Tarawa's neighboring islets, but basically the battle was over, and at 1:12 P.M. Betio was officially declared secured. After almost seventy-six hours of "the bitterest fighting in the history of the Marine Corps," the first land held by Japan before the war had been taken from it.

But Betio had exacted its price. Ensign Kelly realized this as he approached the island in his Hellcat. Corpses bobbed up and down several miles out to sea. In the three days of fighting, out of 12,000 attackers, 2,292 Americans were wounded and 1,056 were killed. Death for most had come brutally—only 565 bodies could be positively identified. Of the 4,836 Japanese defenders, only 17 survived.

Marines were exhausted from their ordeal and, though alive, stared with the eyes of the dead. "I passed boys who had lived yesterday a thousand times and looked older than their fathers," wrote General Holland Smith after touring the battlefield. "Dirty, unshaven, with gaunt almost sightless eyes, they had survived the ordeal, but it had chilled their souls. They found it hard to believe they were actually alive. There were no smiles on these ancient youthful faces; only passive relief among the dead."

Betio, a scenic Pacific island before the war, now resembled a sand-filled trash heap. Blackened stumps of palm trees stuck up through churned coral sand that was littered with spent shells, overturned equipment, bloated corpses, and bits of bodies. Three days after the battle, Admiral Nimitz flew in for an inspection and was reminded of the savagery of Ypres, a World War I battle that had lasted for weeks.

After viewing the carnage, Julian Smith turned to Holland Smith and said, "There was one thing that won this battle, Holland, and that was the supreme courage of the Marines. The prisoners tell us that what broke their morale was not the bombing, not the naval gunfire, but the sight of Marines who kept coming ashore in spite of their machine-gun fire. The Jap machine-gun fire killed many Marines in the water and on the beach. But other Marines came behind those who died." Betio was taken because uncommon bravery was exhibited by common men.

There was controversy after the battle as to whether Tarawa was worth the high number of casualties. Americans back home were shocked when they learned how many men had been lost in such a short time, but most military leaders believed Betio had taught valuable lessons. Surviving participants filed battle reports that were carefully studied, and from these came changes that would be used later in the Pacific campaign.

"There had to be a Tarawa, the first assault on a strongly defended coral atoll," claimed Lieutenant General L. D. Hermle, assistant division commander. "There, untried doctrine was tested in the crucible of actual combat." Military leaders believed that if the bloody assault had not occurred at Betio, it would have taken place somewhere else. Because of the lessons learned at Betio, future attacks on Japanese island strongholds in the Marshalls, the Marianas, the Palaus, and at Iwo Jima were more effective.

Strategic planning benefited from Betio, but most of the Marines who suffered through the three grueling days of fighting and watched fellow Marines die would agree with Robert Sherrod, who, looking back after forty years, wrote, "I regard Tarawa as the most haunting memory of World War II."

28. Hero or Draft-Dodger?
John Wayne and World War II
RANDY ROBERTS

Even today, fifteen years after his death, John Wayne's image appears in restaurants, bars, auction barns, rodeos, television screens, video stores, and homes all across the country. His name is synonymous with patriotism, traditional values, rugged individualism, and conservative politics, and many Americans consider him a hero. They have named airports, streets, and elementary schools after him. Wayne's status as a certifiable superstar developed during and just after World War II, when he starred in such films as Back to Bataan, Flying Tigers, Reunion in France, They Were Expendable, Flying Leathernecks, Operation Pacific, Fighting Seabees, *and* The Sands of Iwo Jima. *For most Americans today, the enduring images of World War II revolve around John Wayne's celluloid exploits against the Japanese.*

But there is an irony to Wayne's status as a superhero. Although given the chance to join the military and fight the Germans and Japanese during World War II, he chose to stay home, making movies and money as a civilian. He was the first real-life person in American history to become a genuine war hero without serving in the military at all. In the following essay, Randy Roberts analyzes John Wayne's life in Hollywood during World War II.

December 7, 1941. The news reached Hollywood at 11:26 on a calm Sunday morning. The Japanese had attacked American naval and air bases in Honolulu. A few people refused to believe the news. It seemed impossible, almost like another "War of the Worlds" broadcast, and they waited for the soothing voice of an announcer to tell them that it was only make believe. Everything about the day clashed with the brutal facts. The weather was perfect, even for a city where ideal weather was the norm. A cool night breeze blew off the desert from the northeast, but by 11:00 it was already in the low 70s. For the Hollywood elite, many of whom had gone to their vacation retreats in Malibu, Palm Springs, or the High Sierras, golf and swimming, not war, was on the day's agenda. Before the news reached Los Angeles, harmony reigned. Only the day before, the UCLA Bruins and the USC Trojans had played to a 7–7 tie, and that very morning a *Los Angeles Times* headline announced "FINAL PEACE MOVE SEEN."

The attack stunned Los Angeles. Responses varied. Some followed normal schedules. Thousands turned up at the "little world championship" football game and watched the undefeated Hollywood Bears, led by Kenny Washington and Woody Strode, defeat the Columbus Bulls. During the game, news updates reminded the spectators that the Bears' victory would probably not be remembered as the day's most important event. In another part of town, several hundred spectators watched Paramount Studio's baseball team defeat an "all-Jap aggregation." After the game, the FBI took the Japanese team into custody. The attack, however, disrupted most schedules. Golfers finished the holes they were playing and returned to the clubhouse. Gossips ended their conversations about Henry Warner's new granddaughter or the removal of Eddie Albert's tonsils or the antiaircraft men who had set up shop at Hollywood Park, and turned to more urgent topics. Thousands simply got into their automobiles—tanks full and rubber treads still good—and drove aimlessly through the city, leading to traffic jams in downtown Los Angeles and Hollywood.

Soon the rumors started to ricochet like bullets. Air defense men had known the attack was imminent. Two squadrons of airplanes—that's thirty planes—had been sighted over the California Coast. Japanese airplanes had reconnoitered the Bay Area. Bombed the Golden Gate Bridge. Pearl Harbor was only a stepping stone. California was next. There would be an uprising of Japanese Americans. Sabotage was certain. Moved to action by the rumors as well as sound precaution, policemen went on 12-hour shifts and sent extra security guards to dams, bridges, and power stations. Most others waited for FDR's announcement that the United States was now at war.

Hollywood and the entertainment industry responded to the attack with sincere feelings of patriotism mixed with an equally sincere desire to cash in on the event. Studios abandoned a few films already in production with poorly timed themes or poorly chosen titles—the musicals *Pearl Harbor Pearl* and *I'll Take Manila* and the comedy *Absent Without Leave*, about a GI who goes AWOL. Just as quickly studios secured the copyrights for more promising titles—*Sunday in Hawaii, Wings Over the Pacific, Bombing of Honolulu, Remember Pearl Harbor, Yellow Peril, Yellow Menace, My Four Years in Japan,* and *V for Victory.* Tin Pan Alley produced topical songs within days of the attack. Although none muscled onto the Hit Parade, such songs as "Let's Put the Axe to the Axis," "We're Going to Find the Fellow Who Is Yellow and Beat Him Red, White and Blue," "They're Gonna Be Playin' Taps on the Japs," "The Sun Will Soon Be Setting for the Land of the Rising Sun," "To Be Specific, It's Our Pacific," "When Those Little Yellow Bellies Meet the Cohens and the Kelleys," and "You're a Sap, Mr. Jap" expressed the angry mood of the country. The Metropolitan Opera Company, sensing that Americans did not want to see a sympathetic portrayal of any Japanese, dropped their production of "Madame Butterfly." The Greenwich Village Savoyards followed the Met's lofty example and dumped their production of "The Mikado."

While Tin Pan Alley turned out their topical tunes and opera companies pruned their repertoires, Americans huddled close to their radios. On Monday morning and Tuesday night FDR delivered his impassioned war speeches before Congress. For a few days, America—and particularly the West Coast—moved through a fog of air raid alarms, blackouts, and tense expectations. They listened as America's foreign commentators broke the news that Germany and Italy had declared war on the United States. They listened to the news that the Germans had sunk two British ships and that the Japanese had followed up Pearl Harbor with attacks in the Philippines, Hong Kong, Wake Island, Guam, and other Pacific strongholds.

Hollywood moaned that the war was a killer at the box office. Certainly flights of parochialism were the standard Hollywood reaction to any event. In 1935 when Mussolini's troops stormed into Ethiopia and the world focused on the League of Nations, a Hollywood producer asked a friend,

"Have you heard any late news?" Yes, the friend replied hotly, "Italy just banned *Marie Antoinette!*" This episode of tunnel vision was surpassed in 1939 when Italy ruthlessly invaded Albania. Louella Parsons, Hollywood's leading gossip writer, began her column that week: "The deadly dullness of the past week was lifted today when Darryl Zanuck announced he had bought all rights to *The Bluebird* for Shirley Temple."

By mid-December Hollywood spokesmen complained that Americans were too interested in the war to go to the movies. Attempting to demonstrate that Hollywood *was* concerned with other events, *Variety* observed that the war had also hurt Christmas shopping, but clearly the box office crisis overshadowed all other concerns. The Wolf Man's *Variety* advertisement announced "Listen to That Box Office Howl!" but the only noise was the studio's howl of financial pain. The same was true for *The Great Dictator, Sergeant York, Citizen Kane,* and the season's other top pictures. Amidst considerable hand wringing, Hollywood leaders speculated on the long-term impact of the war on the industry.

John Wayne shared the industry's general concern, although his worries focused more specifically on the effect the war would have on his own career. After years of struggle with bad scripts and tight budgets, by late 1941 he was moving closer to the fringes of stardom. The reviews he had received for *Stagecoach* and *The Long Voyage Home* had pushed his career to a new level. Republic's head Herbert Yates responded by searching for better scripts, assigning first-line directors, and increasing the budgets for Wayne films. *The Dark Command,* Wayne's first film for Republic under the contract his new agent had negotiated for him, reflected Wayne's new status. Yates allocated $700,000 for the film—more than any previous Republic project—and hired Raoul Walsh to direct it. He also arranged for Claire Trevor and Walter Pidgeon to star in the film with Wayne. And less than four months before the attack on pearl Harbor, Wayne had finished his work on Cecil B. DeMille's *Reap the Wild Wind,* which Paramount had scheduled for a March 1942 release.

New agents, new contracts, better directors, better films—at the age of thirty-four Duke was a player in Hollywood. But he was not yet a major star. In late December 1941, *Variety* issued its annual review of the stars. It set down clearly where an actor or actress stood in the complicated Hollywood pecking order. At the summit of the hierarchy were the performers whose pictures earned the most money for the year: Gary Cooper, Abbott and Costello, Clark Gable, Mickey Rooney, Bob Hope, Charlie Chaplin, Dorothy Lamour, Spencer Tracy, Jack Benny, and Bing Crosby. They had helped make 1941 the best year ever for domestic box office receipts.

Next came the individual studio reports. The stars and featured performers of the individual studios were listed and briefly discussed. The major studios controlled the major talent. MGM led the pack; its stars included Gable, Rooney, Tracy, Robert Taylor, Lana Turner, James Stewart, Hedy Lamarr, Judy Garland, Myrna Loy, William Powell, Joan Crawford, Nelson Eddy, Jeanette MacDonald, Greta Garbo, Norma Shearer, the Marx Brothers, and a host of other leading performers. If the other studios could not match MGM, they could all boast of their proven box office attractions. Warner Brothers, king of the gangster genre, had James Cagney, Humphrey Bogart, Edward G. Robinson, John Garfield, and George Raft, as well as Erroll Flynn, Bette Davis, Merle Oberon, and Ronald Reagan. Twentieth Century Fox had a group of attractive leading men and women which included Tyrone Power, Betty Grable, Gene Tierney, Henry Fonda, Randolph Scott, Maureen O'Hara, and Linda Darnell. Paramount had its comedians—Hope, Crosby, and Benny—as well as Lamour, Claudette Colbert, Veronica Lake, Paulette Goddard, Fred MacMurray, and Ray Milland. RKO featured Ginger Rogers, Orson Welles, Cary Grant, Carole Lombard, Ronald Coleman, and Gloria Swanson. Universal had a great year in 1941 thanks to the success of Abbot and Costello. And Columbia featured Peter Lorre, Boris Karloff, Fay Wray, and the recently acquired Rita Hayworth.

At the bottom of the hierarchy were the smaller studios and their performers. There dwelled Monogram. "No pretenses. No ambitious production. Just bread and butter," noted *Variety*. Its older cowboy and action stars—Jack LaRue, Buck Jones, Tim McCoy, and Bela Lugosi—kept the studio afloat. Finally came Republic. *Variety* listed Gene Autry and John Wayne as Republic's "two corking box-office assets." Wayne's reputation derived from his "loanout" status. Like Monogram, Republic produced films for theaters outside of the major distribution circles, and a star like Wayne who was used by the major studios gave prestige to the Poverty Row studio.

Wayne, always a clear-thinking realist, knew where he stood in the Hollywood hierarchy. He was a star in the third-and-fourth-run theaters in the South and Southwest, in areas with more cattle than people. His success following *Stagecoach* introduced him to the first-and-second-run palaces of the East, Midwest, and West. At the end of 1941 he was nowhere near the summit of the hierarchy, far from the status of such leading men as Clark Gable, Robert Taylor, Tyrone Power, Cary Grant, Gary Cooper, or Henry Fonda. But Wayne was ambitious, and no one in the industry had his capacity for work. The facts were indisputable: his reputation was growing but not yet firmly established, and he was a thirty-four year old leading man. If he enlisted, would his fragile reputation survive two, three, four years in the service? How many years did he have left as a leading man? Enlistment, in the final analysis, would probably end his career.

While Wayne pondered his future and prepared for his next picture, other Hollywood stars put their careers on hold and their lives on the line. Pearl Harbor aroused deep emotions in Hollywood. During the next four years journalists and politicians would accuse the film industry of being cynical, opportunistic, greedy, and worse. The charges were often accurate. But in late 1941 and early 1942 scores of actors, directors, producers, and technicians enlisted out of a deep sense of patriotism. Like millions of other Americans, they were shocked by the Japanese attack and wanted to help win the war.

Henry Fonda, one of Duke's boon companions on the vacations to Mexico, felt the pull of patriotism. He was thirty-seven—three years older than Wayne—and had a wife and three children. For all practical purposes, he was exempt from the draft. But he had a baby face, and he did not want the wives and mothers of soldiers and sailors to see him on the screen and ask, "Why isn't he out there?" Besides, as he told his wife, "this is my country and I want to be where it's happening. I don't want to be in a fake war in a studio or on location. . . . I want to be on a real ocean not the back lot. I want to be with real sailors and not extras." After he finished *The Ox-Bow Incident,* the film in which he was then starring, Fonda drove to the Naval Headquarters in Los Angeles and enlisted. No screen photographers were present; his press agent had not tipped off any reporters. Fonda wanted it simple, no different than other Americans.

John Ford, the man Duke admired the most, also felt the pull. During the late-1930s he had followed with growing uneasiness the spread of fascism in Europe. When Ford's leading writer Dudley Nichols sent him a wire of congratulations for winning the 1940 Academy Award for his direction of *The Grapes of Wrath,* Ford wrote back, "Awards for pictures are a trivial thing to be concerned with at times like these." That spring he organized the Naval Field Photographic Reserve unit, which Washington officially recognized. The forty-six year old Ford was ordered to report to Washington for active duty in the month before Pearl Harbor. Immediately and without publicity he left Hollywood. He left the money, the fame, the career, the glamour.

When the Japanese attacked Pearl Harbor, Ford was eating lunch at the eighteenth-century Alexandria, Virginia, home of Admiral William Pickens. He watched the Admiral take the urgent phone call. He saw the blood drain from his face. After they heard the news, Pickens' wife, Darrielle, showed Ford a scar on their home where a Revolutionary War musket ball had torn through a wall. "I never let them plaster over the hole," she said. Throughout the war and for the rest of his life Ford would remember the story. He wanted to be part of that tradition.

Tradition and patriotism pulled Jimmy Stewart into the war. Stewart's grandfather had fought for the Union during the Civil War. Stewart's father had fought in the Spanish–American War and World War I. In February 1941, Stewart attempted to enlist in the Army Air Corps but was rejected because his 147 pounds was ten pounds too light for his six feet four inch frame. He went on a diet of candy, beer, and bananas. In a month he had put on the ten pounds and he was sworn into the Army. He left his $1,500-a-week movie salary for a private's wages.

Other leading men and Hollywood personalities also felt the pull. Wayne's fellow star at Republic, Gene Autry, joined the Army Air Corps. Robert Montgomery enlisted in the Navy. Tyrone Power joined the Marines. William Holden went into the Army. After the death of his wife Carole Lombard in January 1942, Clark Gable also enlisted in the Army. David Niven, Laurence Olivier, and Patrick Knowles returned to their native Britain and enlisted. Ronald Reagan, Sterling Hayden, Burgess Meredith, and Gilbert Roland all signed up. So too did directors Frank Capra, William Wyler, Anatole Litvak, John Huston, and William Keighley; producers Hal Roach, Jack Warner, Gene Markey, and Darryl F. Zanuck; writers Garson Kanin and Budd Schulberg; cameraman Gregg Toland; and thousands of other Hollywood workers. By October 1942 over 2,700—or 12%—of the men and women in the film industry had entered the armed forces. Some like Fonda and Stewart enlisted quietly and without fanfare. Others like Reagan and Zanuck and Gable made the process of enlistment and service an act of Hollywood. But quietly or loudly they did serve.

In 1941 professional baseball players were the only men who received as much attention and adulation as Hollywood stars. When the war started they laid down their bats and picked up service issue weapons. Joe DiMaggio, Hank Greenberg, Bob Feller, Ted Williams, Bill Dickey, Peewee Reese, and most of the other baseball legends from the 1930s entered the service. More than 4,000 of the roughly 5,700 players in the major and minor leagues served in the armed forces during the war. Some were killed or seriously injured during the conflict. Others experienced the loss of crucial skills because of a lack of practice. And even the players who returned to the big leagues after the war lost several years from a career which at best was painfully short.

Even America's popular comic book heroes enlisted in the war effort. Joe Palooka and Snuffy Smith joined the Army; Mickey Flynn enlisted in the Coast Guard; Dick Tracy received a commission in naval intelligence. Batman, Robin, the Flash, Plastic Man, Captain America, Captain Marvel, the Green Lantern, the Spirit—the cream of the superheroes—fought German and Japanese in the pages of thousands of comic books. The only important superhero who did not enlist was Superman—and he stayed at home for a very good reason. His creators, Jerry Siegel and Joe Schuster, reasoned that Nazis and Japs would be no match for the Man of Steel, and with real Americans fighting and dying in the war it might denigrate their efforts if Superman defeated the Axis. To keep Superman out of the war but still show his patriotism, Siegel and Schuster had Clark Kent—a.k.a. Superman—declared 4-F. Superman's famed X-ray vision malfunctioned during his preinduction physical; instead of reading the eye chart in front of him, Superman accidentally looked through the wall and focused on the one in the next room. Shazam—4-F. Instead of fighting abroad, Superman battled Fifth Columnist activities in the States.

Movie stars and baseball stars, superheroes and boxing champions— they took their place with millions of other less famous Americans. More than any other war in America's history, World War II was a popular, democratic war. In the five years between December 1941 and December 1946, 16.3 million Americans entered the armed forces. All males between the ages of 18 and 64 had to register for the draft, although the upper age limit for service was set at 44 and later lowered to 38. One out of every six American men wore a uniform during the war. The wealthy fought along side the poor, the single beside married men with children. Unlike the Vietnam War, relatively few men tried to avoid military service. For a man in his twenties or thirties not in uniform, the central question was, "Why not?"

It was a question John Wayne had to face for the next four years. Wayne's case was not a matter of draft dodging. Although by late 1941 Wayne's marriage was falling apart and his visits to his home and children were becoming more infrequent, he was technically married and had four children. This coupled with his age meant that he was not a prime candidate for the draft. And in February 1942 General Lewis B. Hershey, Director of Selective Service, called the motion picture industry "an activity essential in certain instances to the national health, safety and interest, and in other instances to war production." In accordance with his statement, he instructed Selective Service officials in California to grant deferments to men vital to the industry. Although Hershey's order was not meant as a blanket deferment, and although the Screen Actors Guild announced that it did not want any privileged status, the California draft board was liberal in its application of the ruling. Many Washington and California officials argued that Gary Cooper was more valuable to the war effort as Sergeant York—a role he played in the top money grosser in 1941 which oozed patriotism—than as Sergeant Cooper.

The most visible Hollywood commodity in need of protection during the war was the leading man. Out of sincere feelings of patriotism or the fear of being branded as a slacker, many of Hollywood's youngest and most famous leading men enlisted. The shortage created a ticklish problem for studio public relation staffs. Leading men were supposed to project youth, sexuality, virility, and strength. But a movie star projecting those traits on the screen during the war faced the painful question, "Why isn't he in the army?" As *Daily Variety* commented, "No more he-man buildup of young men as in the past, for these might kick back unpleasant reverberations. If the buildup is too mighty, [the] public may want to know if he's that good why isn't he in the Army shooting Japs and Nazis. This is a particularly touchy phase and p-r has to be subtle about it." The irony of the situation was best expressed by an agent who told a producer about his latest discovery: "I've got a great prospect for you—a young guy with a double hernia."

A leading man during the war needed a good profile and an adequate voice, but more importantly he had to be either over forty, married with two or more children, or 4-F. Gary Cooper, Bing Crosby, James Cagney, John Garfield, Don Ameche, and Joel McCrea all "had a brood at home to call [them] 'pop'." Warner Baxter, Neil Hamilton, and Nils Aster—all forty to fifty—led the new crop of "semi-romantic" leading men. Sonny Tufts, the handsome, ex-Yale football player who starred in the hit *So Proudly We Hail,* was safely classified as 4-F.

John Wayne's draft status was a family present. Like other actors with two or more children, he could have enlisted. Like his friends Henry Fonda or John Ford, he could have placed his concern for his nation above his concern for his family, status, and career. There were some aspects of his life that Wayne never spoke to the press about; some that he rarely ever even spoke to his family or closest friends about. His decision not to enlist was a part of his life that he did not discuss. Pilar Wayne, whom Duke met and married a decade after the war, said that the guilt he suffered over his failure to enlist influenced the rest of his life. Mary St. John, who worked at Republic during the war and became Wayne's personal secretary after the war, agreed. She recalled that Wayne suffered "terrible guilt and embarrassment" because of his war record. The fact that his brother Robert served in the Navy only exasperated Wayne's sensitivity. His mother, who always openly favored Robert, was not above reminding Wayne that Robert, and not Duke, had served his country during the great crisis. On the screen, Wayne was the quintessential man of action, one who took matters into his own powerful hands and fought for what he believed. Never had the chasm between what he projected on the screen and his personal actions been so great.

Throughout 1942 and 1943, as he made one picture after another and as his reputation as a leading man soared, Wayne flirted with the idea of enlistment. He was particularly concerned about his stature in Ford's eyes, and he suspected that Ford had little respect for Celluloid soldiers. His suspicion was dead right. In early October 1941, shortly after he went on active duty, Ford wrote his wife that Wayne and Ward Bond's frivolous activities were meaningless in a world spinning toward total war. "They don't count. Their time will come." Three months after Pearl Harbor, Ford again mentioned Wayne in a letter to his wife. In a letter soaked in contempt, he remarked that he was "delighted" to hear about Wayne and Bond sitting up all night on a mountain top listening through earphones for signs that the Japanese were attacking California: "Ah well—such heroism shall not go unrewarded—it will live in the annals of time."

A pattern developed in Wayne's letters to Ford during the first two years of the war. Again and again, Wayne told Ford that he wanted to enlist—planned to enlist—as soon as he finished just one or two pictures. In the spring of 1942, Wayne inquired if he could get in Ford's unit, and if Ford would want him. If that option were closed, what would Ford suggest? Should he try the Marines? Plaintively, Wayne insisted that he was not drunk and that he hated to ask for favors, adding, "But for Christ's sake, you can suggest can't you?" A year later, Wayne was still considering enlistment in his letters to Ford. After he finished one more film he would be free: "Outside of that [film] Barkus [sic] is ready, anxious, and willin'."

But Barkus never did enlist. Toward the end of his life, Wayne told Dan Ford, John Ford's grandson, that his wife Josie had prevented him from joining Ford's outfit. According to his story, OSS head and Ford's superior William J. Donovan had sent a letter to Wayne explaining when Duke could join the Field Photographic Unit, but Josie never gave him the letter. He also confessed that he considered enlisting as a private, but rejected the idea. How, he pondered, could he fight along side seventeen and eighteen year old boys who had been reared on his movies? For them, he said, "I was America." In the end he concluded that he could best serve his country by making movies and going on an occasional USO tour.

The problem with any discussion of Wayne's "war record" is that it depends too much on statements made by Duke and others long after the war ended. Did his wife hide Donovan's letter? There is no such letter in Donovan's public and private papers. Did he believe that he was such an American institution by 1942 that he could not enlist as a private? This statement is difficult to take at face value when one considers that Gable, Power, Fonda, and Stewart—far more important stars than Wayne—were willing to share a foxhole or a cockpit or a ship deck with seventeen and eighteen year old American soldiers or sailors. Did, in fact, Wayne try to enlist? Catalina Lawrence, a script supervisor at Republic during the war who sometimes doubled as Wayne's secretary, remembers writing letters for Wayne attempting to get him in the service. "He felt so bad," she recalled, "especially after Robert was drafted into the Navy. Duke wanted to get in, but he just never could."

The closest one can come to the truth is Wayne's Selective Service record, and even here there are a few problems. The government has destroyed full individual records; all letters between Wayne and his draft board having long since been turned into ashes in official government incinerators. The skeleton of Wayne's record, however, remains. When the war started, Marion Mitchell Morrison—Selective Service Serial Number 2815, Order Number 1619—was classified 3-A, "deferred for dependency reasons." A continuation of that classification was requested and granted on November 17, 1943. Local draft boards periodically reviewed all classifications, and depending on their needs the government changed some classifications. To maintain a deferment or obtain a different deferment, a person or his employer had to file an official request. After returning the initial Selective Service Questionnaire, Wayne never personally filed a deferment claim, but a series of claims were filed "by another." Although the records have been destroyed, Republic Pictures almost certainly filed the claims. After Republic's leading money earner Gene Autry enlisted in 1942, studio president Herbert Yates was determined to keep Wayne out of uniform and in front of the camera. Therefore, in April 1944 another deferment claim was filed and granted reclassifying Wayne 2-A, "deferred in support of national health, safety, or interest." A month later Wayne was once again reclassified. With the war in Europe and the Pacific reaching a critical stage, Duke received a 1-A classification, "available for military service." This reclassification generated a series of new deferment claims, and on May 5, 1945, Wayne was once again classified 2-A. His last classification came after the war when he received a 4-A deferment on the basis of his age.

At any time during the war Wayne could have appealed his classification. At no time did he file an appeal. Always an active man, the war years were particularly frantic for Wayne. With his career bolting forward, he worked at four different studios and starred in thirteen pictures. In addition, he divorced his first wife, met and married his second wife, and led an active social life. When he was not working, the absence of a uniform gnawed into Wayne's self-respect and sense of manhood. It was then that he wrote Ford that "Barkus was ready." But then would come another movie, another delay, another link in a chain of delays that stretched from Pearl Harbor to Hiroshima.

Perhaps in his own mind his single-minded pursuit of his career meshed with his sense of patriotism. If so, Wayne was not the only person in Hollywood who expressed such beliefs. In March 1942, shortly after the premiere of *Reap the Wild Wind,* Wayne attended a luncheon for the Associated Motion Picture Advertisers. Cecil B. DeMille addressed the audience on the subject of the role Hollywood should play in the war. DeMille, his voice charged with moral urgency, remarked, "The job of motion pictures is to help bring home a full realization of the crisis and of the deadly peril that lurks in internal squabbles. Ours is the task of holding high and ever visible the values that everyone is fighting for. I don't mean flag waving, but giving the embattled world sharp glimpses of the way of life that we've got to hang on to in spite of everything." In DeMille's mind, the civilians who worked in the motion picture industry had a job and a duty every bit as important to the war effort as the American Marines fighting on Pacific islands or American sailors battling the Germans on the Atlantic. Victory demanded unity and dedication by all Americans—at home and abroad, civilian and military.

The Roosevelt Administration agreed with DeMille. Only weeks after the war began, FDR announced that Hollywood had an important role to play in the war effort: "The American motion picture is one of our most effective media in informing and entertaining our citizens. The motion picture must remain free in so far as national security will permit." Unlike steel, automobiles, and other vital American industries, which were heavily controlled by the government during the war, the controls on the film industry were comparatively light. Although several of FDR's advisors counseled him to take over Hollywood production, he believed that the industry leaders would perform their duty better if they remained in charge. But the subtext of Roosevelt's message to Hollywood was clear. The studio heads could continue to make money, but their product had to serve the war effort. They had to combine propaganda within the entertainment. If they did not, then the government would take over the industry.

Washington's liaison with Hollywood was Lowell Mellett, a former editor of the *Washington Daily News* who had the good looks of an older Hollywood character actor. After considerable bureaucratic reorganization in June 1942, Mellett was placed in charge of the Bureau of Motion Pictures (BMP) which was nominally under the Domestic Branch of the Office of War Information (OWI). While Mellett, dubbed the "white rabbit" for his less than forceful character, administered the BMP from his Washington office, the bureau's Hollywood office was run by Nelson Poynter. A close friend of Mellett's as well as a newspaper man, the dark-haired, frail looking Poynter had unassailable New Deal and interventionist credentials but lacked even basic knowledge of Hollywood and film making. Nevertheless, FDR charged the team of Mellett and Poynter with making sure Hollywood produced the kind of pictures deemed important to the war effort.

If he were uncertain about the process of making pictures, Poynter was very explicit about what kind of films he expected Hollywood to produce. From his tiny office in Hollywood, Poynter and his small staff compiled a blueprint to guide the motion picture industry's wartime behavior. Officially titled *The Government Informational Manual for the Motion Picture Industry*, it set down the official—and ideological—government line. The central question every producer, director, and writer should ask was "Will this picture help win the war?" Every film should contribute to that end by presenting America's effort and cause, its allies and friends, in the most generous possible terms. The manual emphasized that the United States was engaged in nothing less than "a people's war" to create a "new world" where want and fear were banished and freedom of religion and speech were a birthright. Social democratic and liberal internationalist in its intent, the manual was designed to move Hollywood toward its ideological position.

In practical terms, *The Government Informational Manual for the Motion Picture Industry* codified a long list of "do's" and "don'ts" for Hollywood. Whenever possible, for example, films should "show people making small sacrifices for victory"—"bringing their own sugar when invited out to dinner, carrying their own parcels when shopping, travelling on planes or trains with light luggage, uncomplainingly giving up seats to servicemen or others travelling on war priorities." Americans on the homefront should be portrayed as happy, busy, productive, rationing-loving patriots, planting victory gardens, taking public transportation even when they could afford to drive, and generally pitching in to win the war. Heading the list of "don'ts" was disunity on the homefront or the battlefront. America was not to be presented as divided by any racial, class, or gender issue. Scenes of strikes or labor conflict critical of labor were frowned upon; plots which suggested that the United States was anything less than a paradise for black Americans were verboten; and resorts to ethnic or religious bigotry were censored. Similarly, the allies of the United States had to be presented as paragons of national virtue. Hollywood was instructed to use its magic to manufacture a classless Britain, an efficient and incorruptible China, and a democratic Russia. Noting the irony of Hollywood's whitewash of the Soviet Union, *Variety* commented, "War has put Hollywood's traditional conception of the Muscovites through the wringer, and they have come out shaved, washed, sober, good to their families, Rotarians, brother Elks, and 33rd Degree Mason."

During the war, John Wayne starred in movies which fit comfortably within the parameters defined by Mellett, Poynter, and the BMP. To be sure, the producers of the Wayne films occasionally clashed with the BMP, but the conflicts were usually caused by the BMP's narrow ideological interpretation of individual scenes or insistence that a specific propaganda message appear in the film's dialogue. In a larger sense, *The Government Informational Manual for the Motion Picture Industry* described an America—if not a world—that Wayne already held dear. Perhaps the physical world of Hollywood was closer to the ideal presented by the BMP than any other American community. The motion picture industry was populated by WASPs and immigrants, Catholics and Jews, whites and blacks, men and women. A communist might write a screenplay which a liberal would produce and a reactionary direct, but for a time all three would be unified by a common bond—the movie. In Hollywood some of the highest paid stars were women, and a few blacks—very few—earned incomes higher than Southern cotton planters. And nowhere in America was the Horatio Alger ideal of rags to riches so religiously enshrined. Hollywood was an industry that literally manufactured modern American folk heroes. It was America's "last frontier." It was the crossroads where luck, looks, and talent intersected. And in a strange way, it was the America described in the pages of the BMP official manual. Of course Wayne believed in its message. He was its message.

John Wayne's wartime movies portrayed the BMP's message even before the bureau was created and the manual written. During the first four months of 1942, as American forces experienced painful losses in the Pacific and the Atlantic, Wayne made two pictures—*The Spoilers* and *In Old California*. Both films have similar plots. *The Spoilers*, based on the Rex Beach novel, is set in Nome in 1900 during the Alaskan Gold Rush, centers on a claim jumping scheme, and features a love triangle between Wayne, a society woman, and a dance-hall girl. During the course of the film, Wayne thwarts the claim jumping scheme as he discovers that the society woman is heartless and the dance-hall girl has a heart as pure as a Klondike nugget. *In Old California* is set in Sacramento in 1848–1849 during the California gold rush, features a land grabbing scheme, and highlights a love triangle between Wayne, a society woman, and a dance-hall girl. By the end of the film, not only does Wayne foil the land grabbing scheme and discover that the society woman is heartless and the dance-hall girl has a heart as pure as a nugget from Sutter's Mill, but he also saves the entire region from a particularly nasty typhoid epidemic.

ROBERTS / JOHN WAYNE AND WORLD WAR II   323

The message of both films was also similar: defend your property with every fiber of your being. Neither film expresses any sympathy for men who traffic in appeasement or legal niceties. In *The Spoilers* two prospectors announce in a saloon that they were "just working along kinda peaceful like" when at least twenty claim jumpers forced them off their stake. What could we do, they ask. "Ya still have five fingers on your gun hand, ain't ya," comes the immediate reply. All at the bar nod in agreement to the sage advice. Even the sexual innuendo revolves around claim jumping and force. Crooked gold commissioner Alexander McNamara (Randolph Scott) plans to jump both Roy Glennister's (John Wayne) Midas Gold Mine and his woman, Cherry Malotte (Marlene Dietrich). He tells Cherry that he might "move into [Glennister's] territory." "Could be tough going," Cherry cautions. "But worth it," McNamara replies. Glennister's use of brutal force defeats both forms of aggression. In one of the longest fist fights in film history, Glennister outlasts McNamara. Force—not the impotent and even dishonest representatives of the law—proves the only solution to aggression.

The same conclusion is expressed in *In Old California*. When the good but timid citizens of Sacramento are attacked, Tom Craig (John Wayne), the otherwise peace-loving town pharmacist, asks, "Doesn't anybody fight back around here?" "Angry men defending their home," he asserts, can never be defeated. And, of course, they do triumph. Lead by the forceful Craig, "the people" overcome both the land grabbers and the typhoid epidemic. For Americans embroiled in a war to prevent land-grabbing and aggression, the message of *The Spoilers* and *In Old California*—both released in the dark month of May 1942—reinforced official government statements about the causes of the war.

In Old California was little more than an inexpensive Republic formula picture. Without John Wayne, wrote the *New York Times'* reviewer Bosley Crowther, the picture "would be down with the usual run of strays." *The Spoilers,* however, received favorable reviews. "The he-men are back," noted the *New York Times.* "John Wayne is . . . virile," commented *Variety.* "John Wayne is a valuable piece of property," was the judgment of the Chicago *Tribune.* The acting characteristics which Wayne had spent a decade perfecting—the sideways glance and smile at his female lead, the tight-lipped, shark-eyed stare at his evil rival—found worthy recipients in *The Spoilers.* Dietrich's seething sexuality and Scott's oily villainy contrasted nicely with Wayne's cocky masculinity.

Wayne was maturing as an actor, and he knew it. On the set he was more self-confident. He was occasionally rude and impatient with Scott, who took a more artistic approach to his craft than Wayne. Scott, a Southerner with courtly manner, disliked Duke. On and off the set of *The Spoilers,* Dietrich occupied Wayne's attentions. The affair which had begun when Wayne and Dietrich were starring together in *Seven Sinners* had not yet run its passionate course. On and off the set they were constantly together. They dined at Ciros, the Brown Derby, Mocambo, and the Trocadero, Hollywood's trendiest restaurants. They went to sporting events and on weekend hunting and fishing trips together. Dietrich "was the most intriguing woman I've ever known," Wayne later told his wife Pilar. She shared her bedroom and ideas with Duke. And this combination of sexual and intellectual stimulation bolstered Wayne's belief in himself.

At Republic Pictures, Herbert Yates was not as interested in Wayne's emotional and intellectual growth as in his burgeoning box office power. Paramount released *Reap the Wild Wind* in March 1942, and it opened in the first-run theaters and music halls throughout the country. Respected *New York Times* reviewer Bosley Crowther saw the Technicolor epic in Radio City Music Hall. Always a generous reviewer for DeMille's films, he was particularly lavish in his praise for *Reap the Wild Wind*. It was "the essence of all [DeMille's] experience, the apogee of his art and as jam-full a motion picture as has ever played two hours upon a screen. It definitely marks a DeMillestone," Crowther wrote. The review, and others like it, echoed like gold coins in Yates's mind. *Reap the Wild Wind* was a hit—reviewers compared it with that other breezy film, *Gone With the Wind*—and John Wayne was one of its stars, even if he were killed in the movie by a giant squid and therefore failed to win the heroine. And Wayne belonged to Yates and Republic. If Yates had been unimpressed by Duke's success in *Stagecoach* and *The Long Voyage Home,* he now fully understood the worth of his star attraction.

With profits and the war in mind, Yates put Wayne into his first war film. If it were not for the fact that *Flying Tigers* was a shameless rip-off of *Only Angels Have Wings,* the film might be considered as the prototype for World War II combat films. It possessed everything but originality, a point that did not cause serious concern for an action oriented studio like Republic. Howard Hawks's *Only Angels Have Wings* (1939) contained all the motifs that film scholar Robert B. Ray has labeled as basic to Hollywood's World War II combat films: "the male group directed by a strong leader, the outsider who must prove himself by courageous individual action, the necessity for stoicism in the face of danger and death, the premium placed on professionalism, and the threat posed by women."

Only Angels Have Wings centers on a group of pilots in a South American jungle contracted to deliver the mail over a range of dangerous, stalactite mountains of unearthly appearance. In this group of flying mercenaries is a brave leader called "Pappy" who emphasizes teamwork, a man branded as a coward who has to prove his courage to win acceptance, a woman who threatens to destroy the chummy fraternity atmosphere, and pilots who share a common Hemingwayesque code of life and language. They speak with their actions, resist expressing their emotions, and demonstrate their dependency and even love in such nonverbal ways as asking for a cigarette or a match.

Flying Tigers contains all the same elements. This time the mercenary pilots are part of Colonel Claire Lee Chennault's "American Volunteer Group," flying against the Japanese for China on the eve of Pearl Harbor. Once again, the leader stresses the value of teamwork and is called "Pappy" by his men. Once again, there is a suspected coward who must prove himself, a flamboyant individualist who on the surface seems to only care about himself, and a woman who threatens the harmony and effectiveness of the male unit. There is even the same language of cigarettes and matches and painful grimaces when talk turns to matters of the heart. The similarities of plot and structure are so striking that Ray commented that "Hawks should have sued for plagiarism."

But for all the similarities—and there were many—there was a major difference. *Flying Tigers* went into production shortly after Pearl Harbor during America's darkest months in the Pacific War and dealt with the most urgent topic in the world: the war. It was filmed from May to July, 1942, months that saw the Japanese take Corregidor and the United States win the Battles of Coral Sea and Midway. *Flying Tigers* capitalized on the national mood. At a moment when the nation demanded a hero, Republic responded with John Wayne. At a time when the Americans longed for good news from the Pacific, *Flying Tigers* recounted the heroics of Chennault's "American Volunteer Group." During a crisis when the country wanted to believe the best of its allies and the worst of its enemies, the film presented Chinese straight from the pages of Pearl S. Buck's *The Good Earth* and automatous Japanese fresh from hell. In addition, the film touched the rawest of American nerves—Pearl Harbor. FDR's full war speech is replayed in the film, and the climactic scene occurs after the Japanese attack on Pearl Harbor.

The film was an ideal vehicle for Wayne. The role of the solid, quiet leader around whom all the action and all the other parts revolved played to Duke's strengths. Increasingly in his recent films he was developing a palpable screen presence. Without talking, often without moving, he dominated a scene. In one scene, for example, the pilots listen to FDR's war speech on the radio. Slowly the camera moves in for a close-up on Wayne, who stands silent, listening to FDR's message, a cigarette in his left hand. During the entire message, Wayne never moves. His eyes and mouth do not change expression. The only movement is the smoke drifting upward from Wayne's unsmoked cigarette. At the end of the speech, he takes a deep breath and walks off screen. Roosevelt had said it all; Wayne could only have added a trite cliché. Duke played the scene with controlled passion and complete sincerity. It is a powerful scene which underscored Wayne's screen presence.

Republic believed *Flying Tigers* conveyed the message advocated by the Office of War Information's Bureau of Motion Pictures. The film emphasized teamwork. Woody Jason (John Carroll) tells his fellow mercenaries early in the film that he is in China for the $600 a month and the $500 bonus for every Japanese plane he shoots down: "This is not our home. It's not our fight. It's a business. And, boy, I hope business is good." "It's every man for himself, isn't it," he asks just before he bums a cigarette from one man and a match from another. But by the end of the film Woody sacrifices his life in a suicide mission to save Jim "Pappy" Gordon (John Wayne). After Pearl harbor, he realizes that China is as important as his "home street." Scenes that emphasize the importance of non-flying personal and mechanics similarly stress the themes of teamwork and cooperation. And if that did not provide enough propaganda content, *Flying Tigers* is filled with good-hearted, loyal Chinese and cold, ruthless Japanese.

Government officials, however, had mixed reactions to the film. Harry B. Price, a government consultant on China, noted that although the film was generally of a high caliber, it left "much to be desired from the standpoint of an adequate portrayal of our Allies, the Chinese." Like so many other Hollywood films, wrote Price, *Flying Tigers* presented the Chinese as "likable, but slightly ludicrous," and there is "little in the picture to suggest that the Chinese people are human beings just as varied and many sided in their natures as Americans." In addition, the film did not explore Chennault's tactical innovations. The Bureau of Motion Picture staffer who reviewed *Flying Tigers* agreed with Price's assessment. Marjorie Thorson complained that the film's glorification of individual heroics muted its theme of teamwork and cooperation, that the Chinese are presented as harmless and slightly incompetent people, and that the major issues of the war are not discussed. She notes that although there are Chinese nurses and doctors in the movie, only American nurses are shown changing bandages and "the final decision in any matter of a flier's health is left to the *nonprofessional* American squadron leader . . . just being an American presumably qualifies him to make medical decisions over the head of the trained Chinese." Even worse, "no Chinese men are shown fighting." "Altogether," she concluded, the "picture attempts a great deal more than it accomplishes."

Official complaints often demonstrated an ignorance both of filmmaking and the war. Members of the "American Volunteer Group" charged that *Flying Tigers* was "unbelievably bad" because it contained several factual errors and employed two former members of the AVG as technical advisors who had been dishonorably discharged for being "suspected of perversion." Contentions that filmmakers distort history by focusing on the individual or the small group at the expense of historical reality reveal a deep misunderstanding of the industry. As for *Flying Tigers'* treatment of Chiang Kai-shek and the Chinese, blindly generous is the best description. Divided by warlordism and civil war, plagued by corruption and inefficiency, Chiang's Kuomintang government dismissed "aggressive action" against the Japanese before Pearl Harbor and after December 7, 1941, left any serious fighting to the United States. As one American military official noted in late 1941, "The general idea in the United States that China has fought Japan to a standstill and has had many glorious victories is a delusion." If *Flying Tigers'* portrayal of the Chinese is historically inaccurate, it was closer to reality than the line adopted by the BMP. And the assertion in the film that Americans provided the combat muscle in the war did reflect actual conditions.

The entire debate was irrelevant at Republic. Yates was not interested in the veracity of *Flying Tigers*. Republic was a bottom line studio, and its only concern was ticket sales. From its first preview, the film exceeded Republic's usual modest expectations. The *Hollywood Reporter* announced, "*Flying Tigers* marks an all-time production high for Republic. It is a smashing, stirring, significant film. . . . It will be a record grosser in all engagements, and no theater in the land should hesitate about proudly showing it." *Variety* agreed: "In *Flying Tigers,* Republic has its best picture." Even though the film was released late in the year, *Flying Tigers* became one of 1942's leading box office successes and the only picture in the top twenty not produced in one of the major studios.

No one at Republic had to search for the reason. It was John Wayne. If Republic executives needed confirmation, they found it in every major review: *Hollywood Reporter:* "John Wane is at his peak. . . ." *Variety:* "John Wayne matches his best performance. . . ." *New York Times:* "Mr. Wayne is the sort of fellow who inspires confidence. . . ." Republic had a hit and a star. Yates was now convinced. So was the rest of the industry. And during the next three years of war, Wayne would reconfirm again and again his star status as his name alone came to guarantee box office success.

Now more than ever, Yates was determined to keep Wayne. Shortly after the release of *Flying Tigers* the film's producer, Edmund Grainger, and director, David Miller, entered the armed service. Neither would make another picture until the late 1940s. Wayne believed that he too should enlist. Yates refused to release Wayne. The loss of Gene Autry, whose contract to make eight straight pictures for Republic had to be shelved when the singing cowboy enlisted in the Army air service, devastated Yates. He told Wayne that he would sue him for breach of contract if Duke enlisted. Furthermore, Yates announced, if Wayne enlisted he would make certain that Duke would never work for Republic or any other studio again. Although Yates's threat violated government policy—every person in uniform was guaranteed their civilian job once the war ended—Wayne did not press the issue. He feared poverty and unemployment, and perhaps more, he feared losing the status he had achieved and sinking into obscurity. Always a man haunted by the ghosts of his own insecurity, he stayed out of uniform, secure in his home at Republic.

Wayne's home was Republic, but his contract allowed him to make pictures for other studios. With the scarcity of leading men becoming more pressing every month, Duke was never in greater demand. It was an ideal situation for Wayne. He was a man who never made peace with inactivity. He loved his work and he hated the time between pictures. Mary St. John, who worked as Wayne's personal secretary for over twenty-five years, said that part of his problem was that he had no hobbies, nothing to do to fill the empty days. His daughter Aissa commented that he "was a slave to his energy." On location he always awoke by four-thirty or five A.M., and even when he was not working on a picture he was up at dawn. "He never slept late. Ever," Aissa remembered. Once up, and wired by his morning coffee, he was ready for work, and when there was no work, he simply had to endure long periods of restless rest. And in 1942, such stretches were intolerable. His home life was empty, his marriage almost over, many of his friends in uniform. When he worked, his life had structure and purpose. When he was not working, he had time to mull over the irony that without serving a day in the armed forces he was becoming a World War II hero. It was during these periods that he penned "Barkus" letters to Ford.

Throughout 1942 Duke worked at a hectic pace. *The Spoilers* was shot in January and February, *In Old California* in March and April, and *Flying Tigers* in May, June, and July. While *Flying Tigers* was in post-production, Wayne moved on to other films. Between the end of July and September he starred in *Reunion in France* for MGM, and in September and October he starred in *Pittsburgh*, another Universal film with Marlene Dietrich and Randolph Scott. Both *Reunion in France* and *Pittsburgh* were released in December. In one year Wayne had made five films, all released that same year. In addition, *Lady for the Night* and *Reap the Wild Wind* had also premiered in 1942. There were few empty periods.

Like *Flying Tigers, Reunion in France* and *Pittsburgh* were war films. *Reunion in France,* however, was a peculiar sort of war film, the product of MGM's odd but predictable slant on life. MGM, noted Warner Brothers' executive Milton Spalding, "was a studio of white telephones." Quality—or at least the illusion of quality—mattered, and studio head Louis B. Mayer spent money to obtain it. As a result, at MGM nothing was what it seemed, everything was idealized. Reality never entered the MGM lot. Women especially had to look perfect. Cameramen "had to photograph the movie queens and make them look damn good," said MGM director George Cukor. If such MGM women as Greta Garbo, Joan Crawford, Jean Harlow, Norma Shearer, Lana Turner, Greer Garson, and Myrna Loy had individual styles, they all shared a common glamour and elegance. Regardless of the role they were called on to play, they always projected beauty and glamour.

After Pearl Harbor and the start of the war, Hollywood wags exchanged jokes about how the conflict would be portrayed at MGM. "The Japs may take California but they'll never get in to see Louis B. Mayer," quipped one wit. When an industry personality remarked that the United States needed a positive slogan that articulated what the country was fighting for, a less earnest listener replied, "Lana Turner." There was a truth in both jokes. As long as Louis B. Mayer called the shots at MGM, only movies that presented a highly stylized version of World War II would be made. And as long as Mayer approved all projects, MGM would fight a war to make the world safe for Lana.

Reunion in France brought America face to face with the stark glamour of war. The film centers on the trials and clothes of Michele de la Becque (Joan Crawford), a wealthy French socialite who loses her mansion and carefree life when the Germans invade France in 1940. With the swiftness of the Nazi blitzkrieg, her comfortable, insulated world is shattered. Her industrialist fiancé turns collaborationist, her wealth is confiscated, and she is forced to work for her former dressmaker—a job that pays poorly but allows her to remain the best dressed woman in Paris—to pay her bills. Resisting Nazi domination, she befriends Pat Talbot (John Wayne), an American RAF Eagle Squadron flier who has been shot down and wounded behind enemy lines, and helps him escape. The film ends with Michele's reunion with her fiancé, who turns out to be a resistance fighter in collaborationist clothing. Far from helping Germany, the industrialist had been sending the Nazis faulty war materials to foil their efforts to dominate Europe.

The BMP reacted angrily to MGM's sanitized version of the war. "If there were ever a perfect argument for OWI reading of scripts before they are shot, this picture is it," wrote BMP staffer Marjorie Thorson in her review of the film. The picture failed the war effort on a number of counts. Count one: the film presented the Gestapo as "cruel, suspicious, and sadistic" but contained a favorable portrayal of all other Germans. The German military governor of Paris is depicted as a courtly, sweet, and charming older gentleman, an echo of a European aristocracy of decency and integrity. Furthermore, the German soldiers were disciplined and polite. Count two: the film suggests that any greedy, opportunistic collaborationist may really be an upstanding, patriotic member of the French Resistance. "It is a well known fact," the reviewer reported, "that many of the great French industrialists were pro-fascist long before the present war began; that they helped the Nazis conquer France; that they are now reaping the bloodstained rewards of their betrayal." Count three: the film shows nothing of the misery that the Germans have brought to the French people. MGM portrays a France that "falls with great elegance. Everyone we see is beautifully gowned, comfortably housed, and apparently well fed." Nazi occupation of Paris, the film insinuates, only means that the swastika hangs on the railroad stations and dumpy German women get the first crack at the latest Parisian fashions. Count four: the film misses the chance to contrast Nazi and democratic ideologies. Beyond the heroine saying that democracy is not dead and will live again in France, the film fails to explore the vital issue. In the context of the film, democracy suggests only that thin French women will someday reclaim their own fashions.

The serious charges led to the final verdict: *Reunion in France* "is a very poorly conceived picture. It misrepresents France, the French underground, the Nazis. Far more serious, it unintentionally gives aid and comfort to the enemy in the peace offensive that will surely, and perhaps soon, be launched." That was the crux of the matter. The Office of War Information predicted a German peace offensive in January 1943, and it believed *Reunion in France* would work to the benefit of the Germans. At the time when the Office of War Information was pressing the BMP to get producers to seriously discuss the issues of the war in their films, MGM suggested that the war was between fat German and thin French women with fashion hanging neatly pressed in the balance. Reviewing the film, the Office of War Information's Bureau of Intelligence commented, "the most striking feature of France as shown in the picture is a genius for designing and wearing women's clothes. . . . The preservation of this genius from the bad taste of the Germans is the big issue."

Newspaper reviews agreed with the government's assessment. One review commented that Joan Crawford behaves in the film "like nobody except an MGM movie star," and the *New York Times* found Wayne "totally unconvincing as an American flyer." Most reviews emphasized that the war was a serious affair and should not be used as an MGM costume drama. The reviews, however, did not kill *Reunion in France* at the box office. It was one of MGM's top fifteen grossers for 1943. Once again, Wayne had demonstrated his worth. The message in Hollywood was clear: even a bad Wayne film made money.

Wayne's last film of 1942 was his most ambitious attempt to aid the war effort. As originally planned by agent Charles K. Feldman, *Pittsburgh,* like *The Spoilers,* was to be a vehicle for three of his clients—Dietrich, Wayne, and Scott. But it soon turned into a tribute to the industrial home front. Associate producer Robert Fellows worked closely with the BMP to ensure that the film conveyed the government's exact propaganda message. It focuses on the Markham-Evans Coal Company, and its heroes are industrialists and workers in the coal and steel industries. In the film, Wayne plays the flawed hero Charles "Pittsburgh" Markham, a man who rose from the depths of a coal mine to the ownership of the company. In a role that Wayne was to develop more fully in such films as *Red River, Hondo, The Sea Chase, The Searchers,* and *The Man Who Shot Liberty Valance,* he portrays a man obsessed, driven by his own inner demons. Pittsburgh willingly uses anything and anyone to acquire power. On his way to the top, he abandons the woman who loves him (Marlene Dietrich) and his trusted partner (Randolph Scott). But the same ruthlessness that allowed him to rise in the coal business leads to his downfall, causing him to lose his wife, his company, and his self-worth. World War II provides a rebirth for Pittsburgh. Once again, he rises from the mines to manage the company. Only this time he works for his nation, not himself. He is redeemed by submerging his own ego into his nation's crusade for a better world.

When Nelson Poynter and his BMP staff previewed *Pittsburgh* at Universal Studio on December 1, 1942, they were delighted. The picture was a preachy epic of coal and steel that appealed to the BMP's wordy sense of effective propaganda. It contained long semi-documentary sections of the coal and steel industries, and it rarely said anything visually that could be put into flat dialogue. But there was no mistaking its message: every American—soldier and industrial worker alike—can and should contribute to the war effort; victory would only result if "all the people" work and fight as one. The BMP applauded the results. "*Pittsburgh* succeeds in making many excellent contributions to the war information program," noted the BMP review of the film. In fact, much of the dialogue "appears to have been culled directly from the OWI Manual of Information for the picture industry. . . ." Nevertheless, the picture was "highly commended for an earnest and very successful contribution to the war effort." As far as the BMP was concerned, *Pittsburgh* was "one of the best pictures to emerge to date dealing with our vital production front. . . ."

Poynter, who had worked so closely with Bob Fellows on *Pittsburgh,* thought he had scored a real coup. Often ignored by the more important producers, Poynter actually believed that *Pittsburgh* was a good film and that his contributions to the film had been significant. As soon as he saw the final cut, he shot off a series of letters complimenting everyone involved with the movie including himself. "Magnificent. . . . It shows what can be done if the creative unit sets out to help interpret the war and at the same time put on a helluva good show," he wrote Fellows, Faldman, and several Universal executives. Poynter wrote Lowell Mellett, his BMP superior in Washington, telling him to see *Pittsburgh* and to take other Office of War Information and War Production Board people with him.

Mellett went, but he did not share Poynter's enthusiasm. "The propaganda sticks out disturbingly," Mellett responded to Poynter. Most newspaper reviewers shared Mellett's opinion. "This business of instructing and informing intrudes at times at the expense of the entertaining," noted the *Motion Picture Herald,* but the film "yields realistic results when not hampered by dialogue freighted with purpose." From West Coast to East, the reviews were the same. *Pittsburgh* was not exactly a bad film, but it was certainly "not in the inspired class," or, more to the point, it was "routine entertainment at best." In a New York theater, a cartoon entitled *Point Rationing,* which explained the use of the new rationing book, drew a more positive review than *Pittsburgh.*

The critical and financial failures of *Pittsburgh* reinforced the belief in Hollywood that if FDR and alphabet agencies could get America out of the Depression, they certainly could not make a hit movie. The resistance against Poynter and his staff that was present in the industry from the beginning stiffened even more in the months after the release of *Pittsburgh.* Hollywood was right. The BMP was not film-literate. Both Mellett and Poynter were newspaper men who thought in terms of words. They wanted dialogue that sounded like it was straight off an editorial page. As far as they were concerned, if a movie did not use dialogue to present the government's message, then the message was not delivered. They had difficulty thinking visually. The major studio executives realized the government approach toward propaganda would mean death at the box office. They were willing to make propaganda pictures that served the interest of the country, but they wanted to make them in their own way.

No film better demonstrates Washington's lack of understanding of movies than *Casablanca*. The classic film ran into trouble in Washington. Various sections of the Office of War Information were disappointed by the movie. Most were upset with Rick's (Humphrey Bogart's) cynicism. Others were dissatisfied with the treatment of the French, the Germans, and the North Africans. And the last line—"This could be the beginning of a beautiful friendship"—well, as far as the OWI was concerned, it said nothing about the Atlantic Charter or why the United Nations were fighting Fascism. As film historians Gregory D. Black and Clayton R. Koppes observed, Washington "was not content to let meaning emerge from the interaction of the characters and the overall story line . . . it would have preferred a two-paragraph sermonette explaining Nazi aggression and the justice of the Allied cause."

The battle between Washington and Hollywood would drag into 1943 and would last in a more limited way for the rest of the war. It was a war fought by studio heads and producers, not actors, and as in the larger war, Wayne avoided the conflict. But his hectic activity of 1942 had begun to undermine his health. On January 21, 1943, he collapsed on a movie set and was rushed to the hospital. Doctors told him he had influenza and needed rest. That was the bad news. The good news was that his collapse was reported in the *New York Times*. Duke was a star.

ACKNOWLEDGMENTS (continued from copyright page)

8. "Doughboys at Cantigny" by James Hallas. From: James Hallas, "Doughboys at Cantigny," *American History Illustrated* (November 1983). Reprinted through the courtesy of Cowles Magazines, publisher of *American History Illustrated.*

9. "Dinner at the White House." From: "Southern Democrats Berate the President," *New York Times,* October 18, 1901; "Approval in Boston," *New York Times,* October 18, 1901; "The Dinner Incident," *New York Times,* October 19, 1901; "The President's Dinner to Booker T. Washington," *New York Times,* October 27, 1901; "Mr. Roosevelt's Independence," *New York Times,* October 27, 1901; "Negro Guest Entertained by Roosevelt," *Atlanta Constitution,* October 17, 1901; "Will You Walk into My Parlor," Mobile *Weekly Press,* December 24, 1901; "Teddy's Mistake or Booker's Reception," in Louis R. Harlan and Raymond W. Smock, *The Booker T. Washington Papers, Vol. 6, 1901–2* (Urbana: University of Illinois Press, 1977), 333–34.

10. "The Brownsville Affray" by Richard Young. From: Richard Young, "The Brownsville Affray," *American History Illustrated* (October 1986). Reprinted through the courtesy of Cowles Magazines, publisher of *American History Illustrated.*

11. "The Passing of the Great Race" by Madison Grant. From: Madison Grant, *The Passing of the Great Race* (New York, 1916).

12. "Italian Exodus to America" by Alexander DeConde. From: Alexander DeConde, "Italian Exodus to America," *American History Illustrated* (August 1972). Reprinted through the courtesy of Cowles Magazines, publisher of *American History Illustrated.*

13. "The President under Fire" by Richard K. Murray. From: Richard K. Murray, "The President under Fire," *American History Illustrated* (August 1974). Reprinted through the courtesy of Cowles Magazines, publisher of *American History Illustrated.*

14. "'Big Bill' Tilden: Superstar of the 1920s" by James S. Olson. From: An original essay by James S. Olson. Copyright 1993.

15. "Bruce Barton's *The Man Nobody Knows:* A Popular Advertising Illusion" by Edrene S. Montgomery. From: Edrene S. Montgomery, "Bruce Barton's *The Man Nobody Knows:* A Popular Advertising Illusion," *Journal of Popular Culture* (Winter 1985). Published by Popular Press. Reprinted by permission of Popular Press.

16. "The Glamorous Crowd: Hollywood Movie Premieres between the Wars" by David Karnes. From: David Karnes, "The Glamorous Crowd: Hollywood Movie Premieres between the Wars," *American Quarterly* (Fall 1986). Published by the American Studies Association. Reprinted by permission of *American Quarterly* and the author.

17. "The Election of 1932" by David Burner. From: David Burner, *Herbert Hoover: A Public Life* (New York, 1979). Reprinted by permission of the author.

18. "The Indian New Deal" by James S. Olson and Raymond Wilson. From: James S. Olson and Raymond Wilson, "The Indian New Deal," in *Native Americans in the Twentieth Century* (Urbana: Univ. of Illinois Press, 1984). Reprinted by permission of The University of Illinois Press.

19. "John Dillinger: Public Enemy" by Mark Sufrin. From: Mark Sufrin, "John Dillinger: Public Enemy," *American History Illustrated* (February 1970). Reprinted through the courtesy of Cowles Magazines, publisher of *American History Illustrated.*

20. "The Night of the Martians" by Edward Oxford. From: Edward Oxford. "Night of the Martians," *American History Illustrated* (October 1988). Reprinted through the courtesy of Cowles Magazines, publisher of *American History Illustrated.*

21. "The Case for Birth Control" by Margaret H. Sanger. From: Margaret H. Sanger, *The Case for Birth Control* (New York, 1917).

22. "Illegal Operations: Women, Doctors, and Abortion, 1886–1939" by Angus McLaren. From: Angus McLaren, "Illegal Operations: Women, Doctors, and Abortion, 1886–1939," *Journal of Social History* (Summer 1993). Reprinted by permission of the *Journal of Social History.*

23. "'I Want a Girl, Just Like the Girl That Married Harry James': American Women and the Problem of Political Obligation in World War II" by Robert B. Westbrook. From: Robert B. Westbrook, "'I Want a Girl, Just Like the Girl That Married Harry James': American Women and the Problem of Political Obligation in World War II," *American Quarterly,* (December 1990). Published by the American Studies Association. Reprinted by permission of *American Quarterly* and the author.

24. "We Also Served" by Doris Brinker Tanner. From: Doris Brinker Tanner, "We Also Served," *American History Illustrated* (November 1985). Reprinted through the courtesy of Cowles Magazines, publisher of *American History Illustrated.*

25. "America's Nazis" by Susan Canedy Clark. From: Susan Canedy Clark, "America's Nazis," *American History Illustrated* (April 1986). Reprinted through the courtesy of Cowles Magazines, publisher of *American History Illustrated.*

26. "The Making of a Madman" by James S. Olson. From: Ronald Fritze, Randy Roberts, and James S. Olson, eds., *Reflections on Western Civilization to 1600* (New York: HarperCollins, 1992).

27. "Even Hell Wouldn't Have It" by John F. Wukovits. From: John F. Wukovits, "Even Hell Wouldn't Have It," *American History Illustrated* (February 1986). Reprinted through the courtesy of Cowles Magazines, publisher of *American History Illustrated.*

28. "Hero or Draft-Dodger? John Wayne and World War II" by Randy Roberts. From: Randy Roberts and James S. Olson, *American Experience* (New York: HarperCollins, 1994).